# INFORMATION SYSTEMS ENGINEERING:
## A FORMAL APPROACH

# INFORMATION SYSTEMS ENGINEERING: A FORMAL APPROACH

K. M. van HEE

CAMBRIDGE
UNIVERSITY PRESS

Published by the Press Syndicate of the University of Cambridge
The Pitt Building, Trumpington Street, Cambridge CB2 1RP
40 West 20th Street, New York, NY 10011-4211, USA
10 Stamford Road, Oakleigh, Melbourne 3166, Australia

First published 1994

Printed in Great Britain at the University Press, Cambridge

*Library of Congress cataloguing in publication data available*
*British Library cataloguing in publication data available*

ISBN 0 521 45514 6

The illustration for the cover was supplied by Annelies Schott

TAG

# Contents

# Preface

The term *systems engineering* covers a wide area of activities, focused on the development of systems. One of these activities, called *systems modeling*, is the construction of *models* of systems. Models are made and used by systems engineers for various reasons. Sometimes a model is used to document the *functionality* of a system, i.e. the model describes the behavior of a system in an abstract way. For instance this is done in *requirements engineering*, in case it concerns a new system, or in *reverse engineering*, if an old one has to be renovated. In both cases the model is used as a *specification* of the system.

A model can also be used as a *blueprint* of a system that has to be constructed. In this case the description is less abstract than a specification in the sense that it should be easy to map the building blocks of the model onto existing or realizable components.

A third reason to make a model is to *analyze* a system, for instance *performance* or *reliability*. If the system already exists one could in principle observe its behavior. However, it is often not feasible to experiment with a real system, due to the costs or the risks of experimentation. If the system under consideration is new, i.e. it exists only on paper and in the minds of some persons, a model is the only way to study its behavior. Instead of experimenting with the real system the systems engineer may perform experiments with a model.

In many cases it is possible to analyze the models in a formal way, instead of analysis based on experiments. This has the advantage that we are able to prove theorems for the behavior of a system, while experiments allow us only statistical assertions to make and may serve as counter-examples for hypotheses.

The models we consider here are *abstract* or *mathematical* rather than physical. Often we transform these models into a form appropriate for interpretation by a computer. In that case the computer can *simulate* the behavior of the system and experimentation is then called *computer simulation*.

Models are expressed with *formalisms*. A formalism consists of a mathematical *framework* and a *language*. A model is an *instance* of a framework. A model is described in the language, which might be textual or graphical. A description of a model in the language is called a *script*. So the *semantics* of a script is a model.

The formalisms we use apply to all systems that have a countable set of *states* and that make *state transitions* at discrete moments. We call these systems: *transition systems*. A very important type of system is called *information system*, in which the state is formed by a set of *information objects*. The scope of this book is however wider than computer science, and includes systems studied in industrial engineering and electrical engineering as well.

Most books on the development of information systems are focused on the techniques used in practice today. The formalisms they use to make models of systems are very weak. Often *data flow diagrams* and *entity-relationship diagrams* are the only "formalisms" offered. On the other hand these books pay a lot of attention to interview techniques, cost-benefit analysis and planning techniques. In this book we do not consider these topics at all, not because they are unimportant for the systems engineer but because there are already enough books on them.

In this book we concentrate on modeling of systems and therefore we need some formalisms to describe the models. Many formalisms consider only *aspects* of transition systems; for instance *data models* to define *state spaces* of systems, *process models* to define the *interaction* between different components of systems and so-called *specification languages* to define *local state transitions* or *operations*. (Note that data models and process models are in fact formalisms for *defining* models rather than models themselves.) It turns out to be very difficult to integrate these different *views* of a system. Therefore we provide a small set of formalisms here and we show how they may be combined to obtain an *integrated model* of a system. We do not provide a detailed survey of all existing formalisms here, but select a few and extend them a little in order to be able to *integrate* them.

The frameworks we will use are:

- transition systems,
- a binary data model with complex objects,
- timed and colored Petri nets.

The languages we use are:

- a specification language very close to Z,
- graphical languages for defining data models and Petri nets.

The *transition systems* (in fact unlabeled transition systems) provide the highest level of semantics: every model denotes a transition system. A transition system has an *event set* and a function, called *transition law*, that assigns to a (finite) sequence of events a set of possible subsequent events. An event is a pair consisting of a *state* and a *time point*, which denotes the time the system moved to the state.

The *data model* is used to define state spaces of systems. The data model is a binary version of the entity-relationship model with two extensions: there are more facilities for expressing *constraints* and there is a notion of *aggregation* of entities and relationships into so-called *complex objects*. In fact a state is a set of complex objects.

The *transition law* of a system is defined by (timed and colored) Petri nets. In a Petri net we have *places* in which complex objects may reside and *processors* that may *consume* and *produce* complex objects from specific places. (In the Petri net literature processors are called *transitions* and the complex objects are called *tokens*.) Each processor has an *input-output relation*, which determines its consumption/production behavior. The time component of the formalism enables us to model *real-time* aspects of systems.

The *specification language* is a language based on *typed set theory* with a *constructive subset*, that is, a *typed functional language*, which is very close to Z. In fact it is a subset of Z, because we have restricted ourselves to a *countable universe of values* that can be represented by *finite sets*. Functions map values to values. Functions are in general infinite sets, so they are not considered to be values themselves, which implies that we do not allow function-valued functions. These restrictions do not impede the modeling of systems in practice, and make the theoretical treatment more easy; we present a construction for the language, including static type checking and evaluation of expressions. The constructive subset of the specification language is important because we advocate a style of modeling that is adopted from VDM, in which the systems engineer first gives a *descriptive specification* of an entity and afterwards a *construction* in a constructive subset of the language. So, we distinguish descriptive and constructive specifications. (Often it is possible to give a construction that is easy to understand at once, so that a descriptive specification is no longer useful.) Our subset of Z has very few primitive functions, which means that most functions used in specifications, are themselves constructed in the language. Of course the language is extendible in the sense that new primitive types and functions can be added. Our syntax differs from Z on minor points, mainly where we use $\lambda$-expressions. In Z the $\lambda$ symbol is used for function definitions. However, in practice that is not always a convenient notation. (Most functional languages use more familiar ways for expressing function constructions.)

The specification language is used to define the types of the complex objects that *flow* through the Petri net and the input-output relations of the processors in the Petri net. An important language construct is a *schema*. (A schema denotes a subset of a labeled Cartesian product.) Schemas are defined using types, functions and predicates. The complex objects and the input-output relations are defined by schemas. The language also has schema operators to define complex schemas using already defined simpler schemas. Another difference between our specification language and Z is that we allow *partial schemas*, i.e. schemas in which not all *variables* or *attributes* must have a value. This is particularly important for the specification of processors that do not consume from all their input places and that do not produce output for all their output places.

*Constructive* specifications are useful because they are *executable*, which is important when a systems engineer needs to *validate* a model by means of simulation experiments. For information systems a computer model is a *prototype* that can be tested by potential users of the modeled system.

Graphical languages are used to define the structure of the Petri nets and parts of the data model. In these languages descriptions are in fact *graphs*, in which the vertices represent object classes, processors or places and in which the edges represent relationships between object classes or connections between processors and places. The graphical language for the data modeling is close to the usual ones. In the Petri net language we have introduced *hierarchy*, which makes it possible to *decompose* models in a way similar to *data flow diagrams*. This is a useful feature because data flow diagrams are very often used in practice and systems engineers who have experience with data flow diagrams, can use them in our formalism in almost the same way.

Our choice of formalisms is rather arbitrary. A combination of a process algebra, an algebraic specification language and another data model could have worked also. However, we have the experience that so-called *model-based* formalisms, such as we have chosen, are more comfortable with practitioners than *property-based* formalisms, such as the algebraic ones.

The author is leader of a research group at the Eindhoven University of Technology that has developed a software tool called ExSpect. This tool incorporates most of the formalisms introduced in this book and is commercial available by Bakkenist Management Consultants, Amsterdam. The tool has been operational since 1989. It is used by several industrial companies for a variety of applications, such as the modeling and analysis of logistical systems and the prototyping of distributed software systems. (It is also used by software houses in the ESPRIT project EP-5342 called PROOFS.) These experiences have motivated my decision to write this book. The chosen combination of formalisms is useful. It is not necessary to use ExSpect to apply the theory of this book in practice. There are other tools on the market that support our approach as well. The use of a tool is recommended for large systems or if simulation or prototyping is needed. Each tool has its own peculiarities and requires some learning time. Note that our approach is not dependent on any tool however, there are tools that support it.

The book is divided into five parts. The first, called Concepts, introduces most of the concepts a systems engineer needs for modeling systems. The treatment is as informal as possible in order to give the reader an intuitive understanding of these concepts, which are illustrated with realistic examples.

In the second part, called Frameworks, the formalization of these concepts is given as well as the more theoretical details of the frameworks used. This part is interesting for experts; the frameworks are complex and it may take some time to understand them fully. If we expect systems engineers to make formal specifications then they have to understand the formalisms they use! However it is possible to understand many details of later parts of the book without knowledge of this part.

In the third part, called Modeling methods, we give a collection of methods for constructing models. These methods, all illustrated with practical examples, are *actor modeling*, concerning the modeling of (extended) Petri nets and *object modeling*, which is also called *data modeling*. We conclude this part with a chapter on *object oriented modeling*, which is a mixture of actor and object modeling. The modeling methods cover ones for constructing models after reality as well as others for transforming models from one formalism into another. The modeling methods are treated mostly in an informal way, using examples, in order to facilitate the readability.

Actor models and object models are "glued together" with the specification of types for complex objects and processor relations. Here we need the specification language that is introduced in part I and treated in detail in part V.

In part IV, called Analysis methods, we consider several methods for analyzing a model. They cover *invariant methods* and *occurrence graph methods* of Petri nets, methods for verifying *time constraints* and *simulation methods* for validating models by experimentation.

In part V, called Specification language, we define the Z-like specification language. The construction of the language is interesting in itself. Because function construction plays an important role in specifications, this topic is treated extensively. Therefore this part of the book can also be considered as an introduction to *functional programming*.

Each part concludes with an annotated bibliography and a set of exercises. Answers to the exercises are available from the author.

The book ends with three appendices on mathematical notions, the syntax of the specification language and a toolkit of useful functions.

The book is intended for advanced undergraduate and graduate students in computer science, electrical engineering and, industrial engineering as well as for professional systems engineers. The author is convinced that tommorow's systems engineers need an education in formal methods to model systems than is offered in most university courses to day. The only way to cope with the complexity of large systems is to make precise and concise models (of parts) of the systems under consideration. This book offers the foundations for such education.

Prerequisites of the book are: a good understanding of (naive) set theory and predicate calculus. Some experience in functional programming and some knowledge of Petri nets and data bases is useful but not necessary. For a more practical course the instructor could summarize part II and skip part V. Since there are three views presented in the book (the data base view, the Petri net view and the formal specifications view) instructors may decide to emphasize one of these perspectives in a course.

The whole book can be taught in about sixty hours. A course that covers only parts I, II and III can be taught in about forty hours. Exercises with a tool like ExSpect are very useful.

The book will also be of interest for researchers in the areas of formal specifications and systems modeling, in particular the methods part contains many challenges for future research.

## Acknowledgements

The main part of the book is written while I was on a sabbatical leave at the University of Waterloo, Ontario. I thank John Ophel and Farhad Mavaddat from the Computer Science Department of this University and the students of course CS757 (1992) for many useful comments. Furthermore I wish to express my gratitude to Jan Paredaens (University of Antwerp) for several helpful comments.

The book is the result of the research and software development of the ExSpect group at the Eindhoven University of Technology. I thank them all for their contributions, but in particular Wil van der Aalst, Lou Somers, Peter Verkoulen and Marc Voorhoeve.

The research of the ExSpect group was supported by the ESPRIT program (EP-5342) and the TASTE project of the Netherlands organization for applied scientific research, TNO. Therefore I am grateful to the European Commission and TNO as well as the Eindhoven University of Technology for granting me a sabbatical leave.

Last but not least I thank Jane Pullin and Jeroen Schuyt for a large part of the text editing, and Susan Parkinson for excellent copy editing.

Kees M. van Hee,
Eindhoven University of Technology,
e-mail: wsinhee@win.tue.nl
1993

# Part I

# System concepts

# 1

# Introduction

Engineering is the scientific discipline focussed on the creation of new artifacts designed to be of some use to our society. Such artifacts range from buildings to software and from screws to airplanes. Different types of artifacts require different engineering approaches; therefore there exist many engineering disciplines. However, in all these disciplines the *development* of a new artifact is divided into *stages*. Three stages can always be recognized in some form, although the terminology may differ between disciplines or even between schools within the same discipline. These stages are as follows.

**Analysis,** which involves:

- *evaluation* of the existing artifact (if any) that is to be replaced or improved and of the *environment* in which the artifact should fulfill its tasks,
- *specification* of the *requirements* the artifact has to fulfill for its environment.

**Design,** which involves the creation of two models:

- the *functional model*, also called the *specification*, which describes the behavior of the artifact in an abstract way;
- the *construction model*, also called the *blueprint*, which models the artifact in terms of existing components and materials from which the artifact is to be constructed.

The design stage also involves *verification* that the functional model satisfies the requirements specified in the analysis and that the construction model has the functionality described in the functional model.

**Realization,** which involves:

- *construction* of the artifact (or a prototype) according to the construction model,

3

  – *testing* the constructed artifact with respect to the functional model.

These three stages concern the development of an artifact; however the *life cycle* of an artifact involves further stages. If it is a *mass product*, there are two additional stages.

**Production,** in which copies of the realized artifact are produced (note that often the production process itself has to be designed first).

**Distribution,** in which the copies are brought to the environment where they are wanted, often via market mechanisms.

These stages do not occur if the artifact is a unique product. Whether or not the latter is the case, the following stages belong to the life cycle.

**Introduction** of (a copy of) the artifact in the environment where it will be used.

**Maintenance** of the artifact to keep it working or to adapt it to new requirements.

In the present book we only consider the first two stages of the development process. We focus our attention on a specific type of artifact, called a *discrete dynamic system*. Such a system consists of active components or *actors* that *consume* and *produce* passive components or *tokens*. Many complex artifacts in our world can be considered as discrete dynamic systems. Three subtypes will be studied in more detail:

– business systems (such as a factory or restaurant);
– information systems (whether automated or not);
– automated systems (systems that are controlled by an automated information system).

The first subtype is studied by *industrial engineers*, the third by *software engineers* and *electrical engineers*, whereas the second is a battlefield for all three disciplines. We hope that our approach suits these disciplines; we call their union *systems engineering*. The types of discrete dynamic systems on which we focus our attention are described in the next chapter.

During the analysis and design stages of the development process for discrete dynamic systems the systems engineer is working with *models* of these systems. A model is in fact another system, but one that is easier to analyze or observe than the original system. But the model has so much similarity to the original system (in certain aspects at least), that conclusions drawn from the model are assumed to be valid for the original system as well.

We consider *conceptual* models (also called abstract, mathematical or symbolic models), not physical models. The former can be analyzed by formal methods, whereas the latter can be observed by experiments only. However, if the conceptual model can be executed on a computer system, thus *simulating* the original system, we can combine analysis with experimentation. This is what we aim for.

The process of creating a model is called *modeling*. There are two approaches for modeling: *top-down modeling* and *bottom-up modeling*. In both cases one starts with a certain set of primitive submodels or *components*. In the first approach one keeps refining an initially empty model into sub-components until one reaches the primitive components. In the second approach the primitive components are extended and linked together to form less primitive ones and this is continued until a final component is constructed that approximates the real system sufficiently precisely.

The systems engineer involved in analysis and design creates conceptual models in his mind and documents these models. He makes models of existing real-world systems in the evaluation part of the analysis stage and models of a new system to be created in other cases. In all cases the systems engineer needs a set of *concepts* that have an intuitive meaning for him to build his models.

Examples of such concepts within the context of this book are for instance *state*, *event*, *token*, *object* and *actor*. The systems engineer should be able to map real-world entities and phenomena onto these concepts. This process is one of the most important elements of modeling. Reasoning with concepts in our mind is dangerous, because we can easily make mistakes. Therefore the systems engineer needs a *formalism*. A formalism consists of a *mathematical framework* and a *language* (called a modeling language). The mathematical framework attaches a rigorous meaning to the concepts, for instance in terms of sets and functions. This language is used to construct conceptual systems from mathematical concepts and to represent them symbolically. (In the literature, a framework is often erroneously called a model; in fact it is a formalism.)

For instance, an architect has intuitive concepts such as window, roof and wall. The formalization of these concepts is geometrical (in three dimensions). The language by which he makes conceptual models of a building is a graphical one using polygons and other curves. In part I of the book we introduce the concepts we will use for modeling discrete dynamic systems. In the parts II and V we consider formalisms.

A systems engineer needs intuitive concepts as well as their formalization. In fact, each modeling process starts off with an informal model in everyday language (sometimes illustrated by equally informal diagrams). After that the model is formalized. Formalization invariably shows errors in the informal description, so the latter then has to be adapted. Note that the formal description is not enough: we also need the informal one to get the right intuition.

The concepts for modeling discrete dynamic systems are of two kinds. The first kind of concept is used when dealing with a *holistic* view of systems. This means that we do not consider many details of a system but only its main characteristics and also that we consider a system as one entity. This topic is studied in chapter 3 where we introduce, informally, the framework of *transition systems*. According to this framework a system is at each moment in some state and if an event occurs, it makes a transition to another state. This framework contains many important system concepts and enables us to derive general properties for the kind of systems in which we are interested.

In chapter 4, we introduce a *reductionistic* view of systems. Here we make use of the second kind of concept, such as object, token and actor, from which we can construct the concepts of the first framework, as follows. Tokens contain objects and are used to construct states of a transition system. Actors are used to construct the mechanism for changing the state. So, both frameworks fit nicely together. The reductionist approach is used for modeling and the holistic one for analysis.

The language we use to model systems is mathematical. Like the architect using geometry (the language of shapes) to model the artifacts he wants to make, we use the language of sets and functions to model our artifacts. In doing so, we can use mathematics to establish properties of our models.

# 2
# Application domains

The formalisms and methods of this book will be used to model and analyze a broad class of systems, called *discrete dynamic systems*. These systems are characterized by the fact that they are at each moment in a *state* and that there is a sequence of *events* that move the system to another state. So the number of state changes during the course of a system is at most countable, which warrants the adjective "discrete". So, we shall not consider *continuous* systems where the state varies continuously with time. This is not too great a disadvantage: continuous functions can be approximated by step functions with arbitrary precision. Similarly, we can build discrete models for any continuous system.

According to quantum physics, our world (at the sub-atomic scale) has discrete behavior and can be modeled as a discrete dynamic system. Nevertheless, in many cases a continuous model is more appropriate.

Discrete dynamic systems are thus a subclass of all dynamic systems, but a very important one: all computerized systems such as distributed databases, user interfaces, electronic mail systems and decision support systems fall within this class; so do many business systems such as factories, offices and transport enterprises. A more systematic discussion of system classes is given below.

Discrete dynamic systems are built of two kinds of component: *actors* and *objects*. Actors are the active components in the sense that they *consume* and *produce* objects, which are the passive components. In fact they consume and produce *tokens*; tokens are "containers" for objects. Therefore we often speak of "object" instead of "token".

Instead of the consumption/production paradigm we can use the *flow* paradigm: tokens flow through a network of actors. For instance, the production process in a factory can be considered as a flow of orders, materials and semi-finished products. In each production step one or more objects are used to produce new objects.

*Actors* can be human beings, machines, vehicles or networks of other discrete dynamic systems. Actors perform operations on the state of the whole discrete dynamic system although they mostly consume only a subset of the tokens in a state. *Objects* can be material objects such as chairs and cars, or information objects like insurance policies, diagnoses, advice, designs or financial transfers. The produced objects are often strongly related to the consumed ones. For example, they may differ only in some properties like color, form, weight or location. If one consumed object results in one produced object and they differ only in location, we call the operation of the actor *transportation*. If other attributes only are changed we call the operation *transformation*. If more than one object is consumed to produce one new object we call the operation *convergence* or *assembly*. If one consumed object results in several produced ones we call it *divergence* or *decomposition*. Produced objects are called *products*. In many cases an information object is consumed and produced simultaneously with the consumption and production of material objects. The *state* of a discrete dynamic system is formed by the configuration of the tokens (inside as well as outside the actors) at the moment the state is considered. The *transition law* (that says which states are allowed as the next state) is determined by the operations the actors may perform.

We will discuss below three subtypes of discrete dynamic systems: *business systems*, *information systems* and *automated systems* (*see* figure 2.1). These subtypes are not disjoint but represent different views. One should not confuse "subtypes" and "subsystems". Type A is a subtype of type B if all entities that belong to A also belong to B. A system belongs to a type if it has the characteristic properties of the type. System A has a subsystem B if B is a component of A; they may be of different types.

### Business systems

In a *business system* objects have an economical value and for each operation of an actor the sum of the values of produced objects should be larger than or equal to the sum of the values of the consumed objects, although this target is not always met. A business system can be regarded as a "value-adding discrete dynamic system" or "profit center". In industrial engineering one distinguishes many subtypes of business systems. One such subtype (*see* figure 2.1) is formed by *business units* or departments, for example:

**marketing:** actors perform operations to obtain orders to produce or to deliver from stock;

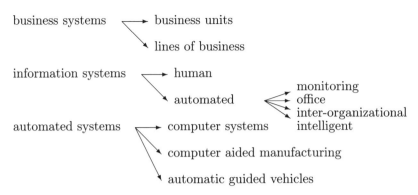

Fig. 2.1 A taxonomy of discrete dynamic systems: "human", "automated", "monitoring", "office", "inter-organizational" and "intelligent" are all types of information system.

**purchase:** operations to obtain raw materials or semi-manufactured materials;

**engineering:** operations to design products and the production process;

**manufacturing:** operations to transform, assemble or dissemble objects and to control quality;

**logistics:** operations to transport objects at the right time and place, including storage;

**maintenance:** operations to keep the non-human actors in good condition;

**personnel:** operations to keep the human actors in good "shape" by recruitment, training, career development and firing;

**data processing:** operations to maintain the computer systems (another subtype of discrete dynamic systems) and to develop new applications (software or computer systems);

**finance:** operations to administrate the financial transactions caused by sales, purchases, wages, rentals, loans, leasing, interest payments, debts, credits and investments.

This subtype "business system" belongs to a *micro-economical* view. It is essential for a systems engineer to recognize the business units in a practical situation and to have an idea of their functionality.

The second subtype belongs to a *macro-economical* view. It is based on the *kind of business*:

**primary industry:** operations to obtain raw material from nature, for example agriculture, fishing, mining and oil drilling;

**secondary industry:** operations to manufacture products from raw materials; products may be such things as food, clothing, buildings, chemicals, mechanical constructs, electrical equipment and software;

**transportation:** operations to move persons or goods via air, water, rail and road;

**trade and distribution:** operations to transfer the ownership of objects in order to match demand and supply, for example the trade in raw materials (such as oil and cereals) and the wholesale and retail business;

**banking and insurance:** operations to transfer, store and invest money and to share financial risks in order to enable the other lines of business;

**services:** operations to produce abstract products, for example consultancy, health care, education, and engineering design.

Of course many companies are involved in a mixture of these lines of business; for instance a large oil company might be a primary industry as well as a distribution company, and a restaurant may belong to retailers as well as to the "food industry".

### Informations systems

Another subtype of discrete dynamic systems is called an *information system* and is characterized by two properties:

(i) all actors in an information system are consuming and producing information objects exclusively;

(ii) an information system is part of another discrete dynamic system (called the *target system* in this context); the role of the information system is to support the target system.

The task of an information system for its target system can be split into a *logistics* part (recording, storage, retrieval and transmission of information objects) and a *management* part (creation of information objects, needed to *control* the target system, on the basis of recorded information objects from the target system). If information objects are the final products of a discrete dynamic system (as is the case in the service industry) then the actors that produce them are clearly no "control actors". Often one does not consider such actors to be part of the information system. We will not restrict ourselves, however, in the use of the term information system.

An information system is formed by two kinds of actor (*see* figure 2.1): information workers who form the *human information system* and *automated information systems*, a subtype of both computer systems and information systems. An information system communicates with other systems by means of *sensors* and *actuators*. Sensors are physical constructs that produce information objects at events that involve the equipment to which they are connected. Actuators are also physical constructs, but they work the other way around: they consume information objects, called control objects, and create events for the equipment to which they belong.

We now consider human information systems. As said before, one of the major tasks of an information system is the control or management of the target system. Management consists of five elements;

**collecting** relevant information (objects) from the target system;
**analyzing** the information to obtain diagnoses;
**generating** control objects to steer the target system to a goal;
**evaluating** the generated control objects;
**selecting** a control object and sending it to the target system.

Control objects are often called *decisions* in this context. Human beings often take care of these tasks, but computer systems also take part in the process. It is usual to distinguish several levels of management. We distinguish four levels, as follows:

**equipment control:** for instance driving a vehicle or tending a lathe; the control objects are sent very frequently (for instance every few seconds);
**operational control:** the control over a production unit, i.e. a small discrete dynamic system consisting of a group of equipment and some human resources; the control objects are sent frequently, with time intervals varying from an hour to several weeks;
**tactical management:** decision making for a business unit; the decisions have a relatively long influence on the system and are made with low frequency, with time intervals varying from a month to some years;
**strategic management:** decision making for a business system; decisions of the same type are made seldom and they have a very long impact on the system.

We now look at *automated information systems*(*see* figure 2.1). This type of information system is exclusively realized by computer systems. We distinguish four subtypes of automated information systems: monitoring information systems, office information systems, inter-organizational information systems and intelligent information systems.

*Monitoring information systems* fulfill the following tasks for their target systems:

**recording** events of the target system in order to obtain an up-to-date image of the state of the target system (called the *stored* state);
**triggering** or **signaling** the target system in the case where the stored state satisfies some condition and a trigger is used to steer the target system;

the system time may be one of the parameters of such a condition, hence
the triggering may for example occur only because the system time passed
some limit;

**reporting** on the stored state, on demand or periodically.

While a trigger does not contain much information on the stored state, a report
gives an outline of it. Often the triggers require complex calculations whereas the
reports do not. An accounting system is an example of a monitoring information
system.

A monitoring information system often uses a *database management system*,
i.e. system software, to organize large collections of structured data. Most monitoring information systems are *on-line systems*, which means that they obtain
their information objects directly from the target system and that their results
are passed immediately to the target system or to some part of the environment.
Examples of on-line monitoring information systems are found for example in
*logistics* systems where they record the movements of vehicles and goods, in
banks where they monitor money flows and in universities where they monitor
the progress of students. If the target system is a piece of equipment, registration
and triggering may have to fulfill some very strict time constraints within short
time intervals. In this case one calls these systems *real-time* systems. Examples
of real-time systems are found in robots, automated guided vehicles, numerically
controlled lathes and telephone exchanges.

*Office information systems* form a relatively young type of automated information system. They are composed of editors for text, diagrams or pictures,
spread sheets, database management systems, electronic mail systems and work-
flow managements systems. The support they give to the information workers
can be characterized by for example the supply of pens, paper, erasers and calcu-
lators, filing and postal services. Office information systems will incorporate more
intelligence in the future and therefore the distinction from intelligent information
systems may disappear.

*Inter-organizational information systems* are also relatively young. They support business communications between autonomous organizations. Examples are
*video-tex systems* and *electronic shopping systems*. Communication between organizations is often realized by *electronic data interchange* via computer networks.

*Intelligent information systems* incorporate "expertise" or "knowledge", which
they use to support creative work. The knowledge is represented as mathematical
formulae such as linear differential equations or logical formulae such as Horn
clauses. The role intelligent information systems play in creative work consists
of the following.

**Design support:** this concerns the design of physical objects. Besides the editing facilities also found in office informations system, an intelligent information system computes quality measures such as strength or resistance and it generates alternative shapes or layouts. Such systems are called *computer aided design systems*.

**Diagnosis or analysis:** this concerns the process of drawing conclusions from complex data. Where the data are numerical, mathematical statistics are used, for instance in forecasting or hypothesis testing. Statistical or numerical software packages are components of such intelligent information systems. Where the data are non-numerical logical data are often involved and then a theorem prover or inference engine is used to derive conclusions; examples of such systems are found in laboratories, hospitals and marketing departments. They are called *expert systems*.

**Decision support:** this concerns management decisions in a business system. As we have seen before there are many levels of management decision. Decision support always concerns the choice of a control object or decision. As in computer aided design systems it involves the following kinds of support:

- checking user defined decisions on feasibility;
- evaluating the quality of decisions;
- generating decisions that satisfy some user defined goals (optimization);
- assisting in the selection process when there are several candidate decisions.

The systems involved in the above are called *decision-support systems*. In a computer aided design system the final product is the design of a physical entity, whereas the final product of a decision-support system is a plan. Therefore a decision-support system is sometimes called a *planning system*.

**Automated systems**

The final subtype of discrete dynamic systems we consider is called an *automated system*. This consists of an automated information system and a physical system. The automated information system is often called an *embedded system*. *Computer systems* are a type of automated system (*see* figure 2.1). Such a system consists of computer hardware and software. Here, the automated information system is called the *operating system*. (Note that automated information systems are, logically, also a type of computer system.)

*Computer aided manufacturing systems* are another type of automated system. A numerically controlled lathe is one example, a robot is another. The last subtype of automated systems we mention is *automatic guided vehicles*.

Now that we have considered the discrete dynamic systems that are relevant to us, we reconsider the informal definition of discrete dynamic systems. A discrete dynamic system always has an information system as a subsystem. Furthermore, there are often subsystems that have to be controlled, such as the biological systems, encountered in agriculture. A discrete dynamic system may also have one or more discrete dynamic systems as a subsystem, so we shall define discrete dynamic systems in a recursive way. A syntactical definition of a discrete dynamic system is as follows:

discrete dynamic system ::= information system $*$ ⟨ controlled system ⟩
controlled system        ::= physical system |
                     discrete dynamic system.

Here $*$ denotes the composition operator for systems and the expression between ⟨⟩ may be repeated zero, one or more times. In figure 2.2 we give an example:

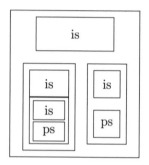

Fig. 2.2 An example of a discrete dynamic system; "is", "ps" refer to "information system" and "physical system".

each rectangle represents a discrete dynamic system. The organization of a discrete dynamic system rules the interaction between its subsystems. The information system takes care of the execution of these rules with respect to its target system and the other subsystems; hence the organization is incorporated in the information system.

Our first interest is the modeling of discrete dynamic systems. Secondly we are interested in the analysis of the (possible) behavior of a system. Models can be used for several purposes, for example, as a *functional model*, as a *construction model* or for *analysis* of an existing system. Models are analyzed for the following:

**verification** of behavioral properties, such as *invariants*, and absence of *deadlocking* (these concepts will be explained later);
**determination** of performance characteristics, such as *efficiency* and *reliability*.

Analysis is useful for models of existing systems that do not perform well. Based on an analysis one may decide to redesign the system. Analysis is also useful to check the design (functional or construction model) of a new system, in order to prevent mistakes: it is always cheaper to adapt a design than to adapt a real system.

# 3

# Transition systems

The systems in which we are interested are subject to changes during their lifetime. At any moment in time the system has a certain *state*; at any later moment this state may have changed. The set of all states that a system may have is called its *state space*.

A system's state can be regarded as a snapshot of the system, showing all relevant details. It may often contain some details that cannot be directly observed. For example, a state may contain temporal information, such as the time at which the current state was reached or the time at which the current state will end.

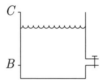

Fig. 3.1. A water reservoir.

Fig. 3.2. The state-time diagram of the water reservoir.

Let us consider a water reservoir as an example system. It is filled by rain and emptied by means of a tap. Figure 3.1 depicts such a water reservoir. The state of this system is defined as the water level. In this case we thus have a single variable. Figure 3.2 is the graph showing the fluctuations of the state during a certain time period. It is an example of a *state-time diagram*. From the structure of the reservoir (if we neglect evaporation) we can derive the following properties of its state: the water level cannot be above $C$ and it cannot decrease if it is below or at $B$. We have displayed the state-time diagram as a continuous function, which is not possible for the discrete systems we consider. Later we shall display a discrete version.

The *time domain* of a system is a set of so-called time points. The state of a system is defined only for the time points in its time domain. We will consider only time domains that are a subset of the real numbers. We normalize our time domain in such a way that the minimal time point is 0. In our example, we regarded an interval of the real numbers as the time domain. Sometimes we will consider subsets of the natural numbers. In this case there is a unique next time point, which is not the case for intervals of the real numbers, for example.

A *path* of a system is a (partial) function from its time domain to its state space. Figure 3.2 depicts such a path for our water reservoir, so the graphical representation of a path is a state-time diagram. The domain of a path must be a (possibly infinite) interval: if the path is defined in $t_0$ and $t_1$, it must also be defined for any $t$ in the time domain $t_0 \leq t \leq t_1$. Usually, the number of possible or conceivable paths a system may follow is very large or even infinite, as in our reservoir, where we cannot predict either rainfall or water consumption.

In this book, we consider systems for which paths are determined by a *trace*, a sequence of *events*. An event signifies the transition of one state to another state at a specific time point; a process is thus a series of state transitions. Paths that can be characterized by a trace are step functions: the state changes when an event occurs, then it stays the same until the next event occurs.

More formally, an event is a pair $(s, t)$, where $s$ is a state and $t$ a time point. An event $(s, t)$ means that the system "moves" to state $s$ at time $t$; $t$ is called the *event time*.

A trace is a *monotonous* finite or infinite sequence of events, starting with time 0. Monotonous means that the event times in a trace form a non-decreasing sequence. Our notation for a trace is $\langle (s_0, t_0), (s_1, t_1), \ldots \rangle$, where $t_0 = 0$. An event $(s, t)$ from a trace is said to *occur* at event time $t$. A *prefix* of a trace $p$ is obtained from $p$ by deleting all events from some point onward. Clearly a prefix of a trace is a trace.

The *empty trace*, the empty sequence of events, is denoted by $\epsilon$. It is a prefix of any non-empty trace. We allow that successive events in a trace may occur at the same time point. A subsequence of a trace with all events having the same time point is called a *multiple event*. Multiple events occur at the same point in time, but nevertheless in a certain order. At first sight it seems to be paradoxical that two or more events may occur at the same time in some order. However, if the

I *System concepts*

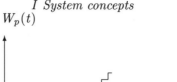

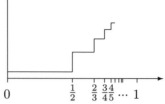

Fig. 3.3. The path of a system with livelock.

time domain is the set of natural numbers, representing weeks, then we consider the system only at the end of each week; so all events that have occurred during a week are observed simultaneously at the end of the week. Two successive events may have the same state, which means that the state of the system does not change. The first event in a (non-empty) trace is called the *initial event* (with time 0). Its state is called the *initial state*.

A trace $p = \langle (s_0, t_0), (s_1, t_1), \ldots \rangle$ determines a path $W_p$. The path $W_p$ is a function on the time domain. For some time point $t$ the state will be $W_p(t)$, where

$$W_p(t) = s_i \text{ if } t \in [t_i, t_{i+1}) \text{ for } i \in \mathbb{N},$$

$$W_p(t) = s_n \text{ if } p \text{ is finite, } (s_n, t_n) \text{ is the final event and } t \geq t_n.$$

(Note that $[a, b) = \{x \in \mathbb{R} \mid a \leq x < b\}$.) Again $t_0 = 0$. If $p = \epsilon$ then $dom(W_p) = \emptyset$.

A pathological situation occurs if the number of events in a trace $p$ occurring before a time point $t$ is infinite. An example of such a trace is one that is infinite with all events occurring at the same time point.

In figure 3.3 another example is displayed. This property of a trace is called *livelock*. If a trace $p$ livelocks, $dom(W_p)$ is a finite interval.

Note that different traces may determine the same path. If two consecutive events in a trace have the same state $(s)$ component the second one may be deleted and if they have the same $t$ component the first one may be deleted in each case without altering the path.

Which traces and therefore which paths a certain discrete dynamic system can have is determined by a function called the *transition law*. A transition law $\mathcal{L}$ can be applied to a finite trace $p$. $\mathcal{L}(p)$ is thus a set of events, the possible next events of the system. The term "next" means that the possible events have an event time that is at least as large as the event time of the last event of the trace.

More formally, the transition law of a system is a function $\mathcal{L}$ that assigns to any finite trace $p = \langle (s_0, t_0), \ldots, (s_n, t_n) \rangle$ a set of events $\mathcal{L}(p)$. A transition law also assigns to the empty trace $\epsilon$ a set of *initial events*. All initial events have an event time equal to zero.

A system with transition law $\mathcal{L}$ will behave as follows. Suppose it already has a history, consisting of the trace

$$p = \langle (s_0, t_0), \dots, (s_n, t_n) \rangle,$$

and that the actual time is $t$, with $t \geq t_n$. The transition law gives a set of possible events $\mathcal{L}(p)$. A next event that will occur must have event time greater than or equal to $t$ and be an element of $\mathcal{L}(p)$. Possibly no further event will occur.

A trace $p$ such that $\mathcal{L}(p)$ is the empty set is said to *deadlock*. This means that no next event is possible.

Another problem is when too large a state space has been defined. This means that there are states that never occur in an event of a trace. In the example of the water reservoir the states in $[0, B)$ never occur. The states that do occur in some event are called *reachable states*.

The *autonomous behavior* of a system with transition law $\mathcal{L}$ is the set of all traces $q = \langle (s_0, t_0), (s_1, t_1), \dots \rangle$ such that

$$(s_0, t_0) \in \mathcal{L}(\epsilon),$$

and for $m \geq 1$

$$(s_m, t_m) \in \mathcal{L}(\langle (s_0, t_0), \dots, (s_{m-1}, t_{m-1}) \rangle).$$

This is the set of all traces that can be produced by the transition law of the system itself. Note that the autonomous behavior is an empty set if and only if $\epsilon$ deadlocks.

If the range of $\mathcal{L}$ contains only the empty set and singletons, $\mathcal{L}$ is called *deterministic*. The reason is that then each finite trace $p$ can either be continued in one way or not continued at all.

If $\mathcal{L}$ is not deterministic, it is called *non-deterministic*. In that kind of system there is a $p$ such that $\mathcal{L}(p)$ contains more than one element. Starting from such a trace $p$, there are several events that can occur.

We have encountered uncertainties above: whether a next event will occur or not and if so, which event will occur. When a system is actually functioning, only one possibility is chosen. Such a choice is made by a "demon" that takes decisions that we do not want to make within our system.

Sometimes there are components within our system that we cannot control or predict. For our reservoir this is for instance the weather. Also human beings (if considered as components of a system) fall within this category. Even (actual) machines have the nasty property that they can malfunction at unpredictable moments.

Sometimes we model a deterministic system, the state of which cannot be observed completely, as a non-deterministic system. Our model's state will contain the information we have about the system's state and our model's transition law will take the incompleteness of our information into account by allowing several alternative paths.

Last but not least, we often make models in which we do not want to prescribe the model's behavior completely. This is the case when modeling a piece of software that is to be made. When the model is turned into an actual system, the constructor may choose whatever he thinks fit from a set of possible alternatives. For instance, if we make a model of a system that sorts items according to the value of one of their attributes, we do not specify in which order items with the same attribute value should appear. So our model can be a non-deterministic system. The constructor, though, may realize it as a deterministic system. Note that it is also possible to describe the model as a deterministic system, although we do not specify how items with the same attribute values should be ordered. In that case our model is incomplete. In the example, it would mean that we ask the constructor to build a deterministic system.

Again, we do not know how the demon chooses. Sometimes a *probabilistic* demon is handy. In such a case, the transition law must be modified, adding a probability distribution to the alternatives offered. The probabilistic demon chooses according to this distribution. If we have a probabilistic demon we often require that it is *fair*, which implies that it gives every possible choice a positive probability. It is sometimes difficult to realize a fair demon.

For practical purposes, we will often postulate the demon to be *eager*. This means that it always chooses an event with the minimal event time, if an event like that exists. For example, suppose that $\mathcal{L}(p)$ for some path $p$ is given by

$$\mathcal{L}(p) = \{(a, 44), (a, 56), (b, 44), (c, 60)\},$$

where $a$, $b$ and $c$ are states. Then an eager demon will select $(a, 44)$ or $(b, 44)$ as next event.

The traces from the autonomous behavior of a system that can be selected by an eager demon form its *eager autonomous behavior*.

We can obtain the eager autonomous behavior of a system as the autonomous behavior of another system with the same state space and a modified transition law. The modification consists of deleting events with a non-minimal event time. In the above example we would obtain

$$\mathcal{L}(p) = \{(a, 44), (b, 44)\}.$$

An eager demon can sometimes turn a non-deterministic system into a determin-istic one, but this is not necessarily the case.

Another postulate we often make for the behavior of the demon is that it is *maximal*, which means that the demon will choose a next event, unless the trace deadlocks.

We have seen how a transition law determines the autonomous behavior of a system, which consists of *internal events*. However, *external influences* may cause *external events*. Consider a finite trace $p = \langle (s_0, t_0), \ldots, (s_n, t_n) \rangle$ and assume that this trace has occurred. Let the actual or current time be $t$ and let $t > t_n$. Then we know that the demon did not choose an event with event time $t'$ such that $t_n < t' \leq t$. Suppose at $t$ there occurs an external event $(s, t)$. After that the demon will forget its former choice and will make a new choice from the event set $\mathcal{L}(p; (s, t))$. So there are two different mechanisms that determine the trace of a system: the demon that chooses from the event sets offered by the transition law and external events arising from some other system.

Let us consider a discrete version of the water reservoir, where a state transition may only occur at natural time points. Again, the state variable is the water level. The system is initialized at time point 0 with a level $i$ between $B$ and $C$. At each integer time point, a quantity up to $p$ of water (if possible) may be consumed. (No consumption is modeled as consumption of a quantity 0.) Then one must wait till the next time point. In the meantime, the water level may have increased due to rainfall with a quantity $a$, if it fits into the reservoir; otherwise the reservoir is filled to capacity. Figure 3.4 might be considered as a path of this system.

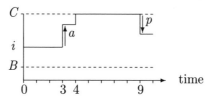

Fig. 3.4. A path of the discrete water reservoir.

We shall now define the transition law of this system:

$$\mathcal{L}(\epsilon) = \{(i, 0) \mid B \leq i \leq C\},$$
$$\mathcal{L}(\langle (s_0, t_0), \ldots, (s_n, t_n) \rangle) =$$
$$\{(s, t) \mid t = t_n + 1 \ \wedge \ max(B, s_n - p) \leq s \leq min(C, s_n + a)\}.$$

The first equation describes the initialization. The second one describes (com-bined) rainfall and consumption ($p$ and $a$ are parameters). Note that identical transitions are possible in this example, but multiple events are not.

A natural requirement for a transition law is that the set of next events generated by a transition law only depends upon the last event, $(s, t)$. This is called a *memoryless* transition law. The name is derived from the observation that such a law does not "remember" the system's earlier events; only its present state and time matter. (Note that a "memory" of previous events may perhaps be stored in the present state.) Sometimes we have an even stronger property, a *strongly memoryless* transition law. In that case the set of next events depends only on the last reached state and not on the time at which it was reached. If a system has a strongly memoryless transition law, then the states should contain time information, since the transition law describes what the next state will be and *when* the transition will happen on the basis of the last state only.

The systems we will consider in the rest of this book will have a strongly memoryless transition law.

We have described the autonomous behavior of a system by means of a transition law. Another approach is to specify directly a set of allowed traces. In practice, this amounts to formulating *constraints*, i.e. predicates that together characterize this set. The set is prefix-closed: a prefix of an allowed trace is also allowed.

One often distinguishes *static* and *dynamic* constraints; static constraints restrict the state space of a system, while dynamic constraints restrict the state transitions that can be made.

We can construct from any set of constraints characterizing a prefix-closed set of finite traces a transition law that characterizes the same set, and vice versa (*see* chapter 9). The choice between a transition law and constraints is a matter of efficiency. In some cases it is easier to say what is possible (the transition law) and in other situations it is easier to say what is forbidden (constraints). We will use the transition law because it is a constructive approach.

The next concepts we consider deal with the *life cycle* of a system. Often one wants to regard the creation and death of a system as two special state transitions. From our point of view a system is always existing, although it may have one special state, "non-exist". This special state has the following properties.

If the system is in its non-exist state only one event may occur, and that event, called *creation*, brings the system into one of its "live" states. From there it evolves according to its transition law. There is one other special event, called *death*, that brings the system back to its non-exist state. No other event brings the system into its non-exist state. The time spent between the occurrence of the creation and death events is called a *life cycle*.

There is another way to deal with life cycles. It occurs when we want to change the transition law itself during the course of a system. Such a situation frequently occurs. Take for instance the water reservoir system when the capacity of the tap is enlarged. In that case we may consider this as the death of the system with a small tap and the creation of a new system with a bigger tap. However, it is also possible to extend the state space of the system by means of a new state variable component, called "tap capacity". An event "tap change" has to be introduced to change this new component of the state variable. Now the system may be considered as living forever with only one transition law. A third way of dealing with such a structural change is to incorporate the new parameters in the transition law. In this solution the transition law is not memoryless but it will depend on the last event that adapted the tap capacity. So there are three ways of dealing with this kind of system change: by extending the state space by a new state (e.g. non-exist); by extending it by a new state variable component (e.g. tap capacity); or by adapting the transition law. Sometimes the kind of change considered here is referred to as the *second order dynamics* of a system. We have shown that these changes may be regarded as normal or first order dynamics.

In the remainder of the book, we assume special structures for state spaces and transition laws. The state of a system will be a set of *objects* or *tokens*. A transition law consists of (consecutively but instantaneously) removing some tokens from the old state and inserting tokens into the new state. Instead of deletion and insertion we often speak of *consumption* and *production* of tokens. We will always assume that produced tokens are "new": they did not occur in the old state. However, we may regard a newly produced token as the *continuation* of a consumed one, which is in fact a way to express that a token has been changed in the event.

So far, we have only considered systems without any outside influences, so-called *closed* systems, which are encountered seldom in practice. Almost invariably, *open* systems, which interact with other systems are being described, constructed or modeled. If we concentrate on one system, we call the systems with which it interacts its *environment*. We can define an open system and its environment in such a way that they form a closed system together.

Next we shall show how two systems are combined to make one new system. This is called *composition*. When describing a complex system, we often *decompose* them into less complex systems called *components*. The original system is then a *compound system*, the composition of the components.

We consider only the composition of systems with strongly memoryless transition laws. If we compose two systems, we will take the union of their states to get the state of the compound system. In the compound system, tokens can be of two kinds: those affected exclusively by either of the components (*private* tokens) and those that can be affected by both components (*shared* tokens).

The transition law of the compound system consisting of two components, is derived from the transition laws of the components in the following way. A new event for the compound system is either caused by a single component or by both simultaneously. In the first case one of the components consumes tokens from the state (shared or private to itself) and produces new ones. In the second case both components consume tokens from the state; however, the consumed sets must be disjoint and the event times of the corresponding events must be the same.

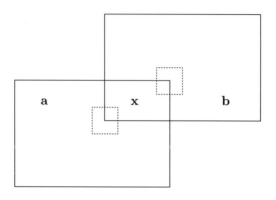

Fig. 3.5. Venn diagram of a composition example.

We will illustrate this in figure 3.5, in which we see the states $a \cup x, b \cup x$ and $S_C = a \cup b \cup x$ of systems $A$, $B$ and their composition $C$ respectively. The dotted squares represent sets of tokens that can be consumed by $A$ and $B$ during events with the same, minimal, event time. For system $C$ three kinds of event are possible: an event from system $A$ that consumes the left-hand dashed square, an event from system $B$ that consumes the other dashed square and an event consuming from both sets of tokens.

It is important to observe that composition is defined to be *commutative* and *associative*, which means that the composition of a complex system from smaller subsystems does not depend upon the order in which they are combined.

An important aspect of system composition is that we can define the concept of *communication* between systems. Two systems can communicate if they are components of a compound system. Communication is the exchange of shared tokens: one system produces them and the other consumes them in different events.

An event of the compound system caused by the transition law of one component is called an *external event* for another component, if it changes the set of shared tokens. If it does not, it is called an *internal event* for the first component. Each component of a compound system is in fact an *open* system, since events external to it can occur.

There are two well-known paradigms of communication, namely *message passing* and *shared memory*. In the first one, a system sends tokens (messages) to another system. In the second one, a system "writes" a common state component that can be "read" by the other. In our formalism, both paradigms are combined. Communication between systems is the production and consumption of shared tokens. This can be considered as the exchange of messages: one component produces tokens that are consumed by the other component in a later event and that also update a common state component.

# 4

# Objects

We have seen how to construct complex systems from more simple systems by composing them. However, it is far from easy to determine the state space and the transition law of a complex system in practice. Therefore we will extend our formalism with an extra layer to facilitate the definition of the state space and transition law of a transition system. Of course, we keep open the possibility of composing systems into a compound system, but we will also see how to construct a system out of more elementary building blocks.

Our approach is based on the observation that discrete dynamic systems can be seen as networks of *actors* that consume and produce tokens (*objects*). (The subtle difference between a token and an object is explained below.) The state of a system at some moment is the set of all tokens in the system at that moment. Events are the consumption of tokens in a state and the production of new tokens.

We assume that objects that are consumed in a transition disappear, although they may be reproduced in the same transition in some other form. As before we assume transitions to be instantaneous. In a system all objects reside at some *place*, also called a *channel* or *store*.

In the literature actors are also called *agents* or *automata*. Actors are able to perform local state transitions in the form of the consumption and production of objects. Actors are connected to places: they may only consume objects from, and produce objects for, places to which they are connected. We assume that the network topology is *static*, i.e. the connection relation between actors and places is fixed. Some other formalisms allow the topology to change; this is called a *dynamic* topology.

In this chapter we will elaborate the structural properties of objects and in chapter 5 we will consider the actors in more detail. The *framework* we use to define a state space will be defined formally in chapter 10; here we give an informal description.

In the literature such a framework is often called a *database model* because the concept arose first in the database area. In this book the term "model" is used for a conceptual system that represents a "real" world. In such a world we do not restrict ourselves to *information objects*, as in the database area, but include the actual objects represented by information objects. The term "data model" is misleading, because it is a framework to define models. (Some authors use the term *meta data model*.) We do not restrict the framework to the modeling of *information systems*, i.e. systems with only information objects, and therefore we use the more neutral term "object framework". This framework is in fact an extension of (the binary version of) the *entity-relationship model*. The extension concerns the clustering of "entities" into complex objects and the *distribution* of the complex objects over *places*. In classical data models one considers only one database, i.e. one set of (information) objects at a time. However, we include many different sets of objects in one model, so our framework is suited for the design of *distributed databases* as well.

Instead of using the term "entity", as in the entity-relationship model, we use the term *simple object* or *simplex*. Simplexes are mutually related by *relationships*. A relationship is characterized by a pair of two simplexes and a name, the name of the relationship. The relationships give meaning to the simplexes: having a relationship can be considered as having a *property*.

The classical data models distinguish *attributes* as a third concept besides entities and relationships. We consider them as (abstract) simplexes, which makes our formalism a little easier and avoids the difficult problem of deciding whether a "thing" is an entity or an attribute.

In our framework simplexes are

- *concrete* or *physical* objects, such as persons, cars and chairs,
- *abstract* or *conceptual* objects, such as orders, jobs and names,
- *information* objects, which *refer* to either a concrete or an abstract object.

Concrete objects can be observed in a physical world. Abstract objects are not observable but are supposed to exist in a world of "thoughts"; however, they can be described by information objects. So we assume there is only one name "John" in a world of thoughts but there are many information objects representing "John". The information objects exist in *information systems*; they describe both concrete and abstract objects. A world of concrete and abstract objects is sometimes called a *real system* in contrast with the information system that describes a real system.

Simplexes are assumed to have the following characteristics:

- they are *atomic*, i.e. we do not consider any internal structure in them,

– they are *distinguishable*, so "water" is not a simplex, but a drop of water is,
– they belong to a *type*, called a *simplex class*,
– in each state of a system the number of simplexes of each class is finite,
– their classes can be named by a noun, as we did with "person" or "job".

Relationships also belong to classes: relationships with the same name connect simplexes of one class to simplexes of another (or it may be the same) class. So, this name determines the *relationship class*.

A structured set of simplexes and relationships is called a *complex object* or, in brief, a *complex*. The set of all possible complexes with the same structure is called a *complex class*. A complex class is characterized by the simplex classes and the relationships classes to which its simplexes and relationships belong. The structure we require is that the relationships should be connected to simplexes that also occur in the complex, so that we do not allow "dangling" relationships. Note that a complex may consist of only one simplex and that simplexes never exist on their own but are always part of a complex.

A complex is like a "molecule", whose "atoms" correspond to the simplexes that are connected by relationships. A complex may represent a set of similar simplexes of the same class, such as a set of school children. However, an example of a different type of complex is the following: the set containing a car and also its parts. In this case there is one simplex in the complex that represents the car itself, while the other simplexes represent parts like wheels, chassis, engine and seats. If a complex consists of information simplexes only, it is an information object itself. Many complexes are mixtures of the three kinds of object mentioned above. Examples of complexes in information systems are databases and messages or files that flow through a channel. The data used for updating a data base form a complex and so do the retrieved data. In classical data base theory one only considers a single data base at a time: the whole data base schema forms one complex class.

Complexes are "stored" or "carried" in "containers" called *tokens*. A token has some additional characteristics: a *place* at which it resides, a *time stamp* that tells when the token may leave the place and a *identity*. A place is either a physical location or a stage in which the token resides. Simplexes are unique within a complex (because a complex is a set of simplexes and relationships), but the simplexes in a set of tokens do not have to be unique. However, if the tokens in a set have unique identities then the simplexes in these tokens can be identified uniquely by the token identity. Figure 4.1 relates the concepts "state", "token" and "complex".

Simplex classes, complex classes and relationship classes are defined in an *object model*, which is called a *database schema* in the database literature. We consider

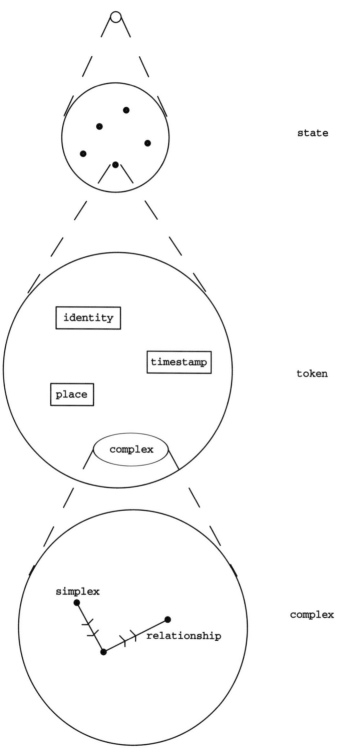

Fig. 4.1 A state is a set of tokens with unique identities. A token consists of a place, time stamp, identity and complex. A complex consists of simplexes and relationships.

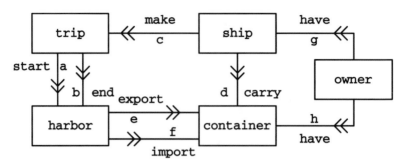

Fig. 4.2. Simplex diagram SeaTransport.

it as a *role* of a simplex to be a concrete, an abstract or an information object; this role may depend on the complex class it belongs to. Representation by means of a labeled diagram known as a graph, for a part of an object model: a simplex class is denoted by a node in the form of a rectangle and the relationship classes are denoted by labeled and directed lines known as edges. Relationship classes have a direction; this is necessary in the case of relationship classes that connect a simplex class with itself (*see* the example in figure 4.4). Complex classes are denoted such as that in table 4.1. For each complex class the simplex classes and the relationships that are contained in the object class are listed. Not all relationships between two simplex classes of an object model have to occur in a given complex class. However, if a relationship class occurs in a particular complex class then both simplex classes it connects should be in the complex class as well. Complex classes may overlap and the set of all simplex classes and all relationship classes is also a complex class. We call this class a *universal complex class*. In one model we only consider complex classes that are subclasses of one universal complex class. A graphical representation of (a part of) an object model is called a *simplex diagram*. In figure 4.2 we see an example of such a simplex diagram.

To a relationship belongs a *verb* in addition to its name. This verb links the two nouns of the connected simplex classes to form a sentence. Consider the example in figure 4.2. If we conjugate the verbs properly we get two sentences for each relationship: one in active form and one in passive form, for instance:

– a ship makes a trip;
– a trip is made by a ship;
– a harbor exports a container;
– a container is exported from a harbor.

Note that we use indefinite articles in these sentences, because we are speaking of

Table 4.1. *Complex classes SeaTransport.*

| Complex class | Simplex classes | Relationship classes |
|---|---|---|
| *Voyage* | *trip* | *c* |
| | *ship* | *d* |
| | *container* | |
| *Cluster* | *harbor* | *e* |
| | *container* | *f* |

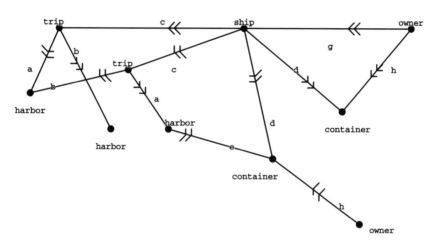

Fig. 4.3. An instance of the universal complex class for SeaTransport.

arbitrary simplexes from a class. The rest of this diagram speaks for itself: on a
trip containers are transported, trips go from one harbor to another and harbors
import and export containers. (It is clear from these examples that particular
form given of the verb is not enough to identify the relationship in a simplex
diagram; therefore we use an arbitrary identifier for each relationship and we use
the verb as an auxiliary name.) The complex classes relating to this simplex
diagram are listed in table 4.1. The universal complex class that contains all
these simplex classes and relationship classes is not listed in this table.

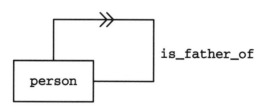

Fig. 4.4. The simplex class *person* and a relationship class.

A simplex is called an *instance* of a simplex class and a complex is an instance of a complex class. As we have seen in figure 4.2, a complex class can be represented by a graph; a complex itself also. Each node represents now a simplex and each labeled edge is again a relationship. In figure 4.3 we see a complex in the universal complex class for the sea transport example. In figure 4.4 we see an example of a simplex diagram with a relationship class that relates a simplex class to itself. An instance of the universal complex class can be represented as a set of sets: for each simplex class a set of simplexes and for each relationship class a set of simplex pairs. For example, for figure 4.4 the two elements are as follows. For simplex class *person* we may have

$$\{John, Peter, Bill, Edward\}$$

and for relationship *is_father_of*

$$\{(John, Peter), (Peter, Bill), (Peter, Edward)\}$$

This example shows that it is important to distinguish the direction of a relationship: John is the father of Peter and not vice versa. The direction is indicated by (one or two) arrowheads on the edges and we call the simplex class at the tail of the arrow the *domain class* and the one at the head the *range class*.

We have represented the simplexes by names in the above example, instead of representing them by nodes as in figure 4.3. In the models we construct we will always use a *symbolic representation* for simplexes and complexes. In fact we will use *finite mathematical values* or *values* for short, to represent simplexes and complexes (*see* part V). All these values can be constructed from a finite set of given constants, which explains the adjective "finite". A value is constructed from other values that belong to some *basic types*, such as the natural numbers or character strings, using *constructors* (*see* section 6.1). For example, $\{(a, 1), (b, 2), (c, 3)\}$ is a constructed value using only natural numbers and alphabetic characters. It denotes a set of pairs. The instance of the simplex diagram in figure 4.4 may be represented by the relationship *is_father_of* alone, because that set of pairs gives all the information we need to construct the instance graph in this case (up to isomorphy).

All values have a type and we associate to each simplex class and to each complex class a type. We have to guarantee that the values represent the simplexes and complexes correctly. Simplexes are uniquely determined by their simplex class name and their value. So we may use the same type to represent simplexes of different classes. The choice of the representation depends on the use we will make of the objects in the actors. This gives us the freedom to use representations that make life easy for the systems engineer. On the other hand, if the systems engineer has to design a database system that is to be implemented by a database management system, then he will choose representations that are close to the data formats of the system. (This will be considered in part III.) The only thing we have to remember here is that simplexes and complexes have a symbolic representation in the form of values in our models, and that each object class has its value type. In principle the systems engineer does not have to use an object model at all, if he is able to define relevant value types for tokens. In this case, however, it might be hard to give a useful meaning to the values, i.e. it might be difficult to represent the real-world entities in a consistent way in a model.

In order to see how complex classes determine a *state space*, we recall that a token is a complex (in fact a value) endowed with a place, a time stamp and an identity. A state is a set of tokens with unique identities. So we allow that in a given state one simplex may occur in two tokens (or complexes). This means that at least one of them represents an information object: it refers to the "real entity" but it does not represent it. In the real world it may happen that two items of identical information reside at different places; for example, somebody's name and address may be stored in two databases. It is possible that the relationships of an information simplex in one complex are different from the relationships in another complex in the same state: two different computers or two different persons may have different views of the same world.

In general we will not allow all possible complexes in a state. For instance, in the example of figure 4.4 we will not allow that a person has more than one father and in the sea transport case we do not allow that a given trip is made by more than one ship. These restrictions are (static) *constraints*. With constraints we give more meaning to a complex class: it has fewer instances but more specific information. Constraints are part of an object model. Some of them may also be represented in a simplex diagram. They are called *standard constraints*.

A constraint for a complex class is in fact an *invariant* for the transition law of a system. A constraint says that only objects satisfying it are allowed in the state. In general we cannot guarantee automatically that a transition relation keeps a constraint invariant: it is a task for the systems engineer to design systems such that constraints are invariants. The systems engineer should prove this!

Consider the example of figure 4.5, which has the following meaning. A task needs some functions ($c$) and a resource is able to perform one or more functions ($d$). An operation is related to a resource and a task: the operation is the execution of the task using the resource. The task requires several functions to be performed, for instance drilling and sawing. Each resource can perform one or more functions. For each function required by a task there should be an operation. An operation is related to a set of time slots: during these time slots the operation is executed. The following requirements are obvious:

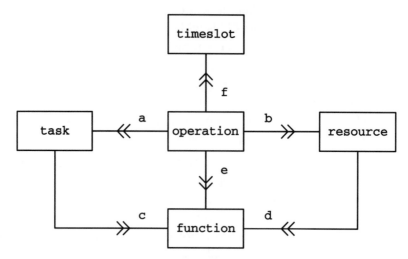

Fig. 4.5. Task assignment.

- each operation belongs to only one task;
- each operation belongs to only one resource;
- each operation belongs to only one function;
- for each required function of a task (by *c*) there is an operation with this function assigned to it (by *e*);
- each function assigned to a resource (by *e*) should be a function the resource is able to perform (by *d*);
- no resource can be involved in two operations at the same time.

In predicate calculus we can express this by:

$$\forall o : operation \bullet \#(a(o)) = 1,$$
$$\forall o : operation \bullet \#(b(o)) = 1,$$
$$\forall o : operation \bullet \#(e(o)) = 1,$$
$$\forall t : task \bullet e(a^{-1}(t)) = c(t),$$
$$\forall o : operation \bullet e(o) \subseteq d(b(o)),$$
$$\forall o_1, o_2 : operation \bullet (o_1 \neq o_2 \wedge b(o_1) \cap b(o_2) \neq \emptyset) \Rightarrow f(o_1) \cap f(o_2) = \emptyset.$$

These predicates should be *true* for every complex. The name *task* should be interpreted as the set of *task* simplexes in that complex and *operation* as the set of *operation* simplexes. The relationship names have to be interpreted as (set-valued) functions that assign to the simplexes of their domain class all the related simplexes of their range class (in the complex); the relationship names with superscript −1 represent inverse functions from the range class to the domain class of the relationship. (In constraints we identify relationships with these functions.) There are several frequently occurring constraints:

– cardinality constraints,
– key constraints,
– exclusion constraints,
– inheritance constraints,
– tree constraints.

Because they occur so frequently, they are represented in the simplex diagram. A *cardinality constraint* puts requirements on the number of simplexes related to a particular simplex in a relationship. (We have met such a constraint in the example of figure 4.5.) In figure 4.6 we see two simplex classes $a$ and $b$ and one relationship class $r$. The domain class of $r$ is $a$ and the range class is $b$, as indicated by the double arrowhead.

If we put a solid circle at the tail of the arrow, as in figure 4.7, we mean that every simplex of $a$ is associated with at least one element of $b$. We call this property *totality* because the (set-valued) function $r$ is total, i.e. for each argument $x$ the set $r(x)$ is non-empty. If we replace the double arrowhead by a single one, we mean that there is at most one element of $b$ associated to each $a$, so that $r$ is a single-valued function. In this case we call $r$ a *functional* relationship, and the constraint is called *functionality*. This is displayed in figure 4.8. These requirements relating to the domain side can also be applied to the range side. A solid circle at the head of the arrow means that every simplex of $b$ is related to at least one simplex of $a$. This means that the (set-valued) function $r$ is *surjective* and therefore we call the property *surjectivity*. This is displayed in figure 4.9. The last cardinality constraint is graphically denoted by a bar, as in figure 4.10. It means that every simplex of $b$ is associated to at most one simplex of $a$, so that the function $r$ is *injective*, and therefore we call the property *injectivity*. These four cardinality constraints (totality, injectivity, surjectivity and functionality) determine 16 ($=2^4$) different constraints on the cardinality of a relationship. With these 16 possibilities we are able to express that a simplex is associated to at least zero, other simplexes or at least one, or exactly one or at most one other simplex. An example of such a combination is shown in figure 4.11. Here we have a *bijective* relationship $r$, which is a relationship that has all four properties. Note that $r^{-1}$ is also bijective.

Next we consider *key constraints*. An example is given in figure 4.12. The solid circle on the curved edge means that the two relationships $a$ and $b$ determine the tasks uniquely: no two tasks belong to the same project and are carried out by the same set of persons. The crossings of the key constraint edge with the relationship edges are marked with a small dot if the relationship participates in

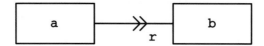

Fig. 4.6. A relationship without constraints.

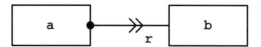

Fig. 4.7. Total relationship.

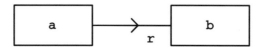

Fig. 4.8. Functional relationship.

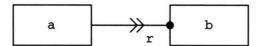

Fig. 4.9. Surjective relationship.

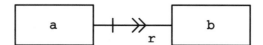

Fig. 4.10. Injective relationship.

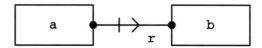

Fig. 4.11. Bijective relationship.

the key constraint. In the example of figure 4.13 relationships $a$ and $b$ form a key constraint and $c$ does not belong to this constraint. In fact this is a *domain* key constraint because all relationships involved have the same domain simplex class. There are also *range* key constraints, in which all relationships involved have a common range simplex class.

Another standard constraint for a set of relationships sharing a domain or range class is called an *exclusion constraint*. In figure 4.14 we see an example of a *domain* exclusion constraint. There are also *range* exclusion constraints: the star

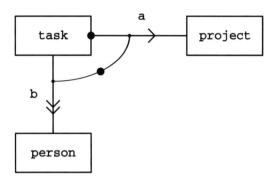

Fig. 4.12. Key constraint.

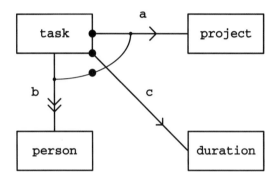

Fig. 4.13. Another key constraint.

on the curved edge means that a person cannot be involved in the relationships *a* and *b* simultaneously. Thus, a *person* always comes to work either with (a) one of his *cars* or (b) with one of his *bicycles*, or without a vehicle at all. So it is excluded that he comes to work with both a car and a bicycle. In general, key and exclusion constraints may involve more than two relationships.

The fourth kind of constraints we consider is an inheritance constraint. An *inheritance relationship* is a total, functional and injective relationship, and an *inheritance constraint* is a subset of relations from a simplex diagram, such that the graph we obtain if we erase all other relationships, is acyclic and directed. In figure 4.15 we display an example. This shows that every student and every teacher "is" also a school person, and that every student is also a library member. A school person is of course a person and so is a library member. Each of these simplex classes may have its own values and we say that a simplex "inherits" all its relationships from the simplexes it is mapped to by the inheritance relationships. So a student inherits the relationships of the (unique) library member, school person and person to which he is connected. In this inheritance approach there

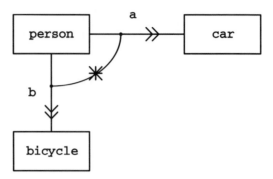

Fig. 4.14. Exclusion constraint.

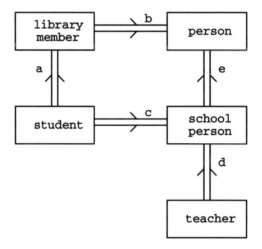

Fig. 4.15. Inheritance constraint.

are different simplexes for each role of a student: the student as library member, as person etc. However, there is a one-to-one correspondence between students and library members who are also students.

There are other approaches to inheritance in the literature in which an inheritance constraint imposes an inclusion requirement, namely that the simplex student and the library member to which it belongs are in fact the same simplexes. (Both approaches have their advantages and drawbacks.) An extra requirement that has to be fulfilled is that if there are two paths from a simplex class $a$ to a simplex class $b$, following the inheritance arrows, then on the instance level these paths should lead to the same simplex of class $b$, if they start in one simplex of class $a$. So the person that relates to a student according to the path via library member should be the same as that according to the path via school person. In

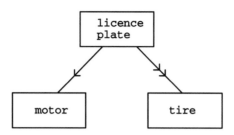

Fig. 4.16. Tree constraint for "CarWithParts".

an inheritance hierarchy only one simplex can be a physical object; the others are abstract objects that represent *roles* of the physical one. Usually the top of the hierarchy is the physical one, as in the example; the person is the physical object and the others are roles.

The last kind of constraint is the *tree constraint*. It is a requirement on a complex class. The requirement is that one simplex class must supply exactly one simplex, called the *root simplex*, to a complex and that all other simplexes in the complex should be connected to the root simplex by means of relationships, either directly or indirectly (via other simplexes in the complex). So every simplex in a tree complex is reachable from the root simplex. Consider for instance the complex class "CarWithParts". We have the constraint that there is only one car in the class and that the graph of the complex is connected, i.e. each part is directly or indirectly connected to the car of the complex. Note that the root simplex class is often an abstract simplex class: a car is more of a concept than a thing! In figure 4.16 we display this example.

So far we only considered constraints on complex classes. We call them *local constraints* because we can verify them for every local state transition of an actor. There are, however, also constraints on states as a whole, i.e. for the set of tokens in a state. We call them *global constraints*. An example of a global constraint is the requirement that only one simplex from a certain simplex class may occur in a state. This is a natural constraint if this simplex class always represents a physical entity.

# 5

# Actors

In the previous chapter we set out the principles of constructing the state space of a transition system: a state is a set of tokens with a unique identity, a place, a time stamp and a complex (*see* e.g. figure 4.1). The place is a concept that may be used to model the physical location where a token (complex) resides or the logical stage in which the token is. The *time stamp* attached to a token is the time at which the token becomes available; it can be regarded as its creation, completion or arrival time. The value is one that represents a complex object. We distinguish two kinds of places, *channels* and *stores*. A channel may contain zero, one or more tokens while a store always contains exactly one token. Usually the token in a store has a more complicated structure than the tokens in channels. The token in a store may represent for instance a complicated data base state or the entire stock in a depot. A store is just a place with a special use: the actors that consume the token of a store have the duty to produce a new one for that store in the same transition. Another property of a store is that its token is always available; it always gets a time stamp equal to the time at which it is produced.

Actors are connected to places by means of *connectors*. So, each actor may be regarded as a "spider" whose legs are connectors. Connectors are connected to places; they have a direction and are *input* or *output* connectors. An actor may be connected to one place by more than one connector; an actor is connected to store by zero or two connectors, in the latter case by means of an input connector and an output connector.

The term actor is used for active entities in a system. We distinguish two kinds of actors. The first kind is called a *processor*; the other kind is a network of actors and is called a *non-elementary actor*. A processor is an elementary actor.

Note that the concept of an actor is defined recursively, since each network is considered to be an actor itself. The connectors of an actor that is part of

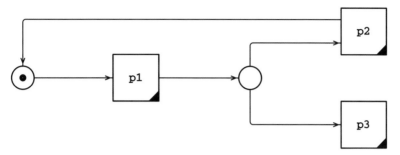

Fig. 5.1. A classical Petri net.

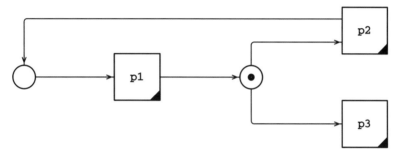

Fig. 5.2. The next state.

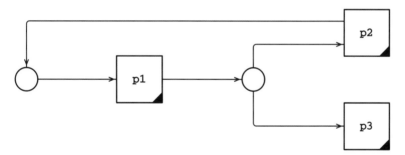

Fig. 5.3. A deadlock.

another actor may be connected to the connectors of the enclosing actor instead
of to a place inside the enclosing actor.

The framework we are using for the modeling of systems is an extension of
the *Petri net* framework. Before we discuss the extensions, we define classical
Petri nets informally. In figure 5.1 we display an example of a classical Petri
net. A Petri net is a directed, bipartite graph with two kinds of nodes, *places*
and *processors*. The latter are called *transitions* in the Petri net literature. The

places are displayed as circles and the processors as rectangles (in our book with a marked bottom right-hand corner). A place is called a *input place* of a processor if there is an edge from the place to the processor. Similarly we call a place an *output place* if there is an edge from the processor to the place. We called these edges input or output connectors. Note that we allow more input or output connectors from a processor connected to one place.

Further, the places are *marked* with zero or more *tokens*. A Petri net determines a strongly memoryless transition system. Note that "time" does not play a role in Petri nets, so all events may occur at the same time, for instance zero. The *state* of the Petri net is the configuration of tokens over the places and is called the *marking* of the net. An *event* is the *firing* or *execution* of a processor. A processor is *enabled* to fire if it can consume one token from of its each input places. The result of the firing of a processor is that all output places of the processor get one token more and that from each input place one token is deleted. In the example only one processor $(p_1)$ is enabled in the displayed state. If it fires then the next state will be as displayed in figure 5.2. Now there are two processors enabled: $p_2$ and $p_3$. If $p_2$ fires then the system returns to the initial state, displayed in figure 5.1. However, if $p_3$ fires, the system moves to the state displayed in figure 5.3. In this state no processor is enabled, so the system deadlocks. In classical Petri nets which processor will execute is not determined, so the classical Petri nets are non-deterministic. Note that tokens in classical Petri nets do not have a value, or if they have one this value does not play any role.

We consider an extension of classical Petri nets, called *timed colored Petri nets*. The main extensions are:

- tokens have a *value*, in the form of a complex, and this value may influence the execution of a processor;
- tokens have a *time stamp*, and the time stamp may influence the execution of a processor as well;
- a processor does not have to consume a token from each input place, and it does not have to produce one for each output place; what happens depends on its *processor relation* (as explained later).

We require that a processor has to consume at least one token in an execution. A processor may execute in an event if it can get enough tokens, depending on their values. A token can be consumed by only one processor. A store always contains one token that should be available for the executing processor, which implies that no other processor connected to this store may execute in the same event. However, two processors that can get enough tokens to execute simultaneously, may do so. We assume that a processor may not execute simultaneously with itself.

Processors execute *instantaneously* and therefore events happen instantaneously. This implies that it is possible for several events to occur at the same time, albeit in some order. In particular, one processor may execute several times at some moment, but in some order.

Processors behave in a *non-deterministic* way: if they consume tokens via their input connectors, the tokens produced for their output connectors are determined by a *processor relation*. Such a processor relation can be represented as a possibly infinite table.

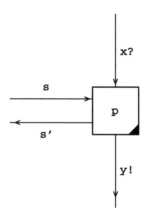

Fig. 5.4. A processor.

We will illustrate the processor relation by means of some examples. All these examples have processors with the same connectors, as displayed in figure 5.4, where we do not display the places to which the connectors are connected. The figure shows a processor $p$ with input connectors $x$? and $s$, and output connectors $y$! and $s'$. The connectors $s$ and $s'$ are supposed to be connected to the same store. (By convention the output connector to a store acquires the name of the input connector "decorated" by $'$.) The complex class of the tokens in these places is supposed to be simple: it has only one simplex class with two simplexes, so the value type of the token can be represented by a set of truth values, here denoted by $\{1,0\}$. We do not consider the identities of the tokens in this case, which means that they are arbitrary. In this processor relation we only consider the values of the tokens. The processor relation for $p$ can be expressed in the following form:

| input | | output | |
|:---:|:---:|:---:|:---:|
| x? | s | y! | s' |
| 1 | 1 | 0 | 0 |
| 0 | 1 | 1 | 0 |
| 1 | 0 | 1 | 1 |
| 0 | 0 | 1 | 0 |

Each connector name represents the value of the token that is consumed from or produced for it. Here $s'$ denotes the value of the stored token after the execution of processor $p$. In this example $y! = \neg(x? \wedge s)$ and $s' = x? \wedge \neg s$. An example of the token values before and after the execution of this processor is given below:

| connector | x? | y! | s, s' |
|:---|:---:|:---:|:---:|
| before | 1 | - | 1 |
| after | - | 0 | 0 |

We assume that the connectors $x?$ and $y!$ are attached to channels $x$ and $y$ respectively. The store connectors $s$ and $s'$ are attached to a store $s$.

We could give an *implicit* definition for the above processor relation as a *schema* (schemas will be defined formally in part V):

$$[x? : \mathbb{B},\ s : \mathbb{B},\ s' : \mathbb{B},\ y! : \mathbb{B}\ \mid\ (s' = x? \wedge \neg s)\ \wedge\ (y! = \neg(x? \wedge s))].$$

The connector names and their types are defined on the left-hand side of the bar. They form the so-called *signature* of the schema. The right-hand side is called the *predicate*. The connector names are also called *variables* or *attributes*, "variables" because they are used as such in the predicate and "attributes" because the meaning of a schema is a set of *tuples* and the connector names play the role of attributes in these tuples. Note that a tuple is a set of pairs, such that the first element of each pair is a different attribute. The meaning of the displayed schema is the set of all tuples of the form:

$$\{x? \mapsto a,\ s \mapsto b,\ s' \mapsto c,\ y! \mapsto d\}$$

where $a$, $b$, $c$ and $d$ are truth values that make the predicate true if the attributes are replaced by these values. If $t$ is a tuple belonging to a schema and $A$ is an attribute then $\pi_A(t)$ denotes the value of the tuple for that attribute. The tuples of a processor relation may be *partial*, which means that the tuples may have less attributes than the schema. If in a tuple of a processor relation an attribute is missing, it means that for the corresponding connector no token is consumed or produced.

In this example we see four properties that will not be the case in general.

- There is a tuple in the table for each combination of input tokens. This property is called *totality*. If the processor relation is not total there is a *precondition*.
- The output is *functionally dependent* on the input, i.e. there are no two tuples with the same input and different output.
- Every tuple has a value for all inputs. If this is so, we call the processor relation *input complete*. In the case where every tuple has a value for all outputs, we call the processor relation *output complete*. If the processor relation is input and output complete, we call it simply *complete*.
- The processor relation can be given by enumeration.

We call the first three properties *processor characteristics*. If all processors of a network are total and complete and if we discard the values and the time stamps of the tokens, the network is a classical Petri net. Note that totality depends on the values of tokens but that completeness depends only on the presence of tokens.

In general we will not be able to enumerate all elements of the processor relation. For example, suppose that the value types of the values are the set of natural numbers and that the processor relation prescribes that

$$y! = 0 \;\; \text{if } s' \text{ is even}$$
$$y! = 1 \;\; \text{if } s' \text{ is odd}$$
$$s' = s + x?$$

Then we cannot give a complete table. So, in this case we can only give the relation in *implicit* form. Here the schema is

$$[x? : \mathbb{N}, \; s : \mathbb{N}, \; s' : \mathbb{N}, \; y! : \mathbb{N} \;\; | \;\; (s' = s + x?) \land (y! = s' \bmod 2)].$$

Now we still have the first three properties (totality, functional dependence on input and completeness). If we change the processor relation a little, the output token is not always specified (the processor relation is then only input complete):

$$[x?, s, s', y! : \mathbb{N} \;\; | \;\; (s' = x? + s) \land (s' \bmod 2 = 0 \Rightarrow y! = 0)$$
$$\land \; (s' \bmod 2 = 1 \Rightarrow y! = \bot)].$$

We have introduced a shorthand notation for the signature of a schema: we have written $\mathbb{N}$ only once. The "value" $\bot$ means that no token is produced for channel $y!$. We will change the example again:

$$[x?, s, s', y! : \mathbb{N} \;\; | \;\; (s' = x? + s) \land (y! = 0 \lor y! = 1)].$$

In this case the value of the output token is not *functionally* dependent on the input any more. So the processor may decide in a non-deterministic way which value $y!$ will get. In the next modification we lose *totality*:

$$[x?, s, s', y! : \mathbb{N} \mid (x? \geq 2) \wedge (s' = x? + s) \wedge (y! = s' \bmod 2)].$$

Not all combinations of input values are allowed now. This should be interpreted as follows: the processor only executes when it can consume an input token for $x?$ with value greater than unity. This is a precondition. A processor will not consume tokens that do not satisfy its precondition.

It is not always required that for each input connector a token is consumed.

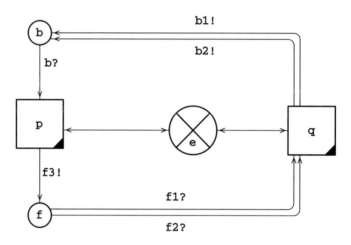

Fig. 5.5. An actor (closed, non-elementary).

To specify a network of processors, channels and stores, we use the graphical representation of classical Petri nets. In figure 5.5 we show a simple network. The squares with marked bottom right-hand corner denote processors, the smaller open circles denote channels and the crossed open circles denote stores. The connectors from processors to channels are denoted by directed edges. As a shorthand we draw a connector with arrowheads in both directions to stand for two connectors from a processor to a store: an input and an output connector.

Actors that are networks of channels, stores, processors and other actors are represented graphically by rectangles (without the marked bottom right-hand corners). These non-elementary actors are useful for representing large networks in a hierarchical way. In a network they are connected to channels and stores, just as processors are, but it is possible to replace them by their defining network. Non-elementary actors are used to hide information or to express our partial knowledge of a system.

In figure 5.6 we see a network with a non-elementary actor $A$ and in figure 5.7

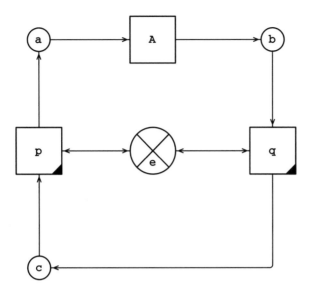

Fig. 5.6. A network containing a non-elementary actor $A$.

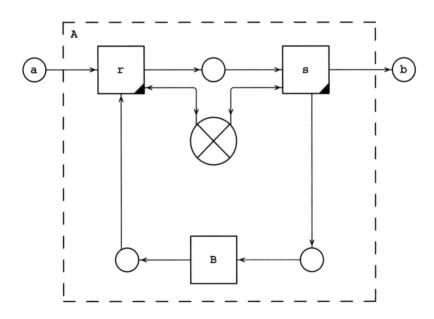

Fig. 5.7. A decomposition of $A$.

we see the network for this actor $A$. Note that a non-elementary actor itself may contain non-elementary actors, such as $B$ in figure 5.7, but it cannot also be true that $A$ is contained in $B$. An actor with connectors, like $A$, is called an *open actor*. It can be influenced by another actor that puts tokens on its connectors or consumes tokens from these connectors. (This is only possible if the connectors are attached to places first.) Then the other actor creates external events.

Actors without connectors are called *closed actors*. Note that processors themselves have connectors, so that a processor is an open actor itself. We often study open actors, for instance if we model an information system that communicates with an environment. However, if we model the environment as an actor too we may combine both into a closed actor. Note that we will not consider a detailed model of the environment in that case, but just a simple model that has the desired processor behavior for the system we study.

Two important features of the execution of a processor not yet discussed are the *timing* and *identification* of produced tokens. We start with the timing. As mentioned before, each token has a time stamp, denoting the time it becomes available. In the model we assume that tokens may be in a channel at a time before their time stamp. This sounds paradoxical. However, since we have assumed that the state transitions are instantaneous, the production of a token does not take any time and the tokens will exist immediately after the state transition that produced them. So, to be able to express that a token needs some time to be produced, we attach a time stamp that could be interpreted as its "creation", "completion" or "arrival" time.

The first rule for execution of a processor is that it may execute if it has *sufficient* input connectors (according to the processor relation) that have one token with a time stamp that is at most as large as the actual time and if the precondition is satisfied. So tokens with time stamps larger than the actual time are neglected. The second rule for execution is that if at some time at least one processor is able to execute then at least one of these processors will execute. This property is called *eagerness*.

With this mechanism it is easy to model that a processor needs a time delay after an execution simply by adding a channel for this processor that is connected to it by one input and one output connector. In figure 5.8 we have added a channel $c$ that always contains one token; the value of the token is irrelevant. For each execution the processor needs the token from this channel. If the new token is given a time stamp equal to the event time plus a delay, the processor behaves as if execution takes time. To see this, let the first token that is consumed via $a$ require a processing time $d$. Thus the token in $c$ acquires a delay of $d$ time units

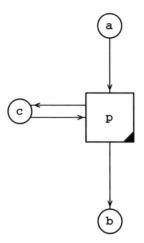

Fig. 5.8. A processor that is not directly available after execution.

and so the next time the processor wants to consume a token from $a$ it has to wait till $d$ time units have been passed.

Although we may assume that there is a clock and a notion of *global time*, we do not need these concepts to define systems in our formalism. Given a state, we can define the *transition time* of this state in a unique way, namely as the earliest time one or more processors may and will execute. This time is uniquely determined by the tokens of the state. A *trace* is, as defined in chapter 3, a sequence of events. In the systems we describe here, each state carries the transition time to the next state, it is the time of the event in which the system will leave the state. So, in each trace $\langle (s_0, t_0), (s_1, t_1), \ldots, (s_n, t_n), (s_{n+1}, t_{n+1}), \ldots \rangle$ we have for all $n$ that $t_{n+1}$ is the transition time of state $s_n$. In other words, the event time of $(s_{n+1}, t_{n+1})$ is the transition time of state $s_n$. This implies that the system has a strongly memoryless transition law. As in chapter 3, we assume that each system has an initial event with event time $t_0$ and an initial state $s_0$. From that moment on the system may run through a trace in a non-deterministic way, without interference from outside. Note that, although it is possible to consider a global time, the processors operate in an *asynchronous* way.

The next feature we consider is the *identification* of newly produced tokens. The produced objects acquire new, unused identifiers and this is done by the processor that produced them. This can be done without any reference to a central identifier base, in a purely distributed way in which processors do not have to remember what identities they have created in the past. (In chapter 10 this will be elaborated.)

We will illustrate the above by means of the sea transport example. We first

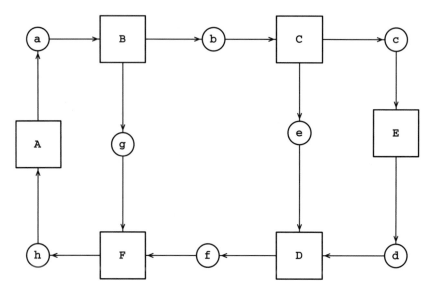

Fig. 5.9. A sea transport network.

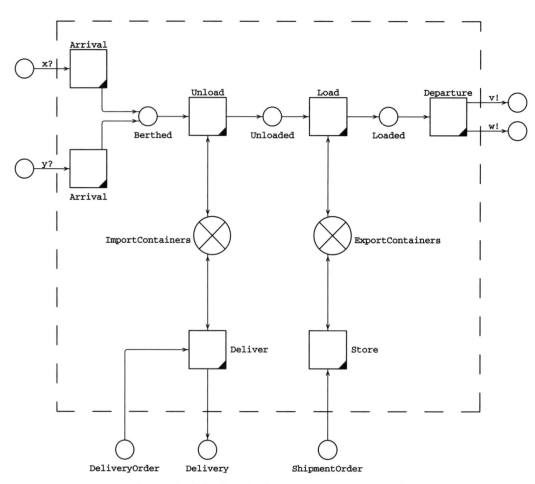

Fig. 5.10. A harbor in the sea transport network.

give a hierarchical network with non-elementary actors. This network models the real-world transportation network and is the counterpart of the object model presented in chapter 4. In figure 5.9 each harbor activity corresponds to an actor and each channel to a sea route. The ships can make several voyages through this network. The channels *a* through *h* may contain tokens with complexes of the complex class *Voyage* of table 4.1. So the tokens moving through the network are ships with their cargo and with the specification of their trip. The actors *A* through *F* are networks built from processors. Each of these actors has a structure similar to the one displayed in figure 5.10. To be precise, the actors *A* and *E* have only one arrival processor and one output connector from the departure processor, *B* and *C* also have only one arrival processor, but both *v* and *w* as output connectors, and finally *D* and *F* have two arrival processors and only one output connector from the departure processor. The names of the channels, stores and processors make a further explanation of the network almost superfluous. The processor *Deliver* is activated by a delivery order for some containers and *ShipmentOrder* is activated by a shipment order. For the channels *DeliveryOrder*, *Delivery* and *ShipmentOrder* we have not defined complex classes. For the stores *ImportContainers* and *ExportContainers* we use the complex class *cluster*. Note that we have to add some constraints: a cluster in *ImportContainers* should not include "export" containers and vice versa. To all other channels and stores we associate the complex class *voyage*, because they represent the various stages a ship passes on its voyage. The only thing we have left unspecified here are the processor relations.

We conclude this chapter with a small, though complete, example of a *system specification*. In this example we consider the production and consumption of items. The system as displayed in figure 5.11 is quite simple. The processor *EndConsumption* takes consumers who have finished their consumption to the wait stage *WaitingConsumers* and creates an order for some arbitrary quantity of items. The processor *StartConsumption* tries to match this with a delivery of items to one of the waiting consumers in *WaitingConsumers* and puts the consumer into channel *ConsumingConsumers* with a delay dependent on the number of delivered items (the more items, the longer the delay). On the other side we see that processor *StartProduction* links an order to a waiting machine and creates an operation with a delay according to its speed and the ordered quantity. Finally, processor *EndProduction* creates a delivery and puts the machine used in the operation from *WorkingMachines* into *WaitingMachines*. The processor characteristics are as follows: all processors are input and output complete and all except *StartConsumption* are total. All but *EndConsumption* are functional.

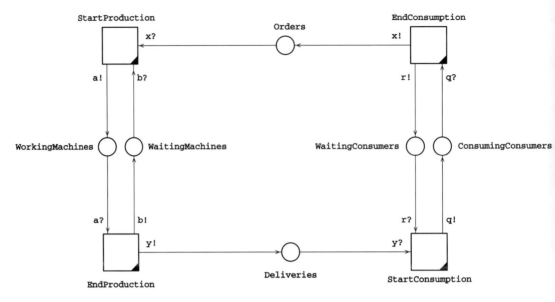

Fig. 5.11. A production/consumption example.

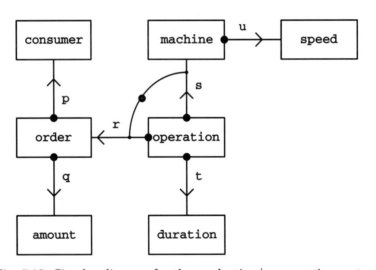

Fig. 5.12. Simplex diagram for the production/consumption system.

We see that some channels represent locations for tokens, such as *Orders* and *Deliveries*, while the other channels represent stages of tokens.

After this informal explanation of the system we give the simplex diagram in figure 5.12. The simplex classes speak for themselves. All relationships are total and functional. Relationship $p$ assigns a consumer to an order, relationship $q$ an amount to an order and relationship $u$ a speed to a machine; the other relationships determine for an operation the machine $(s)$ and the order $(r)$. Further, we see that an operation is uniquely determined by a machine and an order; this will be used to define values later. The duration of an operation can be computed from the order amount and the machine speed, so it is superfluous and therefore it will not be represented in the value types. In our system there are five complex classes: *Consumer*, *Machine*, *Order*, *PendingOrder* and *Operation*. They all satisfy the tree constraint. In table 5.1 the root class of each complex

Table 5.1. *Complex classes for the production/consumption system.*

| Complex class | Simplex classes | Relationship classes | Root class |
|---|---|---|---|
| *Consumer* | *consumer* | | * |
| *Machine* | *machine* | $u$ | * |
| | *speed* | | |
| *Order* | *order* | $q$ | * |
| | *amount* | | |
| *PendingOrder* | *order* | $p$ | * |
| | *consumer* | | |
| *Operation* | *operation* | | * |
| | *machine* | $s$ | |
| | *order* | $r$ | |
| | *amount* | $q$ | |
| | *speed* | $u$ | |

class is indicated by an asterisk.

We have to attach connectors and complex classes to the channels, which is done in table 5.2. Note that each connector acquires the name of the channel to which it is connected, decorated either with a question mark (?) or an exclamation mark (!).

We will use schemas to define value types for the object classes. In this case we do not use a predicate in the schemas, which is in fact the same as always using the predicate *true*. (Note that schemas without a predicate are *tuple types*, as will be explained in part III.) The simplex classes acquire the following value types:

$$
\begin{aligned}
consumer &:= Name, \\
order\ \ \ &:= ID, \\
machine\ &:= ID, \\
speed\ \ \ &:= Speed, \\
amount\ \ &:= Quantity, \\
operation &:= [m : ID, o : ID].
\end{aligned}
$$

Here *ID* denotes a set of identities and *Name* some arbitrary type of names;

Table 5.2. *Assignment of complex classes to channels.*

| abbreviation | channel | class |
|---|---|---|
| (a) | *WorkingMachines* | *Operation* |
| (b) | *WaitingMachines* | *Machine* |
| (x) | *Orders* | *Order* |
| (y) | *Deliveries* | *Order* |
| (r) | *WaitingConsumers* | *PendingOrder* |
| (q) | *ConsumingConsumers* | *Consumer* |

*Speed* and *Quantity* are sets of non-negative real numbers. The complex classes are defined by

$$Consumer \quad := Name,$$
$$Order \quad := [o : ID, h : Quantity],$$
$$PendingOrder := [o : ID, c : Name],$$
$$Machine \quad := [m : ID, s : Speed],$$
$$Operation \quad := [m : ID, o : ID, h : Quantity, s : Speed].$$

It is not difficult to find for each complex class a function that transforms each value into a complex and vice versa. Take for instance *Operation*. The $m$ and $o$ attributes refer to the machine and the order that uniquely determine the operation as a consequence of the domain key constraint for *operation*. Since *Operation* satisfies the tree constraint, there is only one *operation* simplex and since all relationships are functional there are also only one machine and one order. Hence the complete complex is defined by the four attributes of the schema.

Now we are ready to define the processor relation. We use a more convenient notation for schemas: a table format (*see* table 5.3). If $t$ is a tuple and $x$ a component name of $t$, then $\pi_x(t)$ denotes the value of that component. In the processor relations the names of the components and their types are displayed in the upper part (the *signature*) of the processor relation. In the lower part we see the *predicate* of the relation. All lines of the predicate have to be taken in conjunction.

Note that the connector names are interpreted as the tokens that are consumed or produced "through" the connector. The function *New* has "hidden" arguments; it can be used to create new identities without using a database of unused identities. Thus it uses the identity of one consumed token to create, in a pure functional way, a new identity. This only works for values of the type *ID*, the definition of which is not important here. The function *TransTime* computes the maximal time stamp of the consumed tokens, which is the event time. The connector names with subscript $t$ denote the time stamp of the tokens that are

EndConsumption_____

$q?$ : Consumer
$r!$ : PendingOrder
$x!$ : Order

$\pi_c(r!) = q?$
$\pi_o(r!) = \pi_o(x!)$
$\pi_o(x!) = New$
$\pi_h(x!) \geq 1$
$r_t! = TransTime$
$x_t! = TransTime + 1$

StartConsumption_____

$r?$ : PendingOrder
$y?$ : Order
$q!$ : Consumer

$\pi_o(r?) = \pi_o(y?)$
$q! = \pi_c(r?)$
$q_t! = TransTime + \pi_h(y?)$

StartProduction_____

$x?$ : Order
$b?$ : Machine
$a!$ : Operation

$\pi_o(a!) = \pi_o(x?)$
$\pi_m(a!) = \pi_m(b?)$
$\pi_h(a!) = \pi_h(x?)$
$\pi_s(a!) = \pi_s(b?)$
$a_t! = TransTime + \pi_h(x?)/\pi_s(b?)$

EndProduction_____

$a?$ : Operation
$b!$ : Machine
$y!$ : Order

$\pi_o(y!) = \pi_o(a?)$
$\pi_h(y!) = \pi_h(a?)$
$\pi_m(b!) = \pi_m(a?)$
$\pi_s(b!) = \pi_s(a?)$
$b_t! = TransTime$
$y_t! = TransTime + 1$

Table 5.3. *Processor relations for the production/consumption system.*

produced for the connector. (The connector name without a subscript denotes the value of the token.)

An explanation of the processor relation of the different processors is given below. Here we use the connector names (without decoration) as the channel names to which they are connected.

- The processor relation for *EndConsumption* specifies that the consumer from channel $q$ is connected to an order to become a pending order $r$, without delay. For channel $x$ an order is produced with a delay of one time unit. The quantity is not defined, but is specified that to be at least 1.
- The processor relation for *StartConsumption* specifies that this processor may execute only if the identification of the token from $r$ is equal to that of the token from $y$. Furthermore, the consumer part of the token from $r$ is put into $q$ with a delay equal to the number of items that the token from $y$ brings. So, the consumer cannot pass the processor *EndConsumption* before he has consumed all items, one per time unit.
- The processor relation for *StartProduction* shows that a token for channel $a$ is made, composed of the tokens of $x$ and $b$, which is identified by the order

and machine identity. The delay depends on the speed of the machine and the number of items to be produced.

- The processor relation for *EndProduction* specifies that the input token is decomposed into two tokens: the token for $b$ is the machine $a$? and the token for $y$ is the old order.

We remark that this example shows some interesting *invariance properties*:

- The sum of the number of tokens in $r$ and $q$ is constant for each trace, and equal to the number of customers.
- The sum of the number of tokens in $a$ and $b$ is constant for each trace, and equal to the number of machines.
- The sum of the number of tokens in $x$, $a$ and $y$ is always equal to the number of tokens in $r$, which means that for each waiting consumer there is an order in some stage of processing. This property only holds when if it was initially true.

This invariance properties such as these are studied in part III.

Finally we summarize the steps in the development of a complete model:

(i) make a *(hierarchical) net diagram*, including the determination of the processor characteristics;
(ii) make an *object model*, including constraints;
(iii) assign *complex classes* to the places;
(iv) define for each object class a *value type*;
(v) define for each processor a *processor relation*.

We call the first three activities *modeling* and the last two *specification*. Finally we should do some *verification*, for instance that the local and global constraints are satisfied.

# 6

# Specification language

As we have seen in chapter 5 three languages are used for the definition of a complete actor model: a language for object classes, a language for networks of actors and a language to define constraints and value types for complex classes and to define processor relations. The first two languages are graphical and are used for *modeling*, while the third is textual and used for *specification*. In this chapter we give a sketch of this specification language. In part V it is defined more precisely. It is a powerful language: each computable function can be expressed in it. It is a formalization of the language of mathematics, which means that *sets* and *functions* are the building blocks. Sets play two different roles in the language: sets are used as *types* for values and in function and schema definitions also as *signatures*. The values used as complexes are *finite* in the sense that, in principle, they can be represented as finite sets. However, we will use more sophisticated constructs such as tuples and sequences as well. Types, on the other hand, can be infinite.

The language has a *constructive* part, which means that sets and functions can be constructed from a small set of primitive sets and functions. Processor relations are defined by means of *schemas* and in a schema *predicates* play an essential role. The schema part of the language is similar to the language Z. The specification language is *extendable* in the sense that we start with a set of basic types and a set of primitive functions, but the systems engineer is free to add other basic types and primitive functions.

## 6.1 Values, types and functions

**Values and types**

Values used in a model always belong to a type, i.e. a set. There are some well-known basic types: $\emptyset$, the empty type; $\mathbb{B}$, the set of Boolean values $\{true, false\}$; $\mathbb{N}$, the set of all natural numbers; $\mathbb{Z}$, the set of all integers; $\mathbb{Q}$, the set of all rational numbers and the alphabet of (Ascii) characters. Note that we make a difference between the natural number two, the integer two and the rational number two. Of course there are (primitive) conversion functions. In fact we have a different syntax for them: 2, (+2) and (+2/1), respectively. If it is clear from the context what type the number has, we simply write 2 in all these cases (as a "sugaring" of the language). Two types have at most only some special values (such as the empty set) in common, so we may consider them as essentially disjoint. The values of the basic types should be given in some suitable syntax.

New types and new values are introduced by means of *constructors*. So,

$$\{a,\ b,\ c\}$$

is also a value, called a *set*, if $a$, $b$, $c$ are values of the same type, say $T$. This is the well-known set construction. The type of $\{a,\ b,\ c\}$ is

$$\mathbb{F}(T),$$

the set of all finite subsets of values in $T$. In particular $\{\}$ is the empty set. (Note that the empty set is a value in any set type.) Another construction is

$$\langle a,\ b,\ c \rangle,$$

which is a *sequence* or list of the three values. The type of such a sequence is denoted by

$$T^*,$$

which is the set of all finite sequences of type T. In particular, $\langle \rangle$ is the empty sequence. We can also combine values of different types to make new values. Let $a$, $b$, $c$ be values of types $A$, $B$, $C$ respectively. Then

$$(a,\ b,\ c)$$

is called a *vector* and the type of all these vectors is

$$(A \times B \times C)$$

which is called the Cartesian product of $A$, $B$ and $C$. We usually omit the outer parentheses of Cartesian products for notational convenience. So

$$A \times (B \times C)$$

stands for

$$(A \times (B \times C)).$$

Because long vectors are cumbersome if we want to extract an element of them, there is also a "labeled" vector, called a *tuple*. Here we use a set of *attributes* to mark the vector elements. Let $x$, $y$ and $z$ be different attributes; then

$$\{x \mapsto a,\ y \mapsto b,\ z \mapsto c\}$$

is a tuple, and the type of all these tuples is denoted by

$$[x : A,\ y : B,\ z : C].$$

In principle any set of attributes defines another language. Attributes are used only to select values in tuples and therefore calculation with them is not allowed, except for attributes in schema signatures: they are treated as variables. For tuple types there is one other constructor, called a *join* and denoted by $\bowtie$. It is only applicable for tuple types that have the same types for the same attributes (they are called *compatible*). For example,

$$[x : A,\ y : B,\ z : C] \bowtie [v : D,\ y : B]$$

is the same type as

$$[x : A,\ y : B,\ v : D,\ z : C].$$

For tuple types the order of the attributes does not play a role, so two tuple types are the same if they differ in the attribute order only.

The constructions treated above are the only ones that create new values and types. However, we can make very complex values in this way, for example,

$$\{x \mapsto (a,\ b),\ y \mapsto \langle c,\ c,\ a,\ a \rangle,\ z \mapsto \{z \mapsto a,\ x \mapsto c\}\}.$$

**Functions**

With a set of basic types and the type constructors we can generate a (countable) set of values. On these values we define *functions*. Functions should be well-behaved, which means that they satisfy some typing properties.

We distinguish *monomorphic* functions that have some specific type as their domain and another type as their range. For instance the function *minus* has $\mathbb{Q} \times \mathbb{Q}$ as its domain and $\mathbb{Q}$ as its range type. (Note that *minus* is the normal subtraction in this case for rationals, so $minus((+5/3), (+3/2))$ equals $(+1/6)$.) Monomorphic functions are not defined outside their domain type, which is equivalent to saying that their function value is $\bot$ when they are applied to a value outside their domain. Here $\bot$ is called the *nil value*; it is a special value and not a member of any type. There are also functions that have more than one domain type. They are called *polymorphic* functions. For example the *equality* function,

denoted by =, is polymorphic because it can be applied to any two values that
are of the same type. So,

$$= (2,3)$$

is a legal expression and

$$= (\{1,3\}, \{2,4\})$$

is also. (Instead of this prefix notation we usually write = in infix notation:
$\{1,3\} = \{2,4\}$.) Note that = is a primitive function in the language. It has the
property that two sets are *equal* if they have exactly the same elements, so the
order in which they appear in the set expression is irrelevant and so is the number
of duplicates of an element in a set. Similar properties hold for the equality of
tuples. The range type of = is of course $\mathbb{B}$, but there are many domain types.
We express this by a *type variable*, so the domain type of = is $\$ \times \$$, where $\$$
is a type variable. It means that for any substitution of $\$$ by a "normal" type,
the function = can be applied to values of that type. There are polymorphic
functions where the range type also contains type variables.

However, these type variables have to occur also in the domain type. For
example, the function $\cup$ can be applied as follows,

$$\{1, 2\} \cup \{2, 3\},$$

to obtain the set $\{1, 2, 3\}$. So, the range type is $\mathbb{F}(\$)$ because the domain type is
$\mathbb{F}(\$) \times \mathbb{F}(\$)$. The relationship between the domain and range type is expressed
by the *signature* of the function. For $\cup$ the signature is

$$\cup : \mathbb{F}(\$) \times \mathbb{F}(\$) \Rightarrow \mathbb{F}(\$).$$

Note that functions are not values. One reason for this separation is that, in
general, functions are not representable as finite sets, and therefore they (i.e.
their graphs) cannot be computed. So, functions cannot be applied to functions
and functions cannot be the result of a function application.

For primitive functions only the signature is used in the language; the relation
between arguments and associated function values (the *graph* of the function) is
assumed to be known and it is not part of the language. We have already met
some primitive functions ($\cup$ is not primitive but the others are). We will now
introduce some other important primitive functions. A very useful function is
the *selection* function, mostly used in infix notation:

$$if \ b \ then \ a \ else \ c \ fi.$$

This evaluates to $a$ if $b$ is equal to *true* and to $c$ otherwise. The signature of this function is

$$\mathbb{B} \times \$ \times \$ \Rightarrow \$.$$

Functions that select values from rows and tuples are called *projection* functions. They are denoted by $\pi_\ell$, where $\ell$ is a natural number when the function is applied to rows and an attribute when the function is applied to a tuple. For example,

$$\pi_2((a,\ b,\ c))$$

evaluates to $b$ and

$$\pi_z(\{x \mapsto a,\ y \mapsto b,\ z \mapsto c\})$$

evaluates to $c$. The signatures of these functions are

$$\$_1 \times \$_2 \times \$_3 \Rightarrow \$_2$$

and

$$[z : \$_1] \bowtie \$_2 \Rightarrow \$_1$$

respectively. Analogously we have projection functions with more than one attribute or natural number:

$$\Pi_{1,3}((a,\ b,\ c))$$

evaluates to $(a,\ c)$ and

$$\Pi_{x,z}(\{x \mapsto a,\ y \mapsto b,\ z \mapsto c\})$$

evaluates to $\{x \mapsto a,\ z \mapsto c\}$. The signatures of these functions are

$$\Pi_{1,3} : \$_1 \times \$_2 \times \$_3 \Rightarrow \$_1 \times \$_3$$

and

$$\Pi_{x,z} : [x : \$_1, z : \$_2] \bowtie \$_3 \Rightarrow [x : \$_1, z : \$_2].$$

For sets we have the following primitive functions (name and signature):

$$
\begin{aligned}
ins\ &:\ \$ \times \mathbb{F}(\$) \Rightarrow \mathbb{F}(\$),\\
pick\ &:\ \mathbb{F}(\$) \Rightarrow \$,\\
rest\ &:\ \mathbb{F}(\$) \Rightarrow \mathbb{F}(\$).
\end{aligned}
$$

Here $\$$ is again a type variable. The meaning of these functions is, expressed in the meta language, as follows:

$$
\begin{aligned}
ins(a, b) &= \{a\} \cup b,\\
pick(a) &\in a,\\
rest(a) \subseteq a\ &\wedge\ ins(pick(a), rest(a)) = a.
\end{aligned}
$$

Note that *pick* is a selection function that assigns to each non-empty set a (fixed) element of that set. So there is no "random mechanism" hidden in *pick*. For sequences we have the following primitive functions:

$$cat \; : \; \$^* \times \$ \Rightarrow \$^*,$$
$$head \; : \; \$^* \Rightarrow \$,$$
$$tail \; : \; \$^* \Rightarrow \$^*.$$

The meaning of these functions is:

$$cat(\langle a, \, b, \, c \rangle, d) = \langle a, \, b, \, c, \, d \rangle,$$
$$head(\langle a, \, b, \, c \rangle) = a,$$
$$tail(\langle a, \, b, \, c \rangle) = \langle b, \, c \rangle.$$

For tuples we have, in addition to the projection functions, the *tuple update*

$$\oplus : \$_1 \times \$_2 \Rightarrow \$_1 \bowtie \$_2,$$

with meaning

$$\{x \mapsto 1, \, y \mapsto 2\} \oplus \{x \mapsto 3, \, z \mapsto 4\} = \{x \mapsto 3, \, y \mapsto 2, \, z \mapsto 4\}.$$

Note that $\oplus$ is not commutative because if the values in the first and second tuple for the same attribute are different, then the value of the second tuple will "survive".

Finally there are some primitive functions on $\mathbb{N}$, $\mathbb{Z}$ and $\mathbb{Q}$: subtraction $(-)$, integer division $(div)$, rational division $(\div)$, comparison $(<)$ and conversion functions for conversion between naturals, integers and rationals ($toint : \mathbb{N} \Rightarrow \mathbb{Z}$, $torat : \mathbb{Z} \Rightarrow \mathbb{Q}$, $truncint : \mathbb{Q} \Rightarrow \mathbb{Z}$ and $truncnat : \mathbb{Z} \Rightarrow \mathbb{N}$). Note that we use the same symbol for more than one function (for example $\div$). This is called *overloading* and does not give ambiguities as long as the functions have different signatures and only one pair of a domain and a range type can be deduced from the expressions where the function name is used. (For a full list of primitive functions see appendix C.)

Functions are allowed to be *partial*, which means that they do not have a function value for all values in their domain. We give them the value $\bot$ for these domain values. For instance $pick(\{\})$ is $\bot$. On the other hand, some functions may be applied outside their domain; for example *if* $3 < 4$ *then* $3$ *else* $\bot$ *fi* is a legal term that evaluates to *true*. So, $\bot$ may be used explicitly in constructions.

We conclude this section with *type definitions*. As we have seen, type expressions involving type constructors and type variables are used. For notational convenience we may use an abbreviation for such expressions, for example

$$A := \mathbb{F}(\mathbb{N} \times \mathbb{B}).$$

Here $A$ is the name of a new type. We do not allow recursion in type definitions. We call the abbreviations introduced above *defined types*.

## 6.2 Value and function construction

There are several ways to construct new values and functions. We have already seen some value constructions, namely the formation of finite sets, rows, sequences and tuples by explicitly enumeration of their elements. There are three ways to construct new values in an *implicit* way:

(i) function application,
(ii) set restriction,
(iii) mapping construction.

Function application is well-known. Let $f$ be a function with signature $T \Rightarrow S$ and $a$ a value of type $T$, then $f(a)$ denotes the value of the function in $a$. For example, $(+3/4) \div (+4/5)$ is such an application and its result is $(+3/5)$.

Set restriction uses a given set, say $s$ of type $\mathbb{F}(T)$, and a function $f$ with signature $T \Rightarrow \mathbb{B}$. The new set is denoted by

$$\{x : s \mid f(x)\}$$

and is the set of all values of $s$ for which $f(s)$ has the value *true*. For example, the set defined by

$$\{x : \{1, 2, 3, 4, 5, 6, 7, 8\} \mid even(x)\}$$

is the set $\{2, 4, 6, 8\}$. (Note that the function *even* has not yet been defined.)

Map construction is the construction of a finite set of pairs with unique first components. Such a set is itself a function; however, it has a finite domain and therefore it is also a value. We call such a function a *mapping*. An example is the mapping, say $m$, and defined by

$$(x : \{2, 4, 6, 8\} \mid square(x)),$$

which is the set of pairs

$$\{(2, 4), (4, 16), (6, 36), (8, 64)\}.$$

(Note that the function *square* has not yet been defined.) Mappings can by applied to an argument like normal functions, by means of the application function $(\cdot)$; thus $m \cdot 6$ equals 36.

To improve readability it is possible to give value constructions a name as shorthand, for example:

$$a := \{1, 2, 3, 4\}.$$

To construct new functions out of given ones, we introduce *terms*. A term is a construction to form a value in which *variables* are substituted for values. For example, the term

$$\textit{if } x < y \textit{ then } x \textit{ else } y \textit{ fi}$$

is a compound function application (first $x < y$ and then the selection function) where $x$ and $y$ are place holders for values. We construct functions by giving a name to terms that contain variables. The term above defines a function that determines the minimum of its two arguments:

$$\textit{min}(x, y) := \textit{if } x < y \textit{ then } x \textit{ else } y \textit{ fi}.$$

This is a function definition. The variables appearing on the left-hand side of the definition sign (:=) denote that it is a function of two variables. (In fact the domain of the function is a Cartesian product, because we may write $f(\dots)$ instead of $f((\dots))$.) The signature of this function is $\mathbb{Q} \times \mathbb{Q} \Rightarrow \mathbb{Q}$. (We may also define the function for $\mathbb{N}$ and $\mathbb{Z}$, with the same definition.) So we *abstract* the variables $x$ and $y$ from the term that defines the function and we say that the variables in the term are *bound* by the left-hand side of the definition. It is allowed to define functions without arguments. They are constants such as the approximation $\pi := (+22/7)$.

We may also use terms in set restrictions and map constructions. For example, with a set $s$ of rational numbers (i.e. of type $\mathbb{F}(\mathbb{Q})$) we have

$$\{x : s \mid x < 5\},$$

which is the same as

$$\{x : s \mid g(x)\}$$

with

$$g(x) := x < 5.$$

Similarly, for a map construction we may write, for example,

$$(x : s \mid x \div (+2/1)).$$

Note that we have used terms already in these constructions, but only as function applications with variables as arguments.

A function definition always has a signature. In many cases, but not in all, the signature can be derived from the term that defines the function. We always define the signature explicitly, because it is often the start of a definition and it can be used for verification purposes: if the defined type is not equal to the derived type, the systems engineer has made a mistake. Thus, the complete definition of the function *min* becomes

$$min(x, y) := if \ x < y \ then \ x \ else \ y \ fi : \mathbb{Q} \times \mathbb{Q} \Rightarrow \mathbb{Q}.$$

Below we give the construction of some well-known functions.

$$
\begin{aligned}
+(x, y) \quad &:= x - (0 - y) : \mathbb{Q} \times \mathbb{Q} \Rightarrow \mathbb{Q}, \\
even(x) \quad &:= (+2) \times (x \, div(+2)) = x : \mathbb{Z} \times \mathbb{Z} \Rightarrow \mathbb{B}, \\
\wedge \ (x, y) \quad &:= if \ x \ then \ y \ else \ false \ fi : \mathbb{B} \times \mathbb{B} \Rightarrow \mathbb{B}, \\
\vee(x, y) \quad &:= if \ x \ then \ true \ else \ y \ fi : \mathbb{B} \times \mathbb{B} \Rightarrow \mathbb{B}, \\
\Rightarrow (x, y) \quad &:= if \ x \ then \ y \ else \ true \ fi : \mathbb{B} \times \mathbb{B} \Rightarrow \mathbb{B}, \\
\neg(x) \quad &:= if \ x \ then \ false \ else \ true \ fi : \mathbb{B} \Rightarrow \mathbb{B}, \\
\times(x, y) \quad &:= x \div ((+1/1) \div y) : \mathbb{Q} \times \mathbb{Q} \Rightarrow \mathbb{Q}, \\
natrat(x) &:= torat(toint(x)) : \mathbb{N} \Rightarrow \mathbb{Q}.
\end{aligned}
$$

Now we have defined multiplication for rationals, we can use the conversion functions to obtain multiplication for integers and naturals. This is a standard construction and we will omit this here. (The logical operators can be extended to non-domain values involving $\perp$.)

Function construction is very powerful because of *recursive* function definitions, i.e. definitions in which the name of the function is used in the term. Such a definition is in fact an *equation* with the function as unknown variable. There are standard techniques to find a function that solves the equation; however, that is not our aim here. We only have to be sure that there exists a solution. Next, we present the recursive definitions of some useful functions:

$$
\begin{aligned}
size(x) \quad &:= if \ x = \{\} \ then \ 0 \\
&\quad else \ 1 + size(rest(x)) \ fi : \mathbb{F}(\$) \Rightarrow \mathbb{N}, \\
sum(f) \quad &:= if \ f = \{\} \ then \ 0 \\
&\quad else \ \pi_2(pick(f)) + sum(rest(f)) \ fi : \mathbb{F}(\$ \times \mathbb{Q}) \Rightarrow \mathbb{Q}, \\
forall(f) \quad &:= if \ f = \{\} \ then \ true \\
&\quad else \ \pi_2(pick(f)) \wedge forall(rest(f)) \ fi : \mathbb{F}(\$ \times \mathbb{B}) \Rightarrow \mathbb{B}, \\
exists(f) \quad &:= if \ f = \{\} \ then \ false \\
&\quad else \ \pi_2(pick(f)) \vee exists(rest(f)) \ fi : \mathbb{F}(\$ \times \mathbb{B}) \Rightarrow \mathbb{B}, \\
setapply(r, x) &:= if \ r = \{\} \ then \ \{\} \\
&\quad else \ if \ \pi_1(pick(r)) = x \ then \\
&\qquad\qquad ins(\pi_2(pick(r)), setapply(rest(r), x)) \\
&\quad else \ setapply(rest(r), x) \ fi \ fi : \\
&\qquad\qquad\qquad \mathbb{F}(\$_1 \times \$_2) \times \$_1 \Rightarrow \mathbb{F}(\$_2).
\end{aligned}
$$

The function *size* determines the cardinality of a (finite) set. The function *sum* is applied to binary relations and in particular to mappings with the rationals as range. For such a mapping it determines the sum of the function values of all domain values. If the argument of *sum* is not a mapping, the result is the sum over all domain values of one arbitrary function value per domain value. The function *forall* applied to Boolean-valued mappings is the well-known universal quantor and *exists* is the existential quantor. The function *setapply* assigns to a binary relation $r$ and a value $x$ a set of values that form a pair with $x$ in $r$. With *setapply* we can construct the application function $\cdot$ for mappings:

$$\cdot(f, x) := pick(setapply(f, x)) : \mathbb{F}(\$_1 \times \$_2) \times \$_1 \Rightarrow \$_2.$$

Note that the *pick* function selects the unique function value if $f$ is a mapping. (There is a "toolkit" of well-known functions in appendix C.)

## 6.3 Predicates

With the tools developed in the former section we have constructed all the logical operators. However, we do not yet have a complete predicate language, because we have no quantification over infinite sets, in particular over types. We often need this and therefore we introduce predicates as new language elements. Note that, in general, a quantification over an infinite set cannot be evaluated in finite time. For instance,

$$\forall n : \mathbb{N} \bullet n < n + 1$$

is *true*, but we cannot verify this by evaluating $n < n + 1$ for all $n \in \mathbb{N}$. On the other hand, the evaluation of the function *forall* (as defined in section 6.2) is computable in finite time because the domain of quantification is always a finite set.

The basic building blocks of the predicate language are Boolean terms, i.e. terms with a value in $\mathbb{B}$. A *predicate* is recursively defined by following:

   (i) a Boolean term is a predicate;
   (ii) if $p$ and $q$ are predicates then $p \wedge q$, $p \vee q$, $\neg p$ and $p \Rightarrow q$ are predicates;
   (iii) if $p$ is a predicate then $\forall x : D \bullet p$ and $\exists x : D \bullet p$ are predicates, where $D$ is a type.

The set $D$ is called the *domain* of the quantor. An example of a predicate is:

$$\forall x : \mathbb{N} \bullet \exists y : \mathbb{N} \bullet y < x,$$

which has the value *false*. Only if for each variable in a predicate a *domain* over which the variable may run is given does the predicate have a value in $\mathbb{B}$;

otherwise, no value is defined. If a variable has no defined domain it is called a *free variable*, otherwise, a *bound* variable. Note that the logical operators $\neg$, $\wedge$, $\vee$ and $\Rightarrow$ are already defined as functions in the toolkit.

Predicates are used in *constraints* for an object model, in *function declarations* and in *schemas*. A constraint, however, does not have free variables. In a constraint such as:

$$\forall\, t : task \bullet e(a^{-1}(t)) = c(t)$$

the name *task* stands for the set of all tasks in a complex. This is a finite set. The functions $e$, $a^{-1}$ and $c$ can be defined properly in the context of a complex. The use of predicates in function declarations is considered in part V and the use in schemas is considered in the next section.

## 6.4 Schemas and scripts

A schema is a *restricted* tuple type. For example the schema

$$[x : \mathbf{N}, y : \mathbf{N} \mid \exists\, z : \mathbf{N} \bullet x + z = y],$$

denotes the set of all tuples of the form,

$$\{x \mapsto a, y \mapsto b\}$$

where $a$ and $b$ are natural numbers such that $a \leq b$. The general structure of a schema is as follows:

$$[signature \mid predicate].$$

(Note that a schema signature differs from a function signature.) Free variables in the predicate have to occur also in the signature and are thus bound by the signature. The attributes of a tuple are used as variables in the predicate of a schema.

Note that we often use a *table* representation for schemas as we did in chapter 5. If the predicate is a conjunction of several predicates then we may put every predicate on a separate row in the table. So, if in a schema two rows are not connected by a logical operator then these rows are supposed to be connected by the $\wedge$ operator.

In schemas we may use the nil value $\bot$. We have to state explicitly that a variable obtains the value $\bot$. If a variable is not given a value at all in a predicate, it is assumed that it may be any value except $\bot$. Consider for example the schema $s$

$$
\begin{array}{|l}
\hline
\; s \underline{\hspace{10cm}} \\
\quad x : \mathbf{N} \\
\quad y : \mathbf{N} \\
\underline{\hspace{11cm}} \\
\quad (x = \bot \ \wedge \ y < 2) \ \vee \\
\quad (x = 2 \ \wedge \ y = 2) \ \vee \\
\quad (x < 2 \ \wedge \ y = \bot) \\
\hline
\end{array}
$$

The meaning of this schema is the set of tuples

$$\{y \mapsto 0\}, \ \{y \mapsto 1\}, \ \{x \mapsto 2, \ y \mapsto 2\}, \ \{x \mapsto 0\}, \{x \mapsto 1\}.$$

Note that tuples are functions if we ignore type information: the attributes are the arguments and the values per attribute are the function values. The problem is that the function values may be of different types, therefore we treat them differently in the language.

In a *schema definition* we can give a schema a name, just as we give names to types in type definitions. Here type variables are allowed. An example of a schema definition is as follows:

$$A := [x : \mathbf{N}, y : \mathbf{N} \mid x > 2 \ \wedge \ y < x].$$

Schemas can be used to describe processor relations. Then, the attributes represent connectors and we often use the convention that input connectors have names that are "decorated" with a question mark (?) at the end and output connectors end with an exclamation mark (!). An input connector to a store, however, does not acquire a question mark (?) while the output connector to a store is decorated with a prime ('), because $s$ represents the old and $s'$ the new value of the token in the store.

In a schema we may use subscripts $t$ and $i$ for input connectors: $t$ denotes the time stamp of the token (e.g. $x_t$?) and $i$ its identity. Furthermore we may use the functions *New* and *TransTime*, which supply a new token identity and the event time (i.e. the maximal time stamp of the consumed tokens).

Often we are dealing with very large schemas and then it is useful to be able to construct a schema from more elementary schemas. Therefore we have *schema operators*, i.e. operators that combine schemas. We will illustrate them by means of the example of figure 6.1. Consider a simple system having two processors connected to the same store. The processor *update* is connected to the store and has one extra input connector $x$?. The processor *retrieve* is also connected to the store and has one extra input connector $y$? and one extra output connector $z$!. All connectors have the value type $\mathbf{N}$. The first processor is able to update the store by adding the value of the input token to the token in the store. The second

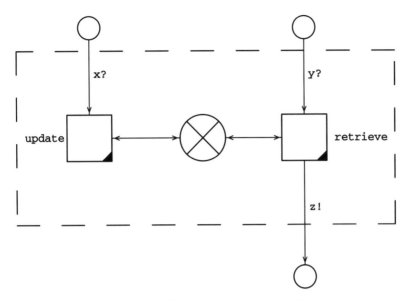

Fig. 6.1. Update/retrieve example, net diagram.

processor is able to retrieve the stored value, multiplied by the value of the input token. So if $y?$ is 1, then the stored value is produced by *retrieve*. There is a requirement: the value of the stored token should always be even. This can be expressed by the following schema:

$$store := [s : \mathbf{N} \mid even(s)].$$

This schema is used to define the type of the store and to formulate a constraint for it: it is a restricted tuple type. Next we give the schema for *update*:

$$update := [x? : \mathbf{N},\ s : \mathbf{N},\ s' : \mathbf{N} \mid s' = s + x?\ \wedge\ even(s)\ \wedge\ even(s')].$$

So *update* consumes a token only if it is even, because otherwise $s'$ cannot be even. Instead of this specification we can use the $\Delta$ operator:

$$update := [\Delta store,\ x? : \mathbf{N} \mid s' = s + x?].$$

This means that the attributes of *store* are added to *update* and that each undecorated attribute now also appears with a prime. Further, the predicate of *store* is copied into *update*. The $\Delta$ symbol indicates that *update* might change a store. For *retrieve* we have:

$$retrieve := [y? : \mathbf{N},\ z! : \mathbf{N},\ s : \mathbf{N},\ s' : \mathbf{N} \mid even(s)\ \wedge\ even(s')$$
$$\wedge\ z! = y? \times s\ \wedge\ s' = s].$$

Instead of this redundant notation we may write

$$[\Xi store,\; y? : \mathbb{N}, z! : \mathbb{N} \mid z! = y? \times s].$$

The $\Xi$ operator does the same as $\Delta$ but it also adds the predicate that all undecorated variables should be the same as the corresponding decorated ones. Note that we have not bothered about time stamps here, because they do not play a role in this specification. Leaving them out means that all delays are zero.

A *script* is a complete specification of a system. It is a list of definitions of one of the following kinds:

- type definitions,
- value definitions,
- function definitions,
- function declarations,
- schema definitions.

A script must satisfy the *define before use* principle, which means that in each definition on the right-hand side of the definition sign ($:=$) only names that have been defined earlier in the script may appear. There is only one exception to this rule: in a function definition the name of the function itself may be used in the defining term (for recursive definitions).

# 7

# References and exercises for part I

This part of the book conveys the basic concepts of systems engineering and therefore here we give references only to the most important foundation works. In later parts of the book we give more specialized references. The list of references given here is not exhaustive: only seminal publications and reference books and articles are mentioned. The *development process* of information systems is studied in the literature in three areas of computer science: *software engineering, systems analysis and design* and *management information systems*. In these areas the problem of the development of information systems is approached from different perspectives. There are many excellent textbooks on software engineering, for example [Pressman, 1987; Sommerville, 1989; Boehm, 1981]. These books still pay relatively little attention to the use of formal models of systems in the development process, although system engineers have a growing belief that making and analyzing models of the systems before constructing them is an effort that repays. More formal approaches to software engineering are based on formalisms such as VDM and Z. For VDM *see* [Jones, 1990; Andrews and Ince, 1991] and for Z *see* [Woodcock and Loomes, 1988; Wordsworth, 1992]. An introduction to a variety of formal approaches can be found in [Cohen *et al.*, 1986]. Most of the books on *systems analysis and design* are very practical and support a specific approach to system development. Important examples of such approaches are [Jackson, 1983; Yourdon, 1989; Ross, 1977].

Books on *information systems* do not restrict their focus to computerized information systems but also consider the *human information workers* as part of an information system. Good references are [Davis and Olson, 1985; Lundeberg *et al.*, 1981; Lyytinen, 1987]. There are many books on the *development of organizations*, for example [Galbraith, 1973; Mintzberg, 1979]. They focus on tasks of human beings in systems. Systems engineering principles for arbitrary systems can be found in [Boardman, 1990; Checkland, 1981; Wymore, 1967].

Surveys of the *application domains* of information systems engineering can be found in the introductory parts of books on systems engineering as mentioned above.

The concepts behind *transition systems* are already very old. There are several roots for these ideas. In computer science *automata* are in fact transition systems. Examples of automata models are the Turing, the Mealy and the Moore machines. They are described in most books on the foundations of computer science, for instance [Lewis and Papadimitriou, 1981; Hopcroft and Ullmann, 1979]. In probability theory a *Markov chain* is in fact a transition system with probabilities attached to each transition. In fact Markov chains can be considered as *stochastic automata*. They are treated in most books on stochastic processes, for example [Ross, 1983] and [Revuz, 1975].

The concept of an *object* is borrowed from *data base theory*. The idea of an object first occurred in the database framework called the *network model* defined by C.W. Bachman, *see* [Bachman, 1969]. Here an object is a record in a file. The first rigorous database framework, developed by E.F. Codd, was the *relational model*, where an object is a *tuple* in a relation; *see* [Codd, 1970; Date, 1990a; Date, 1990b; Ullman, 1988]. In the more advanced *nested relational model* an object can be composed of other objects; *see* [Schek and Scholl, 1986; Paredaens *et al.*, 1989]. The concept of a simplex used in this book is in fact borrowed from the *entity-relationship model*, invented by P.P. Chen; *see* [Chen, 1976]. There are many other database frameworks. In [Tsichritzis and Lochovsky, 1982] a survey is given.

The concept of an *actor* has many roots. The fundamental idea behind this concept is that the state transitions of a complex system are performed by *components* of the system that can work *concurrently*. The "founding fathers" of the modern formalisms of concurrent processes are C. Petri, E.W. Dijkstra, C.A.R. Hoare and R. Milner. The formalism of Petri nets (*see* [Petri, 1962; Petri, 1980]) has been extended fundamentally since their invention by Petri. Specifically, the development of *colored Petri nets* by K. Jensen was a mile stone. Good reference books here are [Peterson, 1981; Reisig, 1985; Jensen, 1992]. Petri nets are very close to the basic idea of the transition system. Dijkstra's article [Dijkstra, 1968] has influenced many researchers in this area. The formalisms of Hoare and Milner, called CSP and CSS respectively, are *algebraic process models*. They describe the behavior of system components by means of (recursive) equations. Good references are [Hoare, 1985; Milner, 1980]. Further useful books on algebraic processes are [Hennessy, 1988; Baeten and Weijland, 1990].

Other frameworks for describing systems with the purpose of *simulating* them can be found in [Zeigler, 1982] and [Ören *et al.*, 1984].

There are formalisms that allow *dynamic reconfiguration* of a system, when the number of actors may grow or shrink during the lifetime of a system. All *object oriented languages* such as *Simula* (*see* [Dahl *et al.*, 1970]) and *Smalltalk* (*see* [Goldberg and Robson, 1983]) have this feature but very few of them have formal semantics. An example of a formal framework with this feature is the *actor model*, described in [Agha, 1986].

The graphical language for hierarchical net models used in this book is very close to the *data flow diagram* technique called DFD, *see* [Yourdon, 1989], SADT, *see* [Marca and McGowan, 1988], and ISAC, *see* [Lundeberg *et al.*, 1981]. Data flow diagrams extended with (informal) semantics for time can be found in [Ward and Mellor, 1985].

The specification language is close to Z. References to the latter are given above [Woodcock and Loomes, 1988; Wordsworth, 1992]. Another reference is [Spivey, 1989]. However, part V of this book is a good reference to Z as well.

## Exercises for part I

(1)   Consider a grocery store, which buys products from suppliers, stores them and sells them to customers.

Identify and describe the business units and determine the tasks of the information system of the company as a whole and of the business units in particular.

(2)   Consider a computer-service company that makes its computer resources available to its customers on a time sharing base, and that maintains databases for public access. Identify and describe the business units and determine the tasks of the information system of this company.

(3)   Consider a transition system with state space $S = \{1, 2, 3\}$ and a memoryless transition law $\mathcal{L}$ characterized as follows:

$$\forall t \in \{x : \mathbf{Q} \mid x \geq 0\} : \quad \begin{aligned} \mathcal{L}(\epsilon) &= \{(1,0)\}, \\ \mathcal{L}((1,t)) &= \{(1,t), (2, t+1)\}, \\ \mathcal{L}((2,t)) &= \{(1, t+1), (3, t+2)\}, \\ \mathcal{L}((3,t)) &= \emptyset. \end{aligned}$$

(Here we write $\mathcal{L}(e)$ instead of $\mathcal{L}(\langle e_1, \ldots, e_n, e \rangle)$ in case $\mathcal{L}$ is memoryless.)

(a) Determine the set of deadlocking traces.

(b) Determine the set of traces with livelock.

(4)    Consider a garage. Customers make appointments for diagnoses and re-
       pair tasks for their cars. A task concerns a standard package of activities.
       A task for one car is performed by one mechanic. The customer receives
       an invoice for the task. Make an object model for this company, as follows.

   (a) Define simplex classes and relationships;
   (b) draw a simplex diagram;
   (c) define some useful complex classes;
   (d) define constraints, either graphical or in natural language.

(5)    Consider the following game. There is an urn with two kinds of ball: red
       and black. A person takes two balls from the urn in each step of the game.
       He cannot *see* the balls before they are out of the urn. If he then has two
       balls of the same color, he returns a black ball into the urn; otherwise, he
       returns a red one. (The player has enough black balls outside the urn to
       play the game.)

   (a) Make a classical Petri net for this game.
   (b) Show that the system always reaches a final state.
   (c) Determine the final state for each possible initial state.

(6)    Consider a *finite state machine* with state space $M$ (a finite set), input
       alphabet $I$ (a finite set) and transition function $T \in M \times I \to M$. If the
       machine is in some state $m \in M$ and it receives some input symbol $i \in I$
       then the machine will move to state $T(m, i)$.

   (a) Model such a machine as a transition system. (Hint: introduce
       two kinds of states, states that represent the states of the machine
       and states that represent pairs of a machine state and an input
       symbol.)
   (b) Now consider a non-deterministic finite state machine, i.e. $T$ is a
       set-valued function $T \in M \times I \to \mathbb{P}(M)$. Answer (a) again.
   (c) Extend the machine with an output alphabet $O$ and a response
       function $R \in M \times I \to O$, and answer (a) again.

(7)    Model the producer-consumer system defined below as a transition sys-
       tem. The system only moves at the end of each period (the periods have
       the same duration).

   – The consumer has a stock of $C$ items.
   – The producer has a stock of $P$ items.
   – There is a set of orders $O$ (an order asks for an arbitrary number of
     items).
   – There is a set of deliveries $D$.

- The consumer orders $S - C$ items if its stock satisfies $C \leq s$ ($s \leq S$, $s$ and $S$ are given).
- In each time period the consumer uses an arbitrary amount of its stock, and if possible at least one item.
- The producer makes in each period $A$ items and puts them in stock.
- The producer sends the requested number of items of the oldest order as soon as it has enough items.
- Items are received one period later than they are sent.

(8) Modify the example of the water reservoir (*see* figure 3.1) such that there is a tap change possible at some point in time. Give two solutions: one with a modified state space and one with a modified transition law.

# Part II

# Frameworks

# 8

# Introduction

In part II we define the formalisms we shall use to model and analyze systems. The concepts have already been introduced in part I. As previously mentioned, a *formalism* consists of a mathematical framework and a language. The mathematical *framework* is represented by a *tuple* of mathematical entities, called *attributes*, and a set of *requirements* to be fulfilled by the attributes.

As an illustration we define the framework of an automaton. An *automaton* is a tuple

$$(S, I, O, T, B)$$

where

- $S$, $I$ and $O$ are sets, called the state space, the input set and the output set respectively,

- $T \in S \times I \twoheadrightarrow S \times O$ is called the transition function,

- $B \subseteq S$ is called the set of initial states.

If we refer to an automaton, we give it a name, for instance $A$, and we may refer to an *attribute* of $A$ by using the name of the automaton as a subscript for the attribute name. For instance $S_A$ denotes the state space of the automaton $A$. If we are considering only one automaton then we drop the dependency of the name. We refer for instance to the "state space $S$ of the automaton" if there is only one (maybe arbitrary) automaton in the context.

Note that a framework is in fact a set of functions with a common domain. Each function of a framework is called a *model*. The elements of the common domain are (traditionally) listed in a tuple. In the example above the framework is called an "automaton" and is formally defined as follows:

$$\{A|A \text{ is a function} \;\land\; dom(A) = \{S, I, O, T, B\} \land$$
$$A(S),\ A(I),\ A(O) \text{ are sets} \;\land$$
$$A(T) \in A(S) \times A(I) \twoheadrightarrow A(S) \times A(O) \land$$
$$A(B) \subseteq A(S)\}$$

However, we will use the shorter notation as given above: note that $S_A = A(S)$. In other situations we often write $f_x$ instead of $f(x)$, but it will always be clear from the context what the function and the argument are.

We use a similar technique for specifying models in the specification language (*see* part V). There we use so-called *schemas* to specify models. The difference between a schema and a framework is, that in a schema each attribute has a *type*, i.e. a set to which the (function) value of the attribute belongs. So, if we had used a schema to specify the automaton, we would have had to specify to which sets $A(S)$, $A(I)$ and $A(O)$ belong. So schemas are "typed" and frameworks not. (Note that the term "tuple" is used in the specification language in a slightly different sense.)

The first framework we present is called the *transition systems framework*. It formalizes the concept of discrete dynamic systems and their properties. The second framework is called the *object framework*. It formalizes the concepts of *simplexes* and *complexes*. These are *static* concepts used for modeling state spaces (or databases). The third framework is called the *actor framework*, because it formalizes the concepts of actors and networks of actors. It generalizes the framework of Petri nets.

The three frameworks fit together, since the object framework is used to define the objects in the actor framework and the actor framework is used to model discrete dynamic systems. More precise: an object model is part of an actor model and an actor model is an instance of the transition systems framework.

Two parts of these frameworks, the *class model* and the *hierarchical net model*, form in fact an *abstract syntax* for the graphical part of the modeling language we used in part I. A software tool for systems engineering should be able to edit and verify graphical representations according to this syntax. The semantics of this syntax is given as well in the other definitions in this part. The syntax and semantics of the textual part of the modeling language is found in part V.

# 9

# Transition systems framework

We start with some notations and preliminary definitions. Let $\mathcal{N}$ be the set

$$\{x \subseteq \mathbb{N} \mid \forall i \in x, j \in \mathbb{N} : j < i \Rightarrow j \in x\}.$$

So $\mathcal{N} = \{\emptyset, \{0\}, \{0, 1\}, \{0, 1, 2\}, \ldots\}$. Also $\mathbb{N} \in \mathcal{N}$.

A *sequence* $p$ is a function such that $dom(p) \in \mathcal{N}$. The sequence is called infinite if $dom(p) = \mathbb{N}$, otherwise it is finite with *length* $\mid p \mid$. The empty sequence with domain $\emptyset$ is denoted by $\epsilon$, other sequences by optional $\langle \, \rangle$ brackets. Thus for example,

$$\langle a, b, c \rangle = \{(0, a), (1, b), (2, c)\}.$$

Note that in fact $\epsilon = \emptyset$. For $i \in dom(p)$ we write $p_i$ instead of $p(i)$. If $p$ is a sequence of length $n > 0$ and $a$ is an arbitrary element, we define

$$(p \, ; \, a) = \langle p_0, \ldots, p_{n-1}, a \rangle.$$

For the sequence of length 0 we define $(\epsilon \, ; \, a) = \langle a \rangle$.

Let $A$ be a set. An $A$-sequence is a sequence with range $A$. $A^n$ is the set of all $A$-sequences of length $n$, $A^*$ the set of all such finite $A$-sequences and $A^\infty$ the set of all infinite $A$-sequences. Further, we define $A^+$ as $A^* \cup A^\infty$.

The *prefixes* of a sequence $p$ are the sequences $p^i = \langle p_0, \ldots, p_{i-1} \rangle$ with $i \in dom(p)$. By convention $p^0 = \epsilon$ and for finite $p$ we have $p^{|p|} = p$. Note that $(p^i \, ; \, p_i) = p^{i+1}$.

A set $D \subseteq A^+$ is called *prefix-closed* if and only if

$$\forall p \in D, i \in dom(p) : p^i \in D.$$

It is called *suffix-closed* if and only if

$$\forall p \in A^\infty : (\forall i \in dom(p) : p^i \in D) \Rightarrow p \in D.$$

It is called *closed* if it is both prefix- and suffix-closed. A prefix-closed set $D$

81

contains all prefixes of its elements; if a suffix-closed set $D$ contains all prefixes of an infinite $p$, it contains $p$ itself. Note that the empty set is closed, $A^*$ is prefix-closed and $A^\infty$ is suffix-closed.

We shall now define *transition systems*. Transition systems consist of possible *events*, from some set $E$. The elements of $E^+$ are called *traces*. The important part of a transition system is a function $\mathcal{L}$, the *transition law*, telling what events come next when a certain finite trace has occurred.

**Definition 9.1** A transition system is a pair $(E, \mathcal{L})$, where

- $E$ is a set, called the *event set*,
- $\mathcal{L} \in E^* \to \mathbb{P}(E)$ is called the *transition law*.

A *trace* of $(E, \mathcal{L})$ is an element of $E^+$. An *autonomous trace* of $(E, \mathcal{L})$ is a sequence $p \in E^+$ such that

$$\forall\, i \in dom(p) : p_i \in \mathcal{L}(p^i).$$

An autonomous trace $p$ is called *maximal* if and only if it is infinite, or is finite and such that $\mathcal{L}(p) = \varnothing$. The set of all autonomous traces of $(E, \mathcal{L})$ is called its *autonomous behavior*. The set of all maximal autonomous traces is called its *maximal autonomous behavior*.

□

For a trace $p$ the set $\mathcal{L}(p)$ is the set of *possible extensions* of $p$. Note that $\epsilon$ is an autonomous trace for any transition system. It is easy to prove that the autonomous behavior of a transition system is closed. (The proof is an exercise.) The next theorem shows that any non-empty closed set of sequences can be described as the autonomous behavior of some transition system. This result is important because it proves that the autonomous behavior of a transition system can be obtained by restricting the set of all possible traces by so-called *dynamic constraints*.

**Theorem 9.1** Let $E$ be a set and let $D \subseteq E^+$ be non-empty and closed. Then there is a transition system $(E, \mathcal{L})$ with $D$ as autonomous behavior.

*Proof* Let $p \in E^*$. Then we set

$$\mathcal{L}(p) = \{e \mid (p\,;\ e) \in D\}.$$

We shall prove that $(E, \mathcal{L})$ has $D$ as autonomous behavior. First let $q \in D$. We shall prove that $q$ is an autonomous trace. Take $i \in dom(q)$. We have to prove that $q_i \in \mathcal{L}(q^i)$. By the definition of $\mathcal{L}$,

$$q_i \in \mathcal{L}(q^i) \Leftrightarrow (q^i;\ q_i) \in D.$$

Because $(q^i; q_i) = q^{i+1}$ we have

$$q_i \in \mathcal{L}(q^i) \Leftrightarrow q^{i+1} \in D.$$

The last assertion is true by the prefix-closedness of $D$. So $q$ is indeed an autonomous trace of $(e, \mathcal{L})$.

Conversely, let $q$ be an autonomous trace of $(E, \mathcal{L})$. We have to show that $q \in D$. Since $D$ is non-empty and prefix-closed we have $\epsilon \in D$. Moreover $q^0 = \epsilon$, so that

$$q^0 \in D.$$

If $q^i \in D$ for some $i \in dom(q)$, then $q_i \in \mathcal{L}(q^i)$, because $q$ is an autonomous trace. Hence, by the definition of $\mathcal{L}$, we obtain $(q^i; q_i) \in D$, i.e. $q^{i+1} \in D$. This proves that

$$\forall i \in dom(q) : q^i \in D \Rightarrow q^{i+1} \in D.$$

By induction, either $q$ (if finite) or all its prefixes (if infinite) are in $D$. By the suffix-closedness of $D$ we conclude that $q \in D$. $\quad\square$

As a corollary, every prefix-closed subset of $E^*$ is the intersection of $E^*$ with the autonomous behavior of some transition system.

The maximal autonomous behavior of a transition system can be obtained by removing all sequences from the autonomous behavior that are prefixes of some autonomous trace. Conversely, the autonomous behavior is derived from the maximal autonomous behavior by adding all prefixes. A maximal autonomous trace has "maximal length", which explains the term "maximal". We shall now define some properties of transition systems.

**Definition 9.2** An autonomous trace $p$ of a transition system $(E, \mathcal{L})$ is said to *deadlock* if and only if $\mathcal{L}(p) = \emptyset$. A transition system $(E, \mathcal{L})$ is called *deterministic* if and only if its maximal autonomous behavior consists of a single sequence.
$\square$

Often we deal with transition systems where only the last event of a finite trace determines the set of next possible events. Such transition systems are called *memoryless* and their transition law can be characterized by a binary relation over $E$, called the *transition law relation*. We denote by $\ell(p)$ the last event of a non-empty trace $p \in E^*$, i.e.

$$\ell(p) = p_{|l|-1}.$$

**Definition 9.3** Let $(E, \mathcal{L})$ be a transition system. If

$$\forall\, p, q \in E^* : (p \neq \epsilon \wedge q \neq \epsilon \wedge \ell(p) = \ell(q)) \Rightarrow \mathcal{L}(p) = \mathcal{L}(q)$$

then $(E, \mathcal{L})$ is called *memoryless*. For such a memoryless transition system the binary relation $T\ell \subseteq E \times E$ satisfying

$$T\ell = \{(e_1, e_2) \mid \exists\, p \in E^* : \ell(p) = e_1 \ \wedge \ e_2 \in \mathcal{L}(p)\}$$

is called the *transition law relation*.

□

**Theorem 9.2** Let $(E, \mathcal{L})$ be a memoryless transition system with transition relation $T\ell$. Then

$$\forall\, p \in E^* : \mathcal{L}(p) = \{e \in E \mid (\ell(p), e) \in T\ell\}.$$

*Proof* If $e \in \mathcal{L}(p)$, then clearly $(\ell(p), e) \in T\ell$. Suppose that, conversely, $(\ell(p), e) \in T\ell$. Then there is a $q \in E^*$ such that $\ell(p) = \ell(q)$ and $e \in \mathcal{L}(q)$. Since $\mathcal{L}$ is memoryless, $\mathcal{L}(q) = \mathcal{L}(p)$, so $e \in \mathcal{L}(p)$. □

Now we shall further elaborate our event set. Events have a *time* and *state* component; we assume that allowed event times are a subset of our standard time domain $T$, the non-negative real numbers. From now on, event sets have the shape $St \times T$, where $St$ is a set called a *state space*. Given an event $e$ in some $E$, $\sigma(e)$ denotes its state component and $\tau(e)$ its time component, so that $e = (\sigma(e), \tau(e))$. We fix the start time of transition systems by setting, for any transition law $\mathcal{L}$,

$$\forall\, e \in \mathcal{L}(\epsilon) : \tau(e) = 0.$$

The sequence of the projections on the state component of the events in a trace is called a *state trace*. Often the adjective "state" is omitted.

We now introduce two behavioral properties of transition systems.

**Definition 9.4** A transition system is *monotonous* if and only if

$$\forall\, p \in E^* \backslash \{\epsilon\} : \forall\, e \in \mathcal{L}(p) : \tau(e) \geq \tau(\ell(p)).$$

An autonomous trace $p$ of a transition system is called *eager* if and only if

$$\forall\, i \in dom(p) : \forall\, e \in \mathcal{L}(p^i) : \tau(p_i) \leq \tau(e).$$

The set of all eager autonomous traces is called the *eager autonomous behavior*.

□

From now on we will only consider monotonous transition systems. The eager autonomous behavior of $(E, \mathcal{L})$ is the autonomous behavior of $(E, \mathcal{L}')$, where $\mathcal{L}'$ is derived from $\mathcal{L}$ by deleting all elements from $\mathcal{L}(p)$ for which the time component is not minimal. Strangely enough, a maximal autonomous trace of $(E, \mathcal{L}')$ does not have to be an eager maximal autonomous trace of $(E, \mathcal{L})$, because it is possible to construct an $\mathcal{L}$ such that $\mathcal{L}(p)$ is an infinite set without minimal element for some $p \in dom(\mathcal{L})$. Then $\mathcal{L}'(p)$ is empty, so $p$ has no eager continuation. However, if $\mathcal{L}(p)$ is finite and non-empty, then $p$ has an eager continuation.

**Definition 9.5** A transition system is called *strongly memoryless* if and only if

$$\forall p, q \in E^* : \sigma(\ell(p)) = \sigma(\ell(q)) \Rightarrow \mathcal{L}(p) = \mathcal{L}(q).$$

□

**Definition 9.6** Let $(E, \mathcal{L})$ be a transition system. A *livelock* of $(E, \mathcal{L})$ is an infinite autonomous trace $p$ such that

$$\exists t \in T : \forall i \in dom(p) : \tau(p_i) \leq t.$$

□

Our concept of a livelock is a trace that makes infinitely many transitions in finite time.

We now define the *path* of a trace as the function giving the state for each point in time. A time point $t$ is mapped to the state resulting from the last event that occurred before or at $t$.

**Definition 9.7** Let $p$ be a non-empty trace of a transition system $(St \times T, \mathcal{L})$. The *path* of p is the function $W_p \in T \to St$ satisfying $W_p(t) = \sigma(p_i)$, where $i$ is defined by

$$i \in dom(p) \,\wedge\, \tau(p_i) \leq t \,\wedge\, \forall j \in dom(p) : j > i \Rightarrow \tau(p_j) > t.$$

□

Thus if a trace contains several events with the same time $\tau(p_i)$ the last-mentioned one determines $W_p$. Note that a trace has no path if it livelocks, since it has no last event for every $t \in T$; we could define its path on a subset of $T$.

We conclude by defining some *similarity relations* on the set of transition systems. They are used later to compare transition systems. For instance, if the events of two transition systems have different names but their autonomous behavior is the same after renaming the events, we would like to call them "similar". In fact they are *isomorphic*, which is the strongest form of similarity.

**Definition 9.8** Let $A$ and $B$ be transition systems. Further, let $X \subseteq E_A \times E_B$ be a given binary relation.

    – $p \in E_A^*$ and $q \in E_B^*$ are called $X$-*similar* (notation $\sim_X$) if and only if

$$dom(p) = dom(q) \; \wedge \; \forall i \in dom(p) : (p_i, q_i) \in X.$$

    – $A$ is called *similar* to $B$ with respect to $X$ if and only if

$$\forall p \in E_A^*, q \in E_B^* : p \sim_X q \Rightarrow$$
$$\forall x \in \mathcal{L}_A(p) : \exists y \in \mathcal{L}_B(q) : (x, y) \in X.$$

    – $A$ and $B$ are called *bisimilar* with respect to $X$ if and only if $A$ is similar to $B$ with respect to $X$ and $B$ is similar to $A$ with respect to

$$X^{-1} = \{(y, x) \mid (x, y) \in X\}.$$

$\square$

    The following theorem establishes an obvious relationship between the autonomous behaviors of two similar transition systems.

**Theorem 9.3** Let $A$ and $B$ be two transition systems such that $A$ is similar to $B$ with respect to $X \subseteq E_A \times E_B$. Further let $P_A$ and $P_B$ be the autonomous behaviors of $A$ and $B$ respectively. Then

$$\forall p \in P_A : \exists q \in P_B : p \sim_X q.$$

*Proof* Let $p \in P_A$. Clearly $\epsilon \sim_X \epsilon$ and $p_0 \in \mathcal{L}_A(\epsilon)$. So $\exists q_0 \in \mathcal{L}_B(\epsilon) : (p_0, q_0) \in X$. We apply induction on the length of an autonomous trace. Assume the assertion holds for autonomous traces of length $n$ in $P_A$. Let $p = (p^n; p_n) \in P_A$. By the induction hypothesis we have the existence of an autonomous trace $q \in P_B$ with length $n$ such that $p^n \sim_X q$. Since $p_n \in \mathcal{L}(p^n)$ we have, by the similarity, the existence of $q_n \in \mathcal{L}(q)$ such that $(p_n, q_n) \in X$. Hence $(p^n; p_n) \sim_X (q; q_n)$ and $(q; q_n) \in P_B$. $\square$

Note that two systems are always (bi)similar with respect to the empty relation. So it is essential to mention the relation for which the similarity holds.
The next theorem establishes two important properties of similarity.

**Theorem 9.4** Similarity is *reflexive*, with respect to the identity relation and *transitive*, with respect to the composed relation.

*Proof* Clearly a transition system $(E, \mathcal{L})$ is similar to itself with respect to the relation $\{(x, x) \mid x \in E\}$. This is reflexivity. To prove transitivity, let $A$, $B$ and

$C$ be transition systems such that $A$ is similar to $B$ with respect to $X$ and $B$ is similar to $C$ with respect to $Y$. Further, let $Z = Y * X$ be defined by

$$Z = \{(x, z) \mid \exists\, y \in E_B : (x, y) \in X \,\wedge\, (y, z) \in Y\}.$$

Finally, let $p \in E_A^*$ and $r \in E_C^*$ such that $p \sim_Z r$. Then there exists a $q \in E_B^*$ with $p \sim_X q$ and $q \sim_Y r$. From the two similarities we derive

$$\forall\, x \in \mathcal{L}_A(p) : \exists\, z \in \mathcal{L}_C(r) : \exists\, y \in \mathcal{L}_B(q) : (x, y) \in X \,\wedge\, (y, z) \in Y.$$

Hence

$$\forall\, x \in \mathcal{L}_A(p) : \exists\, z \in \mathcal{L}_C(r) : (x, z) \in Z.$$

So $A$ is similar to $C$ with respect to $Z$. □

Note that, under the assumptions of the theorem, there is, for each autonomous trace $p$ of $A$, an autonomous trace $q$ of $B$ and an autonomous trace $r$ of $C$ such that $p \sim_X q$ and $p \sim_Z r$. Moreover there is an autonomous trace $\tilde{r}$ of $C$ such that $q \sim_Y \tilde{r}$. However, we may not yet conclude that $q \sim_Y r$. If we know that there is only one $r$ such that $p \sim_Z r$, then this problem is solved. This is the case if the relations over the event sets are *graphs* of functions, i.e. if there is a function $f$ such that $X = \{(x, y) \mid x \in E_A \,\wedge\, y = f(x)\}$ and a function $g$ with $Y = \{(y, z) \mid y \in E_B \,\wedge\, z = g(y)\}$.

Symmetry is lacking in the similarity relation and therefore it is not an equivalence relation. Bisimilarity is symmetrical, so that this relation must be an equivalence relation.

**Theorem 9.5** Bisimilarity is an *equivalence* relation.

*Proof* Reflexivity is trivial. The symmetry follows from the fact that $(X^{-1})^{-1} = X$. Transitivity follows from the fact that $X^{-1} * Y^{-1} = (Y * X)^{-1}$. □

An important case is the situation where $X \subseteq E_A \times E_B$ is the graph of a bijective function $f$. Then bisimilarity of $A$ and $B$ means that $A$ and $B$ are *isomorphic* and $f$ induces a bijective function between the autonomous behaviors of the two transition systems.

According to the definitions so far, the similarity of transition systems establishes relations between autonomous traces of the same length only. However, if one transition system needs several transitions to *simulate* one transition of another transition system, then these transition systems are not (bi)similar according to our definitions. In order to allow transition systems to be called "similar" in such cases, we introduce the notion of an extended transition law.

Let $(E, \mathcal{L})$ be a transition system. The *extended transition law* $\tilde{\mathcal{L}}$ is defined by

$$\tilde{\mathcal{L}}(p) = \mathcal{L}(p) \cup \{\ell(p)\}.$$

Thus we have added "dummy" events, i.e. repetitions of events. We say transition system $A$ is *weakly (bi)similar* to $B$ if the (bi)similarity holds with respect to the extended transition law. In particular $(E, \mathcal{L})$ and $(E, \tilde{\mathcal{L}})$ are bisimilar with respect to the identity relation ($\{(x, x) \mid x \in E\}$).

A nice application of similarity is that there is for each non-memoryless transition system a memoryless transition system that is similar to it.

**Theorem 9.6**  Let an arbitrary transition system $(E, \mathcal{L})$ be given. Then there is a memoryless transition system $(E', \mathcal{L}')$, that is similar to $(E, \mathcal{L})$ with respect to $C$, where

- $E' = E^*$,
- $C$ satisfies: $(e', e) \in C \Leftrightarrow \ell(e') = e$.

*Proof* The proof is an exercise.  □

Similarity is important for system composition: if system $A$ is similar to system $B$ then the composition of system $A$ and system $C$ should be similar to the composition of $B$ and $C$. (In chapter 11 we define a composition operation for systems.)

# 10

# Object framework

In this chapter we introduce a framework to model complexes. Complexes will be used to define tokens and therefore to define the state space of a system. We start with the definition of a *class model*, which contains the information necessary for defining the structure of complex classes. A class model is an *abstract syntax* for simplex diagrams. (In the database literature the term *database model* is also used instead of class model.) Then, we define the concept of an *instance model*, which contains the information necessary for defining simplexes and complexes. Afterwards we introduce *constraints*. Constraints are used to define properties of complexes. Often the systems engineer wants to consider only a subset of a complex class rather than the entire class. The transition law of the system should guarantee that in all reachable states the complexes in the tokens satisfy the constraints. So, the constraints are the *invariants* for the transition law of the system. It is a *proof obligation* for the systems engineer to show that the constraints are indeed invariant. There are several kinds of constraints that occur frequently in models, such as *relationship*, *inheritance* and *tree* constraints. All constraints have a graphical notation in the simplex diagram. There are many other constraints possible (and often necessary) in models; they can be expressed using predicate calculus (*see* part III). A complete *object model* consists of

- a class model,
- an instance model,
- a set of constraints.

**Definition 10.1** A *class model* is a 7-tuple

$$(CN, \; SN, \; RN, \; DM, \; RG, \; CB, \; CR)$$

where the following hold.

(i) $CN$, $SN$ and $RN$ are mutually disjoint sets of names of complex classes, simplex classes and relationship classes respectively. There is one element in $CN$ called the *universal* complex class.

(ii) The functions

$$DM \in RN \rightarrow SN \text{ and } RG \in RN \rightarrow SN$$

give a domain simplex class ($DM$) and a range simplex class ($RG$) to every relationship.

(iii) The functions

$$CB \in CN \rightarrow \mathbb{P}(SN) \text{ and } CR \in CN \rightarrow \mathbb{P}(RN)$$

determine the body simplex classes ($CB$) and the relationship classes ($CR$) contained in a complex class, such that $\forall n \in CN : \forall r \in CR(n) :$

$$DM(r) \in CB(n) \wedge RG(r) \in CB(n).$$

Further, $CB(universal) = SN$ and $CR(universal) = RN$.

□

Note that the bodies of complex classes may overlap. All complex classes are *subclasses* of the universal complex class. A class model is (partly) defined in a simplex diagram, as shown in part I. A simplex diagram may display constraints as well. Note that complex classes may share simplex classes and relationships.

For the production/consumption example with class model $X$, the simplex diagram of figure 5.12 and the table 5.1 show the following (we have written $CN$ instead of $CN_X$, etc.):

$CN = \{Consumer, Machine, Order, PendingOrder, Operation\}$,
$SN = \{consumer, order, amount, machine, operation, duration, speed\}$,
$RN = \{p, q, r, s, t, u\}$,
$DM = \{(p, order), (q, order), (r, operation), (s, operation), ...\}$,
$RG = \{(p, consumer), (q, amount), (r, order), (s, machine), ...\}$
$CB = \{(Consumer, \{consumer\}), (Machine, \{machine, speed\}), ...\}$
$CR = \{(Consumer, \emptyset), (Machine, \{u\}), (Order, \{q\}), ...\}$.

We shall now define the instance model of an object model.

**Definition 10.2** Let a class model be given. An *instance model* is a 2-tuple ($sim$, $com$) where

(i) $sim$ is a set-valued function with $dom(sim) = SN$ and, for $n \in SN$, $sim(n)$ is the set of representations of all possible simplexes in the "world";

(ii)  *com* is a set-valued function that assigns to all $n \in CN$ the set of representations of possible complexes, and

$$com(n) = \{c | c \text{ is a function } \wedge \; dom(c) = CB(n) \cup CR(n) \; \wedge$$
$$\forall \, m \in CB(n) : c(m) \subseteq sim(m) \wedge c(m) \text{ is finite } \wedge$$
$$\forall \, r \in CR(n) : c(r) \subseteq c(DM(r)) \times c(RG(r))\}.$$

$\square$

Note that if all pairs of complex classes differ at least in one simplex class or one relationship class, then we can determine the class of a given complex, because the domain of a complex contains the essential information.

The function *sim* specifies which values are used to denote "atomic" entities of a certain kind in the world. The values have to come from a *value universe U* that will be defined in part V. For instance *sim(chair)* is the set of representations of all possible chairs in the world. Although two different simplex classes may have the same set of representations, we can always distinguish them because we assume the class of a simplex is always known. Given these representations, we can define complex classes by means of the function *com* that determines which "molecular" entities in the world belong to a certain complex class. A complex is defined as a function that assigns a finite set of simplexes to each name of a simplex class and a finite set of simplex pairs to each name of a relationship class. As we have seen in part I, we can consider a complex as a graph with simplexes as nodes and relationships as edges, labeled with the names of the relationships; this is just another way of representing the function. The relationships may only connect simplexes that belong to the complex. The elements of simplex classes and complex classes are called *instances* of these classes.

In the production/consumption example of table 5.1 a possible instance (i.e. a complex) $c \in com(Operation)$ is

$$c = \{(operation, \{operation1\}),$$
$$(machine, \{machine3\}),$$
$$(order, \{order123\}),$$
$$(amount, \{10\}),$$
$$(speed, \{35\}),$$
$$(q, \{(order123, 10)\}),$$
$$(r, \{(operation1, order123)\}),$$
$$(s, \{(operation1, machine3)\}),$$
$$(u, \{(machine3, 35)\})$$
$$\}.$$

In this example the second element of each pair is always a singleton. (This is because all relations are functional and total and because there is a root simplex class due to a tree constraint.)

In specifications it is sometimes cumbersome to use the (function) representation of a complex class as defined above. Depending on the role of the complexes in processors the systems engineer can use a different representation. If he does so, he needs to define for each complex class $n$ a bijective *representation function*

$$RF_n \in U \rightarrow com(n).$$

The next step in the definition of an object model is the definition of constraints. First we introduce, for notational convenience, some auxiliary functions and a set called the *object universe*, which contains all possible complexes in the universal complex class.

**Definition 10.3** Let a class model and an instance model be given.

- $OU = \bigcup_{n \in CN} com(n)$ is the *object universe*.
- $R_{r,c}$ is, for each complex $c \in OU$ and relationship $r$, a function with $dom(R_{r,c}) = c(DM(r))$, that assigns to a simplex $x \in c(DM(r))$ the set of simplexes that have a relationship of class $r$ with it:

$$R_{r,c}(x) = \{y \mid y \in c(RG(r)) \ \wedge \ (x, y) \in c(r)\}.$$

- $D_{r,c}$ is a similar function with $dom(D_{r,c}) = c(RG(r))$, but it concerns the domain of a relationship. For a simplex $y \in c(RG(r))$,

$$D_{r,c}(y) = \{x \mid x \in c(DM(r)) \ \wedge \ (x, y) \in c(r)\}.$$

□

In general, a constraint is a Boolean function (i.e. a function with range $\{true, false\}$) over a complex class. A Boolean function is expressed by a predicate with a free variable that denotes a complex.

Constraints will be expressed in the specification language (*see* part V). Here we will give an example of a constraint. Consider the class model displayed in figure 4.15. There we required that the "person" to which the "student" refers by means of relationships $a$ and $b$ and the "person" to which "student" refers by $c$ and $e$ are the same. This can be expressed by following predicate with $u$ as an arbitrary universal complex:

$$\forall x \in u(student) : R_{b,u}(R_{a,u}(x)) = R_{e,u}(R_{c,u}(x)).$$

Here we have silently extended the domain of $R$ in order to apply the function to sets of complexes in the obvious way. Furthermore, we have not expressed the requirement that $R_{b,u}(R_{a,u}(x))$ and $R_{e,u}(R_{c,u}(x))$ should be singletons. A more concise notation is possible, but in essence every constraint can be expressed like this one. The notation used in part I is more concise; here the dependency on the complex $u$ is deleted, $u(n)$ is replaced by $n$ (for a simplex class $n$) and the functions $R_{n,u}$ and $D_{n,u}$ are replaced by $n$ and $n^{-1}$ respectively. With these conventions the formula above will read, in the specification language,

$$\forall\, x : student \bullet b(a(x)) = e(c(x)).$$

There are several constraints that occur frequently in practice and therefore they have a representation in the simplex diagram, as shown in part I. We call them *standard constraints*; they are the relationship, inheritance and tree constraints. The *relationship constraints* are the cardinality, key and exclusion constraints.

**Definition 10.4** Let a class model and an instance model be given. The function

$$FC \in RN \rightarrow \mathbb{P}(\{total,\ functional,\ injective,\ surjective\})$$

denotes the *cardinality* constraints. The cardinality constraints imply a set of requirements for a relationship $r$ and each complex $c$ with $r \in dom(c) \cap RN$:

- if $total \in FC(r)$ then

$$\forall\, x \in c(DM(r)) : R_{r,c}(x) \neq \varnothing,$$

- if $functional \in FC(r)$ then

$$\forall\, x \in c(DM(r)) : \#R_{r,c}(x) \leq 1,$$

- if $injective \in FC(r)$ then

$$\forall\, y \in c(RG(r)) : \#D_{r,c}(y) \leq 1,$$

- if $surjective \in FC(r)$ then

$$\forall\, y \in c(RG(r)) : D_{r,c}(y) \neq \varnothing.$$

□

**Definition 10.5** Let a class model and an instance model be given. The functions

$$DK \in SN \rightarrow \mathbb{P}(\mathbb{P}(RN)),$$
$$RK \in SN \rightarrow \mathbb{P}(\mathbb{P}(RN)),$$
$$DX \in SN \rightarrow \mathbb{P}(\mathbb{P}(RN)),$$
$$RX \in SN \rightarrow \mathbb{P}(\mathbb{P}(RN)).$$

respectively denote the *domain key* constraints, the *range key* constraints, the *domain exclusion* constraints and the *range exclusion* constraints. They should satisfy

$$\forall\, n \in SN : \forall\, r \in \bigcup DK(n) : DM(r) = n,$$
$$\forall\, n \in SN : \forall\, r \in \bigcup RK(n) : RG(r) = n,$$
$$\forall\, n \in SN : \forall\, r \in \bigcup DX(n) : DM(r) = n,$$
$$\forall\, n \in SN : \forall\, r \in \bigcup RX(n) : RG(r) = n.$$

A domain key constraint is an element of $DK(s)$; analogously for the other constraints. For an arbitrary complex $c$ these constraints imply respectively:

$$\forall\, n \in SN : \forall\, C \in DK(n) : \forall\, x, y \in c(DM(r)) :$$
$$(\forall\, r \in C : R_{r,c}(x) = R_{r,c}(y) \neq \emptyset) \Rightarrow x = y,$$
$$\forall\, n \in SN : \forall\, C \in RK(n) : \forall\, x, y \in c(RG(r)) :$$
$$(\forall\, r \in C : D_{r,c}(x) = D_{r,c}(y) \neq \emptyset) \Rightarrow x = y,$$
$$\forall\, n \in SN : \forall\, C \in DX(n) :$$
$$\forall\, r_1, r_2 \in C : \forall\, x \in c(DM(r_1)) : R_{r_1,c}(x) = \emptyset \ \lor \ R_{r_2,c}(x) = \emptyset,$$
$$\forall\, n \in SN : \forall\, C \in RX(n) :$$
$$\forall\, r_1, r_2 \in C : \forall\, x \in c(RG(r_1)) : D_{r_1,c}(x) = \emptyset \ \lor \ D_{r_2,c}(x) = \emptyset.$$

$\square$

Note that totality and surjectivity are counterparts and so also are functionality and injectivity, in the sense that the roles of $R$ and $D$ are exchanged. Further, note that totality and injectivity together imply a domain key constraint and that similarly surjectivity and functionality imply a range key constraint.

For the production/consumption example, the simplex diagram of figure 5.12 and the table 5.1 show the constraints that are displayed in table 10.1.

The key constraints can be used to find representations for simplexes: we may choose as a representation a combination of the representations of the simplexes involved in a key constraint. If for instance the simplex class *operation* is the domain simplex class of two relationships $s$ and $r$ with range simplex classes *machine* and *order* respectively and if $s$ and $r$ form a domain key constraint, then we can use the pairing of the representations of *machine* and *order* as the representation for *operation*. Note that we cannot combine domain and range key constraints into one "key constraint" since if there were then a relationship that connected a simplex class with itself, it would be ambiguous whether the domain or the range of this relationship should be used.

Table 10.1. *Constraints for the production/consumption system.*

| FC | $\{(p, \{functional, total\}),$ <br> $(q, \{functional, total\}),$ <br> $(r, \{functional, total\}),$ <br> $(s, \{functional, total\}),$ <br> $(t, \{functional, total\}),$ <br> $(u, \{functional, total\})$ <br> $\}$ |
|----|---|
| DK | $\{(consumer, \varnothing),$ <br> $(order, \varnothing),$ <br> $(amount, \varnothing),$ <br> $(machine, \varnothing),$ <br> $(operation, \{\{r, s\}\}),$ <br> $(duration, \varnothing),$ <br> $(speed, \varnothing)$ <br> $\}$ |
| RK <br> DX <br> RX | $\{(consumer, \varnothing),$ <br> $(order, \varnothing),$ <br> $(amount, \varnothing),$ <br> $(machine, \varnothing),$ <br> $(operation, \varnothing),$ <br> $(duration, \varnothing),$ <br> $(speed, \varnothing)$ <br> $\}$ |
| IC | $\varnothing$ |
| TC | $\{(Consumer, consumer),$ <br> $(Machine, machine),$ <br> $(Order, order),$ <br> $(PendingOrder, order),$ <br> $(Operation, operation)$ <br> $\}$ |
| PC | $\varnothing$ |

The next kind of constraint we consider is the *inheritance* constraint. First we introduce the notion of a relationship path.

**Definition 10.6** Let a class model and an instance model be given. A sequence of relationship class names $\langle r_1, \ldots, r_k \rangle$ is called a *relationship path* if and only if all elements are different and

$$\forall\, i \in \{1, \ldots, k-1\} : RG(r_i) = DM(r_{i+1}).$$

□

**Definition 10.7** Let a class model and an instance model be given. A relationship is called an *inheritance relationship* if it is total, functional and injective.

An *inheritance constraint IC* is a set of inheritance relationships $IC \subseteq RN$ such that:

- The graph with nodes in $SN$ and edges $\{(DM(r), RG(r)) \mid r \in IC\}$ is a directed acyclic graph.
- For all complexes $c$ and all relationship paths $\langle r_1, \ldots, r_k \rangle$ and $\langle p_1, \ldots, p_l \rangle$ in $dom(c) \cap IC$, with

$$DM(r_1) = DM(p_1) \wedge RG(r_k) = RG(p_l)$$

the following predicate should hold: $\forall\, x \in c(DM(r_1))$ :

$$R_{r_k, c}(R_{r_{k-1}, c}, \ldots, R_{r_1, c}(x)) = R_{p_l, c}(R_{p_{l-1}, c}, \ldots, R_{p_1, c}(x)).$$

$\square$

An inheritance constraint $IC$ is a set of total, functional and injective relationships with the property that they form a directed acyclic graph. If we follow two different paths formed from inheritance relationships, going from one simplex to another, then it should hold for each complex that if we start in the first simplex and follow the paths, then both paths will end in the second simplex.

An inheritance structure induces a partial order on the simplex classes. Sometimes it is useful to combine the inheritance constraint with the exclusion constraint. For instance, in the example of figure 4.15 we might want to exclude the states in which a school person is a student and a teacher at the same time; therefore, we could add the set $\{c, d\}$ to $RX(schoolperson)$. Note that an inheritance constraint may contain several different class hierarchies. Inheritance can be used to obtain efficient representations in a database. We will discuss this topic in chapter 15.

The last kind of constraint we consider is the *tree constraint*. A tree constraint specifies that the complexes in a class have a tree-like structure, i.e. there is one simplex, called the *root simplex*, from which all the other simplexes can be reached by an *undirected* path of relationships. Furthermore the complex may contain only one simplex of the root simplex class. For a complex $c$ we define

$$cont(c) = \bigcup_{k \in dom(c) \cap SN} c(k),$$

the set of all simplexes enclosed in the complex $c$.

**Definition 10.8** A *tree constraint* is an element of the function

$$TC \in CN \nrightarrow SN$$

where $\forall\, n \in dom(TC)$:

(i) $TC(n) \in CB(n)$ is called the *root simplex class*;

(ii) $\forall c \in com(n) : \#c(TC(n)) = 1$; this element is called the *root simplex*;

(iii) $\forall c \in com(n) : \forall x \in cont(c) :$

there is a sequence of simplexes $\langle z_1, \ldots, z_k \rangle$ in $cont(c)$ such that

- $z_1 \in c(TC(n)) \wedge z_k = x$,
- $\forall i \in \{1, \ldots, k-1\} :$

$\exists r \in dom(c) \cap RN : (z_i, z_{i+1}) \in c(r) \vee (z_{i+1}, z_i) \in c(r)$.

□

Note that $z_1$ is the root simplex.

Having defined class models, instance models and constraints, we are now ready to define an object model.

**Definition 10.9**  An *object model* is a 4-tuple $(CM, \ IM, \ SC, \ PC)$, where

(i) $CM$ is a class model,

(ii) $IM$ is an instance model,

(iii) $SC$ is a tuple of standard constraints, i.e.

$$SC = (FC, \ DK, \ RK, \ DX, \ RX, \ IC, \ TC)$$

where $(FC, \ DK, \ RK, \ DX, \ RX)$ denote the relationship constraints, $IC$ is an inheritance constraint and $TC$ denotes the tree constraints,

(iv) $PC$ is a Boolean function, called the *free constraint*, such that $dom(PC) = CN$ and

$$\forall n \in CN : PC(n) \in com(n) \rightarrow \{true, false\}.$$

□

Instead of the set of all complexes of a class $n$, $com(n)$, we are often interested in the subset of complexes that satisfy the standard and free constraints. In the following chapter an object model is used to define the state space. Note that there may be constraints on states that cannot be expressed as constraints on objects. For instance, the constraint that "no two tokens have a common simplex of a certain class" is such a *global constraint*.

# 11

# Actor framework

In the preceeding chapter we introduced the object framework as a layer on top of the (transition) systems framework to facilitate the modeling of a state space. Here we shall introduce the *actor framework* to make the modeling of transition relations easier. The actor framework may be regarded as the next layer, since it uses concepts from the object framework. However, the coupling between the two frameworks is rather loose, which implies that the systems engineer is free to start with object modeling or with actor modeling as he likes.

First we introduce the concept of an actor. We distinguish *flat nets* and *hierarchical actors*. Inside a flat net all actors are processors, so that there are no actors that represent a (sub)network. A hierarchical actor is a network that contains non-elementary actors also and such a network can be transformed into a flat net. We first define a *flat net model*, which is in fact a formal definition of the actor networks (without hierarchy) as displayed in chapter 5. Secondly we define a hierarchical actor structure. Again this is a formal definition of the actor networks from chapter 5, now also including the non-elementary actors. Then we define the *actor model*, which comprises an object model and a flat net model. Subsequently we define how an actor model determines a transition relation. Finally we give some properties of actor models.

Note that a hierarchical net model is an *abstract syntax* for the diagrams of actor networks we draw and that a flat net model is a special case of a hierarchical net model. The semantics is defined by the actor model, in particular the transition system defined by the actor model.

**Definition 11.1** A *flat net model* is a 6-tuple $(L, P, C, I, O, M)$ where

(i) $L$ (locations) is a finite set of *places*,

(ii) $P$ is a finite set of *processors*,

(iii) $C$ is a finite set of *connector* names,

(iv) $I \in P \to \mathbb{P}(C)$ assigns to a processor a set of input connectors,

(v) $O \in P \to \mathbb{P}(C)$ assigns to a processor a set of output connectors,

(vi) $M \in P \to (C \twoheadrightarrow L)$ (match) assigns the connectors of each processor to places

such that

- $L$, $P$ and $C$ are mutually disjoint,
- $\forall p \in P : dom(M_p) \subseteq I(p) \cup O(p)$,
- $\forall p \in P$: $I(p) \cap O(p) = \varnothing$, i.e. no connector name is input and output for the same processor,
- $\forall p \in P$: $I(p) \neq \varnothing$, i.e. each processor has at least one input connector,
- $\bigcup_{p \in P}(I(p) \cup O(p)) = C$, i.e. there are no "dangling" connectors.

□

It is easy to see how a flat net model can be represented graphically (an example is figure 5.5). Note that the same connector name may occur at different processors and that processors do not need to have output places. Further note that there may be processors with unconnected connectors. Such actors are called *open actors* while the others are called *closed*. Only closed (flat) actors will have a state space and a transition relation associated to them. Open actors are considered to be *components* out of which one can make closed actors. A single processor, without places, is an example of an open actor. A processor and a place may be connected by more than one input or output connector. Note that channels and stores are just special places and therefore we do not consider them here.

We will now define the hierarchical net model; it is just a generalization of the flat net model.

**Definition 11.2** A *hierarchical net model* is a 10-tuple

$$(L, P, A, C, I, O, top, HA, HL, M)$$

where

(i) $L$ (locations) is a finite set of places,

(ii) $P$ is a finite set of processors,

(iii) $A$ is a finite set of actors, $P \subseteq A$,

(iv) $C$ is a finite set of connector names,

(v) $I \in A \to \mathbb{P}(C)$ assigns to each actor a set of input connectors,

(vi) $O \in A \to \mathbb{P}(C)$ assigns to each actor a set of output connectors,

(vii) $top \in A$ is the top-level actor,

(viii) $HA \in A\backslash\{top\} \to A$ assigns every processor or actor to an (enclosing) actor, except for $top$,

(ix) $HL \in L \to A$ assigns every place to an actor,

(x) $M \in A\backslash\{top\} \to (C \twoheadrightarrow L \cup C)$ (match) assigns connectors of actors to places or connectors

such that

- $L$, $A$ and $C$ are mutually disjoint sets,
- $\forall a \in A : I(a) \cap O(a) = \varnothing$, i.e. no connector name is input and output for the same actor,
- $\forall p \in P : I(p) \neq \varnothing$, i.e. all processors must have at least one input connector,
- $\forall a \in A\backslash\{top\} : dom(M_a) = I(a) \cup O(a)$, i.e. all connectors of an actor (except for $top$) are connected,
- $C = \bigcup_{a \in A}(I(a) \cup O(a))$, i.e. there are no dangling connectors,
- $\forall a \in A\backslash\{top\} : \exists k \in \mathbb{N} : HA^k(a) = top$, i.e. all actors are directly or indirectly mapped to the top-level actor,
- $\forall a \in A\backslash P :$

$$\forall c \in I(a) : \exists b \in A : \exists d \in I(b) : M_b(d) = c \ \wedge$$
$$\forall c \in O(a) : \exists b \in A : \exists d \in O(b) : M_b(d) = c,$$

so the connectors of a "high-level" actor are internally connected to an actor, input to input and output to output,

- $\forall a \in A\backslash\{top\} : \forall c \in I(a) \cup O(a) :$

$$M_a(c) \in L \Rightarrow HL(M_a(c)) = HA(a) \ \wedge$$
$$M_a(c) \in C \wedge c \in I(a) \Rightarrow M_a(c) \in I(HA(a)) \ \wedge$$
$$M_a(c) \in C \wedge c \in O(a) \Rightarrow M_a(c) \in O(HA(a)),$$

which means that if a connector is connected to a place then this place belongs to the same higher-level actor as the actor itself and if a connector of an actor is connected to another connector, then the latter is a connector of the higher-level actor and is of the same kind.

□

Since all places are mapped to an actor, they are also (indirectly) mapped to $top$, i.e.

$$\forall \ell \in L : \exists k \in \mathbb{N} : HA^k(HL(\ell)) = top.$$

Note that the second-to-last requirement in the above definition does not imply that a connector of a non-elementary actor $a$ is internally connected to an actor

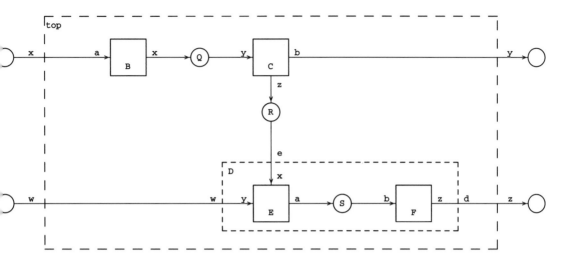

Fig. 11.1. A hierarchical net model.

Table 11.1. *A hierarchical net model, table format.*

| A | I(a) | O(a) | HA(a) |
|---|------|------|-------|
| top | w, x | y, z | - |
| B | a | x | top |
| C | y | b, z | top |
| D | e, w | d | top |
| E | x, y | a | D |
| F | b | z | D |

| L | HL(ℓ) |
|---|-------|
| Q | top |
| R | top |
| S | D |

| A | C | $M_a(c)$ |
|---|---|----------|
| B | a | x |
|   | x | Q |
|   | y | Q |
| C | b | y |
|   | z | R |
|   | e | R |
| D | w | w |
|   | d | z |
|   | x | e |
| E | y | w |
|   | a | S |
| F | b | S |
|   | z | d |

*enclosed* in a: for this we need the last requirement also. The top-level actor (called *top*) is the only actor that may have unconnected connectors. An actor that has unconnected connectors is called *open*, otherwise it is *closed*. Further, note that we have not introduced *stores* yet. A store is just a special place in the sense that it is always connected to one input and one output connector for each processor to which it is connected. We consider it to be "syntactical sugar".

In figure 11.1 we display a hierarchical net model graphically. In table 11.1 the same net model is presented in table format. It is easy to verify that all requirements are satisfied.

Each hierarchical net model determines precisely one flat net model. In fact we define the transition system associated with a closed hierarchical actor to be the one that is associated with a (closed) flat net model. We formulate the transformation from a closed hierarchical net model to a flat net model as a theorem.

**Theorem 11.1** Let $(L, P, A, C, I, O, top, HA, HL, M)$ be a closed hierarchical net model. Let the function $g \in A \backslash \{top\} \to (C \twoheadrightarrow L)$ be defined by $\forall a \in A :$ $\forall c \in I(a) \cup O(a) :$

$$M_a(c) \in L \Rightarrow g_a(c) = M_a(c) \ \wedge$$
$$M_a(c) \in C \Rightarrow g_a(c) = g_{HA(a)}(M_a(c)),$$

where $dom(g_a) = I(a) \cup O(a)$. Then $g$ is defined correctly and

$$(L, P, \tilde{C}, \tilde{I}, \tilde{O}, \tilde{M})$$

forms a flat net model, where $\tilde{C} = \cup_{p \in P}(I(p) \cup O(p))$ and $\tilde{I} = I \upharpoonright P$, $\tilde{O} = O \upharpoonright P$, $\tilde{M} = g \upharpoonright P$.

*Proof* There are two properties to be proven: first, that $g$ is defined correctly by the recursive definition and, second that the defined tuple is a correct flat net model. The proof is an exercise. $\square$

Next we will define the concept of an *actor model*. It encompasses a flat net model and an object model. The definition is given first and an elucidation afterwards. Remember that $OU$ denotes the object universe.

**Definition 11.3** An *actor model* is an 8-tuple

$$(FN, OM, CA, CT, T, ID, F, R)$$

where

(i) $FN$ is a closed flat net model (*see* definition 11.1),

(ii) $OM$ is an object model (*see* definition 10.9),

(iii) $CA \in L \to CN$ is called the *class assignment* function and it determines for each place a complex class,

(iv) $CT \in P \to (C \twoheadrightarrow CN)$ assigns to each connector of a processor a complex class such that

$$\forall p \in P : dom(CT_p) = I(p) \cup O(p) \wedge$$
$$\forall c \in dom(M_p) : CT_p(c) = CA(M_p(c)),$$

which means that a connector and the place to which it is connected have the same complex class,

(v) $T$ is a subset of the non-negative real numbers that contains 0 and it is called the *time domain*,

(vi) *ID* is a countable set of *identities*,

(vii) $F \in ID \twoheadrightarrow ID$ is called the *parent function* and satisfies

$$\forall i \in dom(F) : \exists n \in \mathbf{N} : F^n(i) \in ID \backslash dom(F),$$

(viii) $R \in P \rightarrow \mathbb{P}(C \twoheadrightarrow ID \times OU \times T)$, where $R_p$ is called the *processor relation* of processor $p$ and the elements of $R_p$ are called *firing rules*. The processor relation must satisfy, $\forall p \in P : R_p \neq \varnothing$ and $\forall p \in P : \forall r \in R_p$, the following:

(a) $dom(r) \subseteq I(p) \cup O(p) \wedge dom(r) \cap I(p) \neq \varnothing$,

(b) $\forall a \in dom(r) : \pi_2(r(a)) \in com(CT_p(a))$,

(c) $\forall a \in I(p) \cap dom(r) : \forall b \in O(p) \cap dom(r) : \pi_3(r(a)) \leq \pi_3(r(b))$,

(d) $\exists x \in rng(r \restriction I(p)) : \forall y \in rng(r \restriction O(p)) : F(\pi_1(y)) = \pi_1(x)$,

(e) $\forall x, y \in dom(r) \cap O(p) : x \neq y \Rightarrow \pi_1(r(x)) \neq \pi_1(r(y))$.

$\square$

Note that the sets $R_p$ are almost always infinite because new identities are produced with each execution of a processor. If $T$ is a countable set then $R_p$ is countable as well.

The sets $T$ and *ID* are used to give a complex a *time stamp* and an identity respectively. The function $CA$ assigns the name of a complex class to each place. Objects in a place should always belong to the complex class assigned to the place.

The function $F$ is used to "create" new identities out of old ones. This proceeds as follows: given an identity $i$ a new identity $j$ must satisfy $F(j) = i$. If $F^{-1}$ denotes the inverse of $F$ then $F^{-1}(i)$ is the set of new identities created out of $i$. We will only use a finite subset of this set. The requirement on $F$ implies that no identity is a descendant of itself. The set $ID \backslash dom(F)$ is the set of *start identities*; these do not have ancestors. As an example of an identity set consider the set $\mathbf{N}^*$, the set of all sequences of natural numbers. The "children" created by an identity $i \in \mathbf{N}^*$ are all sequences $(i; j)$ where $j \in \mathbf{N}$ and "; " denotes concatenation. The function $F$ applied to a non-empty sequence gives the sequence with the last element removed. It is also clear that there is an $n \in \mathbf{N}$ for every identity such that $F^n$ applied to this identity gives the empty sequence. Here $dom(F) = \mathbf{N}^* \backslash \{\epsilon\}$. (Later we will derive some properties of $F$.)

The definition of $R_p$ is quite complicated and requires some explanation. Informally, a firing rule in $R_p$ contains connectors of $p$ and "things" (tokens) produced or consumed for these connectors in a firing of $p$. Note that a firing rule contains "things" that are almost tokens, the only difference being, that the place of a token is replaced by a connector, and that the order of components is a little different. This makes it possible to use the same processor relation in an actor several times, in combination with different places. A processor $p$ *executes* (i.e. *fires*), according to one firing rule in $R_p$.

Requirement (a) of $R_p$ states that only tokens are consumed from, or produced for connectors of $p$ and that there is at least one input token (which is important for the activation of the processor and for the identification of new tokens).

Requirement (b) states that consumed or produced tokens should have the right class.

Requirement (c) states that all produced tokens should have a time stamp larger or equal to the time stamps of all consumed ones (which is important for the monotonicity of time, as will be seen later. Note that we usually do not specify the time stamps of the new tokens, but only a *delay* that has to be added to the time of the transition.

The fourth and fifth requirements concern the identification of new tokens. Remember that we have approached the identification of tokens in a constructive way, by introducing a specific identification mechanism. All produced tokens get their identity from one consumed token; this identity $i$ is such that $F(i)$ equals the identity of the consumed token that is selected for identification. So the new tokens get different identities, which are descendants of the identity of the selected token.

Now we are ready to define the state space of an actor model.

**Definition 11.4** Let an actor model be given. The *state space* $St$ is defined by

$$St \subseteq ID \twoheadrightarrow OU \times T \times L,$$

where

- $OU$ is the object universe (*see* definition 10.3),
- $\forall s \in St : \forall i \in dom(s) : \pi_1(s(i)) \in com(CA(\pi_3(s(i)))),$
- $\forall s \in St : s$ is finite,
- $\forall s \in St : \forall i, j \in dom(s) : i \neq j \Rightarrow \neg \exists n \in \mathbf{N} : i = F^n(j).$

Here, a *state* $s$ is an element of $St$; the elements of a state are called *tokens*.
□

So a state is a set of 4-tuples each having a unique first component and denoting the identity, the complex, the availability time (time stamp) and the place of a token respectively. The second requirement states that the tokens in a place should carry a complex that belongs to the class of the place. The last requirement says that in a state no identity is the ancestor of another one.

The next step is the introduction of the transition relation. The transition relation relates a state to a possible successor state. In the definition of a transition relation we use the concept of a *firing assignment*. A firing assignment assigns to a non-empty set of processors a firing rule, i.e. an element of $R_p$, for each processor in the set. So several processors may fire simultaneously, but no processor may fire simultaneously with itself. (In other Petri net formalisms this is sometimes allowed too.)

**Definition 11.5** A *firing assignment f* is a function that satisfies

- $f \in P \twoheadrightarrow (C \twoheadrightarrow ID \times OU \times T)$,

- $dom(f) \neq \emptyset$,

- $\forall p \in dom(f) : f(p) \in R_p$.

☐

So $f(p)$ is a firing rule of processor $p$. Each transition is caused by the firing of one firing assignment; the latter determines one or more firing rules.

Note that a token is of the form $(i, o, t, \ell)$ where $i \in ID$, $o \in OU$, $t \in T$, $\ell \in L$, while a firing rule is of the form $(c, i, o, t)$, with $c \in C$. This is so because in a processor relation the place is not known, but only the connector to which the token corresponds. Further, note that a state is a function of identities and a firing rule a function of connectors. Therefore the structure of a firing rule differs from the structure of a state.

**Definition 11.6** Let an actor model with state space $St$ be given. Further, let $FA$ be the set of all firing assignments. The *transition relation Tr*, with $Tr \subseteq St \times St$, satisfies, $\forall (s, s') \in Tr : \exists f \in FA$, such that

(i) $In(f) \subseteq s$,

(ii) $\forall p, p' \in dom(f) : p \neq p' \Rightarrow in(p, f(p)) \cap in(p', f(p')) = \emptyset$,

(iii) $time(s) = tim(f)$,

(iv) $s' = (s \backslash In(f)) \cup Out(f)$,

where $\forall p \in P : \forall r \in R_p :$

$$in(p,r) = \{(i,(x,t,\ell)) \mid \exists c \in I(p) \cap dom(r) :$$
$$r(c) = (i,x,t) \wedge M_p(c) = \ell\},$$
$$In(f) = \bigcup\{in(p,f(p)) \mid p \in dom(f)\},$$
$$out(p,r) = \{(i,(x,t,\ell)) \mid \exists c \in O(p) \cap dom(r) :$$
$$r(c) = (i,x,t) \wedge M_p(c) = \ell\},$$
$$Out(f) = \bigcup\{out(p,f(p)) \mid p \in dom(f)\},$$
$$tim(f) = max\{\pi_3(x) \mid x \in In(f)\},$$
$$time(s) = min\{tim(f) \mid f \in FA \wedge In(f) \subseteq s\}.$$

A firing assignment $f$ is called *applicable* for state $s$ if it satisfies the requirements (i), (ii) and (iii).

$\square$

Each transition is the firing of a non-empty set of processors according to firing assignment $f$. For each processor $p$ a firing rule in the processor relation is chosen $(f(p))$. The set of all tokens that are consumed by the firing is $In(f)$. This set of tokens should be available in the state $s$ (requirement (i)). Further, no two processors may consume the same token (requirement (ii)). Requirement (iii) states that the set of consumed tokens is the earliest possible set: $tim(f)$ determines the maximal time stamp of the tokens in $In(f)$. Thus requirement (iii) says that we only may use firing assignment $f$ if the maximal time stamp is minimal, so there is no transition possible at an earlier time. This property makes the transition law *eager*. Note that the function *time* assigns to each state the time of the first possible transition. We call this the *transition time* of the state. The definition of $time(s)$ is subtle: it is the minimal firing time of a set of firing rules that consume only tokens from the given state, but we do not require that two different processors do not consume the same tokens (as in requirement (ii) for the used firing rule). The reason is, that, even if two processors would consume a same token, we could delete one of them (from the domain of the firing assignment) without increasing the minimum time. Requirement (iv) specifies how the new state is computed: first delete all consumed tokens, then add the newly produced tokens.

Although we have defined a state space *St* and a transition relation *Tr* for an actor model, we have not defined a *transition law* (*see* definition 9.1). A transition law defines a transition system for an actor model. Here a set of *initial states* has to be given, because otherwise the transition law is undefined. Note that the definition of a transition relation is independent of initial states.

**Definition 11.7** Let an actor model with state space *St*, transition relation *Tr* and set of initial states $S_0 \subseteq St$ be given. The *transition law* $\mathcal{L}$ satisfies

$$\mathcal{L} \in (St \times T)^* \to \mathbb{P}(St \times T)$$

such that

$$\mathcal{L}(\epsilon) = \{(s, 0) \mid s \in S_0\}$$

and $\forall p \in (St \times T)^* \backslash \{\epsilon\}$ :

$$\mathcal{L}(p) = \{(s, t) \mid (\sigma(\ell(p)), s) \in Tr \ \wedge \ t = time(\sigma(\ell(p)))\}.$$

We say the pair $(St, Tr)$ *induces* the transition system $(St \times T, \mathcal{L})$.
□

Here $\ell(p)$ denotes the last event of a non-empty trace $p$ and $\sigma(e)$ and $\tau(e)$ denote the state and time component of an event $e$ (as defined in chapter 9). Note that the *event set* (*see* definition 9.1) is $St \times T$. Instead of giving a set of initial states for an actor model we may also give a transition law; from one we can derive the other.

**Theorem 11.2** Let an actor model with state space $St$ and transition law $\mathcal{L}$ be given. The transition law is *strongly memoryless*.

*Proof* Consider two finite traces $p$ and $q$. Let $\ell(p) = \ell(q) = s$. Then we have

$$\mathcal{L}(p) = \mathcal{L}(q) = \{(s', t) \mid (s, s') \in Tr \wedge t = time(\sigma(s))\}.$$

Hence only the last reached state determines the event set. So, according to definition 9.5, $\mathcal{L}$ is strongly memoryless.
□

Now we know that the transition law is (strongly) memoryless we can apply theorem 9.2, so that the transition law $\mathcal{L}$ is generated by the transition law relation $T\ell$ defined in definition 9.3. The following relationship between $Tr$ and $T\ell$ exists:

$$T\ell = \{((s, t), (s', t')) \mid (s, s') \in Tr \ \wedge \ t \leq time(s) = t'\}.$$

Now we have given the definition of the actor model, we will verify some general properties of the actor model and the autonomous behavior induced by it. For instance, it is not clear whether $s' = (s \backslash In(f)) \cup Out(f)$ is an element of the state space or not. (We will prove that it is.) It obviously is a set of tokens, but it is not clear whether it satisfies all the requirements of a state space. Note that the definition of the transition law remains correct, because if $s'$ is not an element of $St$, then the pair $(s, s')$ does not belong to $Tr$. We also prove that $s \backslash In(f)$ and $Out(f)$ are disjoint, which means that the produced tokens are indeed new.

Further, we will show that the transition relation *Tr* determines a *monotonous* and *eager* transition law. Another property, which appeals to our intuition, is that if processors may fire simultaneously, the next state can also be reached by firing all the processors individually in some arbitrary order. This property is called *serializability*. We also give a sufficient condition for preventing *livelock* in a system. These properties can be considered as proofs that the framework is "sound", in the sense that it corresponds to our intuition.

In the definition of a state space (definition 11.4) we required the property that in a state no identity is the ancestor of another. We will show (in lemma 11.1) that this property is an invariant of the mechanism for creating identities: when a processor fires, one input token is chosen and all new tokens get an identity that is derived from this one, i.e. their identity is mapped by $F$ to the identity of the chosen input token.

**Lemma 11.1** Let the Boolean function $q$ on $\mathbb{P}(ID)$ be defined by $\forall I \in \mathbb{P}(ID)$ :

$$q(I) = \forall i,j \in I, \ n \in \mathbb{N}\backslash\{0\} : F^n(i) \neq j.$$

(The function $q$ states that no identity in $I$ is the ancestor of another.) If for some $J \subseteq ID$ it holds that $q(J) = true$ then

$$\forall j \in J, \ i \in ID : F(i) = j \Rightarrow i \notin J$$

and

$$\forall j \in J : q((J\backslash\{j\}) \cup \{i \mid F(i) = j\}) = true.$$

(So $q$ still holds if one replaces an identity $j$ by its "children" $i$.)

*Proof* Fix some $j \in J$. We start with the first assertion. Assume for some $i \in ID$ with $F(i) = j$ that $i \in J$. This violates the property $q(J) = true$ (with $n = 1$). So the first assertion holds. Next we consider the second assertion. For some $j \in J$

$$J' = (J\backslash\{j\}) \cup \{i \mid F(i) = j\}.$$

Assume that $x, y \in J' \land x \neq y \land \exists n \in \mathbb{N}\backslash\{0\} : F^n(x) = y$. We prove as follows that this implies a contradiction:

- If $x, y \in J\backslash\{j\}$ then the contradiction follows from $q(J) = true$.
- If $F(x) = F(y) = j$ then we have $F^{n+1}(x) = F(y) = j$ and so $F^n(F(x)) = F(x)$, which is a contradiction because of the property of $F$ (*see* definition 11.3).

– If $F(x) = j \land F(y) \neq j$ then $y \in J\backslash\{j\}$ and $y = F^n(x) = F^{n-1}(j)$ which is a contradiction because $y, j \in J$ and $q(J) = true$ (if $n = 1$ we have $y = F(x) = j$, which is a contradiction because $y \in J\backslash\{j\}$).
– If $F(x) \neq j \land F(y) = j$ then $F^{n+1}(x) = j$ and $x \in J\backslash\{j\}$ which is also a contradiction because $q(J) = true$.

So in all cases there is a contradiction, which proves the second assertion. □

**Theorem 11.3** Let an actor model with state space $St$ be given. Let $s \in St$ and let $f$ be an applicable firing assignment. Then we have:

(i) No two processors $p$ and $p'$ ($p \neq p'$) produce the same tokens, i.e.

$$out(p, f(p)) \cap out(p', f(p')) = \emptyset.$$

(ii) The produced tokens are different from the consumed tokens, i.e.

$$(s\backslash In(f)) \cap Out(f) = \emptyset.$$

(iii) Consumption of $In(f)$ and production of $Out(f)$ gives a new state, i.e.

$$(s\backslash In(f)) \cup Out(f) \in St.$$

*Proof* We will prove the theorem for $\#(f) = 2$, i.e. a firing assignment in which two processors fire. The case where only one processor fires and the general case are easily derived from this case. Let $dom(f) = \{p_1, p_2\}$.

We will first prove that all newly produced tokens have a different identity, which implies the first assertion. Note that tokens produced by one processor have different identities, because of property 5 of the processor relation $R_p$ (definition 11.3). Let the tokens selected for creation of new identities in $rng(f(p_1))$ and $rng(f(p_2))$ have identities $j_1$ and $j_2$ respectively. Clearly $j_1 \neq j_2$ (because of requirement (ii) of the transition relation, definition 11.6, and the fact that tokens in state $s$ have different identities). Consider two arbitrary tokens in $out(p_1, f(p_1))$ and $out(p_2, f(p_2))$ with identities $i_1$ and $i_2$ respectively. Then $i_1 \neq i_2$ because $F(i_1) = j_1 \neq j_2 = F(i_2)$.

Next we consider the second assertion. Let $J$ be the set of all identities in state $s$. It follows from the first assertion of lemma 11.1 that neither $i_1$ nor $i_2$ belongs to $J\backslash\{j_1, j_2\}$. This proves the second assertion.

To prove the last assertion we note that $s$ satisfies the constraints of the state space, which means that $q(J) = true$, where $q$ is defined in lemma 11.1. According to that lemma the set

$$J_1 = (J\backslash\{j_1\}) \cup \{i \mid F(i) = j_1\}$$

satisfies $q(J_1) = true$. And similarly satisfies the set

$$J_2 = (J_1 \setminus \{j_2\}) \cup \{i \mid F(i) = j_2\}$$

also satisfies $q(J_2) = true$. However the set of all identities of tokens in the new state is a subset of $J_2$ (the proof of this is an exercise), so this set also has property $q$. This proves the last assertion.                                    □

The following assertion is an immediate consequence of theorem 11.3):

$$\forall (s, s') \in Tr \Rightarrow s \neq s'.$$

The next theorem shows that the induced transition system is monotonous and that every autonomous trace is eager. In particular, if $(s, s') \in Tr$, then

$$time(s) \leq time(s').$$

**Theorem 11.4**  Let an actor model with state space $St$, transition relation $Tr$ and transition law $\mathcal{L}$ be given. Then the induced transition system is *monotonous* and every autonomous trace is *eager*.

*Proof*  We first prove the monotonicity; recall definition 9.4. Let $p = \langle (s_0, t_0), \ldots \rangle$ be an arbitrary autonomous trace. We will prove by induction that, for $n \in \mathbb{N}$,

$$\tau(p_n) \leq time(\sigma(p_n)).$$

We note that $\tau(p_n) = t_n$ and that (by definition 11.7) $time(\sigma(p_n)) = time(s_n) = t_{n+1}$, so we will prove $t_n \leq t_{n+1}$.

We start with $n = 0$. Since all tokens in $s_0$ have non-negative time stamps, we have $time(s_0) \geq 0$. On the other hand $t_0 = 0$ by definition, so we have $t_0 \leq time(s_0) = t_1$.

Assume we have $t_n \leq t_{n+1}$. Then we consider $t_{n+2} = time(s_{n+1})$. We note that for some applicable firing assignment $\tilde{f}$ it holds that

$$s_{n+1} = (s_n \setminus In(\tilde{f})) \cup Out(\tilde{f})$$

where $In(\tilde{f}) \subseteq s_n$. It follows from the definition of the processor relation (definition 11.3, property 3) that

$$\forall p \in dom(\tilde{f}) : \forall x \in in(p, \tilde{f}(p)), y \in out(p, \tilde{f}(p)) : \pi_3(x) \leq \pi_3(y).$$

Therefore:

$$max\{\pi_3(x) \mid x \in in(p, \tilde{f}(p))\} \leq min\{\pi_3(y) \mid out(p, \tilde{f}(p))\}.$$

Note that

$$tim(\tilde{f}) = max\{max\{\pi_3(x) \mid x \in in(p, \tilde{f}(p))\} \mid p \in dom(\tilde{f})\}$$

and that $tim(\tilde{f}) = time(s_n)$. Hence

$$\forall p \in dom(\tilde{f}) : max\{\pi_3(x) \mid x \in in(p, \tilde{f}(p))\} = time(s_n),$$

because otherwise we could delete a processor $p$ from $dom(\tilde{f})$ in order to obtain an $f \in FA$ with a smaller maximum. So we have

$$\forall p \in dom(\tilde{f}) : \forall y \in out(p, \tilde{f}(p)) : \pi_3(y) \geq time(s_n)$$

and therefore

$$\forall x \in In(\tilde{f}), y \in Out(\tilde{f}) : \pi_3(x) \leq \pi_3(y). \qquad (*)$$

We use this property to show that

$$tim(\tilde{f}) = min\{tim(f) \mid f \in FA \wedge In(f) \subseteq s_n \cup Out(\tilde{f})\}.$$

Let $f^* \in FA$ be defined by

$$tim(f^*) = min\{tim(f) \mid f \in FA \wedge In(f) \subseteq s_n \cup Out(\tilde{f})\}.$$

Then $tim(\tilde{f}) \geq tim(f^*)$, because the set over which the minimum is taken for $f^*$ is at least as large as the set for $\tilde{f}$. Assume

$$tim(\tilde{f}) > tim(f^*)$$

which is equivalent to

$$max\{\pi_3(x) \mid x \in In(\tilde{f})\} > max\{\pi_3(x) \mid x \in In(f^*)\}.$$

This is only possible if $In(f^*) \cap Out(\tilde{f}) \neq \emptyset$. However, then there is a $y \in Out(\tilde{f}) \cap In(f^*)$ such that:

$$\pi_3(y) \leq tim(f^*) < tim(\tilde{f}) = max\{\pi_3(x) \mid x \in In(\tilde{f})\}.$$

This contradicts $(*)$. So we have

$$
\begin{aligned}
time(s_n) &= min\{tim(f) \mid f \in FA \wedge In(f) \subseteq s_n\} \\
&= min\{tim(f) \mid f \in FA \wedge In(f) \subseteq s_n \cup Out(\tilde{f})\} \\
&\leq min\{tim(f) \mid f \in FA \wedge In(f) \subseteq (s_n \setminus In(\tilde{f})) \cup Out(\tilde{f})\} \\
&= time(s_{n+1}).
\end{aligned}
$$

The inequality is justified by the fact that the minimum is taken over a larger set on the left-hand side. So this proves, for all traces $p$,

$$\tau(\ell(p)) \leq time(\sigma(\ell(p))).$$

To verify the monotonicity we have to prove that for all events $e$ in the set

$$\mathcal{L}(p) = \{e \mid e = (s, t) \wedge (\sigma(\ell(p)), s) \in Tr \wedge t = time(\sigma(\ell(p)))\}$$

the inequality $\tau(e) \geq \tau(\ell(p))$ holds. This is the case because

$$\tau(e) = time(\sigma(\ell(p))) \geq \tau(\ell(p)).$$

To verify eagerness note that all events in $\mathcal{L}(p)$ have the same event time, which means that one with the minimal time stamp is always chosen.                    □

The next theorem gives the *serializability* property.

**Theorem 11.5** Let an actor model with state space $St$, transition relation $Tr$ and set of firing rules $FA$ be given. Let $f \in FA$ be applicable for state $s$ and $(s, s'') \in Tr$ such that

$$s'' = (s \backslash In(f)) \cup Out(f).$$

If we divide $f$ into two firing rules $g, h \in FA$ such that $f = g \cup h$ and $g \cap h = \emptyset$, then:

- $g$ is an applicable firing rule for $s$,
- $h$ is an applicable firing rule for $s' = (s \backslash In(g)) \cup Out(g)$,
- $time(s') = time(s)$,
- $s'' = (s' \backslash In(h)) \cup Out(h) = (s \backslash (In(g) \cup In(h))) \cup Out(g) \cup Out(h)$.

*Proof* Note first that $In(g) \cap In(h) = \emptyset$, $Out(g) \cap Out(h) = \emptyset$ and that

$$In(f) = In(g) \cup In(h) \ \wedge \ Out(f) = Out(g) \cup Out(h). \qquad (*)$$

Further note that $time(s) = tim(f) = tim(g) = tim(h)$. Hence $g$ (and also $h$) is applicable in $s$. Since $In(h) \subseteq s \backslash In(g)$ we have $In(h) \subseteq s'$, hence $time(s') \leq tim(h)$. By the former theorem we have $time(s) \leq time(s')$. Hence $h$ is applicable for $s'$ and $time(s') = time(s)$. The last assertion follows from $(*)$.                    □

As a consequence of this theorem we may split every applicable firing assignment into a sequence of elementary firing assignments with domains that contain only one processor. The order in which these processors fire is irrelevant for the final result. This property is used in the next theorem, which states that an actor model in which only one processor may fire in each transition is *similar* to the actor model that is the same except that in it several processors may fire simultaneously.

**Theorem 11.6** Let an actor model with state space $St$ and a set of initial states be given. We consider two transition relations for this model: the "standard" transition relation $Tr$ defined in definition 11.6 and the transition relation $Tr'$

defined by
$$Tr' = \{(s, s') \in Tr \mid \exists f \in FA : \#(f) = 1 \wedge$$

$$s' = (s\backslash In(f)) \cup Out(f) \wedge f \text{ is applicable}\}.$$

Let the transition systems induced by $(St, Tr)$ and $(St, Tr')$ be $A$ and $B$ respectively. Then $B$ is similar to $A$ with respect to the identity relation on $St \times T$.

*Proof* It is obvious that $B$ is similar to $A$ , because each transition of $B$ is also a transition of $A$. $\qquad\square$

Note that $A$ is not similar to $B$.

The next theorem gives a sufficient condition to avoid livelock. Remember that a trace has livelock if it can make infinitely many transitions in a finite time interval. Hence no livelock means that the system makes *progress*.

**Theorem 11.7** Let an actor model and a transition law be given such that, for some $\epsilon \in \mathbb{R}^+$, the processor relation satisfies $\forall p \in P : \forall r \in R_p :$
$$max\{\pi_3(r(a)) \mid a \in I(p) \cap dom(r)\} + \epsilon \leq$$

$$min\{\pi_3(r(b)) \mid b \in O(p) \cap dom(r)\}.$$

The system is then *livelock free*.

*Proof* Let $p$ be an infinite autonomous trace. Note that $\sigma(p_i)$ contains only finitely many tokens for all $i \in \mathbb{N}$, since all states are finite. For $n \in \mathbb{N}$, let $k_n$ be defined by
$$k_n = \{i \in dom(p) \mid 0 \leq \tau(p_i) < n\epsilon\}.$$

Hence $k_n$ is the set of (indexes of) events happening before $n\epsilon$. First we show $k_1$ is finite. Note that, for all applicable firing rules $f$ in the initial state,
$$max\{\pi_3(x) \mid x \in In(f)\} + \epsilon \leq min\{\pi_3(y) \mid y \in Out(f)\}$$

because of the requirement on $R$. Hence all tokens, produced in events $k_1$ have a time stamp greater or equal to $\epsilon$ and cannot be consumed in an event during $[0, \epsilon)$. So, all events in $k_1$ are caused by tokens in $\sigma(p_0)$ and form a finite set. Suppose we have proven that $k_n$ is finite. Then the number of tokens produced before $n\epsilon$ is finite. In all events occurring in $[n\epsilon, (n+1)\epsilon)$ only tokens produced before $n\epsilon$ are consumed, since tokens produced after $n\epsilon$ are not available before $(n+1)\epsilon$. Hence the number of events in $[n\epsilon, (n+1)\epsilon)$ is finite and therefore $k_{n+1}$ is finite. So, we have proven by induction that $k_n$ is finite for all $n \in \mathbb{N}$. $\qquad\square$

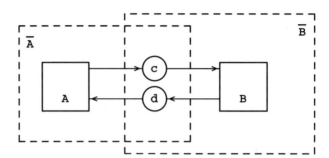

Fig. 11.2. The composition of two open systems.

The next topic we consider in this chapter is the composition of two actor models. The composition of actor models is used to make complex systems out of simple ones. As an example let us start with two open net models $A$ and $B$. We add places and connect the input and output connectors of $A$ and $B$ to these places. Thus we have made the *closures* $\bar{A}$ and $\bar{B}$ of $A$ and $B$ respectively. The composition is denoted by $\bar{A} * \bar{B}$. In figure 11.2 we illustrate this. Here $A$ and $B$ both have two unconnected connectors. These are connected to two channels $c$ and $d$. An event in which the contents of $c$ or $d$ are changed by a processor of $B$ is called an *external event* for $\bar{A}$. In order to define the composition of two actor models we have to define the composition of two object models and the composition of two flat net models first, because an actor model encompasses these entities.

**Definition 11.8** Let $A$ and $B$ be two object models. They are *composable* if and only if the following conditions hold:

- $\forall r \in RN_A \cap RN_B : DM_A(r) = DM_B(r) \;\wedge\; RG_A(r) = RG_B(r)$,
- $\forall n \in CN_A \cap CN_B : CB_A(n) = CB_B(n) \;\wedge\; CR_A(n) = CR_B(n)$,
- $\forall n \in SN_A \cap SN_B : sim_A(n) = sim_B(n)$.

Their *composition*, denoted by $A * B$, is defined as their component-wise union. (So, if $C = A * B$ then $SN_C = SN_A \cup SN_B$, $sim_C = sim_A \cup sim_B$ etc.)
□

**Lemma 11.2** Let $A$ and $B$ be two composable object models and let $C = A * B$. Then

- $C$ is a correct object model, i.e. it satisfies all requirements of definitions 10.1 and 10.2,
- $\forall n \in CN_A \cap CN_B : com_A(n) = com_B(n)$.

*Proof* The proof is an exercise. (Check the appropriate definitions.) □

**Definition 11.9** Let $A$ and $B$ be two flat net models. They are *composable* if and only if

- $P_A \cap P_B = \emptyset$,
- $L_A \cup L_B$, $P_A \cup P_B$, $C_A \cup C_B$ are mutually disjoint.

Their *composition*, denoted by $A * B$, is their component-wise union. (So if $C = A * B$ then $L_C = L_A \cup L_B$ and $M_C = M_A \cup M_B$ etc.)
□

**Lemma 11.3** Let $A$ and $B$ be two composable flat net models and let $C = A*B$. Then $C$ is a correct flat net model.

*Proof* The proof is trivial because all requirements concern $P$ and $P_A \cap P_B = \emptyset$. So if the requirements hold for $A$ and $B$ they hold for $C$. □

**Definition 11.10** Let $A$ and $B$ be two actor models such that

- $FN_A$ and $FN_B$ are composable,
- $OM_A$ and $OM_B$ are composable,
- $\forall \ell \in L_A \cap L_B : CA_A(\ell) = CA_B(\ell)$,
- $T_A = T_B \wedge ID_A = ID_B \wedge F_A = F_B$.

Then $A$ and $B$ are *composable* and their composition, denoted by $A*B$, is defined by

$$(FN_A * FN_B, OM_A * OM_B, CA_A \cup CA_B, CT_A \cup CT_B, T_A, ID_A, F_A, R_A \cup R_B).$$

□

**Lemma 11.4** Let $A$ and $B$ be two composable actor models and let $C = A * B$. Then $C$ is a correct actor model.

*Proof* We only have to verify the requirements for $CT_C$ and $R_C$. For $CT_C$ the requirement follows from $P_A \cap P_B = \emptyset$ and the composability of $OM_A$ and $OM_B$. In order to verify the requirement for $R_C$ note that

$$OU_C = \bigcup_{n \in CN_C} com_C(n) = \bigcup_{n \in CN_A} com_C(n) \cup \bigcup_{n \in CN_B} com_C(n).$$

By the second assertion of lemma 11.2 we have

$$OU_C = OU_A \cup OU_B.$$

Since $ID_A = ID_B$ and $T_A = T_B$ we have

$$R_C \in P_C \to \mathbb{P}(C_C \twoheadrightarrow ID_C \times OU_C \times T_C).$$

The rest of the requirements follow from the fact $P_A \cap P_B = \emptyset$. □

The composition operators, all denoted by $*$, are associative and commutative. This is very important for the design of systems, because it gives us freedom in the way we want to decompose a complex system.

**Theorem 11.8** The composition operators $*$ for object models, flat net models and actor models are *associative* and *commutative*.

*Proof* The proof is an exercise. □

Now we know how to compose actor models, we would like to know the relationship between the state spaces and transition relations of a composed system and its components. The next theorem gives an answer.

**Theorem 11.9** Let $A$ and $B$ be composable actor models and let $C = A * B$. (The subscripts $A$, $B$ and $C$ are used to distinguish the model attributes.) If $(s, s') \in Tr_C$ then $\exists\, s_A, s'_A \in St_A, s_B, s'_B \in St_B$ :

(i) $s_A \cap s_B = \emptyset \land s'_A \cap s'_B = \emptyset$,
(ii) $s = s_A \cup s_B \land s' = s'_A \cup s'_B$,
(iii) for $i \in \{A,\, B\}$:  $s_i \neq s'_i \Rightarrow (s_i, s'_i) \in Tr_i \land time_i(s_i) = time_C(s)$.

*Proof* (For notational convenience we shall drop the subscript $C$ sometimes.) Let $(s, s') \in Tr_C$ and let $f \in TA_C$ be applicable in $s$, such that

$$s' = (s \backslash In(f)) \cup Out(f).$$

Further, let $f_i = f \upharpoonright P_i$. The following four assertions are easy to verify:

(i) $f_A \cap f_B = \emptyset$ and $f = f_A \cup f_B$;
(ii) $In(f) = In(f_A) \cup In(f_B)$ and $Out(f) = Out(f_A) \cup Out(f_B)$;
(iii) $In(f_A) \cap In(f_B) = \emptyset$ and $Out(f_A) \cap Out(f_B) = \emptyset$;
(iv) $In_i(f_i) = In(f_i)$ and $Out_i(f_i) = Out(f_i)$.

So we have

$$s' = (s \backslash (In_A(f_A) \cup In_B(f_B))) \cup Out_A(f_A) \cup Out_B(f_B).$$

By the third and fourth assertions above and the fact that $In(f) \subseteq s$, we can find $s_A$ and $s_B$ such that

$\quad - s = s_A \cup s_B,$

- $s_A \cap s_B = \emptyset$,
- $In_i(f_i) \subseteq s_i$.

Let $s_i' = (s_i \setminus In_i(f_i)) \cup Out_i(f_i)$. Then clearly $s' = s_A' \cup s_B'$ and $s_A' \cap s_B' = \emptyset$, which proves the first two assertions of the theorem. If $f_i \neq \emptyset$ then, using the same arguments as in the proof of theorem 11.3,

$$time_C(s) = tim_C(f) = tim_C(f_i) = tim_i(f_i) = time_i(s_i),$$

which proves that $f_i$ is applicable for $s_i$ and therefore $(s_i, s_i') \in Tr_i$. Finally, we note that $f_i \neq \emptyset \Leftrightarrow s_i \neq s_i'$, which completes the proof. □

Note that the opposite of this theorem is not true: if each of the components of a system can seperately have events at a certain time, then it does not follow that both can have these events (either simultaneously, nor in some order).

Next we consider *processor characteristics*. They are important for the modeling of actors, because they are often known in an early stage of design, i.e. before the processor relation is specified. They are also important for the analysis of actors, because some analysis methods are only applicable for actors where the processors have certain specific processor characteristics.

**Definition 11.11** Let an actor model be given. The *processor characteristics* are defined by the following.

**Totality,** which means that a processor will be enabled if and only if there are enough input tokens, independently of their values. Formally a processor $p$ is total if and only if for all functions $g$ with

$$dom(g) \subseteq I(p) \ \wedge \ \forall a \in dom(g) : g(a) \in CT_p(a))$$

it holds that

$$(\exists h \in R_p : dom(h \upharpoonright I(p)) = dom(g \upharpoonright I(p)))$$
$$\Rightarrow \exists f \in R_p : f \upharpoonright I(p) = g \upharpoonright I(p).$$

**Input completeness,** which means that the processor consumes in each event via all input connectors. Formally a processor $p$ is input complete if and only if

$$\forall f \in R_p : dom(f) \supset I(p).$$

**Output completeness,** which means that the processor produces for every output connector in each event. Formally a processor $p$ is output complete if and only if

$$\forall f \in R_p : dom(f) \supset O(p).$$

We call a processor *complete* if it is both input and output complete.

**Functionality,** which means that the produced tokens are functionally dependent of the consumed ones. Formally a processor $p$ is functional if and only if

$$\forall f, g \in R_p : f \upharpoonright I(p) \subseteq g \upharpoonright I(p) \Rightarrow f = g.$$

□

Note that a total processor does not need to be input complete; however, if it is enabled for some subset of input connectors it is enabled for all possible values of input objects. Functionality does not imply input completeness either; however, if a "functional processor" is enabled for some set of input objects it is not enabled for any subset. Further, functionality implies that two firing rules with the same input have the same output.

As stated in the introduction, the actor framework is a generalization of the Petri net framework. With the processor characteristics we can express precisely in what sense it is a generalization: a (classical) Petri net can be defined as an actor model in which all processors are complete and total. In fact in classical Petri nets the identities, values and time stamps of tokens do not play any role. In classical Petri nets we are only interested in the number of tokens in each place of a state; this set of numbers is called the *marking* of the state. In fact we may use trivial choices for the processor relations and the complex classes: all complex classes are the same and contain only one complex and the processors give all produced tokens a delay equal to zero.

We conclude this chapter with some remarks on *stores*. As already mentioned from a formal point of view they are just places with some special properties, and therefore we have not considered them before in this chapter. A store always contains exactly one token and will always be available, which means that for all $\ell \in L$ such that $\ell$ is a store the following requirements hold:

$$\forall s \in St : \#\{i \in dom(s) \mid \pi_3(s(i)) = \ell\} = 1 \wedge$$
$$\forall i \in dom(s) : \pi_2(s(i)) \le time(s).$$

These requirements can be met if a consumed token of a store is replaced by a produced token with a delay 0.

If we assume that each processor has at least one input *channel*, i.e. a non-store input place, then we may generalize theorem 11.7 by requiring that the processor relation $R$ satisfies

$\forall p \in P : \forall r \in R_p :$

$$max\{\pi_3(r(a)) \mid a \in I(q) \cap dom(r) \wedge a \ is \ a \ channel\}$$

$$\leq$$

$$\epsilon + max\{\pi_3(r(a)) \mid a \in O(q) \cap dom(r) \wedge a \ is \ a \ channel\}.$$

The proof is an exercise.

# 12
# References and exercises for part II

In the references for part I we have given already some references for the formal frameworks used in the book. Here we give some more specialized references.

Our theory of *transition systems* stands on its own, although similar ideas can be found in the literature. For example, transition systems are studied in detail in [Hesselink, 1988]. A survey paper is [De Nicola, 1987]. Also, the concept of *similarity* is considered in these papers. The first paper is [Park, 1981] An important book on transition systems is [Olderog, 1991]. In literature often labeled transition systems are studied instead of unlabeled, as we do. It is easy to transform a labeled transition system into an unlabeled one by adding extra states for each labeled arc.

The theory of *traces* is studied in detail in [Mazurkiewicz, 1984] and [Snepscheut, 1985]. There is some related literature on *process algebras*, as mentioned at the end of part I. [Hoare, 1985; Milner, 1980; Baeten and Weijland, 1990]. In process algebra, similarity relations, for example *bi-simulation*, are studied as well.

*Timed* transition systems are related to process algebraic formalisms with time by for example [Reed and Roscoe, 1988]. Another formalism that supports the notion of time is *temporal logic*, in which assertions about the behavior of a system can be proved; *see* [Pnueli, 1977] or a more general treatise on time in logic for example [van Benthem, 1983]. The idea of a *transition law* and the concept *memoryless* are borrowed from the theory of Markov chains, *see* for example [Revuz, 1975].

The *object framework* is closely related to the entity-relationship model ([Chen, 1976]). There are many extensions of this framework, for example [Parent and Spaccapietra, 1985]. A survey is provided in [Spaccapietra, 1987]. Another important original framework is presented in [Abrial, 1974]; it has only binary relations, as we have here. Binary relations can be considered as set-valued functions and therefore our framework is also closely related to the *functional data model* of [Shipman, 1981]; *see* also [Buneman and Frankel, 1979]. (Note that we will use the term "functional data model" in a more restrictive sense later.) All these data models are often called *semantic data models*. However, there is also an object framework referred to this; *see* [Hammer and McLeod, 1981]. A survey of semantic data models is given in [Hull and King, 1987]. The concept of complexes was first introduced in [van Hee and Verkoulen, 1991; van Hee and Verkoulen, 1992]. There are many other frameworks that have the notion of complex objects, for example the nested relational model, *see* [Schek and Scholl, 1986], and GOOD, *see* [Gyssens *et al.*, 1990]

The *actor framework* is the classical Petri net model extended with time, object identities and complex values for the tokens. It is not borrowed from other authors. A predecessor of this framework is presented in [van Hee *et al.*, 1989a] and the first version of the actor framework can be found in [van Hee *et al.*, 1989b; van Hee *et al.*, 1991]. The framework has many similarities with others, for example with the *colored Petri nets* of [Jensen, 1992]. The differences are that in our framework tokens may have a value that belongs to an infinite type, that tokens have a time stamp and an identity, and that transitions are defined by a processor relation instead of arc and transition inscriptions. The colored Petri net model is an improvement of the *predicate/transition nets* of [Genrich, 1987; Genrich and Lautenbach, 1979]. Ideas relating to Petri nets with distinguishable tokens first appeared in [Schiffers and Wedde, 1978]. Other frameworks of Petri nets with time can be found in [Sifakis, 1977; Sifakis, 1980; Ajmone Marsan *et al.*, 1985].

There are many papers on Petri nets and their analysis. The books of [Reisig, 1985; Jensen, 1992; Peterson, 1981] offer more detailed references. In [Pless and Plünnecke, 1980] a bibliography is given of the literature up to 1980. There is a Petri net news letter that gives up-to-date information on new articles: Petri Net Newsletter, Gesellschaft für Informatik, Bonn (ISBN 0173-7473).

The concept of *serializability* also plays an important role in distributed databases, *see* [Ceri and Pelagatti, 1984].

## Exercises for part II

(1)   Prove that the autonomous traces of a transition system form a closed set.

(2)   Prove theorem 9.6.

(3)   Prove theorem 11.1.

(4)   Prove the assertion in the proof of theorem 11.3 that all identities of tokens in the new state are in $J_2$.

(5)      Prove lemma 11.2.

(6)      Prove theorem 11.8.

(7)      Generalize theorem 11.7 to the following cases:

- tokens in stores do not have a delay;
- not all processors satisfy the requirement of the theorem, but in each *cycle* (i.e. a cycle in the bipartite graph of a flat net model) there is at least one processor that gives its output tokens in the places occuring in the cycle a positive delay.

(8)      Consider an arbitrary transition system and transform it into a memory-less transition system such that the systems are bisimilar.

(9)      Give a formal description of the following actor model and list the behavior of this actor model (i.e. the set of all possible processes starting in the initial state). The actor model has one processor $p$, two channels, called $a$ and $b$ and one store $s$. The object classes of the three places are simple: there is only one complex class and the complexes can be represented by natural numbers. Channel $a$ is an input channel and $b$ an output channel. The processor relation of $p$ is such that the value of the complex in store $s$ is the sum of the values of the input of $p$ modulo 4 and the output objects have a value that is 0 if the store value has become even in an event and 1 if it has become odd. In the initial state the store value is 0 and in channel $a$ reside three objects with values 2, 3 and 0. All time stamps and all delays are 0.

(10)     A *Turing machine* is a finite state machine extended by an infinite tape from which it can read symbols and on which it can write symbols. It is characterized by a 4-tuple $(M, \Sigma, T, m_0)$, where

- $M$ is the finite state space, not containing $h$ the so-called *halt state*,
- $m_0$ is the initial state,
- $\Sigma$ is a set of symbols not including the characters $L$ and $R$, which are used to direct the tape head to the left and right respectively,
- $T$ is a transition function such that

$$T \in M \times \Sigma \rightarrow (M \cup \{h\}) \times (\Sigma \cup \{L, R\}).$$

If the machine is in state $m$, if symbol $a$ is read by the head and if $T(m, a) = (n, b)$ then the new state will be $n$ and

- if $b \in \Sigma$ then the symbol on the tape becomes $b$,
- if $b \in \{L, R\}$ the tape head will move to the left or right respectively.

The machine stops if the state $h$ is reached. (For more information on Turing machines see for instance [Lewis and Papadimitriou, 1981]).

A generally accepted definition of a computable function is, that for each domain value the function value can be computed by a Turing machine. A formalism to express computations is called *Turing complete*, if every computable function can be expressed in the formalism.

Prove that the corresponding actor framework is Turing complete. (Hint: design an actor model for an arbitrary Turing machine.)

(11)  Consider an arbitrary actor model $N$. Show there is another actor model $M$ with the same object model and the same set of places and with only one processor $p$, such that $N$ and $M$ are bisimilar with respect to the identity relation. (Hint: give $p$ an input connector for every input connector occurring in $N$ and connect it to the same place as in $N$, after some renaming to avoid name clashes. Further let the processor relation $R_p$ be the (modified) union of the processor relations of the processors of $N$.)

(12)  A hierarchical net model is defined by

$$
\begin{aligned}
N.L &= \{p,\ q,\ r,\ s,\ t,\ v,\ w\}, \\
N.P &= \{C,\ D,\ E,\ F\}, \\
N.A &= \{top,\ A,\ B\} \cup N.P, \\
N.C &= \{p?, p!, q?, q!, r?, r!, s?, s!, t?, t!, v?, v!, w?, w!, x?, x!, y?, y!\}.
\end{aligned}
$$

Further the functions $N.I$ and $N.O$ are given by

|   | I | O |
|---|---|---|
| A | $p?$ | $q!$ |
| B | $q?$ | $p!$ |
| C | $x?, w?$ | $v!$ |
| D | $v?$ | $y!, w!$ |
| E | $s?, t?$ | $x!, r!$ |
| F | $r?, y?$ | $s!, t!$ |

The function $N.M$ maps every connector with a ? or a ! to the place with the same name (without ? or !) if it exists. Further,

$$
\begin{aligned}
N.M_C(x?) &= p!, \\
N.M_D(y?) &= q?, \\
N.M_E(x!) &= p?, \\
N.M_F(y?) &= q!.
\end{aligned}
$$

And the functions *HA* and *HL* are given by

$$\forall i \in \{A, B\} : HA(i) = top,$$
$$\forall i \in \{C, D\} : HA(i) = A,$$
$$\forall i \in \{E, F\} : HA(i) = B,$$
$$\forall i \in \{p, q\} : HL(i) = top,$$
$$\forall i \in \{v, w\} : HL(i) = A,$$
$$\forall i \in \{s, r, t\} : HL(i) = B.$$

Draw a diagram, determine the errors in this definition and give a correction.

(13)   A *data dictionary* is a *data base* that stores the actor models (including object models) of a system. So in a data dictionary the processors are objects, and object classes and the relationship classes of the object models as well!

 (a) Make an object model for a data dictionary in which only flat net models can be represented.
 (b) Extend this model to enable it to represent also hierarchical net models.
 (c) Make an object model in which an arbitrary object model can be represented, including the graphically expressible constraints.
 (d) Integrate both object models to obtain a model for a "complete" data dictionary.

(14)   Consider an arbitrary actor model. Introduce a store called *time* and connect it to a processor called *clock* that triggers itself via one channel called *step*, which is both an input and output channel for *clock*. The delay of the token in *step* is one time unit. The value of the object in *time* is a natural number that is increased by one in every firing. In the initial state the value in *time* is zero.

   Prove that in each state of an arbitrary trace, store *time* indicates the "right" time (with an error of at most one time unit).

# Part III

# Modeling methods

# 13

# Introduction

In this book a *method* is a set of *guidelines* and *techniques* that can be used for the following tasks.

**Construction** of a model for a system. We distinguish **two** cases:

(i) Making a model after *reality*, i.e. the systems engineer has an informal description of the system or has formed an idea of the system in mind based on observations of the system, and out of this he makes a model in terms of the formalisms given in the preceding part.

(ii) *Transforming* a given model into another one, in which case the second model is formulated in another formalism or in the same formalism but with more structure (i.e. it has properties the first model does not have) or in a different way.

**Analysis** of a model. Again we distinguish **two** cases:

(i) *Verifying* properties of a model by means of a formal proof.

(ii) *Validating* a model by means of *simulation* of the behavior of the model, i.e. testing hypotheses or calculating the characteristic values of a model based on the simulation experiments.

Making a model from scratch is one of the most difficult tasks because the input for this task is "sloppy". Therefore methods for these tasks are not very rigorous. However, every analysis in practice starts with this task, so it is very important.

Transformation of a model is done for several reasons. One reason to transform a model into another one could be that for the second model better analysis tools or techniques are available. Another reason could be that the second model is better suited for construction of the real system. This is the case if the second model is regarded as the blueprint for the real system. Consider for example an object model made in our formalism, for which the corresponding real system is to be constructed with a relational database management system. We can transform our first model into a second one that satisfies requirements of the database management system. The reason why we do not start with the second model immediately is that the first model is more concise, better understandable and may be easier to analyze. Another example is an actor model where stores are shared by several processors. If we have to realize the system on a computer network without shared memory, we can transform our model into a model that has only *private* stores, i.e. stores used only by one processor.

Of course the systems engineer has to prove that the transformed model is sufficiently "similar" to the original one. Here the similarity relations of part II are useful.

The possibilities for verifying properties of realistic models are limited. There are two kinds of properties that can be verified:

(i) internal consistency;
(ii) requirements formulated for construction of the system.

The property of internal consistency means that there are no "logical" errors in the model, for instance that the syntax of the model is correct, that the used types are consistent and that the system does not have any deadlocks. For some of these questions methods are available. The internal consistency of a model is no guarantee that the model describes the system that the systems engineer or his principal has in mind! To make sure the model describes what we want, we have to verify the properties formulated in the requirements specification. Often these properties are written down informally and the systems engineer has to translate them into some formal language first, for instance some form of logic. This translation is also a source of errors. A good strategy is to start with an informal description, then a translation to a formal one and finally a translation of the formal one into an informal description. The two informal descriptions should be consistent; this can be checked by non-specialists.

This kind of verification is a hot research topic and there are not many results yet that can be applied to practical cases. Therefore in many cases the systems engineer has to use experimentation by simulation (validation) with the model in order to obtain confidence instead of certainty: experiments can give counter-examples for a property, but cannot prove that the property holds. However, if a model passes many tests, we obtain a degree of confidence that can be quantified with probability theory.

Methods cannot be regarded as algorithms; they are not sequences of unambiguous instructions to make or analyze a model. The distinction between guidelines and techniques is not very sharp. One could say that a technique is more rigorous, or "closer" to an algorithm than a guideline. In a technique the final result as well as intermediate results are precisely specified, however, the way to go from one step to another is not. As examples of techniques, we mention the following:

- the representation of the history of a system in an object model that only considers the current state of that system;
- the transformation of an object model in our framework to a relational model;
- the verification of an invariance property in an actor model.

Examples of guidelines are:

- hints to represent a practical situation as a model;
- a checklist to perform a modeling task, in fact a *systems development life cycle* may be considered as a checklist too;
- conventions to be followed during a modeling task, for instance conventions for notation that renders models readable, or conventions for the use of specific constructions that render models "well-structured".

For a complex system we cannot make a complete actor model at the outset; we have to construct it in steps. There are three well-known guidelines to develop a model. They have traditional names, that we will use here.

The *process oriented approach* In this approach the steps are as follows.

(i) A hierarchical net model is designed up to the processor level. Neither the processor relations for the processors, nor the object classes for the places (including stores) are defined in this step in a formal way, but are described informally. We give all processors their properties and if necessary, constraints corresponding to the delays of produced tokens. This activity will be called *actor modeling* and we will call the result of this activity an *incomplete actor model*, because term "actor model" is used for a complete formal description of a system. In the information systems community the same activity is called *process modeling*. We, however, use the term "process" for an element of the behavior of a system. Instead of "incomplete" actor model, we will use the term "actor model" where no confusion is possible.

(ii) An object model is designed for the whole system. In this object model all complex classes that play a role within the system or in communication with the environment have to be defined. The object model should include all relevant constraints, either expressed graphically or in predicate calculus and natural language. This activity is usually called *data modeling*. However, we will use the term *object modeling*, because we are not modeling information objects only, but also physical and conceptual objects. Complex classes are defined as in chapter 10, so no sophisticated value type is defined at this stage.

(iii) Complex classes are assigned to places.

These first three steps are called *modeling*.

(iv) For each complex class a value type is specified.

(v) For each processor a processor relation is specified.

The latter two steps are called *specification*.

The *data oriented approach*. Here the same steps are performed, but in a different order.

(i) An object model, including constraints, is designed.

(ii) An incomplete actor model in the sense explained above is designed.

(iii) Complex classes to places are assigned.

(iv) Value types for complex classes are specified.

(v) Processor relations are specified.

The *object oriented approach*. This approach is different from the preceding ones in the sense that the three steps are performed simultaneously, however, for each complex class separately. So the modeling task is not divided up according to the different aspects of the actor model but according to the different complex classes. Note that in the terminology of the object oriented approach, the concept of an object is used differently: a token is there an actor or a combination of an actor and tokens.

In the following chapters we first consider methods for making and transforming models. We distinguish methods for

- actor modeling,
- object modeling,
- specification of value types and processor relations, with as final result a complete actor model as the final result,
- object oriented modeling.

We often mention the properties of a (type of) model, but we do not give proofs here, because we want to concentrate on modeling issues first.

So, in part III we consider methods for the construction of models and in part IV methods for analyzing models.

# 14

# Actor modeling

Actor modeling is the activity of making an incomplete actor model, as explained in the previous chapter. In this chapter we will consider only incomplete actor models and therefore we use the term "actor model" as an abbreviation. Remember that the possible processor characteristics are *totality*, *functionality* and *completeness*. Further the *timing* of tokens is considered in the process model, if this is relevant. Note that we do not consider verification of the properties of models in this chapter.

We distinguish making *an actor model after reality*, i.e. without any formal description to start with, from transforming a given actor model into another one which has structural properties that the first one does not have.

## 14.1 Making an actor model after reality

There are two cases: one where the systems engineer makes a model of an existing system; the other where he models a system that he has (partly) in mind. In the first case he can observe the existing system and check whether his model has the same properties as the real system; in the second case he can only check whether the system he has in mind fits into the environment in which it should operate. From a modeling point of view these cases are not different: only the source of information is different.

We will consider several modeling problems. To illustrate these problems we take two examples: order processing in the sales department of a company that delivers items from stock to customers, and traffic control at a railroad station.

In the order processing system customers send a request $a$ to the sales department to make an offer for the delivery of items. (The letters refer to places in figure 14.1.) Then the sales department produces an offer $b$, taking into account the inventory information which is shared with the environments. The customer then decides to send an order $c$, which starts several activities in the sales de-

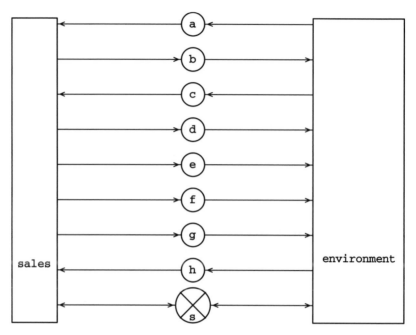

Fig. 14.1. Order processing, context diagram.

partment, and which results in an order confirmation $d$. The sales department then sends a delivery order $g$ to the distribution department. If the distribution department is ready to deliver it sends a message to the sales department $h$ and the sales department notifies the customer and sends an invoice $e$. At the same time the sales department sends a copy of the invoice $f$ to the finance department, which ends this *transaction* for the sales department. Of course there might be some communication between the customer and the finance department concerning the payment of the invoice but that does not bother us here. We also neglect that the customer might be unhappy with the received items and that he contacts the sales department again about this order.

The railroad station has the layout displayed in figure 14.2. Trains are traveling in one direction (from left to right). One track divides into two at the entrance to the station. It is possible to load and unload passengers from both tracks at the platform. One train can pass another at the station. This system needs an information system that controls the use of the tracks at the station safely. The station master may decide when a train is able to leave the station, but the information system should not allow the station master to give two trains a green light at the same time. Sensors along the railroad produce information objects that are sent to the railroad station to notify that a train has passed the sensor.

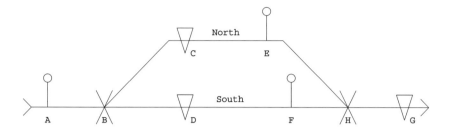

Fig. 14.2. Railroad station, physical layout.

Sensors $C$, $D$ and $G$ produce an information object when a train has completely passed one of these points. Further, there are signals along the tracks: $A$, $E$ and $F$. If a signal is red a train has to wait; if it is green a train may pass. There is one switch $B$ before the station and one join $H$ after the station. The switch $B$ is important because it can be altered from outside the system; $H$ is always pushed into the right position by the trains.

Using these two examples, we will now show how to make an actor model of a discrete dynamic system. We always consider systems at the highest level to be closed; *top* is the actor at the highest level. The first step is to *decompose* (split, refine) *top* into a network of two actors, one representing the discrete dynamic system in which we are interested and the other representing the environment. The latter is called a *context actor*. So the first question to be answered is: what is the boundary of the system we are studying? To answer this we have to define the places through which the system of interest communicates with the context actor.

In figure 14.1 we see the first decomposition of *top* for the order processing example. The only interesting thing on this diagram is the communication with the environment, here by means of four input places, four output places and one store $s$. We often decompose the context actor once because it allows us to structure the communication with the environment. In figure 14.3 we have decomposed it. Here we see some new actors: *finance*, *customers* and *distribution*. They belong to the environment; we call them also context actors. We have left out all communication between the context actors because it is not of interest for us.

The second step, i.e. the first decomposition of the discrete dynamic system that we are studying, (often) gives two actors: one representing the target system and one representing its information system. The *target system* is the system in relation to which the information system works.

An actor model showing the target system and the information system as one actor each and some context actors as well is called a *context diagram*, so figure

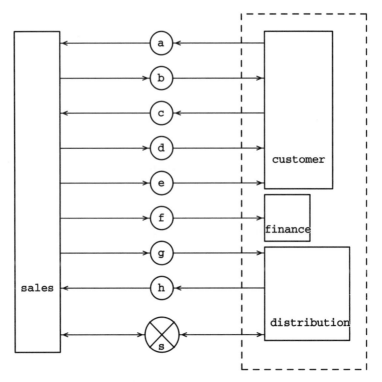

Fig. 14.3. Order processing, first decomposition of the environment.

14.1 and figure 14.3 are both context diagrams. The practice is to start from one of these diagrams.

If we want to *simulate* the system we study, we have to simulate the environment as well. However, it is impossible to do this exactly because this would require us to specify the environment in detail. Instead of doing this we make models of the context actors as if they were operating in isolation. This means that we design a consumption/production behavior for them that is an *approximation* of the behavior of the real environment. Sometimes we may model a context actor by means of a *random generator*, which may imply that the context actor behaves more unpredictably than the real environment. This in turn means that we test the system under circumstances that are more demanding than those which the real system will encounter.

Often we are modeling only an information system, as in the order processing example. In this case the system we want to model is an information system, exchanging information objects only with the context actors. The actor *customers* represents all customers of the company; only the exchange of information objects with the sales department is relevant. Of course, we could have modeled

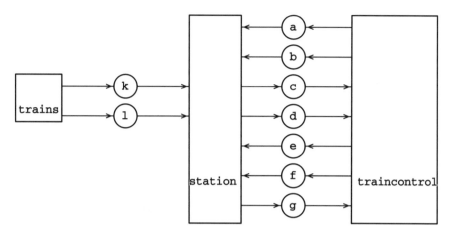

Fig. 14.4. Railroad station, context diagram.

all customers separately by context actors, but this would make the model vulnerable: if there were a change in the customer population, our model would not be correct any more. (How the customers are modeled by one actor is discussed later.)

In the railroad example the object of study is a discrete dynamic system involving physical systems (the trains, the tracks, the semaphores). We distinguish the information system and the target system (which is a discrete dynamic system itself). The information system has two characteristic properties: all tokens are information objects and many tokens in the target system have a "counter-part" in the information system, since the information system maintains an image of the state or history of the target system. The context diagram for the railroad example is displayed in figure 14.4. Here we see three actors: the *station*, which is the target system, *traincontrol*, which is the information system, and a context actor called *trains*. The context actor *trains* has a simple behavior: it will produce trains for place $k$ and it will consume trains from place $l$ (and we not that trains have a direction). So there remain two actors that we will detail to some extent. Channel $a$ gives control tokens to semaphore $A$, $b$ to the switch $B$, $c$ and $d$ pass sensor information from $C$ and $D$ respectively, $e$ and $f$ give control tokens to $F$ and $G$ respectively and by $g$ the sensor information of $G$ is passed.

Besides the target system, its information system and the context actors we often introduce some other actors in the context diagram: *measurement actors*. These actors are used to obtain statistical information of the behavior in the model of the other actors. So these measurement actors only consume tokens from the other actors and they have no influence on their behavior. Often a systems engineer has a "library" of measurement actors at his disposal with which he can collect information on the actors he studies. Note that the measurement actors only play a role in the model and not in the real system.

Summarizing, we may find the following actors in a context diagram:

- the target system,
- the information system,
- context actors,
- measurement actors.

In the next modeling steps the target system and the information system are further decomposed. It is sensible to start with the target system, because the information system has to fit it. If the information system is our focus point, we do not model the target system in much detail. It is difficult to give a general rule how far to go. Often we encounter actors that we are not able to describe completely. For instance, we may have to model human beings. This is, at least for systems engineers, an impossible task. Human beings may also be part of the information system if we decompose it. This kind of actor is not further decomposed. We regard such actors as *black boxes* and call them also context actors. So if we need their external behavior we replace them by simple actors with behaviors at least as "rich" as those of the black-box actors.

In general it is not wise to have many levels of decomposition because this makes a system difficult to understand. Ten levels seems to be a maximum while two to five levels seems to be "normal". There is also a guideline for the size of the network into which we decompose an actor: this should not contain more than ten actors, while five is a good size. (Combining these two limits would imply that models with a few hundred processors are "normal" and that models should never include more than $10^{10}$!) Making a model is more an *art* than a science, there are no "hard" techniques. Some guidelines for doing the decomposition are the following.

- If modeling an existing system, use the functional decomposition that is already there in the real system, for instance the partitioning into departments, business units or task forces.
- If the system is delivering various different products or services, follow their path through the system to find tasks that can be performed by a single actor.
- Do not consider the task of an actor in detail, but only its input-output behavior; draw a "boundary line" and see what kind of tokens are passing the line.
- Let the task of an actor be easy to understand and to describe in natural language. If the task is too complex it might be divided into several tasks, in this case the so-called *cohesion* of the actor was too low.

– Avoid too many connections between two actors, which is called *coupling*. If there are many connections the partitioning of tasks over the actors could probably be improved.
– Often it is useful to work bottom-up: first make a detailed model and then cluster actors into higher-level actors.

When we are refining actors we often discover that we have made errors at higher levels in the actor model, mostly because we have forgotten some communication between actors or because we have considered different types of tokens as one type. This is not a problem although systems engineers hate to modify diagrams that are already made. However, it is very important to keep diagrams consistent, which is often called *balanced* and which means that the diagrams together form one hierarchical net model.

At a certain point the actors become *elementary*, which means that they are processors and will not be decomposed further. A good check to see whether an actor can be considered as elementary is that it should operate in a *memoryless* way and should be able to perform its operation(s) in one event. Hence the tokens it will produce may only depend on the tokens consumed, and we must be able to consider its operation as one transition of the system. Note that it is often possible to consider the stepwise processing of a task as one event. For instance, the execution of a computer program can be described as the evaluation of one function application. In a functional model it is sufficient to represent such a program by one processor. If we want to make a construction model it is necessary to model a program by a processor network in which the processors correspond to elementary program constructs. In actor modeling we do not determine the types of tokens and the functionality of processors in detail, we specify only the processor characteristics. If a processor relation is total and complete (i.e. input and output complete) the actor behaves as a classical Petri net (*see* chapter 5) if we discard the values of the tokens. So, even without completing our model we are able to do some analysis. In many cases it is possible to model systems as classical Petri nets, but these networks become very large and confusing. So we should avoid refining too far and stop at a level where we discover memoryless actors that perform operations in one event.

For the two examples we considered above, we will give a decomposition to the processor level. For each processor we will determine the processor characteristics.

First, we consider the order processing example. In figure 14.5 we show the decomposition of the sales actor. Here we see processors only, so we are already at the lowest level of decomposition. The processor *infoservice* answers questions $a$ of customers by sending them an offer $b$. The processor *ordering* consumes orders $c$ and produces a delivery order $g$ for the distribution department, a confirmation

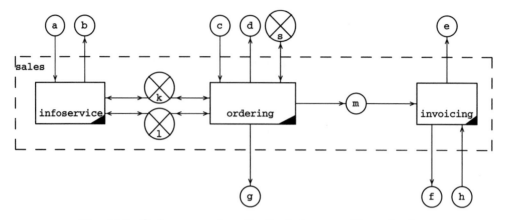

Fig. 14.5. Order processing: the final decomposition of *sales*.

*d* for the customer and the necessary data for delivery and invoicing. This is an information object sent to place *m*. The processor *ordering* also uses the inventory information *s* (which is shared with the distribution department), the customer information in store *l* and the price list in store *k*. In fact *ordering* is updating *s* and *l* as well as retrieving information from them. The processor *invoicing* is triggered by a delivery notice *h* from the distribution department saying when the ordered products will be delivered. It selects the correct order-information object from *m* in the same event. So *invoicing* will not be total, since it is only able to process combinations of tokens from *h* and *m* for which the order identifications match. Note that the distribution department may have very little information about the order, for instance it may not know the prices for which the products are delivered or who is paying for them. The processor *invoicing* also produces a booking for the finance department. All processors are complete; *invoicing* is functional and *infoservice* too. However, *ordering* may be non-deterministic and therefore non-functional. This is the case if there is some flexibility in the determination of volume reductions.

This is our functional model of the sales department. Note that it is not known yet whether persons play a role in this system. For instance, if the communication with the context actors is realized by means of *electronic data interchange* there is no need for persons. However, in today's practice persons will be involved. Each processor is perhaps realized by several persons or all the processors by one person. Here we are only interested in a functional model. If we consider a construction model of this system it should be consistent with this functional model. Note that there are several ways to decompose the higher level of the actor model. The decomposition is adding information. The original informal

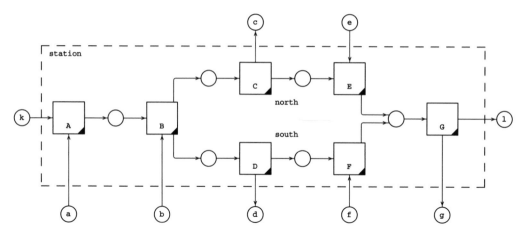

Fig. 14.6. Railroad station, functional model of the actor *station*.

description of the system was not detailed enough to validate the model. The model merely describes the system as it appears to the systems engineer. Finally we remark that this model is far from complete, for instance there are no facilities modeled for updating the price list.

Now we will look again at the railroad station. In figure 14.6 we give a functional model of the target system, the station. Here we see that the signals $(A, E, F)$, switch $(B)$ and sensors $(C, D, G)$ are modeled as processors. The join $H$ appears as a place, the input place of $G$. As we have seen in figure 14.4 the places $a$ through $g$ model the exchange of information between station and train control. Of these places, only place $b$ has a type that has at least two values, namely the strings "north" and "south", while the values of the others are not relevant (only the fact that there is a token is relevant here). The other places are used by trains. So their type is "train". Note that the processors consume or produce physical objects as well as information objects. This often occurs in models, because transformations or translations of physical objects require information. The switch processor $B$ will use the value of the token of $b$ to determine whether the switch should go to the north track or to the south track. Only processor $B$ has incomplete output: it allows a train to go to only one of the tracks. Furthermore $B$ is total, input complete and functional. All other processors are very simple here: they have all the processor characteristics, and their function is the identity function for all the places of the train-type, so they reproduce the train they consume. In the initial state there are tokens only in $k$.

Next we consider the functional model of the information system for the target system: the train control, *see* figure 14.7. This model looks very similar to the

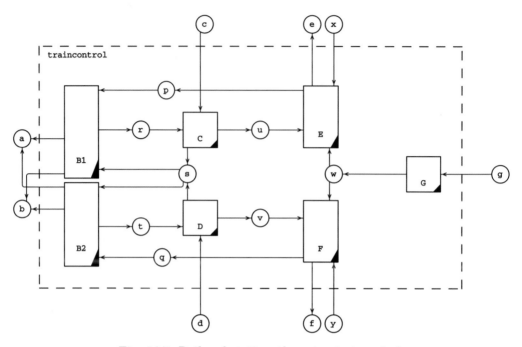

Fig. 14.7. Railroad station, the actor *traincontrol*.

model of the target system! Places with the same labels in figure 14.6 and in figure 14.7 are supposed to be the same.

This is often the case: the information system should maintain all relevant details of the state of the target system, so from the state of the information system we should be able to derive the state of the target system.

Now we will study the model of figure 14.7 in more detail. The names of the processors in the model correspond to the names of the processors in the model of the target system. Only processor $B$ of the target system, the switch, is divided into two processors here: $B_1$ and $B_2$. This is not necessary but makes it possible to model the information system as a classical Petri net: all processors satisfy the three properties and all token values are irrelevant except for the tokens produced by $B_1$ and $B_2$ that give their token the value "north" and "south" respectively. (This can be done in many cases.) The figure also shows the places for the exchange of information objects with the target system. Places $x$ and $y$ are used by the station master, so they have to be connected to a context actor representing this person. Places $p$ and $q$ are used for *feedback* so that if processor $E$ has fired, processor $B_1$ can be enabled again to allow a train onto the north track.

We assume that in the initial state there are tokens in $s$, $p$, $q$, $w$ and $k$ only.

In $k$ their number is arbitrary and in each of the other places there is one. This means that $B_1$ and $B_2$ are enabled and that there are no trains in the station. It is decided by the demon which track will be opened for a new train, i.e. whether $B_1$ or $B_2$ will fire. It is easy to modify the model in such a way that the station master can make this decision. (This is an exercise.)

It is easy to see that the amount of tokens in the places $p$, $r$ and $u$ together is equal to one in any reachable state. The same applies to $t$, $v$ and $q$. Such a property is called an *invariant*, to be precise a *place invariant*.

If there is a token in $p$ then the north track is free and if there is a token in $r$ then a train is entering the north track and has not yet passed the switch completely (i.e. the train has passed sensor $C$). If there is a token in $u$ this means that there is a train at the north platform and switch $B$ can be used by a train that goes to the south track. In this case the invariants are easy to verify. In part IV we will meet a method to find and prove their validity. Another invariant is that places $r$, $s$ and $t$ have exactly one token in total (if the initial state has this property), which means that at most one of the processors $B_1$ and $B_2$ is enabled in each event. If there is a token in $r$ then the switch is open for a train to go into the north track and only after this train passes the sensor $C$ will there again be a token in $s$; this allows the switch to be set to the south track (if this track is free, which is indicated by the existence of a token in $q$). Note that $B_1$ and $B_2$ enable the switch and the signal $A$ in the same event, which will occur if it is safe to enter the station.

The station master may decide which train will leave the station first by putting a token in $x$ or $y$. If he erroneously puts a token both in $x$ and $y$ no harm has been done: there is at most one token in $w$, so the signals $E$ and $F$ cannot both fire. Furthermore, $E$ and $F$ are only enabled if sensor $G$ has given a signal that the preceding train has passed the intersection, i.e. switch $H$. To prove that the whole system works correctly requires more argument; we give it in part IV. However, it is easy to simulate the system informally to get a feeling for it and to detect mistakes.

Note that there are other ways to represent the state of the target system, for instance with one store containing one complex object, as in figure 14.8. Here the store $i$ represents the contents of the places $p$, $r$, $u$, $w$, $t$, $v$, $q$ and $s$ of figure 14.7. The processors $P$, $Q$, $R$, $S$ and $T$ of figure 14.8 are triggered only by external places, i.e. by the sensors of the railroad or by the station master. Although this actor model is much simpler than the one displayed in figure 14.7, the processors are more complicated here, and the verification of correctness more difficult.

In the examples so far we have not considered the timing of tokens. In many cases this aspect is also important at an early stage. For instance, there could be

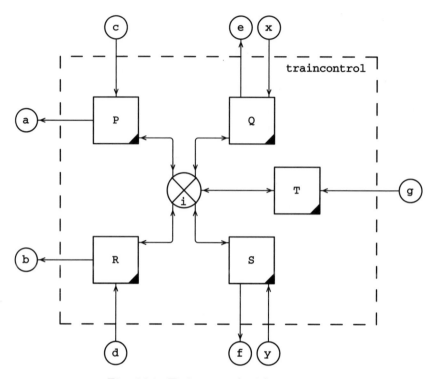

Fig. 14.8. Train control with a store.

an actor representing a clock, which creates *triggers* (tokens) for processors that have to be activated at particular times. In general it is undesirable for the time aspects of the tokens to play an essential role in an information system, i.e. for the functionality of an information system to depend on the processing speed of its components, although in real-time systems this is sometimes the case. There is a trend towards designing information systems that are *delay insensitive*, which means that their functionality is independent of processing speed.

We conclude with some more guidelines.

– Give actors a name that reflects *action*, for instance: "updating" or "painting", and give places names representing a passive state, for instance "waiting for shipment".

– If there is only one connection from a place to an actor, we may use the name of the place for the connector.

– It makes sense to give actors a number in such a way that their descent can be traced.

– It is always important to have an informal description of a model in every stage of development and this description should be updated after further refinement or formalization; always list the assumptions made.

- Check whether in a model every place has at least one input and one output actor; if not, this place might become empty or the number of tokens in it might have unlimited growth, which is seldom what we want.
- Check whether actors have input and output connectors; if not, these are probably context actors.
- In refining a model only use stores that are shared by more than one actor. On the lowest level, however, where we have only processors, we use stores that are private for one processor.
- Try to make simple couplings between actors, so that the knowledge one actor has to have of another with which it communicates is a minimum.
- Make, as far as possible, *reusable* actors, by keeping interfaces simple and using polymorphic functions and type variables in the specifications of places and processors (*see* chapter 6).

## 14.2 Characteristic modeling problems

We will now consider several problems that occur in many modeling situations. We will illustrate these problems, as far as possible with the two examples given above.

### 1. The roles of objects and actors

Objects or tokens can play different roles in a model. They may represent

**physical objects,** such as trains,

**clusters** of physical objects, such as cars in a garage,

**messages,** such as order confirmations,

**databases,** i.e. a complex object that represents (a part of) the state of a system such as a customer file. Often these objects reside in a store, but not necessarily,

**stage indicators** that represent the stage or state of some "entity", such as the objects (tokens) in the places of the train control system (*see* figure 14.7). In these cases the places may contain at most one token and its type is irrelevant,

**signals** such as those exchanged by the station and the train control system; here, only the processors $B_1$ and $B_2$ produce messages and all other interface places contain signals. A signal is like a stage indicator: its value is irrelevant but there may be several signals in one place.

The role of actors and processors, in particular, is one of the following:

**complete systems** that consume and produce tokens, with or without memory
and *self-triggering* (self-triggering means that the processors produce their
own input tokens); in particular human beings can be modeled as actors;

**transformers** or **transporters** of tokens;

**markers of activities** in networks where places represent stages and tokens
represent stage indicators.

It is important to indicate in an early stage of the development of a model what
the role of an actor, a token (type) or the place it resides is. This may determine
properties of the actor model that can be verified at later stages in the development.

## 2. Modeling an entity as a token or as an actor

Often we have the choice of modeling a real-world entity as a token or as an actor.
We start with an example.

In a production system it is quite natural to model the products as tokens,
but for resources this is not so clear. Consider for instance a simple production
system in which a product is taken in one production step from raw material to
the final product by one machine, as illustrated in figure 14.9. Here $A$ denotes a
context actor that produces raw material and $C$ a context actor that consumes
final products, while $B$ represents the machine. It is clear that the quantities of
raw material needed for one product are modeled as tokens and so also are the
products. The machine is a single processor here. A disadvantage of modeling
machines as actors is that the model is vulnerable to changes in the number of
machines, as we saw in the order processing example above in respect of the
modeling of customers. Consider the same production system but with three
machines instead of one; this is displayed in figure 14.10. In figure 14.11 we have
a model with arbitrarily many machines. Note that $B$ now represents a *machine
operation* instead of a machine. The machines reside in place $q$; now they are
tokens too. This model is only of interest if the manufacturing of products takes
time since otherwise there is not much difference between this model and the first
one.

Now we modify the problem a little: we assume that there are two types of
operations, $B$ and $E$, and that the production process requires the use of first a
machine of type $B$, then one of type $E$ and finally one of type $B$ again. We can
model this in two ways: there is still only one actor for each machine operation
(*see* figure 14.12) or there is an actor for each step in the production process (*see*
figure 14.13). In the model of figure 14.12 processors $B$ and $E$ decide whether
the produced token is ready or whether it needs another production step. So, the
tokens should contain this information. In the model of figure 14.13 the tokens

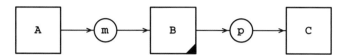

Fig. 14.9. A simple production system.

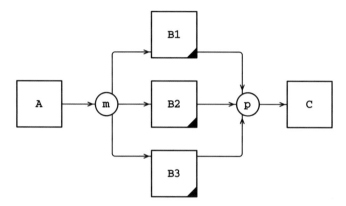

Fig. 14.10. The same production system with three machines.

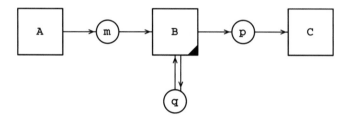

Fig. 14.11. The same production system with arbitrarily many machines.

do not need to contain any processing information at all. Note that, in these models, places $q_1$ and $q_2$ represent the machines of type $B$ and $E$ respectively. There is always a trade-off between a complex network with simple object types and simple processor relations for processors, and a simple network with complex object types and complex processor relations.

The construction presented here can be applied in general. If a processor represents an entity that operates on objects, then we can modify the model so that the processor becomes the *activity* of the entity instead of the resource itself. Then we have to add a place which is connected bidirectionally to the processor and which contains a token that represents the entity. If we do this systematically, we obtain a model in which all entities that live for a time period are represented

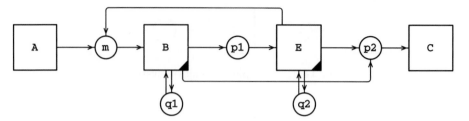

Fig. 14.12. One processor per machine operation.

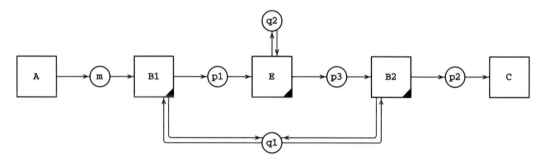

Fig. 14.13. One processor per type of production step.

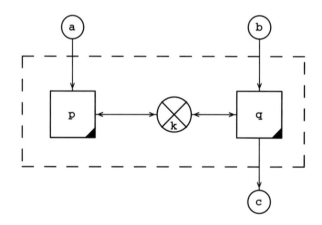

Fig. 14.14. File maintenance with a store.

as tokens and all processors represent instantaneous activities.

## 3. Modeling a file as one token or as a set of tokens

Consider a file of items; this can be used to represent a warehouse containing one type of physical object. We can model this file as a place containing a token for

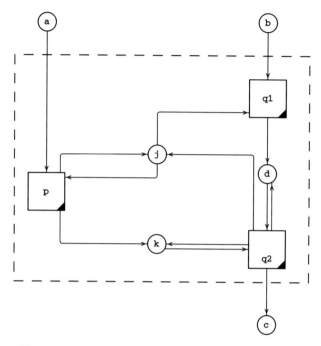

Fig. 14.15. File maintenance without a store (1).

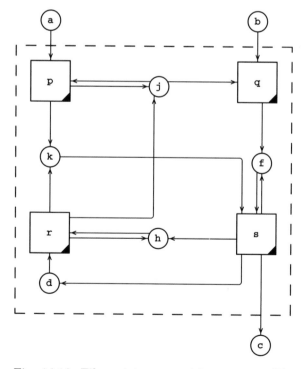

Fig. 14.16. File maintenance without a store (2).

every item in the file, or a store with one complex object representing the whole file. Often we need to inspect all the items in the file and this is quite difficult because processors have no means of checking whether a place is empty or not.

In figure 14.14 we see a simple file-management system. Processor $p$ adds a token of type $\mathbb{N}$ from place $a$ to the file stored as one token in store $k$. The type of this store is $\mathbb{N}^*$. Processor $q$ inspects this store and computes the sum of the values of the items, whenever it receives a signal in place $b$. The processor relation for both processors is quite easy.

However, if we want to avoid the use of a store to model the file, we may replace the store by a channel where each "stored" item is modeled by a token. Using preconditions we may select the right token for an operation. However, if we want to perform an operation on *all* items, we need a more complicated solution, such as that displayed in figure 14.15. We assume that each query token in $b$ has as value some unique number $Q$. Store $k$ has been replaced by a place $k$ containing a token for each "stored" item. Place $j$ has a token in the initial state with a value indicating the number of items in the file (i.e. tokens in place $k$). Each token in $k$ has a value that represents the stored item and the stage in the inspection process ("inspected by query $Q$", where $Q$ denotes the last query in progress). Processor $q_1$ consumes a token from place $b$ and the token from $j$ and produces a token for $d$. The value of the token in $d$ is a vector $(m, n, o, z)$, where $m$ denotes the total amount of items, $n$ the amount of items already inspected, $o$ their sum and $z$ the query identification ($Q$). Then processor $q_2$ consumes all tokens from place $k$ and puts them back with status changed into "inspected by query $Q$". When all tokens have been treated the answer is produced at place $c$ and the token for place $j$ is restored.

If we do not want to add processing information to the "stored" items we need an even more complicated solution such as that displayed in figure 14.16. Again place $k$ contains the file in the initial state as individual tokens, one for each item. Also, place $j$ has a token in the initial state with a value indicating the number of items in the file. No other place has a token in the initial state. Processors $p$ and $q$ are complete, while $s$ and $r$ are only input complete. All processors are total and functional. As long as no request appears in place $b$, processor $p$ may add items to $k$, while updating the token in $j$. When a request arrives in $b$ a rather complex process is started. First the token in $j$ is transferred to $f$ and then processor $s$ transfers all items from $k$ to $d$, while inspecting their values and adding these values to the token in $f$. The value of the token in $f$ is a vector $(m, n, o)$, where $m$ is total amount of items, $n$ the number of items seen so far and $o$ their sum. As soon as the items are counted, i.e. $m$ equals $n$, processor $s$ produces the accumulated file value in place $c$ and puts a token in place $h$ with the number of items in the file as the value (which is known from $f$). Further, it does not return the token that was in $f$ as was done in the preceding firings. Now processor $r$ starts and carries out a process similar to $s$: it returns the items to place $e$, while counting the items seen so far, and ends with the return of a token to place $j$.

This example shows that it is very convenient to use a store to represent a file and that rather complicated constructions are needed otherwise.

## 4. Knowledge in a processor or a store

The processor relation of a processor often uses constants, such as a number or a finite binary relation. Consider for example a processor that produces the amount of taxes to be paid when an income tax return is "consumed". The tax table will be used. The question is, should we put this tax table in the processor specification or should we define a store from which the processor reads the table? If there will be no updates of the tax table it makes sense to put the table in the processor specification, because it simplifies the actor model. However, if updates of the tax table are possible we have to introduce a store and also an actor (maybe a context actor) that updates the store. It is useful to check whether stores in an actor model are updated or not. If not there is probably something wrong: either the updating actor is missing or the store could be incorporated in all the processors that are using the constant. Note that in practice very few constants occur; in most cases the "constants" turn out to be variables. However, we may consider them as constants: changing them would then be understood as a change of the system, which is a *second-order dynamics*.

## 5. Direct addressing or broadcasting

We try to make models that are as modular as possible in order to be able to *reuse* parts of them for other models or to be able to adapt a model easily. Therefore actors have connectors that can be attached to places in a later stage without changing the actor itself. If we have an actor that sends messages to other actors, in fact to their input places, then we have to know precisely which actors will get messages, in order to specify the connectors of the sending actor. This might be cumbersome because we do not know the number of addressees yet, or the number might change in the future. This solution is called *direct addressing*.

A better solution is to send all the messages to one place (so we just need one output connector in the actor) and let the receiving actors consume only messages that are addressed to them. Of course this requires the use of a precondition in the receiving actors. This solution is called *broadcasting*. The messages have to

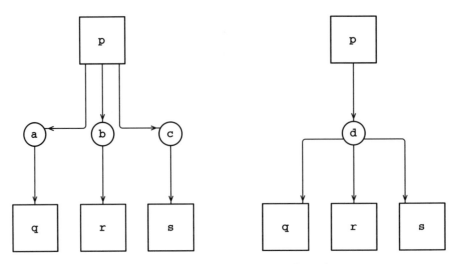

Fig. 14.17. Direct addressing versus broadcasting.

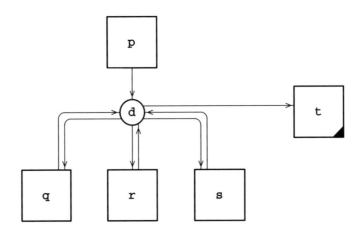

Fig. 14.18. "Real" broadcasting.

carry an address and each receiving actor has to know its own address, which is not the case if we use direct addressing.

In figure 14.17 the two cases are displayed: on the left, direct addressing; on the right, broadcasting. Actor $p$ is the sender and $q$, $r$ and $s$ are the receivers.

In the second, right-hand, solution the sender still has to know all the addressees. If we want a more realistic model of broadcasting the sender should not have to know the addressees nor their number. There are two possible solutions to this problem: either add an actor between the sender and receivers that performs the addressing task (i.e. split $p$), or use a solution like the one displayed in

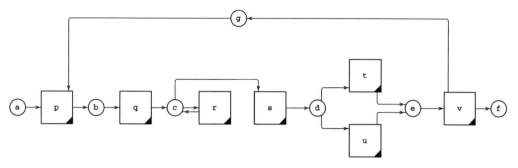

Fig. 14.19. A sequential process.

figure 14.18. In figure 14.18 a message in $d$ is "read" (consumed) by a receiver and then put back. Each receiver has a precondition saying that he should not read the same message twice: for this the type of $d$ is now enhanced with a set indicating which receivers have already read the message. Initially this set is empty. When the size of this set is equal to the number of receivers, the message is discarded by a special processor $t$.

## 6. Sequential processes

A *sequential process*, like the execution of a computer program or a production process in a factory, can be modeled as a network in which every processor represents a processing step and every place a stage in the process. A characteristic of these networks is that every processor (except for the first and the last) has exactly one input place and one output place. (This is the property of a *state machine net*, a kind of actor discussed later.) One of the characteristic features of an actor model representing a sequential process is the fact that the total number of tokens in the network is constant and equal to the number of processes that might be active simultaneously. This number is equal to the number of resources that can work simultaneously. (In traditional computer systems this number is equal to one.) In figure 14.19 a sequential process is displayed. We may interpret this example as a computer program with the well-known constructs *selection*, *iteration* and *assignment*. In fact we may consider this actor model to be a *flow chart*. (Although flow charts are not used in software engineering any more, they still are used in other engineering disciplines.) Processor $p$ represents the buffer control of the process: only if places $a$ and $g$ have a token may it fire. The tokens in $g$ denote the number of free resources that may perform a sequential process. Processors $r$ and $s$ represent an *iteration*. They have preconditions to determine whether the iteration is complete. So only one of them will be enabled to consume the token in place $c$. Processors $t$ and $u$ form a selection. Their

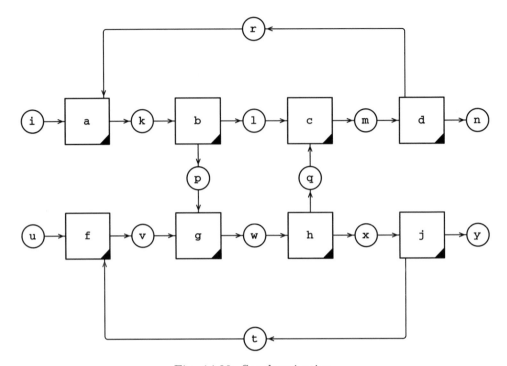

Fig. 14.20. Synchronization.

preconditions form the *if then else* construct. Processor $q$ represents an assignment. All processors are complete and functional. Processors $p$, $q$ and $v$ are
total. Processor $v$ marks the end of the process and returns the resource to place
$g$ to allow processor $p$ to start a new job. So the process itself is the network between processors $p$ and $v$. In the initial state there are only tokens in $g$. We may
replace all processors except for $p$ and $v$ by an actor that satisfies the property
that it has exactly one input and one output connector and that it will produce
one token if and only if it has consumed one token.

Sequential processes can be used to model *object life cycles* in the object oriented modeling approach. Then there is for each complex class one sequential
process. They can also be used to model *transaction processing*: for instance in
a database system each transaction can be considered as an object having a life
cycle.

### 7. Synchronization
Here we consider two sequential processes that may communicate. If one process
needs the processing of another it will send its "job" to the other process and
wait until it returns. This is called the *synchronization* of sequential processes.

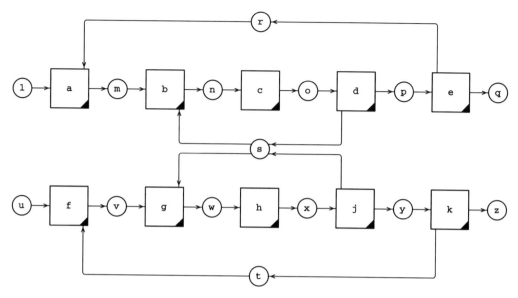

Fig. 14.21. Mutual exclusion.

In figure 14.20 we see two sequential processes. All processors are complete and total. In the first process actor $b$ produces a token that needs further processing in the second process, which is also a sequential process. Processor $g$ of this process waits until the token to be processed arrives in place $p$ and the result is delivered to place $q$ by processor $h$. The first process waits; this is expressed by the completeness of processor $c$. Since the two sequential processes have almost the same structure, we can give a similar description for the second process. Note that processors $b$, $c$, $g$ and $h$ each have exactly one input and output place within their sequential processes.

## 8. Mutual exclusion
Mutual exclusion is a frequently occurring form of communication of processes, which share a resource that can be used by only one processor in one event. In the train control system (*see* figure 14.7), we already find such a situation: the token in place $s$ represents the lever of switch $B$, which can be set to the north or the south track but not to both in the same event. Another form of mutual exclusion is the use of a store by two processors: only one of them can use it in one event or during a given time period. Here the network takes care of the problem!

A more general case of mutual exclusion is displayed in figure 14.21. All processors are complete and total in this example. In the initial state there are tokens

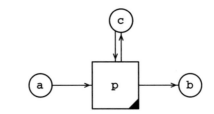

Fig. 14.22. Modeling processing time (1).

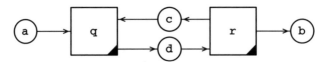

Fig. 14.23. Modeling processing time (2).

in $r$, $t$ and $s$ only. Here both sequential processes need the (single) token in place $s$. Processors $b$ and $g$ are waiting for this token and $d$ or $j$ returns it after $c$ or $h$ has used it. Note there is no guarantee that a system that needs the resource will get it: the other system might always take it just before the first system takes it. Using the time mechanism it is easy to obtain *fairness*, i.e. to guarantee that every request is satisfied. We have to require only that the tokens produced for $r$ and $t$ get a positive delay and that the resource has no delay in place $s$.

## 9. Processing time and time-out

We have already seen in part I how we may represent the fact that processors need time to perform their operations. In figures 14.22 and 14.23 we show two constructions. In the first one processor $p$ produces a token for place $b$ and gives it a delay $t$ which is equal to the delay of the produced token for place $b$. This delay represents the processing time. Although the token in $b$ is immediately there, it is only available to other processors after the delay. In the second solution (figure 14.23) we see two processors $q$ and $r$. The firing of $q$ represents the start of the processing and the firing of $r$ the end of it. In this solution only the token in place $d$ is given a delay equal to the processing time.

The processing time can be used to solve a problem that we encountered before: when we modeled a file as a set of tokens, we found that it was impossible to test whether a place was empty. So we had to use another solution to see if we had inspected all tokens (*see* page 148 where we "stored" the number of tokens in a separate place). With a *time-out* construction it is possible to determine whether

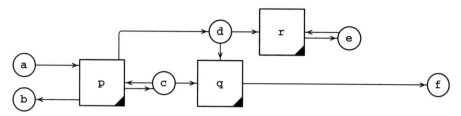

Fig. 14.24. Inspecting a place using a time-out.

a place is empty or not without counting the number of tokens in the place. A time-out is a way to decide whether a processor is enabled to fire, based on the time that has passed since its last firing. In figure 14.24 we consider a part of the file maintenance problem. All processors are total, functional and complete. The delays the processors give to their output are as follows: the tokens in $c$ and $e$ are delayed three time units, by processors $p$ and $r$ respectively, and the tokens in $d$ are four time units behind. Channel $a$ contains the file with items and after inspection the items are put into place $b$. The intermediate result of the inspection of the file is put into place $c$ by processor $p$ and the final result, if the whole file is inspected, is put into place $f$ by processor $q$. The initial state of this system is important: in $a$ is the file, in $c$ there is a token with delay zero, in $d$ there is a token with delay one, in $e$ there is a token with delay two and the other places are empty. Then, as will be proved below, processor $p$ inspects an item every three time units, and processor $q$ cannot take the token from place $c$ before place $a$ is empty because this token is "stolen" by processor $p$ before $q$ is enabled.

To verify this statement, we show by induction the existence of tokens in places $c$, $d$ and $e$ that become available at time points $3k$, $3k + 1$ and $3k + 2$ for $k \in \{0, 1, 2, ...\}$ respectively, as long as place $a$ is not empty. For $k = 0$ this is guaranteed by the initial state. Suppose the statement is true for $k$. Then processor $p$ will fire at $3k$ and it will produce tokens for $c$ and $d$ that are available at $3(k+1)$ and $3(k+1)+1$ respectively. Note that there is still a token in $d$ that is available at $3k + 1$. At $3k + 2$ processor $r$ is enabled because of the token in $e$; it will consume the token in $d$ and reproduce a token for place $e$ that is available at $3(k + 1) + 2$. Now there is again only one token in $d$. So the statement holds for $k + 1$. Only if processor $p$ consumes the last token from $a$, say at time $3k$, will processor $q$ then be enabled at $3k + 4$, because there is a token available in $c$ at $3k + 3$ and in $d$ at $3k + 4$, while processor $r$ has to wait until $3k + 5$ to be enabled. So if $q$ is enabled we know that $a$ is empty, because the time has expired for processor $p$.

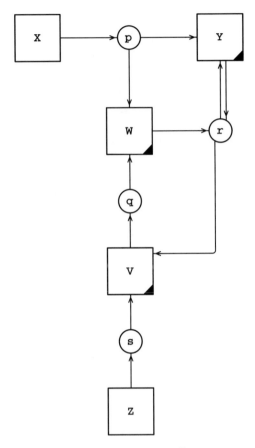

Fig. 14.25. Token cancellation.

This example shows how powerful the time mechanism is, but one should be careful with it because the realization of systems when the functionality of the model is using time aspects is difficult: systems become real-time systems!

## 10. Token cancellation

Sometimes the following situation occurs: a token with a delay is put into a place by some actor $X$ to be consumed by some processor $Y$ and before the delay has expired another actor $Z$ wants to prevent the token from being consumed by $Y$. So $Z$ sends a *cancellation* token that should activate some other processors to consume the token. However, these processors are of course not able to consume the token before the delay has expired. In figure 14.25 a solution is displayed. We have introduced two extra processors $V$ and $W$ and some extra places $q$, $r$

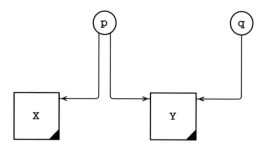

Fig. 14.26. Token selection.

and $s$. As soon as $Z$ puts a token in $s$, processor $V$ consumes the (only) token from $r$ and puts a token in $q$. Now $Y$ is not able to execute because there is no token in $r$. (We assume that all processors are complete.) As soon as the delay of the token in $p$ expires, $W$ consumes the token in $p$ and $W$ resets the system by putting a token in $r$. (So in the initial state there is one token in $r$ and tokens in $r$ have no delay.) Note that we have had to modify processor $Y$ by connecting it to $r$; it is easy, though, to modify the model and thus avoid modification of $Y$.

The above construction only works for cases where $Z$ wants to cancel an arbitrary token in $p$. If $Z$ is more selective in the sense that it will only cancel a token in $p$ with a particular value, then the construction has to be adapted. (This is an exercise.)

## 11. Priority in token selection

Consider the situation displayed in figure 14.26. If there is one token in $p$ and one in $q$ such that the time stamp of the token in $p$ is greater than that of the token in $q$, then the demon will decide whether $X$ or $Y$ will execute. If we want to give $Y$ priority over $X$, we can modify the model as displayed in figure 14.27. All processors are complete. In the initial state there is one token in $r$. As soon as the token in $q$ is available, $Z$ will consume it, together with the token in $r$. So $X$ is not enabled if the token arrives in $p$. Processor $Z$ also duplicates the token in $q$ by placing an a token with identical value in $s$. Now $Y$ is enabled and after its execution there is again a token in $r$ so that the system returns to its initial state. Note that if the tokens in $p$ and $q$ arrive at exactly the same time the demon still decides between executing $X$ or $Y$. (It is easy to modify the model in such a way that $X$ and $Y$ do not themselves have to be modified.)

## 12. Continuous processes

Sometimes we want to model a process that is typically continuous. In part I we

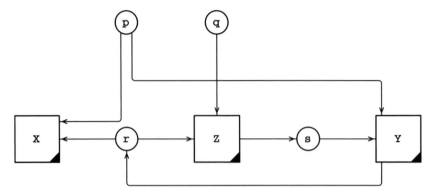

Fig. 14.27. Priority in selection.

said that we would restrict ourselves to discrete systems; however, we are able to model certain continuous systems as well. Consider for example the chemical process displayed in figure 14.28, which shows the production of salt from $NaOH$ and $HCl$. We have modeled each reservoir by a store; the value of the token in the store represents the amount of chemical in that reservoir. All processors are using self-triggering and the tokens in the self-triggering tokens have delays that represent the time necessary for the chemical reactions to take place. In figure 14.29 an arbitrary continuous process is displayed. Stores $a$ and $b$ contain the raw material that is transformed into the required material in $c$. Note that we cannot see the direction of the process in the diagram because we use stores. Let us consider the processor relation of processor $p$. Suppose a fraction $\alpha$ of a unit of $c$ is made of the material of $a$; thus a fraction $1 - \alpha$ of a unit of $c$ is made of the material of $b$. Further, suppose that the processing time for a unit of $c$ is $\beta$ time units. Then the processor relation satisfies the following equations:

$$
\begin{aligned}
h &= min\left\{\frac{a}{\alpha}, \frac{b}{1-\alpha}\right\}, \\
c' &= c + h, \\
a' &= a - \alpha \times h, \\
b' &= b - (1-\alpha) \times h, \\
delay(d) &= \beta \times h.
\end{aligned}
$$

Note that $h$ is the maximal amount of $c$ that can be produced and that we may break up the process into more steps by not producing the maximal amount of the token in $c$.

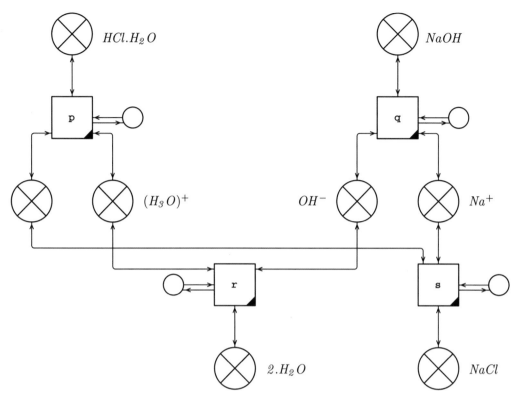

Fig. 14.28. A continuous process: salt production.

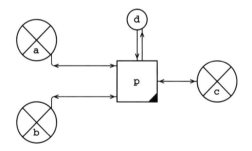

Fig. 14.29. An arbitrary continuous process.

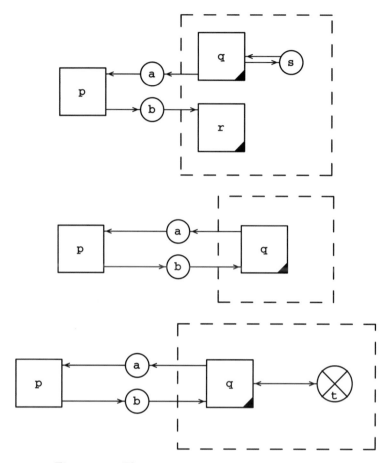

Fig. 14.30. Three ways to model an environment.

## 13. Communication with an environment

As we have remarked before, we have to replace the environment of a (model of a) system by approximations to the context actors in order to be able to simulate the behavior of the system. These approximations to the context actors should have a behavior that is at least as "rich" or varied as the behavior of the real environment in order to be able to test the system. There are in principal three different ways to model the context actors as displayed in the **three** cases of figure 14.30:

   (i) without feed back as displayed in the first case,
  (ii) with memoryless feed back, as in the second case,
 (iii) feed back with memory, as in the third case.

In all three cases $p$ represents the system for which we have to create an environment. The processors $q$ and $r$ are both total and complete. In the initial states we assume tokens in places $a$ and $s$ only.

In the first case processor $r$ simply consumes the output of the system and processor $q$ produces input without any reference to the output of $p$. Note that $q$ fires because of self-triggering via place $s$. In $s$ there may be one or more tokens, and $q$ produces a new one in every firing. A slight variation of this solution is one in which processor $q$ does not produce tokens for $s$. In that case the environment at some point in time stops producing new input. This case can also be modeled by putting all the input tokens in place $a$ at the outset with an appropriate time stamp.

In the second case we see that the environment only produces input after it has received output from the system: the communication follows a simple protocol. In this case the new input may depend on the last output but not on the history of outputs of the system.

In the third case the new input is allowed to depend on the whole history of the output of system $p$. Note that the third solution has a store $t$, which may of course be changed into a place as in the first case. However, in the first case we may not replace place $s$ by a store since we do not want processors to be triggered by stores.

## 14.3 Structured networks

The actor framework describes a very large class of models. It is useful to distinguish *types* of actor models, i.e. subsets of the set of all actor models having some common properties. Such a division into types may be based on:

**class model** An important type here is formed by the *valueless actor models*; these actor models only have one object class, which contains only one object.

**delay structure** An important type here is formed by the *timeless actor models*; in these actor models the tokens in the initial state have a time stamp equal to zero and all delays assigned by processors are zero too.

**processor characteristics** An important type here is that in which all processors are complete, total and functional.

**network structure** Here the division into types is based on the structure of the graph only; there are several important types having different graph structures.

**state structure** Here the division into types is based on the maximum number of tokens per place.

We will now describe several types of actor model and we will consider transformations of actor models belonging to one type into another type.

The first type we will consider is the *classical Petri net* type of model (they are also called *place/transition nets*). We recall that a classical Petri net is a *timeless* and *valueless* actor model, i.e. all tokens have time stamp zero and there is only one complex class with only one complex in it. Furthermore all processors are complete and total. Note that for valueless actor models the functionality of the processor relation is not important. For this type of actor model elegant and useful analysis techniques are available, as studied later; we give here some intuitive ideas about some of these properties. However, the expressive power and comfort are very small. Nevertheless, it is sometimes possible to transform actor models where tokens have values to classical Petri nets, which allows analysis of these actor models by the techniques for classical Petri nets. The intersections of the actor model types we define below and classical Petri nets are well-documented in the literature. They have interesting behavioral properties.

The definition of an actor model is given in part II. Here we only need to know that $L$ denotes the set of places, $P$ is the set of processors, $I(p)$ is the set of input connectors of processor $p$, $O(p)$ is the set of output connectors of processor $p$ and $M_p$ is a function assigning the connectors of $p$ to places. Let $L'$ denote the set of all channels in a flat net model (so $L \backslash L'$ is the set of all stores). We exclude stores from the structural properties, because they do not influence the enabling of processors: they are always available. In order to define properties of actor models we need some definitions. For $p \in P$ the symbol $p\bullet$ is the set of output channels:

$$p\bullet = \{l \in L' \mid \exists x \in O(p) : M_p(x) = l\}$$

and $\bullet p$ is the set of input channels:

$$\bullet p = \{l \in L' \mid \exists x \in I(p) : M_p(x) = l\}.$$

For $l \in L'$ the symbol $l\bullet$ is the set of processors for which $l$ is an input place:

$$l\bullet = \{p \in P \mid \exists x \in I(p) : M_p(x) = l\}$$

and $\bullet l$ is the set of processors for which $l$ is an output place:

$$\bullet l = \{p \in P \mid \exists x \in O(p) : M_p(x) = l\}.$$

The actor models we will consider now are called *free-choice nets*. We assume the processors are total and complete when we are dealing with free-choice nets. A *free-choice net* is an actor model such that

$$\forall p \in P, l \in L' : \#\{x \in I(p) \mid M_p(x) = l\} \leq 1$$

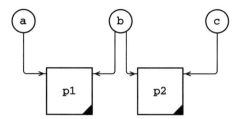

Fig. 14.31. A "non-free-choice" net.

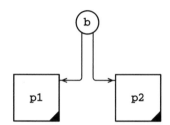

Fig. 14.32. A free-choice net.

and

$$\forall l \in L' : (\#(l\bullet) \leq 1 \vee \forall p \in P : p \in l\bullet \Rightarrow \bullet p = \{l\}).$$

In words, in a free-choice net every processor is connected to an input place by at most one connector and every place is either an input place for only one processor, or it is the input place for more than one processor, but then these processors have only this place as input place.

In figure 14.31 an example of a "non-free-choice" net is displayed. In a free-choice net (which has by definition complete and total processors) the demon is free to choose the processor that will consume a token if there is more than one possibility on the basis of the network. This is not the case in the example of figure 14.31, in which the token in place $b$ cannot be consumed by processor $p_2$ but only by $p_1$, in the state where $a$ and $b$ both have one token and $c$ is empty.

Next we consider three subtypes of free-choice nets: conflict free nets, state machine nets and activity networks.

A *conflict free net* is an actor model satisfying

$$\forall l \in L' : \#(l\bullet) \leq 1.$$

In words, each place is an input place for at most one processor. It is easy to verify that a conflict free net is a free-choice net.

In a conflict free net processors never have to compete for a token: there is no choice about to which processor a token of a place will go. So a useful

property of conflict free nets is that all processors that are enabled at some point
in time may fire at the same time, and if they do not share stores they may even
fire simultaneously. Compare this property with the serializability property (*see*
theorem 11.5): this theorem states that if two or more processors may fire at the
same moment, they may also do this in an arbitrary order. However, for conflict
free nets we do not have to determine which combinations of processors may fire
simultaneously, we just have to find all processors that may fire in isolation at
some moment; we know that they may fire all at that moment! An example of a
conflict free net is a sequential process as studied above.

A *state machine net* is an actor model with the property that

$$\forall p \in P : \#(\bullet p) = \#(p \bullet) = 1.$$

In words, each processor is connected to exactly one input and one output place.
It is easy to prove that a state machine net is a free choice net.

State machine nets can be used to model *finite state machines*. A finite state
machine is a state machine net with an initial state that only has one token and
no stores. All processors are complete and total. Each place represents a state of
the machine and each processor represents a possible transition of the machine to
another state. The token indicates the state in which the machine is. It is easy to
see that in all states of the actor model (not to be confused with the state of the
finite state machine) the number of tokens remains at one if it was so initially.

Finite state machines are often used in theoretical computer science and in
software engineering. In software engineering they are for instance used to specify the functionality of actors, protocols and user interfaces. Since finite state
machines constitute a special type of actor model we may apply our framework
in all cases in which finite state machines are used.

An example of a finite state machine is given in figure 14.33. Note that a state
machine net can be regarded as a graph with one kind of node, namely places,
in which the processors are considered to be edge labels. Here we see an actor
model that "counts" the number of 1's in a binary sequence, i.e. it counts up
to three and if it has counted three 1's it remains in its state, if it gets a 0 it
jumps to its initial state $a$. Channel $a$ denotes the state of the machine after
having seen a 0, $b$ after one 1, $c$ after two 1's and $d$ after three or more 1's. If
a 1 is received processor $p$ fires and the machine will move to state $b$ and if a 0
is received processor $m$ will move the machine to $a$ again. Similarly processors
$q$ and $r$ move the state to places $b$ and $c$ respectively. Processor $n$ moves the
state to place $d$ when a 1 is received. The other processors move the state if
a 0 is received. To understand this model we need a lot of extra information,
such as the process of receiving the binary sequence, which is not displayed in

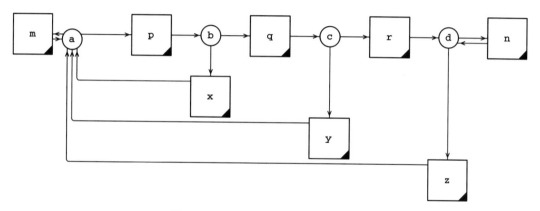

Fig. 14.33. A finite state machine.

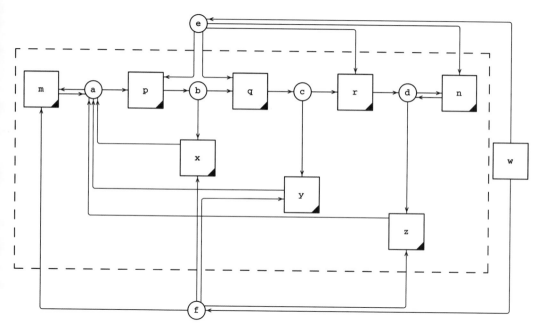

Fig. 14.34. The finite state machine in an environment.

figure 14.33. However, in our framework it is easy to extend the model using an environment to model the extra information. In figure 14.34 the augmented model is displayed. Here places $e$ and $f$ get the 1's and 0's respectively from an actor $w$. The processors $p$, $q$ , $r$ and $n$ consume the 1's while the other processors consume the 0's if they are enabled. We assume that actor $w$ selects the elements of the binary sequence for inspection and that $w$ produces the tokens for $e$ and $f$

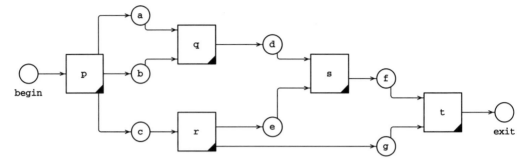

Fig. 14.35. A PERT network.

with a delay larger than the time needed by the finite state machine to perform the transitions.

An *activity network* is an actor model with the property that

$$\forall l \in L' : \#(\bullet l) = \#(l\bullet) = 1.$$

In words, each place is an input place for exactly one processor and an output place for exactly one processor. It is easy to prove that an activity network is a conflict free net.

An activity network is also known under the names *marked graph* or *PERT network*. (PERT is an acronym for Program Evaluation and Review Technique.) The latter name is used only if the network is a-cyclic and if there are extra two places, say *begin* and *exit*, such that $\bullet begin = \emptyset$ and $exit\bullet = \emptyset$. (Formally a PERT network is not an activity network, due to the extra places.) Each processor represents the start or the end of an activity while each place represents the execution of an activity. Activity nets can be used to model *parallel processes* with *precedence constraints*. When we give each token a delay that corresponds to the time an activity takes, the simulation of the model gives us the *earliest* possible completion time of the set of activities, also called the "project". In figure 14.35 an example is displayed. Note that such an activity network can be seen as a graph with processors as nodes and edges labeled with places. In this network the initial state has one token in *begin*. Then processor $p$ marks the start of the activities $a$, $b$ and $c$ in parallel. Only if $a$ and $b$ are complete can processor $q$ start activity $d$. Finally when all activities are complete processor $t$ produces a token for *exit*.

Another important type of actor model, based on the state structure, is called a *bounded net*. These actor models are characterized by properties of the maximal number of tokens per place.

A *k-bounded net* is an actor model where each place has at most $k$ tokens in each state, provided the initial state has this property. A *safe net* is a 1-bounded net.

We have already seen example of safe nets: a state machine net is safe, because there is at most one token in the network; an activity net is also safe. If the number of values the tokens may acquire in a $k$-bounded net is finite, then the number of states is finite too and it will be possible to model the network as a finite state machine.

## 14.4 Net transformations

We will now consider several ways of transforming an actor model into one with another structure.

**Transforming actor models into models with only self-triggering**

Suppose that we have an arbitrary actor model and that we do not want communication by means of places. A reason for this could be that it might be easier to realize a system in which processors inspect memory in their own time without having synchronization problems. Then we can transform such a network into a network with only one place per processor, used exclusively by this processor both as input and output place. The transformation proceeds along the following lines.

(i) Replace each place by a store.
(ii) Give the store a complex class such that tokens of the original place can be clustered into a complex of this class and that the complex can be decomposed into the original components. That is, if the complex class is represented by a value type $T$, then the complex in the store can be represented by $\mathbb{F}(T)$ or $T^*$.
(iii) Introduce for every processor a place that contains in the initial state only one object, which is a valueless complex.
(iv) Modify the processors by adding a *pre-processing* phase in which they select one token from the complex in each of their stores that is an input place and a *post-processing* phase in which they pack the objects they produce into the complexes of the stores that are output places.

If time plays a role it is necessary to represent the time stamps of the original tokens in the complexes of the stores in order to be able to pick them in the right order. The new network should be similar to the original one; *see* definition 9.8. In it stores are inspected by means of self-triggering or *polling*. The tokens in

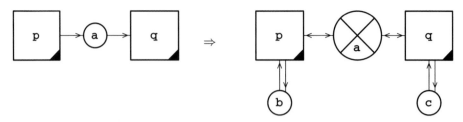

Fig. 14.36. Transforming an actor model into one with only self-triggering.

the new private places may be given delays to model the polling intervals. An example is given in figure 14.36.

In a similar way we can transform an actor model to have only one input place that is either a self-triggering place as above or is an output place of some other processor, which means that some processors are only activated by others and some by self-triggering.

### Transforming actor models into models without shared stores

Now we consider a situation that is almost the complement of the previous one: we have a network in which processors share stores and we would like to transform this net into a net in which stores are particular to a processor. A store can thus be accessed by only one processor in an event, so we should incorporate to the transformed network a mutual exclusion mechanism.

In figures 14.37 and 14.38 we see an example. In the network of figure 14.37 processors $p$ and $q$ share a store $s$. We assume both processors are complete. The transformed network, as shown in figure 14.38, should keep the values of the two tokens in $s_1$ and $s_2$ the same, as far as possible. In the transformed network processor $p$ is replaced by two processors: $p_1$, which takes care of access control, and $p_2$, which performs the update of the store $s_1$. The latter has the same type as $s$. For processor $q$ we see a similar transformation. In the initial state, place $m$ contains two valueless tokens that are needed both by $p_1$ and $q_1$ if they want to initiate an update. After $p_2$ and $q_2$ have performed the updates they return one (valueless) token to place $m$. Further, we see in the figure two new places $d$ and $e$ that are needed to transfer the update of one processor to the other. (Note that $p$ and $q$ may perform totally different kinds of update.) Processors $p_1$ and $q_1$ are complete but $p_2$ and $q_2$ are not input complete: $q_2$ consumes a token either from place $n$ or from $d$. The same applies to $p_2$. However, they always give a token to place $m$. So, if the two tokens of $m$ are consumed by, for instance, $p_1$ then one token is returned by $p_2$ after the update of $s_1$ and the other one by $q_2$ after the update of $s_2$. Processors $p_1$ and $q_1$ have a very simple

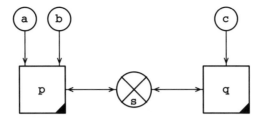

Fig. 14.37. Network with shared store.

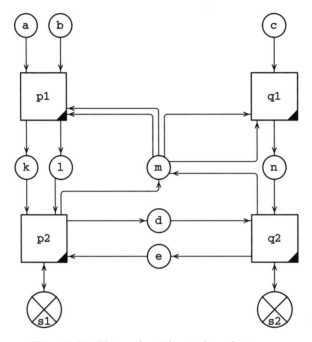

Fig. 14.38. Network without shared store.

processor relation: they pass the tokens they consume from $a$, $b$ and $c$ to $k$, $l$ and $n$ respectively. For processors $p_2$ and $q_2$ there are several transformations possible, depending on what the original processors $p$ and $q$ do. A trivial, but in many cases impractical solution is to let $p_2$ give the new value of the token in store $s_1$ to $q_2$ and vice versa. This modification of $p_2$ and $q_2$ is easy. If the token in the stores is a set and the update is just the addition or deletion of an element of that set, processors $p_2$ and $q_2$ have to exchange only their updates and not the new value of the stored token.

The solution we have considered here can easily be generalized to three or more processors that shares one store. Another generalization is to the case in which

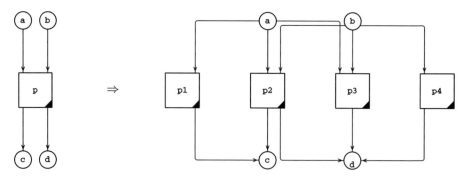

Fig. 14.39. Transforming an incomplete processor.

we have three processors that share two different stores pairwise. We can use a similar transformation here too.

## Transforming incomplete processors into complete ones

Sometimes it is useful to have an actor model with complete processors, for instance to analyze the behavioral properties of a classical Petri net after discarding the values of tokens. If we start with a net with incomplete processors we can transform it into one with only complete processors. Consider the processor relation $R_p$ of a processor $p$. (In definition 11.3 $R_p$ is defined as a set of firing rules; each firing rule describes a possible firing of processor $p$, i.e. a possible combination of consumed and produced tokens and the corresponding input and output connectors.) For all different combinations of input and output connectors involved in a transition we define a new processor.

In figure 14.39 we see on the left-hand side that $p$ has two input and two output places. Assume its processor relation prescribes that it may fire for the following combinations of connectors: $\{a, c\}, \{a, b, c, d\}, \{a, b, d\}$ and $\{b, d\}$. This results in the net on the right-hand side in a processor for each combination of connectors.

In general, let

$$K = \{dom(f) \mid f \in R_p\}$$

denote the sets of combinations of connectors for which $p$ is able to fire, then we have to create a processor $p_k$ for each element $k \in K$ with processor relation

$$R_{p_k} = \{f \in R_p \mid dom(f) = k\}.$$

Note that $K$ is always finite, even if $R_p$ is infinite. Processor $p_k$ has $k$ as its connectors. The following property is easy to verify.

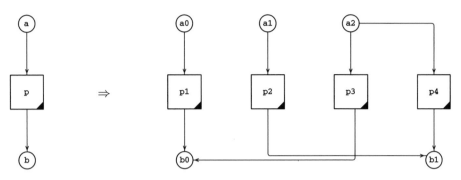

Fig. 14.40.  Transforming a net into a valueless net.

**Theorem 14.1** If processor $p$ is functional then for all $k \in K$ processor $p_k$ is functional.

Processor $p$ may be total but it does not follow that then $p_k$ is necessarily total too. Instead of decomposing a processor as we did here, we may also *cluster* processors by taking the union of their processor relations in order to reduce the number of processors! In fact we can transform each net into a net with only one processor.

Note that in the transformed model two processors that are derived from one processor in the original model, may fire simultaneously, which corresponds to two firings of the processor in the original model!

**Theorem 14.2** An actor model with incomplete processors and the corresponding transformed complete actor model are bisimilar with respect to the identity relation over $St \times T$, if we consider for both actor models the transition relation that allows only one processor firing in each event. (This transition relation is defined theorem 11.6.)

*Proof* First note that both systems have the same state spaces. Every transition of one system can also be made by the other, because we allow only one processor firing in each event. □

**Transforming nets into valueless nets**
As said before, there are some useful analysis methods for classical Petri nets. If we want to apply them to nets in which tokens have values we may discard these values. However, then we lose information. If the number of values that play a role in the transition relations is finite, we may transform the actor model into another actor model with only valueless tokens, without loss of information.

The transformation is analogous to the one above. In figure 14.40 an example is displayed, on the left the original net and on the right the transformed one. The processor relation of this net is given in table 14.1

Table 14.1. *Processor relation table*

| $f$ | $a$ | $b$ |
|---|---|---|
| 1 | 0 | 0 |
| 2 | 1 | 1 |
| 3 | 2 | 0 |
| 4 | 2 | 1 |

From this table we see that place $a$ gets values only from $\{0, 1, 2\}$ and $b$ from $\{0, 1\}$ (we assume that the environment gives no other values). We call these sets the *active domains* of the places, i.e. the subsets of their types that are actively used. In the transformed net each place is "copied" as many times as the size of its active domain. Further, we create a new processor $p_f$ for each function $f \in R_p$ and connect it to the places according to the domain of $p$. We can apply this transformation when the object universe is finite.

**Theorem 14.3**  Let an actor model $A$ with a finite object universe $OU_A$ be given and let $B$ be the actor model to which $A$ is transformed, according to the rules above. Further, assume that both systems have a transition relation that allows only one processor firing per event. (This transition relation is defined in theorem 11.6.) Then

(i) $OU_B$ is a singleton,
(ii) $St_B \subseteq ID \to OU_B \times T \times (L \times OU_A)$,
(iii) $A$ and $B$ are *bisimilar* with respect to
$$C = \{((s, t), (s', t')) \mid s \in St_A \wedge s' \in St_B \wedge t \in T \wedge dom(s) = dom(s') \wedge$$
$$\forall i \in dom(s) : \pi_2(s(i)) = \pi_2(s'(i)) \ \wedge \ \pi_3(s(i)) = (\pi_3(s(i)), \pi_1(s(i)))\}.$$

*Proof* The state spaces are isomorphic and each transition of one system can be made by the other (to the corresponding state).                                    □

# 15

# Object modeling

Object modeling is the activity of making an object model, and includes the definition of value types for simplex classes and constraints but not the definition of "clever" value types for complex classes. The assignment of complex classes to places is made when the actor model is available, and the value types of complex classes are determined in the specification phase; both activities are studied in the next chapter. In this chapter we consider the process of making an object model after reality, some characteristic modeling problems, and methods to transform an object model from one framework into another. We start with some techniques for specifying constraints.

## Constraint specification

Constraints are very important because an object model without constraints is often not sophisticated enough to express the structure of the real-world state space. Constraints are expressed either graphically or in the specification language. We distinguish *local* and *global* constraints. The local constraints concern all complexes of a complex class, while the global constraints concern all states. Each state determines one universal complex in the following way. Let $d$ and $e$ be two arbitrary complexes of complex classes $m$ and $n$ respectively. Then we define a universal complex $c$ as the *union* of $d$ and $e$:

$$\forall\, x \in SN \cup RN : c(x) = d(x) \cup e(x)$$

where we define $d(x) = \emptyset$ if $x \notin CB(n) \cup CR(n)$ and $e(x)$ is defined similarly. (Note that the union of two complexes of the same class is itself a complex of the same class, although constraints might be forced.) So, for a state $s$ we define a universal complex $c$ as the union of all complexes in $s$:

$$c = \bigcup_{i \in dom(s)} \pi_1(s(i))$$

An important global constraint is that this universal complex satisfies the graphical constraints for the universal complex class. We call this the *universal constraint*. This global constraint can be treated as a local constraint, although the universal complex class does not have to be assigned to a place.

A local constraint for a complex class $n$ is a predicate over that class, which means that the predicate should be evaluated in the *context* of each complex that has to be verified. To specify constraints for a complex class $n$ in the specification language we fix a complex $c$ and use the following conventions.

– We associate with every simplex class name $a \in CB(n)$ a type $T_a$ such that the type of the simplexes in $sim(a)$ are represented by values in $T_a$, and we use the symbol $a$ for the representations of simplexes in $c(a)$. In most cases the choice for $T_a$ is free because we do not apply any particular function to the values of $T_a$. In a few cases we require that $T_a$ is a quantity ( for instance represented by $\mathbb{N}$) or that it is a set of time slots (for instance represented by $\mathbb{N} \times \mathbb{N}$).

– We associate with every relationship class $r \in CR(n)$ with $DM(r) = a$ and $RG(r) = b$ a binary relation $R$ that is obtained from $c(r)$ by replacing the elements of the pairs in $c(r)$ by their representations. Further, we associate four functions with $r$ and call them, temporarily, $r_1$, $r_2$, $r_3$ and $r_4$. We distinguish two cases: one where $r$ is total and functional and one where $r$ is not total and not functional. In the first case we can use the relationship as a single-valued function (because it always has one value).

The four functions are defined as follows.

(i) Let $r$ be functional; then $r_1$ is defined by

$$r_1(x) := R.x : T_a \Rightarrow T_b,$$

if $r$ is not total and not functional, then

$$r_1(x) := setapply(R, x) : T_a \Rightarrow \mathbb{F}(T_b).$$

(ii) $r_2$ is derived from $r_1$, because it is the *set-version* of $r_1$.
Let $r$ be functional; then
$r_2(x) := $ *if* $x = \{\}$ *then* $\{\}$ *else*

$$ins(r_1(pick(x)), r_2(rest(x)))\ fi : \mathbb{F}(T_a) \Rightarrow \mathbb{F}(T_b).$$

Let $r$ be not total and not functional; then
$r_2(x) := $ *if* $x = \{\}$ *then* $\{\}$ *else*

$$r_1(pick(x)) \cup r_2(rest(x))\ fi : \mathbb{F}(T_a) \Rightarrow \mathbb{F}(T_b).$$

(iii) $r_3$ is defined by

$$r_3(y) := inverse(R, y) : T_b \Rightarrow \mathbb{F}(T_a).$$

(iv) $r_4$ is the set-version of $r_3$:
$r_4(y) := if\ y = \{\}\ then\ \{\}\ else$

$$r_3(pick(y)) \cup r_4(rest(y))\ fi : \mathbb{F}(T_b) \Rightarrow \mathbb{F}(T_a).$$

Note that the functions *apply* (denoted by "."), *setapply* and *inverse* are defined in appendix C. We will use the overloading facility of the specification language by renaming these functions as follows: $r_1$ and $r_2$ are called $r$, and $r_3$ and $r_4$ are called $r^{-1}$.

From the application of the functions $r$ or $r^{-1}$ the right signature can be deduced, so there will be no confusion. This overloading is very useful because now we do not have to distinguish between applying a function to an element or to a set. Now we may write, for example for (not functional) relationships $r$ and $q$, with $DM(r) = a$, $RG(r) = d$, $DM(q) = b$ and $RG(q) = d$,

$$\forall x : a \bullet \exists y : b \bullet y \in q^{-1}(r(x))$$

which means, in the meta-language,

$\forall c \in com(n) :$
$\quad \forall x \in c(a) : \exists y \in c(b) : \exists z \in c(d) : y \in D_{q,c}(z) \wedge z \in R_{r,c}(x).$

Note that this constraint must hold for all the complexes in the complex class $n$.

The functions for relationships can be derived (also by a tool) from the class model. Therefore, we assume they exist as soon as we have defined the class model.

The types we use for the simplex classes are not important here. In a few cases we will assume that a simplex class is a set of time slots, in which case we assume for it the type $\mathbb{Q} \times \mathbb{Q}$. Each pair of rationals will be interpreted as an interval. Sometimes we assume the simplex class is a set of numbers, in which case the type will be $\mathbb{Q}$. Further we only use set-theoretical functions in constraints (such as $\subseteq$ and $\in$).

The relationship constraints, the inheritance constraints and the tree constraints can be expressed in the specification language for each specific object model; however, these predicates may be quite complex and have a standard structure. In principle it is possible to generate these predicates automatically.

There are more frequently-occurring constraints and they will be discussed in the next section as "characteristic modeling problems". We will not specify global constraints that cannot be treated as a local constraint. (If we want to do so, we have to define a type for a state space.)

## 15.1 Making an object model after reality

We will start with the description of two examples. They are related to the order processing and railway station examples of chapter 14. These two descriptions determine the complex classes of the state spaces of two different systems.

### Example: Factory

Consider a factory that produces a product only if there is an order for it. Each product requires several construction tasks and in each task one or more components have to be assembled. The tasks for a product have a partial ordering. Each task requires some resources for a certain length of time, called the duration, in order to perform the task. Examples of resources are machines, vehicles and human beings. It is assumed that these resources are available for the whole duration of the task. There are several resources that may perform the same function. So in fact a task is specified by certain functions instead of resources. A resource can be used for one task at a time, so there is no resource sharing. Components are bought from suppliers. Several suppliers may sell the same component for their own price. The factory keeps components in stock. The production schedule is just a set of operations. An operation is the execution of a task for some particular order with some particular set of resources in a particular time slot. There are two kinds of orders: customer orders and supply orders. Each order has a delivery date. An order may concern several items of several products. For components we distinguish the total number of items in stock at some day, and the number of free items, i.e. the number of items that is not assigned to an operation yet. Components of the same kind are not distinguishable, only their number counts.

□

### Example: Railroad system

Consider a railroad network where track segments are defined between nodes. A node is a crossing, a switch or a signal. (Track segments are simply called tracks.) They are directed, i.e. trains can only use a track in one direction. A switch connects three tracks: one fixed track, one straight track and one branching track. The fixed track is always part of the route, and so is just one of the other tracks. The straight track and the fixed track form a straight line in the neighborhood of the switch, while the branching track and the fixed track form an angle. (*see* figure 15.3.) Further, there are trains. A train is a temporary "cluster" of a locomotive and a sequence of wagons. A switch has at each moment one of two positions, "straight" or "branching", and a signal has one of three status values, "green", "orange" or "red". A train also has a position at each moment, defined by the track segment on which it is to be found; only one train is allowed per track.

□

## Stepwise development

The development of an object model proceeds along the following steps:

Step 1: Determine the relevant *entities*.

All entities that can be named by a *noun* are either objects or actors. If they are objects, they can be either simplexes or complexes. In fact the nouns indicate *classes*. So the noun "horse" refers to the class (or set) of all horses. In a sentence we use it as "'Runner' is a horse" or "the horse that wins the race". In the last case the sub-sentence (clause) determines a unique element in the set of all horses. Entities have an identity (like the name 'Runner' for a horse). A way of finding the relevant classes is to collect together all nouns that appear in documentation over the system to be modeled, i.e. in forms, instructions, reports etc. This is a *syntactical analysis* of written or spoken text. Of course, if the systems engineer has already some knowledge of the type of system to which the system to be modeled belongs, he probably knows most of the relevant nouns already. The first step ends with the exclusion of actors. An entity is regarded as an actor in each of the following cases.

- It is in the system during the whole life of the system, so the set of actors of a certain class is fixed.
- It is active, i.e. it consumes and produces other entities (in fact objects).
- It is an event, i.e. it occurs at some point in time and it does not "live" for a time interval.
- It does not have relationships with other entities that may change over time.
- It cannot be described by a finite mathematical value, but it needs a function as description.

All other entities are objects. Remember from chapter 14 that processors that represent some physical entity can be split into a processor that represents the *activity* of the entity and a place in which the token represents the physical entity itself. (The token is consumed and (re-)produced in every execution of the processor.) So, all "things" can be modeled as objects, in which case all the processors represent activities. We distinguish *compound* or *molecular* objects, called *complexes* and *atomic* objects, called *simplexes*. Actors are further studied in actor modeling.

Step 2: Determine the *simplex classes*.

We distinguish *concrete* simplexes like the resources and the locomotives in the examples above, and *abstract* simplexes like a task, an operation, a time slot or a train position. A third category of simplexes consists of *information* simplexes. These refer to either concrete or abstract entities. Concrete simplexes are physical entities, while abstract simplexes are activities, events, qualifications, quantities, agreements, instructions or concepts.

   To decide which objects are simplexes we give the following rules:

— simplexes have a unique value that is independent of other objects and that can be used to identify them;

— simplexes are *atomic*, i.e. we cannot "look inside" them to discover other objects, so we do not allow functions that produce values of other simplexes if applied to the value of a simplex;

— in different states of the system the set of simplexes of the same class may be different, may contain more than one simplex and must be finite.

Even if an object consists of parts that are also considered as objects, it can be considered as a simplex if it can be given an independent, atomic value ("train" is an example of this). In this case we model its components as simplexes as well and we use relationships to express that one is part of another.

We may classify simplex classes into three groups.

(i) *Attribute* simplex classes.

   A simplex class $n$ is an attribute simplex class if $n$ is not a domain class of any relationship class, i.e. $\forall r \in RN : n \neq DM(r)$. Attribute simplex classes do not play an important role because their simplexes have no properties of their own. Therefore we neglect them, sometimes, in the first stages of development of an object model.

(ii) *Association* simplex classes.

   A simplex class $n$ is an association simplex class if all relationship classes with $n$ as domain class together form a corresponding minimal key constraint. Further, it is required that $n$ is not the range simplex class of some relationship. Simplexes of these classes have only one role: the coupling of other simplexes. They usually are found in a later stage of the development process.

(iii) *Entity* simplex classes.

   A simplex class $n$ is an entity simplex class if it is not an attribute simplex class or an association simplex class. Simplexes of these classes are important simplexes; they represent the entities we see in the real world.

(It is useful to distinguish these different types of simplex class by different graphical symbols: for attributes circles are often chosen and, for associations, diamonds.)

This classification is useful in the design process; one should start with the entity simplex classes, then the association simplex classes and finally the attribute simplex classes.

Step 3: Determine the *relationship classes*.
Relationships connect simplexes. If a simplex is connected to another simplex we consider this as a *property* of these simplexes. Relationships are labeled with a *verb*, often in two forms, active and passive (*see* chapter 4). Relationships express a *status quo*, for instance "is made of", "belongs to" or "located at". Relationships belong to classes as do simplexes and all relationships of one class connect only simplexes of a given simplex class to simplexes of another given (not necessarily different) other simplex class. Relationships have a *direction*: we choose the verb such that the sentence made of the noun at the domain of the relationship followed by the verb and the noun at the range of the relationship form a sentence in active form. There is some freedom in the choice of the direction of a relationship class. (Remember that the inverse of a functional relationship is an injective relationship.) The choice is based on the intuitive meaning of the relationship: it is a property of the domain class of the relationship class. Further the choice may be influenced by the use of the relationship in key, exclusion and tree constraints.

Step 4: Determine the *complex classes*.
A complex is a cluster of simplexes and relationships. The relationships should connect only simplexes that belong to the complex. Complexes are usually defined if an actor model is already available, because the complex classes partition the simplex and relationship classes over the places.

Often a set of simplexes of the same class forms a complex, for example a set of trains can be a complex in the railway system. Many complex classes satisfy a *tree constraint*, which means that complexes of such a class have one *root* simplex that identifies the complex and that gives "access" to all other simplexes in the complex. In the railway system for instance, there is a complex class called *TrainCluster* the complexes of which have a train simplex as root and a locomotive and a set (in fact a sequence) of wagons in the *body*. So, here we distinguish the locomotive connected to the wagons from the train itself, which implies that there might be different trains with the same locomotive and the same set of wagons. (Of course these different trains will not exist at the same time, but that is not relevant here.) It is also possible to use the noun *Train* only for the cluster consisting of wagons with a locomotive as root; then two trains are identical if they have the same locomotive and the same set of wagons. So, we are free to introduce a simplex class to identify a cluster of simplexes connected by relationships. We distinguish concrete, abstract and information complexes as well as combinations.

All the simplex classes and all the relationship classes should occur in at least one complex class, since only the complex classes in a state are considered. So if for instance a relationship class does not appear in a complex class, then either the relationship class is irrelevant or the complex classes are not defined completely. This requirement provides a check point for the systems engineer.

Step 5: Determine *value types* for the simplex classes.
This activity may occur immediately after the definition of simplex classes; however, we only need these value types sometimes in constraints. Note that the value types for simplex classes define the function *sim* of the instance model of an object model (*see* definition 10.2).

Many constraints do not refer to the values of simplexes at all, but sometimes we need some *properties* of the values of the simplexes. For instance if the simplex class denotes quantities or time slots we may need a value type to express the constraints because we have to apply functions to the simplexes. The values of the simplexes are the only things we know about the simplexes, so the simplexes are identified by their values. We do not give value types for simplex classes in examples where they are irrelevant for constraints. We avoid the use of simplex values in constraints as much as possible for the same reasons that we avoid hard-coded parameters in programs. Note that complex classes are completely defined if the value types of the simplex classes are known. In fact we have a "default" value type for them. However, in specifications we might want to use another, more sophisticated, representation for complexes. (This will be clarified in the next chapter.) In object modeling we need no other representations of complex classes.

Step 6: Determine *constraints*.
First, we consider *relationship constraints*, which have a graphical representation. They are presumed to hold for all relevant complex classes, i.e. complex classes that contain the relationships involved. If we discover a key constraint we always look for a *minimal key constraint*, i.e. if $n$ is a simplex class then $a \in DK(n)$ is

a minimal domain key if

$$\forall\, b \in DK(n) : b \subseteq a \Rightarrow a = b.$$

For range keys the definition is similar. In the same way we search for *maximal exclusion constraints*, i.e. for exclusion constraints that are not contained in larger exclusion constraints.

Next we determine *inheritance constraints*. We use inheritance to distinguish different subclasses of a simplex class in the case where simplexes of a subclass have special relationships that the first simplex class does not have. For complex classes we determine the *tree constraints* as discussed above.

Next we search for constraints that cannot be expressed as one of the above mentioned constraints; for these we use predicates in the specification language. We mention four ways to find (some of) them.

(i) Search for *cycles*.

If there is a cycle in the class model, then we can start with a simplex in one of the simplex classes and follow two different routes to a simplex or a set of simplexes in another simplex class (in the cycle). Are these simplexes the same or should these (sets of) simplexes be disjoint? One cycle gives rise to many of these questions. Here the direction of the relationships is irrelevant.

(ii) Search for *time orders*.

If *time* or *time slot* is a simplex class, then often the simplex classes related to them have constraints with respect to time. For instance if two operations have the same time slot then the resources connected to them should not be the same, because a resource can be involved in only one operation at a time.

(iii) Search for *balances*.

If the quantities are simplex classes then there is often some balance required. For instance if there is a simplex class *order*, which is related to a simplex class *quantity* and if there is a simplex class *orderitem* which is also related to *quantity*, then there might be a constraint that requires the quantity of an order to be the sum of the quantities of the related order items. (Note that an order consists of order items.) Such constraints can be avoided if there is no relationship between order and quantity. This relationship is indeed superfluous because the sum can be computed. However, if not all order items have a quantity (yet) we have to keep both relationships with *quantity*.

(iv) Search for *temporal inconsistency*.

Often we consider a complex in several stages of development. For instance, suppose that an order is already defined but not all of its order items. In such cases we have to *drop* constraints to allow for complexes that will be correct after some modifications. (We use inheritance to solve this problem (*see* section 15.2.).)

Finally we look for global constraints, such as the *universal constraints* and constraints that require that simplexes representing physical entities are unique in a state (i.e. a physical entity cannot be in two different places in the same state).

We will illustrate this development process for the two examples described above.

### Example: Factory (continued)

We start by listing the relevant nouns of the description: product, order, task, component, resource, function, supplier, price, stock, schedule, operation, time slot, duration and delivery date. Note that "factory" is not a relevant noun because there is only one factory, which stays the same during the whole lifetime of the system. The factory may be considered as the top-level actor. We decide that a "schedule" is just a set of "operations" so we will not define a simplex class for it. In figure 15.1 we see all the other nouns as simplex classes. Two simplex classes require some elucidation: *customerorderitem* and *supplyorderitem*. At first sight they seem to be superfluous because we have already *CustomerOrder* and *SupplyOrder*. However, an order is in fact a complex object and it contains for each product or component a "sub-order", which is an object itself. Further, we see a number of relationship classes labeled by characters. It is not difficult to find suitable verbs for each relationship class; for instance *a* is described as *intended–for*, *b* as *belongs–to*, *d* as *concerns* and *e* as *executed–for*. Only relationship *k* requires some clarification; it is called *predecessors* and assigns to a task the set of all tasks that are immediate predecessors of the task. With relationships we should be as thrifty as possible. We could for instance define a relationship between *product* and *component* that denotes the components from which the product is made; however, that relationship is derivable from *h* and *l* because *h* gives all the tasks to be performed for the product and *l* gives all the components needed for these tasks. In other words the relationship is *redundant*. There is considerable freedom in the choice of relationship classes. However, if we should introduce redundant relationships we would find that we have also introduced constraints! For instance, if we had introduced a relationship class *hl* from *product* to *component* then this would have defined the constraint

$$\forall\, p : product \bullet l(h(p)) = hl(p).$$

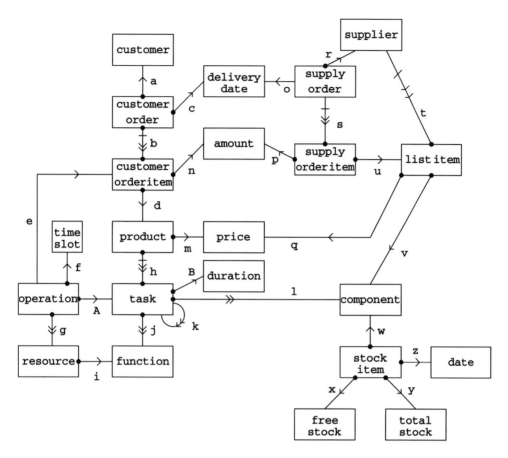

Fig. 15.1. Simplex diagram for the factory example.

Instead of introducing the relationship *hl* and discovering the constraint, we may consider the constraint as the *specification* of the function *hl* and use this function in other constraints or in processor specifications. So, we do not need the relationship *hl* in the object model.

The next step is the determination of the complex classes. They may be indicated in the simplex diagram; however, the diagram then becomes very crowded. Therefore, we list them in the table 15.1. The choices of the complexes may dependent on the actor model, in fact on the "processing". So in general it is not possible to fix the complex classes in the data modeling phase if the actor model is not ready. However, some useful complex classes are listed in the following below. These complex classes have straightforward interpretations. A *BillFor-Material* complex, for instance, gives for a specific product all the tasks needed to construct the product and also the required functions and components per

Table 15.1. *Complex classes for the factory example.*

| Complex class | Simplex classes | Relationship classes | Root class |
|---|---|---|---|
| *CustomerOrder* | *customerorder* | | * |
| | *customer* | *a* | |
| | *customerorderitem* | *b* | |
| | *deliverydate* | *c* | |
| | *amount* | *n* | |
| | *product* | *d* | |
| *Schedule* | *operation* | | |
| | *timeslot* | *f* | |
| | *resource* | *g* | |
| | *task* | *A* | |
| | *customerorderitem* | *e* | |
| *BillOfMaterial* | *product* | | * |
| | *task* | *h, k* | |
| | *component* | *l* | |
| | *function* | *j* | |
| | *price* | *m* | |
| | *duration* | *B* | |
| *SupplyOrder* | *supplyorder* | | * |
| | *supplyorderitem* | *s* | |
| | *supplier* | *r* | |
| | *listitem* | *u* | |
| | *deliverydate* | *o* | |
| | *amount* | *p* | |
| | *price* | *q* | |
| | *component* | *v* | |
| *PriceList* | *supplier* | | * |
| | *listitem* | *t* | |
| | *component* | *v* | |
| | *price* | *q* | |
| *StockItem* | *stockitem* | | * |
| | *date* | *z* | |
| | *component* | *w* | |
| | *freestock* | *x* | |
| | *totalstock* | *y* | |
| *Resource* | *resource* | | * |
| | *function* | *i* | |

step. It looks as though we do not need the simplex classes *customerorder* and *supplyorder* any more, because we have complex classes that contain all relevant information. However, this is not true because an order has a unique identity that is a property of all the order items in the order. This unique identity is given by the "order" simplex classes. Thus it is for instance possible to have two different *CustomerOrder* complexes with the same *deliverydate*, the same *amount*, the same *customerorderitems* etc.

It is easy to verify that all relationship and simplex classes are covered by complexes. The value types for simplex classes are easy to define. Simplex classes with names like *amount*, *price*, *freestock* and *totalstock* have the rationals or integers as type. The simplex class *date* could have the product $\mathbb{N} \times \mathbb{N} \times \mathbb{N}$ as value type, denoting the day, the month and the year respectively. Similarly, *time slot* has the value type $\mathbb{Q} \times \mathbb{Q}$ denoting the interval bounds of the time slot.

The final step in this example is to determine the constraints. The relationship constraints speak for themselves. We have not yet required that relationships are surjective. This may be added. At least for the complex class *Schedule* this would avoid for instance *dangling tasks* in a *Schedule* complex. There are no key, exclusion or inheritance constraints here and the tree constraints are already indicated in table 15.1. So we are only looking for additional constraints. We start by looking for *cycles*. Consider for instance the cycle formed by the relationships $\langle A, j, i, g \rangle$. If we follow two paths from *operation* to *function*, one via $\langle g, i \rangle$ and one via $\langle A, j \rangle$, then we should obtain the same set of functions in both cases. The specification of this constraint is

$$\forall\, x :\ operation \bullet i(g(x)) = j(A(x)).$$

This constraint is defined for the *universal complex class*. Another cycle is $\langle e, d, h, A \rangle$. This cycle gives

$$\forall\, x :\ operation \bullet A(x) \in h(d(e(x))).$$

Yet another cycle is caused by relationship $k$. Indeed, we find two new constraints here. The first constraint says that for each task of a product all predecessor tasks should be tasks of the same product:

$$\forall\, x :\ product \bullet \forall\, y :\ task \bullet y \in h(x) \Rightarrow k(y) \subseteq h(x).$$

The second constraint is more complicated. It concerns the *transitive closure* of the relationship $k$, i.e. a task can never be preceded by itself:
$trans(x) := if\ x = \{\}\ then\ x\ else$

$$x \cup trans(k(x))\ fi : \mathbb{F}(task) \Rightarrow \mathbb{F}(task).$$

The function *trans* computes the transitive closure of the relationship $k$. The correctness of its definition follows from the fact that iterated application of the right-hand side of the equation (*see* chapter 28) gives a non-decreasing sequence $x,\ x \cup k(x),\ x \cup k(x) \cup k^2(x) \ldots$ and there is an $n$ such that $k^n(x) = \varnothing$ (note that we use superscript $n$ to denote the nth iteration). The constraint thus becomes

$$\forall\, x :\ task \bullet x \notin trans(k(x)).$$

This kind of constraint occurs frequently if there is a cyclic relationship path. Not all cycles give constraints, for instance the cycle $\langle c, o, s, p, n, b \rangle$ does not give a constraint. As a last constraint we compare the duration of a task and the time slot of an operation:

$$\forall x : \; operation \bullet B(A(x)) = \pi_2(f(x)) - \pi_1(f(x)).$$

We are never sure that we have formulated all constraints, because we are in fact defining the laws that states or complexes have to fulfill.

□

### Example: Railroad system (continued)

Again we start by listing all relevant nouns in the description. So, we find: (railroad) network, track (segments), node, crossing, switch, signal, train, locomotive, (sequence of) wagon(s), switch position, signal status, route and train position. We decide to consider "railroad network" as a set of tracks and nodes and so we

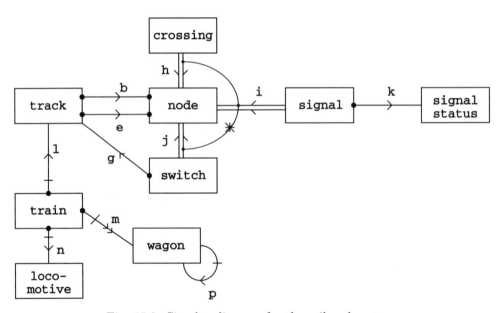

Fig. 15.2. Simplex diagram for the railroad system.

will not introduce a simplex class for it. The noun "route" is only used to explain the function of a switch and is considered to be irrelevant. All other nouns appear in the simplex diagram of figure 15.2, except for "switch position" and "train position". It turns out that it is possible to express the positions of trains and switches by means of relationships! However, it is still possible to introduce

Table 15.2. *Complex classes for the railway system.*

| Complex class | Simplex classes | Relationship classes | Root class |
|---|---|---|---|
| *TrainCluster* | *train* | | * |
| | *wagon* | *m, p* | |
| | *locomotive* | *n* | |
| *Network* | *track* | *b* | |
| | *node* | *e* | |
| | *crossing* | *h* | |
| | *signal* | *i* | |
| | *switch* | *j* | |
| *SwitchPos* | *switch* | | * |
| | *node* | *j, g* | |
| *SemaphorePos* | *signal* | | * |
| | *node* | *i* | |
| | *signalstatus* | *k* | |
| *TrainPosition* | *train* | | * |
| | *track* | *l* | |

simplex classes for them (as will be seen later) but it makes the model unnecessarily complicated. In this object model we assume that in different states the sets of tracks and nodes may be different. We have chosen to represent in this model only the actual state of the railroad system and not the history or the future. (Later we will see how to transform this model to express also the history and future.) The relationship classes require some clarification in this case. On a crossing four track segments come together and are part of two tracks. Each track (segment) has a direction and $b$ indicates the beginning node of a track while $e$ denotes the end node of the segment. Relationship class $l$ denotes the position of the train and a suitable verb for $l$ is " is at". Similarly the switch position is expressed by $g$. Relationship class $p$ determines the predecessor of each wagon, except that the first wagon does not have a predecessor (or in fact the locomotive is its predecessor). The next step is the definition of the complex classes. In table 15.2 the complex classes are given.

These complex classes have a straightforward interpretation. The value types of the classes can be chosen arbitrarily except for *signalstatus*, which will get a basic type with values "green" and "red". The final step is determination of the constraints. All standard constraints are already given in the diagram or the complex table. Note that no two trains may occupy the same track owing to the injectivity of relationship $l$. The injectivity of $m$ and $n$ implies that no two trains share locomotives or wagons. The tree constraints are given by the table. Next, we consider additional constraints. First we look for cycles. One cycle is caused by $p$. This gives the constraint that a predecessor of a wagon belongs to the same train:

$$\forall\, t : train \bullet \forall\, v : wagon \bullet v \in m(t) \Rightarrow p(v) \subseteq m(t).$$

The next constraint due to $p$ is that there is only one wagon without a predecessor per train:

$$\forall\, t : train \bullet size(\{w : m(t) \mid p(w) = \{\}\}) = 1.$$

Finally we observe that $p$ should give an ordering such that no wagon precedes itself, i.e. the transitive closure of $p$ does not enclose the identity function. This can be expressed in the same way as for the "task" precedence in the example above.

The next set of cycles we observe are formed by the simplex classes *track*, *node* and *switch*. A node connects two tracks if it is a signal, three tracks if it is a switch and four tracks if it is a crossing: thus

$$\forall\, x : signal \bullet size(b^{-1}(i(x))) = 1 \;\wedge\; size(e^{-1}(i(x))) = 1,$$

$$\forall\, x : switch \bullet (size(b^{-1}(j(x))) = 2 \;\wedge\; size(e^{-1}(j(x))) = 1)$$

$$\vee$$

$$(size(b^{-1}(j(x))) = 1 \;\wedge\; size(e^{-1}(j(x))) = 2),$$

$$\forall\, x : crossing \bullet size(b^{-1}(h(x))) = 2 \;\wedge\; size(e^{-1}(h(x))) = 2.$$

For a switch there are two different situations displayed in figure 15.3. In the

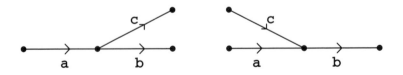

Fig. 15.3. Two different switches.

case on the left the switch is the beginning point of two tracks and the end point of one and in the right case the opposite. This is expressed above. We also obtain a constraint on the relationship $g$: it always points to one of the two tracks that either end (right case) or begin (left case) at the switch. This is expressed by

$$\forall\, x : \; switch \bullet j(x) = e(g(x)) \lor j(x) = b(g(x)),$$
$$\forall\, x : \; switch \bullet e(g(x)) = j(x) \Rightarrow \exists\, t : track \bullet t \neq g(x) \;\land\; e(t) = j(x),$$
$$\forall\, x : \; switch \bullet b(g(x)) = j(x) \Rightarrow \exists\, t : track \bullet t \neq g(x) \;\land\; b(t) = j(x).$$

Finally we have to require that are no loops:

$$\forall\, t : track \bullet b(t) \neq e(t).$$

Note that we have excluded the possibility that a track comes to a dead end.
□

These two examples show how to perform the steps given before. They demonstrate the kinds of problem that appear in making an object model.

## 15.2 Characteristic modeling problems

Next we will consider several problems that occur in many modeling situations. Some of them have appeared already in the examples above.

### 1. Relationships having properties

Often we have defined a relationship $r$ between simplex classes $a$ and $b$ and then discover that it is not sufficient to express that there is for each simplex of $a$ an associated set of simplexes of $b$; we have to indicate also some *property* of the associated simplexes. This situation can be found in the factory example. A simplified case is displayed in figure 15.4. At first sight an "order" was associated to a set of products. Later, though, we required that each associated product has its own amount. A solution is to introduce a new simplex class to replace the relationship class and connect this simplex class to both original simplex classes. In figure 15.4 we have introduced the simplex class *orderitem*. This simplex class can be related to the simplex class *amount*, which was not possible with the relationship $b$ in the left-hand diagram. So, we introduce a key constraint immediately; in the example $a$ and $b$ could form a key constraint.

### 2. Items and kinds

Sometimes we have to distinguish simplexes that represent a *kind* (or type) of object from the objects (called *items* here) themselves. In fact, in the factory example the object class *product* represents kinds of products and not the product items. Examples of product kinds are chair, car and bicycle. Examples of items of these kinds are specific chairs, cars and bicycles identified by their unique value (for instance their serial number). In figure 15.5 the general structure is displayed. The *item* simplex class always refers to the *kind* class with a total and

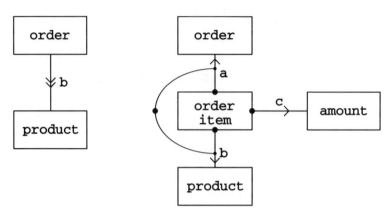

Fig. 15.4. A relationship with properties.

functional relationship. A way to discover the difference between items and kinds

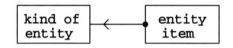

Fig. 15.5. Items and kinds.

is to consider the value of a simplex: if it is a common noun, a brand name or a trade mark it is probably a kind, and if it is a proper noun or a serial number it is probably an item.

## 3. Graphs and recursive structures

In the railroad system example we have in fact already modeled a geographical network (although we did not mention the coordinates of the nodes). In many examples we encounter *recursive* structures such as the tree of tasks in the factory example. Here we will study these structures in isolation. In figure 15.6 we see a general graph structure and two specializations for *trees* and *sequences*. The

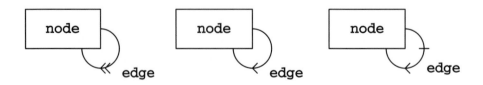

Fig. 15.6. Graphs, trees and sequences.

graph is the general case (left-most figure). Here no relationship constraints apply. The *edge* relationship determines the predecessors of a node. This choice is arbitrary; we could have decided that *edge* determines the successors of a node. The only constraint we could add is that each node is connected to at least one other (not necessarily different) node:

$$\forall\, x : node \bullet \exists\, y : node \bullet x \in edge(y) \lor y \in edge(x).$$

A subtype of the graphs is the set of *acyclic* graphs. To constrain the set of instances to acyclic graphs we introduce auxiliary functions as in the factory example.

$Trans(x) :=$
    *if* $edge(x) = \{\}$ *then* $x$ *else* $x \cup Trans(edge(x))$ *fi* $: \mathbb{F}(node) \Rightarrow \mathbb{F}(node).$

The constraint to acyclic graphs is

$$\forall\, n : node \bullet n \notin Trans(edge(n)).$$

*Trees* are acyclic graphs with the property that the relationship *edge* is functional and assigns to every node a unique parent node. Further, there is one root: the common ancestor. This is expressed by means of an auxiliary function $f$.

$$f(x) := if\ edge(x) = \{\}\ then\ x\ else\ (pick(edge(x)))\ fi : node \Rightarrow node.$$

So for $x \in node$, $f(x)$ denotes its oldest ancestor. Note that this function is correctly defined since we know that the graph is acyclic and therefore repeated application of *edge* results in the empty set. Also note that we have used *pick* because *edge* is not total, so the function value might be the empty set. The constraint becomes

$$\forall\, x : node \bullet \forall\, y : node \bullet f(x) = f(y).$$

The specialization of trees to *sequences* is simply obtained by adding the injectivity constraint to *edge* and the constraint that only one simplex does not have a predecessor (we have seen this constraint before). When the edges of graphs have properties of their own we have to introduce simplex classes as demonstrated above. (This was in fact the case in the railroad system example, where *track* was the class of edges.) Then the constraints have to be reformulated for the particular cases.

Trees play important roles in many practical cases. A bill for material, for instance, is a tree structure. Often a message in electronic data interchange is a tree. Since tree structures occur frequently we have introduced (in part II) the standard *tree constraint* for complex classes. With this constraint we can define a tree structure without additional constraints. To see how we could use this standard constraint, consider the example of figure 15.7. Here the *root* forms the

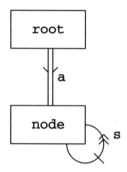

Fig. 15.7. Tree constraint.

root simplex class. Further *s* determines all successors of a node. The injectivity constraint for *s* and the constraint that the root is not a successor of any node,

$$\forall\, x :\; root \bullet \forall\, y :\; node \bullet a(x) \notin s(y),$$

guarantee that there are no cycles even if we discard the direction of the edges. The fact that there is one root (of class *root*) and the fact that each simplex is reachable from this root constrains the complex class to trees.

We consider an example of a *recursive structure* involving trees. In this example a complex class represents a syntax definition for arithmetical terms:

$$term ::=\; constant\,|\; variable\,|\, \underline{(term\; binop\; term)}\,|\, unop\underline{(\; term\,)}$$

where *binop* is a binary operator and *unop* a unary operator. An example of a term is

$$(f(v) + (g(w) \times (x \div y))).$$

This term should correspond to one complex of the class. In figure 15.8 the object model is displayed. Each "node" in the diagram represents a node in the parse tree of a term and relationship class *p* points to the predecessor of a node in the tree. In figure 15.9 the parse tree for the term above is displayed. A node has two branches, one branch, or no branch, corresponding to the different specializations of *node*: *binnode*, *unnode* and *leafnode* respectively. This is expressed by the following additional constraints. (Note the range exclusion constraint.)

$$\forall\, n :\; node \bullet a^{-1}(n) \neq \{\} \Rightarrow size(p^{-1}(n)) = 2,$$
$$\forall\, n :\; node \bullet b^{-1}(n) \neq \{\} \Rightarrow size(p^{-1}(n)) = 1,$$
$$\forall\, n :\; node \bullet c^{-1}(n) \neq \{\} \Rightarrow size(p^{-1}(n)) = 0.$$

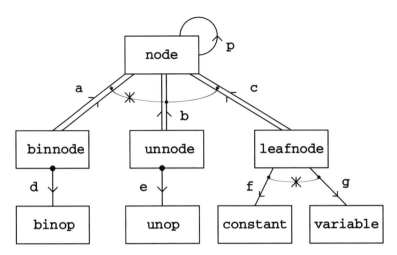

Fig. 15.8. Syntax as complex class.

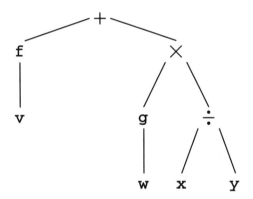

Fig. 15.9. Parse tree.

Further we have to require that *node* and *p* form a tree as shown above. Finally we want to exclude the possibility that there are dangling nodes:

$$\forall x : node \bullet a^{-1}(n) \neq \{\} \vee b^{-1}(n) \neq \{\} \vee c^{-1}(n) \neq \{\}.$$

## 4. Representing history and future

We often start with an object model in which we represent the *actual* situation of a system, i.e. the simplexes represent the entities that are in the system and the relationships represent their actual properties. In the railroad system, for example, the actual positions of the train and the switch were represented. In information systems we often consider the *history* of a process, which means that we store information objects that represent a part of a state of a target system in the past. Rather than information objects that refer to the past, information systems often have information objects that refer to the *future*. These information objects are used for a *planning* for the future of the system. The future does not have to behave as planned; however, the information objects represent what we think or wish to be the future. To transform an object model for an actual situation to one for the history or the future, we have to determine all the *time dependent* simplex classes, i.e. the simplex classes for which the simplexes may come and go during the course of the system. (Most simplex classes have this property.) For all these simplex classes we introduce a new functional relationship connecting the simplexes to simplexes of a class called *timeslot*. The meaning of this relationship is that for each simplex the corresponding time slot indicates when the simplex was, is or will be "alive". If the time at which the simplex will die is not known then the upper bound of the time slot is not specified or is set to some sufficiently large number. Further, we look for time dependent relationships, i.e. relationships that may change during the course of the system independently of the lifetime of the simplexes they connect. For instance relationship $l$ in figure 15.2 is time dependent because it may connect a train to different tracks during the lifetime of the train. The way to solve the problem for time dependent relationships is in fact the way to deal with relationships with properties: we introduce a new simplex class for such a relationship and we connect it to the simplex classes that were connected by the original relationship. Further we connect the new simplex class to the *timeslot* class. In figure 15.10 an example of this construction is displayed. Note that the time slots may refer to the history as well as to the future. If the original time-dependent relationship was functional, we obtain a constraint that the simplexes that replace the relationship may not be connected to more than one simplex of the domain simplex class of the original relationship at the same time. A second constraint states that the time slot of a *relationship* simplex is contained in the time slots of the original simplexes connected by the relationship simplex. In the example of figure 15.10 this means that the time slot of a "position" should be contained in the time slots of the "track" and the "train" to which it is connected by $a$ and $b$ respectively. To express these constraints formally we have to define a value type for time slots: $\mathbb{Q} \times \mathbb{Q}$, denoting the left and right bound of the time slot. Further, we need two auxiliary functions:

$$intersect(x, y) :=$$
$$max(\pi_1(x), \pi_1(y)) \leq min(\pi_2(x), \pi_2(y)) : (\mathbb{Q} \times \mathbb{Q}) \times (\mathbb{Q} \times \mathbb{Q}) \Rightarrow \mathbb{B}$$

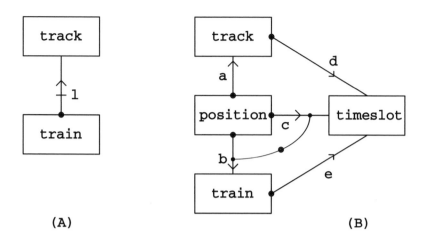

Fig. 15.10. Time dependence.

$contain(x, y) :=$

$\qquad \pi_1(x) \geq \pi_1(y) \ \wedge \ \pi_2(x) \leq \pi_2(y) : (\mathbb{Q} \times \mathbb{Q}) \times (\mathbb{Q} \times \mathbb{Q}) \Rightarrow \mathbb{B}.$

The first constraint becomes

$\qquad \forall \, x : position \bullet \forall \, y : position \bullet$

$\qquad\qquad (x \neq y \ \wedge \ b(x) = b(y)) \Rightarrow \neg intersect(c(x), c(y)),$

and the second becomes

$\qquad \forall \, x : position \bullet contain(c(x), e(b(x))) \ \wedge \ contain(c(x), d(a(x))).$

To guarantee that no two trains are on the same track, which is expressed by the injectivity of $l$ in the first model, we require

$\qquad \forall \, x, \ y : position \bullet$

$\qquad\qquad a(x) = a(y) \ \wedge \ intersect(c(x), c(y)) \Rightarrow x = y.$

## 5. Properties as values or relationships

Sometimes we have to choose between including a property of a simplex in the representation of the simplex, i.e. in the value of the simplex, and including it in a relationship to another simplex class. Consider the example displayed in figure 15.11. Here we see that there are two total and bijective relationships $a$ and $b$. We could decide to delete for instance relationship $a$ and give *person* the set of *names* as value type. If $a$ were not total and bijective this would not be possible (because if it were not total then there would have been persons without (known)

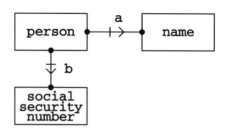

Fig. 15.11. Properties as relationships.

names, if it were not functional a person could have more than one name and if it were not injective there could have been two persons with the same name). As a guideline we recommend the use of the values of simplexes as little as possible, since this gives us most freedom in the specification stage; the construction is then of the type displayed in figure 15.11. In particular if there are several total bijective relationships (as in this case), it would be difficult to decide which one to incorporate in the value.

## 6. Aggregates

Sometimes a simplex is just an *aggregate* of other simplexes. Consider the example displayed in figure 15.12. Here we see a simplex class *address* and intuitively

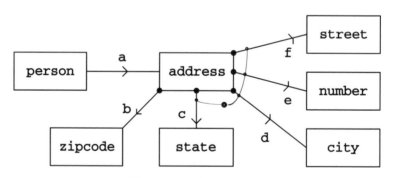

Fig. 15.12. Aggregates.

we feel that an address is just a combination of a street, a number, a city and a state. So, we could consider defining a complex class *Address* which would have *street*, *number*, *city* and *state* as its body. With the constraint that there is only one of each simplex class in the complex, the definition would be complete. However, then we would neither be able to define relationships for *Address* such as that to the *zipcode*, nor we could relate other simplexes such as *person* to *Address*. Besides that, *Address* is a distinct concept and for these reasons we introduce a simplex class *address*. The value type of this simplex class is irrelevant because we can always identify an address by its key constraint. Note that there is another domain key constraint for *address*, not displayed in figure 15.12, the relationships {*b*, *e*}.

It is still useful to define a complex class, say *Address*, which satisfies a tree constraint with *address* as root.

### 7. Use of inheritance constraints

Inheritance gives us the possibility of *differentiating* a given simplex classes into several simplex classes, each with its own relationships. Consider for instance the example displayed in figure 15.13. Each vehicle has an *owner* and a *licence*

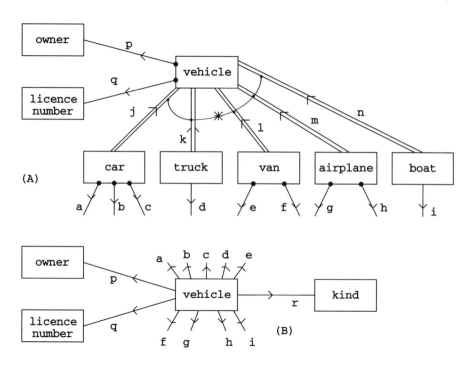

Fig. 15.13. Use of inheritance.

*number*; however, cars have other properties, peculiar to them, as do airplanes or vans (displayed by relationships $a - i$). In solution (B) there is a simplex class *kind* that has a value type that is represented by the set

$$\{car,\ truck,\ van,\ airplane,\ boat\}.$$

Further, *vehicle* has all the relationships $a - i$. Although diagram (B) is simpler than diagram (A) there are many more constraints in solution (B). Besides this,

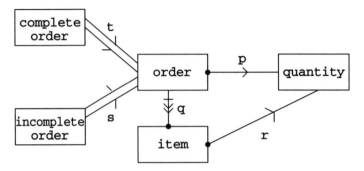

Fig. 15.14. Temporally inconsistent orders.

these constraints use values! For instance we would have to require that if a *vehicle* is not a *truck* then it should not have simplexes connected to it via relationship $d$:

$$\forall\, x : vehicle \bullet truck \neq r(x) \Rightarrow d(x) = \{\}.$$

So, inheritance can be used to avoid non-total relationships (which is important for the *relational data model* as explained in the next section) and to avoid constraints that refer to simplex values. Note that we can easily use the relationships $p$ and $q$ for the specialized simplex classes *car*,...,*boat* by defining auxiliary functions $pj$, $qj$, ..., $pn$, $qn$ as follows:

$$pj(x) := p(j(x)) : car \Rightarrow \mathbb{F}(owner).$$

Another example of the use of inheritance is the treatment of temporal inconsistency. For example consider the class model of figure 15.14. Complete orders should satisfy the balance constraint

$$\forall\, o : order \bullet p(o) = sum(r(q(o))).$$

(Here *sum* is the function that adds the values in a set.) However, not all orders are completely defined and therefore we require this for the complete ones only. For that reason we have introduced the two simplex classes *completeorder* and *incompleteorder* and we require the constraint only for the complete ones:

$$\forall\, o : completeorder \bullet p(t(o)) = sum(r(q(t(o)))).$$

## 8. Derivable relationships

Sometimes we discover that a constraint is so strong that a relationship can be *derived* from the constraint. Consider the example displayed in figure 15.15, which speaks for itself. The constraint that should hold is expressed using an

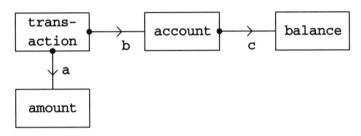

Fig. 15.15. A derivable relationship.

auxiliary function:

$$s(t) := if\ t = \{\}\ then\ 0\ else\ a(pick(t)) + s(rest(t))\ fi :$$

$$\mathbb{F}(transaction) \Rightarrow \mathbb{Q}.$$

It is assumed that the value types of *amount* and *balance* are equal to $\mathbb{Q}$. The constraint becomes

$$\forall\, y : account \bullet s(b^{-1}(y)) = c(y).$$

So the question is whether it is not better to delete relationship *c* and to define an other auxiliary function:

$$balance(x) := s(b^{-1}(x)) : account \Rightarrow \mathbb{Q}.$$

If there are no other relationships connected to the simplex class *balance* we could delete it too. Avoiding constraints means that we have fewer proof obligations in the specification phase!

## 9. Representing a finite function

Often we have to represent a finite function in an object model. For example the price list of a hotel is a function that lists the prices of hotel rooms, which depend on the season, the number of persons in the room and the number of days for which the room will be taken. The price is uniquely defined by these variables. In figure 15.16 we display a solution to this problem. In general there

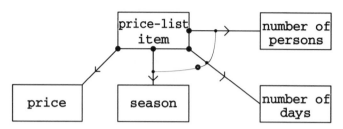

Fig. 15.16. Price list.

will be one simplex class for the (elements of the) function, one for every argument of the function and one for the result. The simplex class that represents the function is related to the other simplex classes by means of total and functional relationships. The relationships with the variables as range simplex classes form a (minimal) domain key. (If the result of the function is compound, there may be more than one simplex class to represent the result.)

## 10. Object model of an actor model

Let an actor model be given. Now we will construct an object model that represents the actual state and the history of the actor model. This is useful in the context of the modeling of *monitoring information systems*. When we make a model of such an information system, we often start with a (complete) actor model of the target system and then make an object model for the event history of this actor model. This object model may serve as a design for a database system in which the events of the actor model will be stored.

The method of constructing an object model from an actor model proceeds along the following steps.

   (i) Create for every processor a simplex class (with the same name).
  (ii) Create for every place two simplex classes (one with the same name and one with the name decorated by a prime).
 (iii) Create a place called *id* and a place called *time*.
 (iv) Create for every connector a relationship, with the same name as the connector, if no name clash occurs, between the simplex class of the processor and the (undecorated) simplex class of the place to which it is connected by this connector. This realionship is independent of the direction of the connector. The domain class of the relationship is the simplex class that represents the processor. The relationship is always functional, and it is total if the processor always consumes or produces a token via this connector. (In the case of a name clash suitable names have to be chosen.)

(v) Create, for every (undecorated) place simplex class, two total and functional relationships to the places *id* and *time*, the one going to *id* should also be injective.

(vi) Create a total and functional relationship from each undecorated place simplex class to the corresponding decorated simplex class.

(vii) For each simplex class $n'$ that represents a place $n$ we define

$$sim(n') = com(CA(n)).$$

(viii) For the simplex classes *id* and *time* we define

$$sim(id) = ID \ \wedge \ sim(time) = T,$$

where $ID$ is the set of identities and $T$ the time domain.

(ix) For each other simplex class $n$ define an arbitrary set for $sim(n)$.

(x) Create a complex class for each simplex class that represents a processor and let this complex class include all the simplex classes that are connected by a directed path of functional relationships; let the complex class satisfy a tree constraint with the processor simplex class as root.

Here we assumed that there is at most one connector between a processor and a place. This assumption is needed to be able to determine if a token is consumed or produced by a processor. ( It is not difficult to modify the object model to allow also multiple connections between processors and places.)

The relationship between the actor model and the object model is as follows: whenever in the actor model a processor $p$ executes, there will be a complex created (with simplex class $p$ as root) and with four simplexes (belonging to a place) for every token that is consumed or produced during the execution of the processor: one simplex (of the undecorated simplex class) that denotes the token, one simplex (of the decorated simplex class) that denotes the complex of the token, one that denotes the identity and one that denotes the time stamp of the token.

Note that it is always possible to reconstruct the transition time: it is the maximum of the time stamps of the consumed tokens. To distinguish the consumed and produced tokens we have to inspect the actor model. (It is in fact easy to modify the object model to incorporate the necessary information.) We will illustrate this method by an example. The actor model represents a resource sharing system. In figure 15.17 the actor model is displayed and in figure 15.18 the corresponding object model. Note that the object model does not contain information about the way processors execute, so it cannot be used for forecasting or simulation but only for monitoring the actor model. To derive the actual state

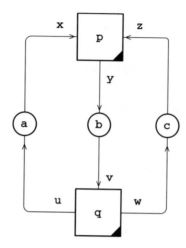

Fig. 15.17. Actor model

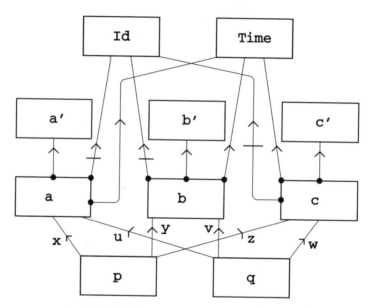

Fig. 15.18. The corresponding object model.

of the actor net we have to determine all the simplexes that represent tokens not occurring as input tokens.

If we want to construct such a monitoring information system we have to modify the processors in the target system to enable them to produce the complexes defined above.

## 15.3 Transformations to other object frameworks

In this section we study methods for transforming object models in our framework into object models in other frameworks and vice versa. The transformations are often only partial because some frameworks have specific requirements or lack some notions (for instance the notion of a complex). In the usual database terminology a framework is defined by a *schema* and a *set of instances* that belong to the schema. (Note that the term "schema" is used here in a different way from that in the specification language.) In our framework, which we simply call the *object framework*, a *schema* is a class model plus the function *sim* that assigns a value type to each simplex class. The set of instances of a schema in the object framework is the set of instances of the universal complex class.

For an arbitrary framework a schema plus its instances is called a *model* and is almost what we called an *object model*.

Formally these transformations proceed along the following lines.

(i) Construct a (partial) function $F$ from schemas in one framework into schemas of another framework.

(ii) Construct a (partial) *injective* function $f$ that transforms an arbitrary instance $a$ of a schema $A$ in the first framework into an instance $f(a)$ of a schema $F(A)$ in the other framework.

The requirement that function $f$ should be injective is very important: it ensures that $f$ is *information preserving*, i.e. that it has a (partial) inverse. So if it is possible to transform an instance $a$ of framework $A$ into an instance $b$ of framework $B$ we can reconstruct $a$ from $b$. Note that in general the function $f$ will depend on $F$ and that there are several choices for $F$ and $f$.

We only consider the cardinality and key constraints in these transformations; however, it is possible to transform some other constraints as well.

Transformations of object frameworks are important for a number of reasons. First of all it is important to be able to communicate an object model to other persons who are more used to another object framework. Second it might be the case that an object model is already available in another framework. Last but not least it might be necessary to implement an object model by means of a database management system that is based on another object framework. Most database management systems used in practice are based on the *relational data model*, so this will be one of the frameworks we consider. Other frameworks are the *functional data model*, the *entity-relationship data model* and the *nested relational data model*, which is an extension of the relational data model. (Note that we have called the entity-relationship data model "the entity-relationship model" in part I.) There are several versions of each of these frameworks; however, we have chosen only one of them. There are some other object frameworks, but except for *object oriented frameworks*, the ones presented here are the most important in practice.

The strategy we follow in this section is displayed in figure 15.19. Here "ERM",

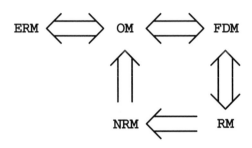

Fig. 15.19. Strategy of transformations.

"OM", "FDM", "RM" and "NRM" denote object models in the entity-relationship data model, (our) object framework model, the functional data model, the relational data model and the nested relational data model, respectively. A double arrow head means that we consider a transformation in both directions. Since we are not expressing specifications but framework transformations we use here meta-language.

## 1. Functional data model

The version of the functional data model we consider here is just a restriction of our framework in which only functional relationships are allowed. So, the only problem in transforming it into our framework is to get rid of the non-functional relationships. In practice most relationships are already functional (see for instance the examples in this chapter). However, if there is a non-functional relationship then we can transform the schema as follows. We define the function $F$ from schemas in our object framework into schemas of the functional data model. We call an object model of the functional data model a *functional object model*.

– If there is a non-functional, non-injective relationship we use again the "trick" of modeling relationships by properties. Thus, we introduce a simplex class for every relationship that is non-functional and connect it to the domain and range classes of the original relationship by total and functional relationships having the new simplex class as their domain class; these relationships have to form a domain key for the new simplex class.

− If a relationship is non-functional but injective, we may exchange the domain and range classes of this relationship and thus obtain a functional relationship.

− The new simplex classes should have a value type, i.e. the function *sim* has to be defined for these classes; since there is a domain key constraint it does not really matter how we define these value types, because the simplexes are uniquely determined by their relationships, however we will use the following definition.

Let *r* be a relationship in the functional object model that is replaced by simplex class *d*; then

$$sim(d) = sim(DM(r)) \times sim(RG(r)).$$

In figure 15.20 we see an example that shows these transformations. Note that

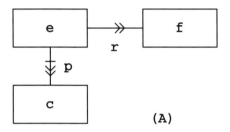

**(A)**

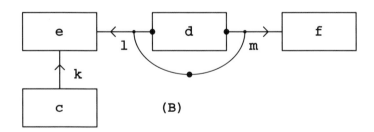

**(B)**

Fig. 15.20. Transformation to a functional model.

*p* is replaced by *k*, and *r* by *l*, *d* and *m*. Now we have seen how to transform the schema. However, we also have to transform instances of our schema into instances of a schema of the functional data model. We only consider universal complex classes, because the functional data model does not have the notion of complex classes. So we consider an arbitrary universal complex $a$ of an object model in the object framework and transform it into a universal complex $b$ of the functional data model. We will call the schemas respectively $A$ and $B$, so that $B = F(A)$. The transformation $(f)$ proceeds along the following lines.

(i) For each simplex class $n$ of schema $A$ we have $b(n) = a(n)$.

(ii) For each functional relationship $r$ of model $A$ the same relationship occurs in schema $B$, i.e. $b(r) = a(r)$, and $r$ has to satisfy the same cardinality constraints.

(iii) For each non-functional but injective relationship $p$ of schema $A$ there is a relationship $k$ of schema $B$ with

$$b(k) = \{(x, y) \mid (y, x) \in a(p)\}.$$

If $p$ is total then $k$ is surjective and if $p$ is surjective then $k$ should be total.

(iv) For each non-functional, non-injective relationship $r$ of schema $A$ there is a simplex class $d$ and two relationship classes $l$ and $m$ such that

$$DM_B(l) = DM_B(m) = d,$$
$$RG_B(l) = DM_A(r),$$
$$RG_B(m) = RG_A(r),$$
$$b(d) = a(r) \quad \wedge \quad b(l) = \{((x, y), x) \mid (x, y) \in a(r)\}$$
$$\wedge \quad b(m) = \{((x, y), y) \mid (x, y) \in a(r)\}.$$

Note that $b(d) = a(r)$ is justified by the choice of $sim(d)$. It is clear that $F$ is not injective. To verify this note that models (A) and (B) of figure 15.20 are both mapped to model (B). However, $f$ is injective. (The proof of this assertion is an exercise.) In fact we may consider the function $F$ as a reduction to a *normal form* of the object framework. Therefore this framework is sometimes called the *irreducible data model*, while in the literature our object framework is itself sometimes called the *functional data model*, because the binary relationships may be considered as (set-valued) functions.

To transform an object model defined as a functional data model into one in our framework, we have to do nothing because it is already an object model in the object framework i.e. the functions $F$ and $f$ are the identities.

## 2. Relational data model

In order to describe the transformations we need a definition of the relational data model. We call an object model of the relational data model a *relational model.* A relational model is defined by a *relational schema* and a set of *instances* of this schema.

**Definition 15.1** A *relational schema* is a 5-tuple

$$(T, \ A, \ \alpha, \ \beta, \ \gamma)$$

where $T$ and $A$ are mutually disjoint sets and where

(i) $T$ is the set of *relation* names,
(ii) $A$ is the set of *attribute* names,
(iii) $\alpha : T \rightarrow \mathbb{F}(A)$ assigns to every relation name a set of attributes such that

$$\forall \, t_1, t_2 \in T : t_1 \neq t_2 \Rightarrow \alpha(t_1) \cap \alpha(t_2) = \varnothing,$$

(iv) $\beta$ is a function that assigns to every attribute a set called an *attribute domain* (note that $dom(\beta) = A$),
(v) $\gamma : T \rightarrow \mathbb{F}(A)$ assigns to every relation one *primary key*, which is a subset of the attributes assigned by $\alpha$, such that

$$\forall \, t \in T : \gamma(t) \subseteq \alpha(t) \ \wedge \ \gamma(t) \neq \varnothing.$$

□

(The terminology used here is the usual one for the relational data model; however, note that some of the terms have a slightly different meaning in the rest of this book.) Note that if the attribute names of two relations are not disjoint we can make them disjoint by combining their names with the names of the relations in which they occur. In table 15.3 we display a relational schema. The code "y" means that the attribute is part of the primary key of the relation and "n" means that it is not part of the primary key. Next we have to define instances

Table 15.3. *Relational schema*

| relation | attribute | domain | key |
|----------|-----------|--------|-----|
| $r_1$ | $a_1$ | $A_1$ | n |
|  | $a_2$ | $A_1$ | y |
|  | $a_3$ | $A_2$ | y |
| $r_2$ | $a_4$ | $A_2$ | y |
|  | $a_5$ | $A_3$ | y |
|  | $a_6$ | $A_3$ | n |
| $r_3$ | $a_7$ | $A_3$ | y |
|  | $a_8$ | $A_4$ | y |
|  | $a_9$ | $A_4$ | n |

of a relational schema that are comparable with our universal complex class (*see* 10.2). The set of instances is defined by the following.

**Definition 15.2** Let a relational schema be given. An *instance* of a relation database schema is a function $b$ with $dom(b) = T$ and

$$\forall t \in T : b(t) \subseteq \Pi(\beta \upharpoonright \alpha(t)) \ \wedge \ (\forall x, y \in b(t) : x \upharpoonright \gamma(t) = y \upharpoonright \gamma(t) \Rightarrow x = y).$$

□

For $t \in T$ and an instance $b$ the set $b(t)$ is a set of functions, called a *relation*, with a common domain $\alpha(t)$. These functions are called *tuples*. The primary key identifies a tuple in an instance. (Note that it is a minimal key, because we have no other keys defined.) The relational data model has several standard constraints: *functional dependence*, *multi-valued dependence* and *referential integrity*. Referential integrity is equivalent to our surjectivity constraint. A key constraint is the most important example of a functional dependency; the multi-valued dependences do not have an equivalent in our framework, therefore we do not consider them.

Note that the concept of a complex does not exist in the relational data model so we have to restrict the transformation to the universal complex class. For the relational data model there exist two *query languages*: the *relational algebra* and the *tuple calculus*. In the next part we show how the relational algebra can be expressed in the specification language.

Let us consider transformations from relational models and object models. In figure 15.21 we see the object model corresponding to the relational schema in the table above. Let us define the function $F$ that maps a relational schema $A$ into a schema for the object framework $B$:

   (i) $SN = T \cup rng(\beta)$, so every relation and every attribute domain become simplex classes,

   (ii) $RN = A$, so all attributes become relationships,

   (iii) $\forall a \in RN, t \in T : DM(a) = t \Leftrightarrow a \in \alpha(t)$ (note that $t$ is uniquely determined),

   (iv) $\forall a \in RN : RG(a) = \beta(a)$,

   (v) $\forall t \in T : DK(t) = \{\gamma(t)\}$,

   (vi) $\forall t \in T : sim(t) = \Pi(\beta \upharpoonright \gamma(t))$,

   (vii) $\forall r \in rng(\beta) : sim(r) = \beta(r)$.

Next we consider transformations on the instance level. The transformation $f$ that maps an instance $a$ of $A$ into a universal complex $b$ of $F(A)$ is defined as follows.

   (i) $\forall t \in T : b(t) = \{x \upharpoonright \gamma(t) \mid x \in a(t)\}$, so all primary keys of a relation form the simplexes of a simplex class with the same name as the relation,

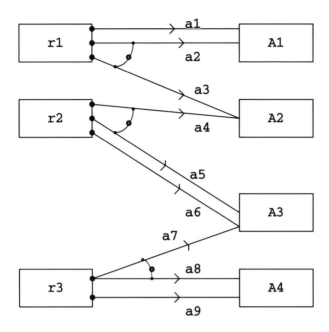

Fig. 15.21. Transformation of a relational schema.

(ii) $\forall d \in rng(\beta) : b(d) = \{x \restriction r \mid \exists t \in T : x \in a(t) \land r \in \alpha(t) \land \beta(r) = d\}$,
so all attribute values of an attribute domain that occur in $a$ form the
simplexes of a simplex class with the name of the attribute domain,

(iii) $\forall r \in RN : b(r) = \{(x, y) \mid \exists z \in a(DM(r)) : x = z \restriction \gamma(DM(r)) \land y \in x(r)\}$; note that $b(r)$ is total and functional because of the property of the
primary keys of the relational data model.

It is clear that these rules define a function. However, we still have to prove that
this function, $f$, is injective.

**Lemma 15.1** The function $f$ defined by the three rules above is *injective*.

*Proof* Let $a_1$ and $a_2$ be two instances of the relational schema $A$ and suppose
that $f(a_1) = f(a_2) = b$. We have to prove that $a_1 = a_2$. Take an arbitrary $t \in T$.
We have (by rule (i) in the list before the lemma):

$$\{x \restriction \gamma(t) \mid x \in a_1(t)\} = \{x \restriction \gamma(t) \mid x \in a_2(t)\}.$$

Let $x_1 \in a_1(t)$ and $x_2 \in a_2(t)$ such that $x_1 \restriction \gamma(t) = x_2 \restriction \gamma(t)$. (Note that this does
not imply $x_1 = x_2$, since $x_1$ and $x_2$ belong to different instances.) Then, for all

$r \in \alpha(t)$ (by rule (iii) in the same list),

$$(x_1 \upharpoonright \gamma(t), x_1(r)) \in b(r) \ \wedge \ (x_2 \upharpoonright \gamma(t), x_2(r)) \in b(r).$$

However, $r$ (as a relationship) is functional and therefore $x_1(r) = x_2(r)$. This proves that $x_1 = x_2$. So we have proven that $a_1 = a_2$.                      □

We continue by considering the transformation the other way around. So, we start with a schema $A$ of an object model and first transform this into the schema $B$ of a relational model (via function $F$); afterwards we define the transformation $f$ that maps an instance of a universal complex class onto an instance of the relational schema. However, we first transform the object model into a functional model as before. So we assume that $A$ is a functional model and in addition that all relationships are total, because this avoids the problem of nil values in the relational model. Note that $F$ is partial now! Transformation $F$ is defined as follows.

   (i) $T = rng(DM)$, so only simplex classes with "properties" become relations,
   (ii) $A = RN \cup \{t' \mid t \in T\}$, so all relationships become attributes and for each
        relation $t$ there is one new attribute $t'$ (assume primes were not used in
        names of $A$),
  (iii) $\forall\, t \in T : \alpha(t) = \{t'\} \cup DM^{-1}(t)$,
  (iv) $\forall\, r \in RN : \beta(r) = sim(RG(r))$,
   (v) $\forall\, t \in T : \beta(t') = sim(t)$,
  (vi) $\forall\, t \in T : \gamma(t) = \{t'\}$, so the new attributes form the primary keys.

In figure 15.22 we see a schema of a functional model and in table 15.4 we see its transformation into a relational model.

   The next step is the definition of $f$. Let a universal complex $a$ be given; the instance $b = f(a)$ should satisfy

$$\forall\, t \in T : \{x(t') \mid x \in b(t)\} = a(t),$$
$$\forall\, t \in T : \forall\, r \in \alpha(t) : \{(x(t'), x(r)) \mid x \in b(t)\} = a(r).$$

It is not a priori evident that these rules determine $b$ uniquely.

**Lemma 15.2** The two rules above define a function.

*Proof* Let $a$ be given. We have to show that $a$ determines only one $b$. Suppose that $b_1$ and $b_2$ satisfy the rules above. We will show that $b_1 = b_2$. Choose some $t \in T$; let $x_1 \in b_1(t)$. Then $x_1(t') \in a(t)$, which implies

$$\exists\, x_2 \in b_2(t) : x_2(t') = x_1(t').$$

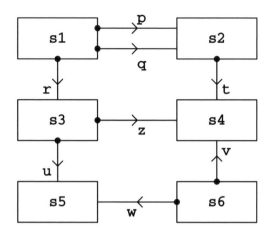

Fig. 15.22. Transformation of a functional model into a relational model.

Table 15.4 *Transformation of a functional model into a relational model, table form*

| relation | attribute | domain | key |
|----------|-----------|--------|-----|
| $s_1$ | $s_1'$ | $sim(s_1)$ | y |
|  | $p$ | $sim(s_2)$ | n |
|  | $q$ | $sim(s_2)$ | n |
|  | $r$ | $sim(s_3)$ | n |
| $s_2$ | $s_2'$ | $sim(s_2)$ | y |
|  | $t$ | $sim(s_4)$ | n |
| $s_3$ | $s_3'$ | $sim(s_3)$ | y |
|  | $u$ | $sim(s_5)$ | n |
|  | $z$ | $sim(s_4)$ | n |
| $s_6$ | $s_6'$ | $sim(s_6)$ | y |
|  | $v$ | $sim(s_4)$ | n |
|  | $w$ | $sim(s_5)$ | n |

Further,

$$\forall r \in a(t) : (x_1(t'), x_1(r)) \in a(t) \Rightarrow$$
$$\exists x_3 \in b_2 : (x_3(t'), x_3(r)) = (x_1(t'), x_1(r)).$$

The fact that $t'$ is a primary key for $b_2(t)$ implies that

$$\forall r \in a(t) : x_3(t') = x_2(t') = x_1(t') \wedge x_3(r) = x_2(r) = x_1(r).$$

This implies that $x_1 = x_2$ and so $x_1 \in b_2(t)$. Therefore $b_1 = b_2$.          □

Finally we have to show that $f$ is injective.

**Lemma 15.3** The function $f$ defined by the rules above is injective.

*Proof* The proof is an immediate consequence of the specification of $f$: if $a_1$ and $a_2$ are two universal complexes with $f(a_1) = f(a_2)$ then the specifications for $a_1$ and $a_2$ by the rules above are identical (namely $b = f(a_1) = f(a_2)$) and so $a_1 = a_2$. □

Note that if we transform a relational schema into an object schema and afterwards this object schema into a relational schema, then the last schema is identical to the first one except that each relation has one extra attribute.

## 3. Entity-relationship data model

As in the case of the relational data model we start with a definition of the entity-relationship data model.

**Definition 15.3** An *entity-relationship schema* is a 7-tuple

$$(E, R, A, \alpha, \beta, \gamma, \delta)$$

where

  (i) $E$ is the set of *entities*,
 (ii) $R$ is the set of *relationships*,
(iii) $A$ is the set of *attributes*,
 (iv) $\alpha : E \to \mathbb{F}(A)$ assigns to every entity a set of attributes,
  (v) $\beta$ is a function that assigns to every attribute a set called the *attribute domain*,
 (vi) $\gamma : E \to \mathbb{F}(A)$ assigns to every entity a *primary key*, such that

$$\forall\, e \in E : \gamma(e) \subseteq \alpha(e),$$

(vii) $\delta : R \to \mathbb{F}(E)$, which assigns to every relationship a set of entities.

□

Like the relational data model, this model does not have the notion of complex classes either, so we restrict ourselves to the universal complex class as before. Normally the entity-relationship data model is used as an aid to define a relational schema and in that case one does not have to define instances of entity-relationship schemas. However, we want to transform an *entity-relationship schema* into a schema of an object model and so we define indirectly instances for entity-relationship schemas as instances of the universal complex class of the corresponding object model! Therefore we do not have to specify the function $f$

that transforms instances. Note that the term "relationship" is used here differently, and therefore we will call it "er-relationship". The transformation proceeds along the following lines.

(i) $SN = E \cup R \cup A$,

(ii) $RN = \bigcup_{e \in E}\{(e, a) \mid a \in \alpha(e)\} \cup \bigcup_{r \in R}\{(r, e) \mid e \in \delta(r)\}$,

(iii) $\forall(x, y) \in RN : DM((x, y)) = x \;\wedge\; RG((x, y)) = y$,

(iv) $\forall e \in E : DK(e) = \{\{(e, a) \mid a \in \gamma(e)\}\}$,

(v) $\forall r \in R : DK(r) = \{\{(r, e) \mid e \in \delta(r)\}\}$,

(vi) all relationships of the object model are total and functional,

(vii) the function $sim$ is defined by:

$$n \in A : sim(n) = \beta(n),$$
$$n \in E : sim(n) = \Pi(sim \upharpoonright \gamma(n)),$$
$$n \in R : sim(n) = \Pi(sim \upharpoonright \delta(n)).$$

In figure 15.23 we display an entity-relationship schema (A) and its transformation into an object model (B). Sometimes it is possible to transform a schema of an object model into an entity-relationship schema with an *isomorphic* graph, i.e. there is a bijective mapping $f$ between the nodes and edges of the two graphs, such that each edge $e$ connects two nodes $m$ and $n$ if and only if $f(e)$ connects $f(m)$ and $f(n)$. This is for instance the case if we consider object models that are made of entity-relationship models by the former transformation. Then we can invert the mapping. For the general case there is also a transformation. Let an object model be given; then the corresponding entity-relationship schema is as follows.

(i) $A = \{n' \mid n \in SN\}$, so we create new names out of $SN$,

(ii) $E = SN$,

(iii) $R = RN$,

(iv) $\forall n \in E : \alpha(n) = \gamma(n) = \{n'\}$,

(v) $\forall n' \in A : \beta(n') = sim(n)$,

(vi) $\forall r \in R : \delta(r) = \{DM(r), RG(r)\}$.

Hence we obtain only binary relationships and each entity has only one attribute. As stated in part I, the object framework may be considered as an extension of the binary version of the entity-relationship model, which means that $\forall r \in R :$ $\#(R(r)) = 2$. This is what we have shown here.

## 4. Nested relational data model

The nested relational data model is a generalization of the relational data model. This framework enables us to model "non-atomic" attributes in an easier way.

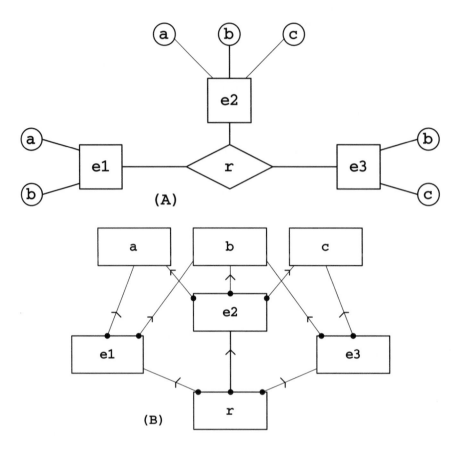

Fig. 15.23. Transformation of an entity-relationship schema.

We start with the example given in table 15.5. To indicate that a "nest" (in fact a vector) of attributes may be repeated we use curly brackets, so the attributes of the table above can be coded by

$$\{(Order, \{(Item, Total, \{(Supplier, Price, Quantity)\})\})\}$$

In the table we see only one nested relation. There is no need for more than one because we can combine two to form a third. For instance, two non-nested relations $T_1$ and $T_2$ with attribute sets $\{A, B, C\}$ and $\{D, E, F\}$ respectively, can be combined into one nested relation, coded by

$$(\{(A, B, C)\}, \{(D, E, F)\}).$$

So, a relational model can be transformed, in an information preserving way, into a nested relational model (the proof is an exercise). We start with the definition

Table 15.5. *Example: nested relational model*

| Order | Item | Total | Supplier | Price | Quantity |
|---|---|---|---|---|---|
| $o_1$ | $i_1$ | 100 | A | 3 | 50 |
|  |  |  | B | 5 | 30 |
|  |  |  | C | 4 | 20 |
|  | $i_2$ | 50 | B | 7 | 20 |
|  |  |  | D | 6 | 30 |
| $o_2$ | $i_3$ | 60 | B | 8 | 40 |
|  |  |  | E | 10 | 20 |
|  | $i_4$ | 80 | A | 10 | 50 |
|  |  |  | D | 12 | 30 |

of a *nested relational schema* and afterwards give the definition of an instance of such a schema.

**Definition 15.4** A *nested relational schema* is a 3-tuple

$$(A,\ \beta,\ T)$$

where

  (i) $A$ is a finite set of attributes,
 (ii) $\beta$ is a function that assigns to every attribute a set called the *attribute domain*,
(iii) $T$ is an *attribute nest*; attribute nests are defined using a syntax (*see* appendix B) by

  – *Nest* ::= *Attribute* | $\underline{(}Nest\langle\underline{,}Nest\rangle\underline{)}$ | $\underline{\{}Nest\underline{\}}$;
  – *Attribute* $\in A$;
  – no attribute may occur twice in an attribute nest.

An *attribute nest* is an entity that can be represented by *Nest*.

□

Next, the set of instances of a nested relation schema is defined.

**Definition 15.5** Let a nested relation schema be given. An *instance* of such a schema is defined recursively using the set $X$ of all *sub-attribute nests* of $T$: $X$ is the set of all attribute nests that are represented by a sub-string of $T$. The set of all instances of $x$, where $x \in X$, is denoted by $I(x)$. The function $I$ is (recursively) defined by

$$\forall\, x \in X \cap A : I(x) = \beta(x),$$
$$\forall\, x, x_1, \ldots, x_n \in X : x = (x_1, \ldots, x_n) \Rightarrow I(x) = I(x_1) \times \ldots \times I(x_n),$$
$$\forall\, x, y \in X : x = \{y\} \Rightarrow I(x) = \mathbb{F}(I(y)).$$

□

So, in the table above the instance

$$\{(o_1, \{(i_1, 100, \{(A, 3, 50), (B, 5, 30), (C, 4, 20)\}),$$
$$(i_2, 50, \{(B, 7, 20), (D, 6, 30)\})\}),$$
$$(o_2, \{(i_3, 60, \{(B, 8, 40), (E, 10, 20)\}),$$
$$(i_4, 80, \{(A, 10, 50), (D, 12, 30)\})\})\})\}$$

is displayed.

As noted before, the relational data model can be transformed into the nested relational data model. We have seen how to transform an object model of our framework into the relational data model. The final step to close the circle is to show how a model in the nested relational data model can be transformed into our framework. Then we will also have shown that a nested relational model can be transformed into a relational model. (Of course it is possible to give a more direct transformation than we present here.)

We first consider the transformation of a nested relational schema into a schema of an object model. It proceeds along the following lines.

(i) Create for each sub-attribute nest in $X$, including the attributes themselves, a simplex class and give it a suitable name (use for example the elements of $X$ as names).

(ii) Create for every simplex class with a name of the form $\{x\}$ a total relationship class $r$ that satisfies

$$DM(r) = \{x\} \ \wedge \ RG(r) = x.$$

(iii) Create for every simplex class with a name of the form $(x_1, \ldots, x_n)$ relationship classes $r_1, \ldots, r_n$ that are total and functional and that satisfy

$$\forall i \in \{i, \ldots, n\} : DM(r_i) = (x_1, \ldots, x_n) \ \wedge \ RG(r_i) = x_i.$$

(iv) $\forall n \in SN : DK(n) = \{DM^{-1}(n)\}$,

(v) For each simplex class $n$ that represents attributes we take $sim(n) = \beta(n)$, for the others we may chose the value types arbitrarily.

In figure 15.24 the transformation of the example given in the table is displayed. (Note that we have represented the names of attributes by their initials.) In fact the simplex classes with numbers 3 and 5 are redundant. In figure 15.25 we have transformed (injectively) the object model in order to obtain a simpler one containing the same information. (The proof of this statement is an exercise.)

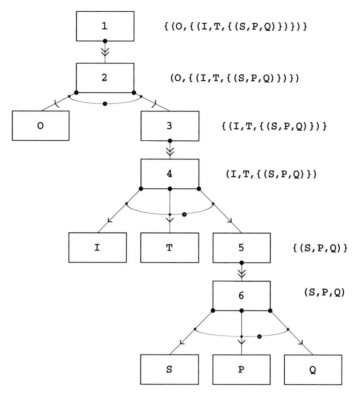

Fig. 15.24. Transformation of a nested relational schema.

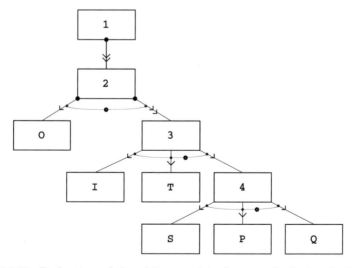

Fig. 15.25. Reduction of the object model of a nested relational schema.

# 16

# Object oriented modeling

As said before, we shall consider *object oriented modeling* as a method of constructing a complete actor model in an integrated way. The method uses a specific paradigm of a system (the object oriented paradigm), which can easily be mapped onto our frameworks. This paradigm is quite informal, and there are many ways to formalize it. We will start with the main ideas of the object oriented paradigm and afterwards we will show how these ideas can be incorporated into our frameworks.

The basic idea of the object oriented paradigm is that there are classes of *active objects*. (Note that we now use the term "object" a little differently.) Each object has a (structured) value and may have *knowledge* of other objects; it has a *life cycle* that starts with its *birth* and ends with its *death*; these are also called the *creation* and *deletion* of the object. During its life an object can change its value and can exchange *messages* with other objects of the same or different classes. The structure of the life cycle is the same for all objects of a specific class and the type of communication with other objects is also determined by the class of the object. A system is considered as a "dynamic set" of objects, which means that at each moment there is in each object class a finite number of objects, each with a particular value and some particular knowledge of other objects, and that there are pending messages destined for specific objects. This "dynamic set" changes over time because the objects may change their values, receive messages and send messages. A change of value of an object may be triggered by a message but this is not necessarily the case; it may also change its value autonomously. The operations that change the value and the knowledge of an object are usually called *methods* and are specific to an object class. The value of an object and the knowledge it has of other objects at a particular time can be considered as the *state* of the object. There are several situations that should be avoided, such as that there exist messages for objects that have already died or that two or more objects are waiting for messages from each other (deadlock).

The idea of object oriented modeling is that a systems engineer can define an object class completely in *isolation*, i.e. without knowledge of other object classes. Object oriented *languages* have facilities for using inheritance relationships between object classes, which may decrease the effort required to model a system.

If we compare the object oriented paradigm with our actor framework we see an important difference: objects in our framework are *passive* components of a system and actors are *active* components but are fixed, i.e. there are no births and deaths of actors! So it is not immediately clear if we should identify the "object oriented" objects with our objects or with our actors. To distinguish object oriented objects from ours, we will call them *o-objects*. It turns out that we have for each *o-object class* a *complex class* and an *actor*.

Object oriented modeling proceeds along the following lines.

- For each o-object class there is a complex class that satisfies a tree constraint and for which the root simplex identifies the o-object (of type ID); we call it an *o-complex class*.
- For each o-object class there is one actor that represents the life cycle of the o-object, we call it an *o-actor*.
- Every o-actor has internally the structure of a *state machine*, i.e. each processor is connected to at most one input and one output place within the actor. A processor may have other input and output connectors that are connected to the connectors of the o-actor.
- The input and output connectors of an o-actor are used for the exchange of messages with context actors or with o-actors.
- For each connector of an actor there is a complex class that represents a message type. We call it an *m-complex class*.
- The life cycle of an o-object can only start with a message from outside. There may be live o-objects in the initial state, so an o-actor does not have to have an input connector for life cycle creation. A message that starts the life of an o-object may be sent by a context actor or by an o-actor. In the latter case it may be the same o-actor, which means that o-objects of one class may create new ones from the same class. A life cycle may end or may continue for ever.
- The o-complexes have two kinds of simplex class: those that are root simplex classes of other o-complex classes and those that are not. The first kind of simplex represents the knowledge of another o-object: if an o-complex contains the root simplex of another o-complex it means that it knows of the existence of the other o-complex. We call it a *knowledge simplex* (k-*simplex* for short).

The second kind of simplex in an o-complex denotes the value of the o-object. We call it a *value simplex* (v-*simplex* for short). In many cases the k-simplexes will have relationships only with the root simplex in an o-complex.

– Newly created o-complexes obtain their identity ( in the root simplex) from the token containing the message that initiated their life. So at the start the identity of the o-object and the identity of the token that contains it are equal. During the life of the o-object the identity of the containing token changes but the identity of the o-object remains the same.

– An m-object contains the identity of the sending o-object (the return address), and in some cases also that of the receiving o-object. There are, however, cases in which the receiving object is not known because the message may be handled by any o-object of the addressed class.

– The *state* of an o-object is determined by the value in the o-complex plus the place in the o-actor where the o-complex resides. So in fact the *token* that carries the o-complex represents the state of the o-object, since a token contains the place information. (Note that the places in an o-actor are *stages* in the life cycle of the o-object. It is the systems engineer's decision which part of an o-object's state is represented by the value of a token and which part by the places in the o-actor.)

– The processors inside an o-actor perform the state changes. They may be triggered by an incoming message and may produce an outgoing message. They may be considered as the *methods* of an o-object.

– The communication between two o-objects needs a *protocol*, i.e. a token exchange pattern. There are two kinds of communication. The first kind concerns the creation of an o-object by some other o-object. The second kind concerns a *client-server* behavior. Here one o-object (the *client*) asks a service of another o-object (the *server*). The server may ask another o-object to perform a part of this service. So the server may behave as a client as well and one request for service may create a cascade of requests.

In most cases a message is answered by an other message. A simple protocol is that an o-object has at most one message pending at a time. So after it has sent a message it may perform *internal steps* (i.e. steps without sending messages) only until it receives an answer from the receiving o-object.

Note that what is here called an o-object, can also be considered as a *transaction*. A transaction in a database system, for instance, also has a life cycle, may initiate other transactions and may wait for the reactions of other transactions. So the object oriented paradigm is applicable to transaction processing systems in a natural way.

As mentioned before the object oriented modeling method develops a model by considering one o-object class at a time. This means that for each class the following activities have to be carried out.

(i) An o-complex class, i.e. an object model, is defined.
(ii) An o-actor, i.e. an incomplete actor model, is defined. The places inside the o-actor mark the stages in the o-object's life cycle.
(iii) For each connector of this o-actor an m-complex has to be defined, if it has not been defined previously for another class.
(iv) Suitable value types for the complex classes involved are specified.
(v) The processor relations for the o-actor are specified. Usually these will be functional; the corresponding functions are called methods.

Note that we have not used the hierarchy of actors in this method. Of course this hierarchy can be used to "hide" part of the life cycle in an actor. The actor then has, internally, the state machine structure and also has one input and one output connector. So it can be considered as a processor, because it behaves as such.

Stores can also be used, but they do not fit very well into the object oriented paradigm. In practice it is good to start with an overall actor model of the system in which the context actors and o-actors are displayed. The use of inheritance that is supported by most object oriented languages is not directly translatable to our framework. Of course we have polymorphic functions, and type variables that give us the possibility of reusing already defined constructions, but we have no inheritance relationships between actors or complex classes.

The question that remains is: how do we find the o-object classes? There is no "waterproof" answer to this question. If the paradigm is carried through too far, every "thing" is considered as an o-object and this means that we obtain many o-object classes with a simple structure but with complicated interactions between the objects of these classes. For example, if we take a library system and consider each simplex of an object model in our framework as an o-object then we have o-object classes for books, for authors, for publishers, for dates etc. This would mean that if a library user wants to ask a question about a book, he has to send a message to the book and then the book has to send a message to the author(s) and to the publisher and to the date (of publication). Of course, the library system can be modeled in this way, but it is not a natural way of modeling and certainly not a simple model. A good approach is to consider only those entities in the real world as o-objects that behave as o-objects, i.e. they have their own life cycle and they communicate with other entities. These entities should belong to classes, which means that there could be more instances of the class in existence at the same time. So in fact there is a simple answer to the question: if real-world entities can be identified as o-objects in a natural way,

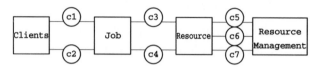

Fig. 16.1. Jobshop: top level.

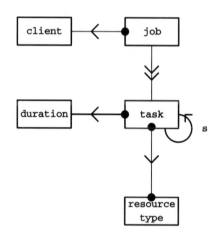

Fig. 16.2. o-complex class for *Job*: *ShopOrder*.

then they should indeed be modeled in this way, or otherwise as simplexes to be incorporated in o-complexes or m-complexes.

We will illustrate the object oriented modeling method by a small example. Consider a jobshop, i.e. a factory that has resources that can be used to perform tasks; clients send jobs consisting of one or more tasks to the factory. (Note that this model is a simplification of the factory example considered in chapter 15.) In figure 16.1 we show the top level of the system. There are two context actors, called *Clients* and *ResourceManagement*. The first one sends jobs to the jobshop and the second one adds new resources, takes resources out and reserves time for the maintenance of resources. We have connected them by channels; however, in this early stage of development it is not certain via how many connectors the o-objects will communicate. (We use for connectors the names of the places to which they are attached.) The context actors are not considered in detail so we concentrate on the two o-object classes, *Job* and *Resource*. We start with *Job*. The o-complex class for *Job* is displayed in figure 16.2. The simplex class *job* is the root of the complex. Tasks have an ordering, which is expressed by the

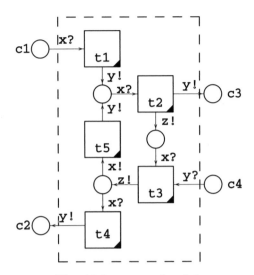

Fig. 16.3. o-actor for *Job*.

functional relationship $s$ that assigns to a task its successor. It needs a constraint as we have seen in section 15.2. We call this complex class *ShopOrder*. The next step is the o-actor for *Job*. It is displayed in figure 16.3. Processor $t_1$ creates a new job from a message of a client and $t_4$ deletes a job. All processors are functional and complete, but only $t_1$ and $t_2$ are total. The other processors have preconditions: $t_3$ selects pairs of input tokens that belong to the same job, and $t_4$ and $t_5$ select tokens on the existence of unfinished tasks in the jobs. Note that from each job only one task at a time can be executed. However, several jobs may be processed concurrently. The m-complex classes for the connectors are displayed in figure 16.4. They all satisfy a tree constraint with *client* or *job* as root. The m-complex class for connector $c_1$ is almost the same as the o-complex class; the only difference is the job identification that is attached to an incoming message, which we call *ClientOrder*. The root of *ClientOrder* is *client*; so, a client may send as many jobs as he likes and they will obtain their own identification internally. The m-complexes for $c_3$ have *job* as root; those for connector $c_4$ consist of one simplex *job* that is also the root simplex. We call these m-complexes *TaskOut* and *TaskIn* respectively. Finally, the m-complex for $c_2$ has *client* as root; we call it *Product*. Note that all internal places have *ShopOrder* as complex class. It is assumed that the client gets the product symbolically in the form of the job identity. Note that *job* and *client* are k-simplexes, while all the others are v-simplexes.

The next step is the definition of appropriate value types for the complex

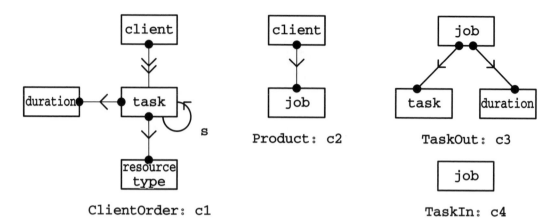

Fig. 16.4. m-complex classes for *Job*.

classes. It is straightforward in this case:

$$
\begin{aligned}
ClientOrder &:= [\, c : ID,\ t : (RT \times DU)^* ], \\
ShopOrder &:= [j : ID,\ c :\ ID,\ t : (RT \times DU)^* ], \\
TaskOut &:= [j :\ ID,\ t : RT \times DU], \\
TaskIn &:= ID, \\
Product &:= [c : ID,\ j : ID].
\end{aligned}
$$

Here $RT$ denotes the resource types and $DU$ is the type for the durations of tasks. We may choose for these $\mathbb{Q}$ or a restricted form of it that allows only non-negative values. Note that attribute $t$ denotes the set of tasks. Since a task is identified by its successor task (except for the last one), we may use this representation. We now specify the processor relations in tabular form (*see* table 16.1). They also are straightforward.

Note that we have only displayed the main schemas for these processors. The time does not play a role in this part of the system.

The next o-object we consider is *Resource*. The o-complex class for *Resource* is displayed in figure 16.5. We call this class *Machine*. It satisfies a tree constraint with *resource* as root. The simplex class *job* is needed to memorize for which job the resource is working, if it is not idle. The simplex class *timeslot* represents free time slots for the resource to work for tasks. A time slot is a pair of rational numbers. The o-actor for *Resource* is displayed in figure 16.6. All processors are functional and complete. Only $t_2$ and $t_3$ are total. The others have to find a correct resource, which is their precondition. Processor $t_3$ creates a new machine by sending a message that has the same format as the machine data. Processor

Table 16.1. *Main processor relations*

---

$t_1$

$x? : ClientOrder$
$y! : ShopOrder$

$\pi_j(y!) = New \ \wedge \ \pi_c(y!) = \pi_c(x?) \ \wedge \ \pi_t(y!) = \pi_t(x?)$

---

$t_2$

$x? : ShopOrder$
$y! : TaskOut$
$z! : ShopOrder$

$\pi_j(z!) = \pi_j(x?) \ \wedge \ \pi_c(z!) = \pi_c(x?) \ \wedge \ \pi_t(z!) = tail(\pi_t(x?))$
$\pi_j(y!) = \pi_j(x?) \ \wedge \ \pi_t(y!) = head(\pi_t(x?))$

---

$t_3$

$x? : ShopOrder$
$y? : TaskIn$
$z! : ShopOrder$

$y? = \pi_j(x?) \ \wedge \ z! = x?$

---

$t_4$

$x? : ShopOrder$
$y! : Product$

$\pi_t(x?) = \langle\rangle$
$\pi_c(y!) = \pi_c(x?) \ \wedge \ \pi_j(y!) = \pi_j(x?)$

---

$t_5$

$x? : ShopOrder$
$y! : ShopOrder$

$\pi_t(x?) \neq \langle\rangle$
$y! = x?$

---

$t_4$ deletes a machine with an identity given by *ResourceManagement*. (Note that *ResourceManagement* should be able to remember the machines it has created.)

The m-complex classes for the connectors $c_3$ and $c_4$ are *TaskOut* and *TaskIn* respectively. The m-complex classes for connectors $c_5$ and $c_6$ are the same as the o-complex class for *Resource*, because we assume that *ResourceManagement* gives and takes complete resources. The m-complex class for connector $c_7$ is trivial: only the identity of the resource is in the message. We call this class: *Retrieve*.

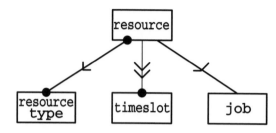

Fig. 16.5. o-complex class *Machine* for *Resource*.

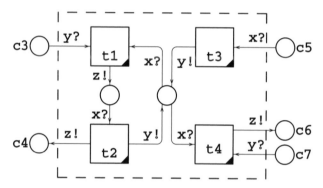

Fig. 16.6. o-actor for *Resource*.

The value types for the complex classes are as follows:

$$Machine := [r:\ ID,\ k:\ RT,\ j:\ ID,\ s: \mathbb{F}(\mathbb{Q} \times \mathbb{Q})],$$
$$Retrieve := ID.$$

Now we are ready to specify the four processors of *Resource* (*see* table 16.2.) They are very simple in this case. Processor $t_1$ selects a suitable resource for a task and determines the delay of it (by means of $z_t!$).

This example is quite simple; even so, it demonstrates the object oriented method well. Note that we have encountered different models for almost the same real-world systems in which *jobs* are asking for *resources*. Sometimes we model the system so that the resource is "carrying" the job (as here) and sometimes we define a new object class *operation* (as in chapter 15). The second procedure has the advantage that the choice of whether to add the job to the resource instead of the resource to the job is avoided. The example we have considered shows that there are many ways to model reality.

Table 16.2. *Processor relations for Resource*

$t_1$

$x?$ : *Machine*
$y?$ : *TaskOut*
$z!$ : *Machine*

$\pi_1(\pi_t(y?)) = \pi_k(x?)$
$\exists\, t : \mathbb{Q} \times \mathbb{Q} \bullet t \in \pi_s(x?) \ \wedge$
$\qquad \pi_1(t) \leq TransTime \ \wedge \ \pi_2(t) \geq TransTime + \pi_2(\pi_t(y?))$
$z! = x? \oplus \{j \mapsto \pi_j(y?)\}$
$z_t! = TransTime + \pi_2(\pi_t(y?))$

$t_2$

$x?$ : *Machine*
$y!$ : *Machine*
$z!$ : *TaskIn*

$y! = y \oplus \{y \mapsto \perp\}$
$z! = \pi_j(x?)$

$t_3$

$x?$ : *Machine*
$y!$ : *Machine*

$y! = x?$

$t_4$

$x?$ : *Machine*
$y!$ : *Retrieve*
$z!$ : *Machine*

$\pi_r(x?) = y?$
$z! = x?$

# References and exercises for part III

There is not much literature on methods for *creating* a model ab initio; most of the literature is about *frameworks* for modeling and about *phasing* the modeling process (the development *life cycle*). The reason that there is so little theory on modeling methods is that modeling is an *art* rather than a *science*. For actor modeling [Genrich and Lautenbach, 1981], [Peterson, 1981] and [Jensen, 1990] are good references. Further, there are many modeling examples published; for example [Brauer, 1980].

A special modeling method based on Petri nets is found in [David and Alla, 1989]. The modeling of time aspects can be found in [van der Aalst, 1992] and the modeling of continuous processes in [David and Alla, 1990]. In [van der Aalst, 1992] a modeling approach for *logistic systems* is presented. Structured actor models (such as free-choice nets) are in fact Petri nets and [Reisig, 1985] and [Peterson, 1980] are good references. The transformation to valueless models, often called *unfolding*, is due to K. Jensen, *see* [Jensen, 1992]. In the Springer-Verlag Series *Advances in Petri Nets 19XX* and in the *Proceedings of the XX-th International Conference on Applications and Theory of Petri Nets* many applications are recorded.

For *object modeling* there is a method based on a slightly different binary data framework, called NIAM, *see* [Nijssen and Halpin, 1989]. Another approach is offered in [Rishe, 1988]. In most books on data models the transformation to the relational data model is considered. In [Spaccapietra, 1987; Teorey *et al.*, 1986] many aspects of modeling with the entity-relationship data model are studied. In [Brodie *et al.*, 1984] several different approaches in object modeling and in particular constraint specification are given. For the transformation of (our version of) the functional data model to the relational data model, *see* [Aerts *et al.*, 1992]. The transformation of the nested relational data model to the relational data model can be found in [Paredaens *et al.*, 1989] and [Schek and Scholl, 1986]. Note however that our formulation of the nested relational model is a bit different.

*Object oriented modeling* is a popular topic. In [Sibertin-Blanc, 1991] an approach for object oriented modeling with Petri nets is given. In [Coad and Yourdon, 1990] and [Rumbaugh *et al.*, 1991] two approaches are offered based on informal frameworks; however, many ideas can be translated to our frameworks. In [Sernadas *et al.*, 1991] and [van Assche *et al.*, 1991] several ideas for object oriented modeling of information systems are given. For database systems to be object oriented there is a set of requirements formulated in [Atkinson *et al.*, 1989]. Many ideas in object oriented programming can be applied to modeling; *see* [Meyer, 1988; Booch, 1991]. There is an object oriented method, that has some similarity with ours, called HOOD; *see* [Di Giovanni and Iachini, 1990].

In [Jackson, 1983] a different but "complete" modeling method (for actor and object modeling) is given. In [Ward and Mellor, 1985] a modeling method for an (informal) framework based on data flow diagrams, on the entity-relationship model and on time is treated. In [Sol and van Hee, 1991] different modeling methods for complete systems are given, among which is the approach given in this book.

## Exercises for part III

(1)    Model a flip-flop circuit as a classical Petri net.

(2)    Model a machine that can count up to $n$ digits objects coming from some generator in a $p$-ary number system up to $n$ digits, as a classical Petri net.

(3)    Consider a cash machine, i.e. a machine that operates according to the following functions:

   – to get money a person has to put his card into the machine, and then enter his personal code;
   – if his code is correct he may enter the amount he wants;
   – if his balance is larger than or equal to the amount he gets the money and the amount is subtracted from his account; otherwise, he gets no money.

   Assume the machine has an infinite money capacity and that entering a wrong code or amount cannot be corrected by the user.

   (a) Model this system as an actor model.
   (b) Extend the functionality by allowing people to put money into the machine, which will result in an update of the account. Answer (a) again.

(c) Extend the machine by allowing people to transfer money to the account of somebody else. Answer (a) again.

(4)  Consider a simple railroad system with one track that consists of a closed curve without intersections. The track is divided into five sections, each ending with a signal that is either red or green. Each signal has a sensor that tells whether a train has (completely) passed the signal. There are two trains traveling in the same direction. The information system has to guarantee that

- no two trains are allowed to be in the same section,
- if the section after a signal is empty the signal is green,
- there is no deadlock.

Assume these requirements hold in the starting state.

(a) Model the railroad system including its information system as a classical Petri net. Explain what the objects, places and processes represent in reality.
(b) Modify the system so that the track intersects with itself and add the requirement that collisions should be excluded.

(5)  Consider a medical care system in which ill persons see a family physician first. The family physician can take one of the following decisions:

- he can give the patient a medicine and request that after a while he wants to see the patient again;
- he can decide that the patient cannot be treated (then the patient leaves the system);
- he can send the patient to a consultant physician.

The consultant can also take the first two of these decisions but in addition he can do some further medical examination: a blood test or X-ray photographs or both. He wants to see the patient back only if all examinations have been done. An extra decision he can make is that he can send the patient back to the family physician. The physicians base their decisions on the number of visits, the medicines used and the blood tests and X-rays of the patients.

(a) Make an (incomplete) actor model for this system.
(b) Modify the model in such a way that there is an arbitrary number (of both types) of physician and that each patient has to be seen by the same physician at each successive visit.

(6)  The Car Rental Company (CRC) has many stations in the country, where cars are stored and maintained.

– Customers make a reservation for a type of car at some station for a specific period of time.

– When the customer arrives at the station on the first day of the rental period, a car of the right type is assigned to the client.

– The client may also cancel a reservation; however, this must be done before the rental period starts.

– A client may return a car to another station at the end of his rental period (a charge is made for this).

– If a client wants to extend his rental period, this is considered as a new rental.

– Cars are either available for service, are being rented or are being shipped from one station to another (by CRC).

– The information system must be able to keep track of the cars and the reservations and must support the process of car assignment and invoicing.

Make two parts of an actor model as follows.

    (a) Make an object model for CRC, including graphical constraints and (if necessary) additional constraints both in natural language and predicate calculus.

    (b) Make an (incomplete) actor model.

(7)     Make an actor model for the following Resource Reservation System (RRS). The system receives requests from clients for an arbitrary resource on a particular date. (Resources are for instance seats in a concert hall or on airplane.) The client receives an acknowledgement of his request. If there is a resource free for that particular date, a reservation is made and the client receives a confirmation giving details of the resource. If no resource is available the request will wait until somebody else cancels his reservation. Clients may cancel their requests or their reservations. The systems administrator should have facilities to delete all the reservations and requests if the date has expired. Consider two cases: one where the unsatisfied requests are assigned to a resource in an arbitrary way and one in which they are assigned in a first-come-first-served order.

(8)      Make an object model for the Resource Reservation System of the previous exercise that can be used to define the database of a monitoring information system for the system (i.e. the universal complex class belongs to the store of the monitoring information system).

(9)      Make a (complete) actor model of a university using an object oriented approach. Consider the following o-classes: student, instructor and course. Choose appropriate o-complex classes and life cycles.

(10)     Modify the actor model of the railroad station (*see* text) in such a way that the station master decides to which track a new train will go.

(11)     Modify the construction for token cancellation (*see* text) such that actor $Z$ can select tokens to be cancelled.

(12)     Make an object model for the store of the train control system displayed in figure 14.8.

(13)     Transform the example of the nested relation in table 15.5 into a relational model.

(14)     Define an injective function that reduces instances of a nested relational model as indicated in figures 15.24 and 15.25.

(15)     Show that the instance transformation for the functional data model that belongs to the schema transformation of figure 15.20 is injective.

(16)     Make an actor model that may simulate simultaneously the behavior of many classical Petri nets, in the following way:

  – define a complex class to represent an arbitrary classical Petri net and its state,

  – define a proper value type for this complex class,

  – define a processor (relation) that consumes tokens with these values and that produces new tokens with a value that represents the same classical Petri net as the consumed one, but with a next state if possible,

  – define an actor model using the complex class and processor defined above, that may receive tokens representing a classical Petri net and a state from an environment and that returns the computed new states of these nets to the environment.

# Part IV

# Analysis methods

# 18

# Introduction

There are several methods for analyzing a model. We distinguish verification methods and validation methods: verification methods are based on proofs and validation methods on experiments. The questions we want to answer concerning a model are as follows.

- Is the model correctly defined?
- Is the model a faithful representation of the system under consideration (existing in the real world or in a person's mind)?
- Are some specific properties invariant (i.e. if they hold in an initial state, do they hold in all reachable states)?
- Are there sequences of processor firings that bring the system back to its initial state or to an equivalent state?
- Are states with certain (for instance undesirable) properties reachable?
- What time is needed to reach certain states?

For the first question we have to know what "correct" means. This is not easy and we will restrict correctness to *type correctness*. Therefore *type checking* is one of the most important verification methods. Type checking is the verification of function definitions, processor definitions and actor definitions with respect to type. Because the specification language is *strongly typed* it is possible to check the types without evaluation of functions and without execution of processors. The type checking of actors means that we verify whether the types of places match the types of processor connectors that are connected to them. Type checking rules are considered in part V. There are *type checking algorithms* based on these rules and therefore type checking can be done by tools. Another aspect of correctness concerns the definition of recursively defined functions. We will treat some methods of verifying this in chapter 28.

The only way to check whether a model is a faithful representation is by means of *simulation*. Here hard proof is not possible, but only the detection of errors.

So, simulation is a form of validation. For interactive simulation a software tool is required that can execute a specification. In chapter 22 we present some guidelines and techniques for performing simulation experiments; however a full treatment would require a complete book.

To verify invariant properties we have two kinds of invariant method: the methods of *place invariants* and of *transition invariants*. Place invariants can be used to prove properties that hold in each reachable state. A transition invariant is a characterization of (finite) traces that bring an actor back to its initial state or to an equivalent one. These methods are studied in chapter 19.

In chapter 20 we consider *occurrence graph* methods. They are used to check whether a system can reach states having certain properties. We specialize these methods in chapter 21 to study the *time behavior* of systems, specifically to compute *throughput* or *response* times. Note that all the verification methods have a limited applicability either because they require structural properties that the system we study does not have or because they ignore structural properties of our model such as the values or the time stamps of tokens.

Two other properties of systems that are worthwhile to verify are *fairness* and absence of *starvation*. For these desirable properties we do not offer special methods; nevertheless we will define them informally. A system is *fair* if the demon makes unbiased choices in the sense that each possible choice will obtain a positive probability. This implies that if two processors share an input place in a free choice actor model, a fair demon will fire both processors infinitely often if there is an infinite stream of tokens to this common input place. Another implication of a fair demon is that tokens in a place will be selected for consumption if it is possible to consume them. If there are tokens that will never be consumed, the system is said to suffer from *starvation*. It is seldom the wish of a systems engineer to have starvation in a system, so we have to verify that all tokens will be consumed in end, may be under the assumption of a fair demon.

We assume throughout this part that the actor model we consider has a flat net model $(L, P, C, I, O, M)$, a processor relation $R$, a state space $St$ and an object universe $OU$. Further all traces considered in this part are state traces, but we call them traces.

# 19

# Invariants

Invariant methods were first developed for classical Petri nets. For classical Petri nets invariants can be found or tested by means of simple linear algebra techniques. We start with a simple example of a classical Petri net.

**Example 1**
Consider the actor model of figure 19.1. It is a simple system that transfers

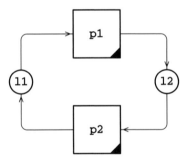

Fig. 19.1. Example 1.

"valueless" tokens from one place two another and vice versa. The processors are complete. Because we consider valueless tokens the other characteristics of the processors are irrelevant.

It is obvious that the number of tokens in this system is constant, i.e. it remains the same as in the initial state for each trace. It is also clear that the system returns to its initial state if processors $p_1$ and $p_2$ fire the same number of times. (Here we neglect the identities of tokens as well as their time stamps.) For this system we can define a so-called *flow matrix* $N$; it is displayed in table 19.1. The value $N(l, p)$ of an entry in this matrix denotes the change in the number of tokens in place $l$ caused by the firing of processor $p$. To find the place invariants

Table 19.1. *Flow matrix for example 1.*

| $N$ | $p_1$ | $p_2$ |
|-----|-------|-------|
| $l_1$ | $-1$ | $1$ |
| $l_2$ | $1$ | $-1$ |

we have to solve the matrix equation

$$w^T N = 0.$$

($w^T$, a row vector, denotes the transpose of the column vector $w$.) A solution $w$ of this equation should be interpreted as follows: the number of tokens in place $l_1$ times $w(l_1)$ plus the number of tokens in place $l_2$ times $w(l_2)$ is constant. (An equivalent formulation is

$$N^T w = 0,$$

where $N^T$ is the transpose of $N$.)
To find the transition invariants we have to solve the equation

$$Nw = 0.$$

A solution should be interpreted as follows: if processor $p_1$ fires $w(p_1)$ times and processor $p_2$ fires $w(p_2)$ times in a trace, then the system returns to its initial state (neglecting the identities of tokens). Note that a trace is defined in chapter 9 as a sequence of pairs, the first component of which is a state and the second component of which is the transition time of this state. Since the transition time is completely determined by the state, we can characterize traces as sequences of states. That is what we will do in this chapter.
□

We prove these properties for the actor model. We start with some definitions. First we introduce the concept of a *filter*. A filter makes it possible to identify tokens that have some common characteristics. Remember that, for a state $s$ and an identity $i$, $\pi_1(s(i))$ is the value, $\pi_2(s(i))$ is the time stamp and $\pi_3(s(i))$ is the place of a token with identity $i$. Also remember that for a firing rule $r$ and a connector $x$ $\pi_1(r(x))$ is the identity, $\pi_2(r(x))$ is the value or the complex and $\pi_3(r(x))$ is the time stamp.

**Definition 19.1** Let an actor model be given. Further, let $f$ be a function such that $dom(f) = OU$. Let $V = rng(f)$. The function $f$ is called a *filter* and $V$ is called a *filter set*. A *marking* is a function $m$ such that

- $m \in St \to (L \times V \to \mathbf{N})$,

$- \forall s \in St,\ l \in L:$

$$m_s(l, v) = \#\{i \in dom(s) \mid f(\pi_1(s(i))) = v \ \wedge \ \pi_3(s(i)) = l\}.$$

□

The invariants do not consider individual tokens but equivalence classes of them. A filter $f$ with filter set $V$ determines such an equivalence relation: two tokens are equivalent if $f$ maps their complexes to the same value in $V$. Therefore we can consider the elements of $V$ as equivalence classes. So, a marking counts the number of tokens in a particular place and a particular equivalence class. A trivial, but important, filter maps all tokens to one value, i.e. $V$ is a singleton. In this case a marking just counts the number of tokens in a place and the case has reduced to a classical Petri net. Therefore we call this filter the *Petri filter*.

Another obvious filter for actor models is the identity function (i.e. $\forall x \in OU :$ $f(x) = x$). We call this the *identity filter*. Note that this filter conserves all information of the tokens except for the time stamps and identities.

Next, we consider functions that characterize the processor relations in terms of a filter. We do not consider the processor relation in full detail; we consider only the relationships between the filtered values of the consumed and produced tokens. The time stamps are ignored as well as the identities.

**Definition 19.2**  Let an actor model with filter $f$ and filter set $V$ be given. Functions $N, N^+, N^-$ are defined by:

$$N, N^+, N^- \in \{(l, v, p, r) \mid l \in L \ \wedge \ v \in V \ \wedge \ p \in P \ \wedge \ r \in R_p\} \rightarrow \mathbf{N};$$
$$N^+(l, v, p, r) = \#\{x \in O(p) \cap dom(r) \mid f(\pi_2(r(x))) = v \ \wedge \ M_p(x) = l\};$$
$$N^-(l, v, p, r) = \#\{x \in I(p) \cap dom(r) \mid f(\pi_2(r(x))) = v \ \wedge \ M_p(x) = l\};$$
$$N(l, v, p, r) = N^+(l, v, p, r) - N^-(l, v, p, r).$$

$N$ is called the *flow function*, $N^+$ the *production function* and $N^-$ the *consumption function*.

□

If processor $p$ executes with firing rule $r$ then $N(l, v, p, r)$ will be the difference between the numbers of tokens in equivalence class $v$ in place $l$ in the old and in the new states. Note that we do not know whether $p$ is able to fire $r$ even when

$$m_s(l, v) \geq N^-(l, v, p, r),$$

because of the time stamps and the possible precondition of $p$.

In general the domain of $N$ is in countably infinite. Since the identities and time stamps of tokens do not play a role in the flow function we define an equivalence relation for firing rules. Two firing rules are equivalent if they have the same domains and the same values (or complexes) for the same connectors.

**Definition 19.3** Let a processor relation $R$ and a processor $p$ be given. Two firing rules $r_1$ and $r_2$ are *equivalent* if and only if the following conditions both hold.

$$dom(r_1) = dom(r_2),$$
$$\forall x \in dom(r_1) : \pi_2(r_1(x)) = \pi_2(r_2(x)).$$

□

In computations involving $N$ we need consider for each *equivalent class* only one firing rule. For actor models with the Petri filter the domain of the flow function can be reduced to a finite set.

**Lemma 19.1** Let an actor model be given. For the Petri filter the flow function $N$ has the following form:

$$\forall l \in L, \ p \in P : \forall r \in R_p : N(l, v, p, r) =$$
$$\#\{x \in O(p) \cap dom(r) \mid M_p(x) = l\} -$$
$$\#\{x \in I(p) \cap dom(r) \mid M_p(x) = l\}.$$

If in addition, all processors are complete, we obtain, $\forall i \in L, \ p \in P :$

$$N(l, v, p, r) = \#\{x \in O(p) \mid M_p(x) = l\} - \#\{x \in I(p) \mid M_p(x) = l\}.$$

*Proof* Since the Petri filter is used, we may delete the condition $f(\pi_2(r(x))) = v$ in the definitions of $N$, $N^+$ and $N^-$. In the case where all processors are complete we have $I(p) \cap dom(r) = I(p)$ and $O(p) \cap dom(r) = O(p)$. □

Since $V$ is a singleton in these cases, we drop the dependency on $v$ in the notation for $N$ and since $r$ either does not play a role at all or plays a role only via $dom(r)$ we may write:

- $N(l, (p, dom(r)))$, in the case of the Petri filter,
- $N(l, p)$ in the case of only complete processors and the Petri filter.

Note that this function $N$ has a finite domain in both cases. As shown in chapter 14 it is always possible to transform an actor model with incomplete processors into a similar one with only complete processors. So we can always reduce the flow function for an actor model with the Petri filter to the case in the lemma where all processors are complete. For this case we consider $N$ sometimes as a *matrix* with a *column* per processor and a *row* per place. We call it the *flow matrix*. Also note that an actor model with finite types can be reduced to a similar actor model with an object universe that is a singleton (chapter 14). For such a model the Petri filter is equal to the identity filter.

## 19.1 Place invariants

Next we define the concept of a *place* invariant.

**Definition 19.4** Let an actor model with filter $f$ and filter set $v$ be given. A *place invariant* $w$ is a function such that

$$w \in L \times V \to \mathbb{Z},$$
$$\forall p \in P : \forall r \in R_p : \sum_{l \in L, v \in V} w(l, v) \times N(l, v, p, r) = 0.$$

This set of equations is called the *flow balance*. (Here we assume that the sum is defined, i.e. that the sum of absolute values is finite. If $V$ is finite this property holds.) The values $w(l, v)$ of a place invariant are called *weights*.
□

Note that the range of a place invariant is $\mathbb{Z}$ while the range of a marking is $\mathbb{N}$. Also note that a function $w$ with zero weights is always a place invariant. It is obvious that linear combinations of invariants are also invariants.

**Theorem 19.1** Let $w_1$ and $w_2$ be place invariants for some actor model and some filter. For all $a$, $b \in \mathbb{Z}$,

$$a \times w_1 + b \times w_2$$

is also a place invariant.

A place invariant determines an invariant for all reachable states of an actor model. The next theorem is the main result of this section. It says that if the system is in a state $s$, and if by execution of firing rule $r$ of processor $p$ the state transforms into $s'$, then a weighted sum of the number of tokens with filtered values remains the same. We start with a lemma.

**Lemma 19.2** Let an actor model with filter $f$ and filter set $V$ be given. Let $s, s' \in St$ and let there be an applicable firing assignment $\{(p, r)\}$, where $p \in P$ and $r \in R_p$, such that

$$s' = (s \backslash in(p, r)) \cup out(p, r).$$

Then $\forall l \in L, v \in V$ :

$$m_{s'}(l, v) = m_s(l, v) + N(l, v, p, r).$$

*Proof* By definition 11.6 $(s, s') \in Tr$. It follows from theorem 11.3 that $in(p, r)$ and $out(p, r)$ are elements of $St$ (so they are functions on $ID$) and that they are mutually disjoint and both disjoint with $s$. So

$$dom(s') = (dom(s) \backslash dom(in(p, r))) \cup dom(out(p, r)).$$

Therefore we have for the marking $m$:

$$m_{s'}(l, v) = m_s(l, v) - m_{in(p,r)}(l, v) + m_{out(p,r)}(l, v).$$

We recall that

$$in(p, r) = \{(i, (y, t, l)) \in ID \times (OU \times T \times L) \mid$$
$$\exists x \in I(p) \cap dom(r) : r(x) = (i, y, t) \ \wedge \ M_p(x) = l\}.$$

Therefore,

$$dom(in(p, r)) = \{i \in ID \mid \exists x \in I(p) \cap dom(r) : \pi_1(r(x)) = i\}.$$

So,

$$m_{in(p,r)}(l, v) = \#\{i \in ID \mid \exists x \in I(p) \cap dom(r) :$$
$$\pi_1(r(x)) = i \ \wedge \ f(\pi_1(in_{(p,r)}(i))) = v \ \wedge \ \pi_3(in_{(p,r)}(i)) = l\}.$$

Since $r$ has for each connector $x$ a different identity $i$, we have

$$f(\pi_1(in_{(p,r)}(i))) = f(\pi_2(r(x))) \ \wedge \ \pi_3(in_{(p,r)}(i)) = M_p(x).$$

So,

$$m_{in(p,r)}(l, v) = \#\{x \in I(p) \cap dom(r) \mid f(\pi_2(r(x))) = v \ \wedge \ M_p(x) = l\}.$$

For $m_{out(p,r)}(l, v)$ we obtain a similar expression, and therefore we obtain

$$N(l, v, p, r) = m_{out(p,r)}(l, v) - m_{in(p,r)}(l, v).$$

$\square$

**Theorem 19.2** Let an actor model with filter $f$ and filter set $V$ be given. Let $s, s' \in St$ and let there be an applicable firing assignment $\{(p, r)\}$, where $p \in P$ and $r \in R_p$, such that

$$s' = (s \backslash in(p, r)) \cup out(p, r).$$

Further, let $w$ be a place invariant for this model. Then we have

$$\sum_{l \in L, \, v \in V} w(l, v) \times m_{s'}(l, v) = \sum_{l \in L, \, v \in V} w(l, v) \times m_s(l, v)$$

for all cases where the sums are properly defined.

*Proof* The former theorem gives

$$m_{s'}(l, v) = m_s(l, v) + N(l, v, p, r).$$

From this, and because $w$ is an invariant, we obtain

$$\sum_{l \in L, v \in V} w(l, v) \times m_{s'}(l, v)$$

$$= \sum_{l \in L, v \in V} w(l, v) \times (m_s(l, v) + N(l, v, p, r))$$

$$= \sum_{l \in L, v \in V} w(l, v) \times m_s(l, v) + \sum_{l \in L, v \in V} w(l, v) \times N(l, v, p, r)$$

$$= \sum_{l \in L, v \in V} w(l, v) \times m_s(l, v).$$

This is the desired result. □

The equation

$$\sum_{l \in L, \ v \in V} w(l, v) \times m_s(l, v) = \text{constant}$$

is called an *place invariant property*. If $L$ and $V$ are finite it is often written in matrix format, as mentioned at the start of the chapter:

$$w^T N = 0.$$

The following theorem is an obvious corollary of theorem 19.2.

**Theorem 19.3** Let an actor model with a filter $f$ and filter set $V$ be given. Further let $w$ be a place invariant for this model. For all autonomous traces $\langle s_0, s_1, s_2, \ldots \rangle$ and $\forall i \in \{0, 1, 2, \ldots\}$,

$$\sum_{l \in L, \ v \in V} w(l, v) \times m_{s_i}(l, v) = \sum_{l \in L, \ v \in V} w(l, v) \times m_{s_0}(l, v).$$

*Proof* We first note that by the serializability theorem 11.5 there is for each pair $(s_i, s_{i+1})$ (with $i \in \{0, 1, 2, \ldots\}$) a sequence of states and corresponding firing rules with only one processor, such that this sequence forms an autonomous trace that starts in $s_i$ and ends in $s_{i+1}$. For each pair of successors in this sequence we can apply the former theorem, which gives

$$\sum_{l \in L, \ v \in V} w(l, v) \times m_{s_i}(l, v) = \sum_{l \in L, \ v \in V} w(l, v) \times m_{s_{i+1}}(l, v).$$

Repeating this argument for each $i$ we obtain the desired result. □

The reverse of this theorem would be that from the fact that all reachable states have the place invariant property we may conclude that the flow balance is true. This conclusion only holds if all processors are *live*.

**Definition 19.5** A processor $p$ is called *live* if each finite autonomous trace $p$ is the prefix of at least one autonomous trace for which $p$ executes after the given prefix. An actor model is called *live* if all its processors are live.
□

**Theorem 19.4** Let a live actor model with initial state $s_0$, filter $f$ and with filter set $V$ be given. Let $w$ satisfy the place invariant property for all reachable states $s$:

$$\sum_{l \in L,\, v \in V} w(l, v) \times m_s(l, v) = \text{constant}.$$

Then $w$ is a place invariant.

*Proof* The proof is an exercise.                                    □

For an actor model with the Petri filter we obtain for the place invariant property a simpler expression,

$$\sum_{l \in L} w(l) \times m_s(l) = \sum_{l \in L} w(l) \times m_{s'}(l),$$

because we may drop the dependency on $v$. For this case we have some useful properties of actor models if the place invariants have only non-negative or positive values. We first introduce some notation and two concepts: *dead set* and *trap*.

**Definition 19.6** Let an actor model be given. For a set $D \subseteq L$ we define sets of processors $\bullet D$ and $D \bullet$:

  (i) $\bullet D = \{p \in P \mid \tilde{M}(O(p)) \cap D \neq \varnothing\}$;
  (ii) $D \bullet = \{p \in P \mid \tilde{M}(I(p)) \cap D \neq \varnothing\}$,

where $\tilde{M}$ is the set version of $M$ ( i.e. $\tilde{M}_p(a) = \{M_p(x) \mid x \in a\}$).
A set of places is called a *dead set* if and only if

$$\bullet D \subseteq D \bullet.$$

A set of places is called a *trap* if and only if

$$D \bullet \subseteq \bullet D.$$

□

In the literature a dead set is usually called a *deadlock*. However, we have used this term in a different way. We may consider $\bullet D$ as the set of *producers* for $D$, and $D\bullet$ as the set of *consumers* for $D$. So, a dead set is a set for which each producer is also a consumer and a trap is a set for which each consumer is also a producer. It is easy to verify that the union of dead sets is a dead set and the union of traps is a trap. (The proof is an exercise.) The first property says that if there is a *non-negative place invariant* then the set of places with positive weights is a dead set as well as a trap.

**Theorem 19.5** Let an actor model with only complete processors and the Petri filter be given. Further, let $w$ be a place invariant for this model with only non-negative values (i.e. $\forall l \in L : w(l) \geq 0$) and let $L' = \{l \in L \mid w(l) > 0\}$ be non-empty. (Such a place invariant is called *non-negative*.) Then

$$L'\bullet = \bullet L'.$$

*Proof* Let $p \in L' \bullet \setminus \bullet L'$. Then $p$ consumes from $L'$ but it does not produce for it. So, there is a $l' \in L$ such that $N(l', p) < 0$ because $p$ consumes from at least one place in $L'$. Further, $\forall l \in L' : N(l, p) \leq 0$, since $p$ does not produce for $L'$. Hence

$$\sum_{l \in L} w(l) \times N(l, p) < 0.$$

This contradicts the fact that $w$ is an invariant. A similar argument holds for the case where is a $p \in \bullet L' \setminus L' \bullet$. Therefore $\bullet L' = L' \bullet$. $\qquad \Box$

The following properties of dead sets and traps are easy to verify.

**Theorem 19.6** Let an actor model with only complete processors and an autonomous trace be given. Let $s$ be a state on this trace. If a dead set does not have tokens in $s$ then the same property holds for all successor states on the trace. If a trap contains tokens in $s$ then the same property holds for all successor states on the trace.

*Proof* The proof is an exercise. $\qquad \Box$

The next theorem gives a sufficient condition for the existence of a positive place invariant.

**Theorem 19.7** Let an actor model with the Petri filter be given. Further, let there be a non-negative invariant $w$ for every place $l$ such that $w(l) > 0$. Then there is a place invariant $\tilde{w}$ such that

$$\forall l \in L : \tilde{w}(l) > 0.$$

(This is called a *positive place invariant*.)

*Proof* Since linear combinations of place invariants are also place invariants, we may select for each place $l$ a place invariant $w_l$ with $w_l(l) > 0$. Hence we may define $\tilde{w}(l) = \sum_{l \in L} w_l(l)$.                                                □

The next theorem shows that actor models with a positive place invariant are *bounded* (c.f. section 14.3).

**Theorem 19.8** Let an actor model with the Petri filter be given. Let $s_0$ be the initial state. Let $w$ be a positive place invariant. Then there is a $n \in \mathbb{N}$ such that, for all reachable states $s$ and all places $l$,

$$m_s(l) < n.$$

*Proof* For each reachable state $s$ we have

$$\sum_{l \in L} w(l) \times m_{s_0}(l) = \sum_{l \in L} w(l) \times m_s(l).$$

Hence, for any $l' \in L$,

$$w(l') \times m_s(l') \leq \sum_{l \in L} w(l) \times m_{s_0}(l)$$

and

$$m_s(l') \leq \frac{\sum_{l \in L} w(l) \times m_{s_0}(l)}{w(l')}.$$

Finally, we choose $n$ to be equal to the maximum over all $l' \in L$ of the right-hand side of the last inequality.                              □

Next, we will consider the use of place invariants. There are two approaches.

   (i) Compute place invariants (automatically) and try to interpret them in terms of properties of the actor model.
   (ii) Transform a desired property of an actor model into a (potential) place invariant and verify whether the place invariant holds.

The first approach seems to be more attractive because it gives the possibility of *discovering* properties. However, there are some problems: for arbitrary filters and in particular for the identity filter there are no algorithms known to generate all place invariants and furthermore, the number of invariants is in general infinite due to theorem 19.1. Another problem is that an arbitrary place invariant does not always have a meaningful interpretation. For the Petri filter there are techniques to determine a finite set of *independent place invariants* such that each place invariant is a linear combination of invariants of this set. In a set of independent place invariants no invariant is a linear combination of the others. (In the next section we consider these techniques.)

We claim that the second approach is the most practical one, specifically for filters other than the Petri filter.

We will illustrate the techniques for finding and using place invariants by some examples. We start with the classical case: actor models with the Petri filter.

**Example 1, continued**

Consider the actor model of figure 19.1 again. Now we assume that it is a "normal" actor model with only complete processors and we use the Petri filter. To find a place invariant we have to solve the equations

$$w(l_1) \times N(l_1, p_1) + w(l_2) \times N(l_2, p_1) = 0$$

and

$$w(l_1) \times N(l_1, p_2) + w(l_2) \times N(l_2, p_2) = 0.$$

The solutions satisfy

$$-w(l_1) + w(l_2) = 0, \quad w(l_1) - w(l_2) = 0.$$

Hence the set of all place invariants is

$$\{w \in L \to \mathbb{Z} \mid w(l_1) = w(l_2)\}.$$

Without loss of generality we may consider $w(l_1) = w(l_2) = 1$. The place invariant property is therefore

$$m_s(l_1) + m_s(l_2) = \text{constant}$$

for all reachable states. This property is obvious and without the invariant analysis we would have found this property immediately. However, now we have a proof!
□

**Example 2**

Consider the actor model of figure 19.2. The processors are complete and we use the Petri filter again. The flow matrix is displayed in table 19.2. It is easy to

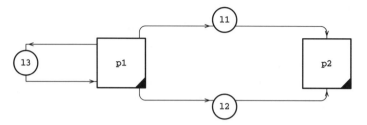

Fig. 19.2. Example 2.

Table 19.2. *Flow matrix for example 2*

| $N$ | $p_1$ | $p_2$ |
|---|---|---|
| $l_1$ | 1 | $-1$ |
| $l_2$ | 1 | $-1$ |
| $l_3$ | 0 | 0 |

verify that each place invariant satisfies the following property:

$$w(l_1) = -w(l_2).$$

There are no requirements for $w(l_3)$, which means that the number of tokens in $l_3$ is constant (which is obvious). If we take $w(l_1) = 1$ then we have proven that the difference between the numbers of tokens in places $l_1$ and $l_2$ is constant. However, there is no bound on the amount of tokens in these places. Of course, if we know that the tokens produced for these places have bounded delays then we can derive an upperbound on the number of tokens in these places, but that is another kind of analysis.

□

### Example 3

We consider a simplification of the train control case of chapter 14. In figure 19.3 the actor model is displayed. All processors are complete and the Petri filter is used. Places $a$, $b$ and $c$ represent the tracks and processors $p$, $q$ and $r$ the signals. Places $d$ and $e$ represent the "memory" of the control system. The flow function $N$ is given in table 19.3. The flow balance gives the following three equations, which have five unknown variables

$$-w(a) + w(b) - w(d) = 0,$$

$$-w(b) + w(c) + w(d) - w(e) = 0,$$

$$w(a) - w(c) + w(e) = 0.$$

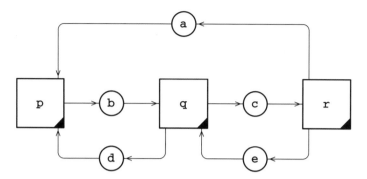

Fig. 19.3. Example 3.

Table 19.3. *Flow matrix for example 3*

| $N$ | $p$ | $q$ | $r$ |
|---|---|---|---|
| $a$ | $-1$ | $0$ | $1$ |
| $b$ | $1$ | $-1$ | $0$ |
| $c$ | $0$ | $1$ | $-1$ |
| $d$ | $-1$ | $1$ | $0$ |
| $e$ | $0$ | $-1$ | $1$ |

Note that the columns of the matrix $N$ are dependent: the sum of the three columns gives a column of only zeros. So there are in fact two independent equations with five unknowns. So we may choose three of these as variables; the others are then determined. Let $x$, $y$ and $z$ be integer variables such that

$$w(a) = x, \ w(b) = y, \ w(c) = z.$$

Then $w(d) = y - x$ and $w(e) = z - x$. Hence the general form of the invariant place property is (for arbitrary $s$):

$$x \times m_s(a) + y \times m_s(b) + z \times m_s(c) + (y - x) \times m_s(d)$$

$$+(z - x) \times m_s(e) = \text{constant}.$$

Not all choices for the variables $x$, $y$ and $z$ have a useful meaning. It is recommended to start by choosing for one of the variables the value 1 and for all the others 0. This gives the place invariant properties (for the first, $x = 1$, for the second, $y = 1$ and for the third, $z = 1$):

$$m_s(a) - m_s(d) - m_s(e) = \text{constant},$$

$$m_s(b) + m_s(d) = \text{constant},$$

$$m_s(c) + m_s(e) = \text{constant}.$$

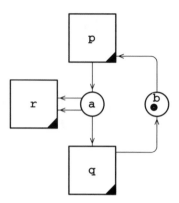

Fig. 19.4. Example 4

The first property does not have a natural interpretation at first sight; however, the second and third do. If the system starts with two tokens, one in $b$ and one in $c$, there will be at most one token in $b$ and at most one in $c$, which means that these tracks are safe. Further, we see that if $b$ is empty then $d$ has a token to enable processor $p$ and similarly, if $c$ is empty then $e$ has a token to enable $q$. A fourth place invariant property can be obtained by choosing $x = y = z = 1$:

$$m_s(a) + m_s(b) + m_s(c) = \text{constant}.$$

This means that the number of trains is constant. Let us consider the first property again. If the system starts in the initial state defined above, there will be at most one token in $d$ and at most one in $e$. So the first property implies that the number of tokens in $a$ is at most two. (It is easy to modify the model to guarantee that $a$ will have at most one token.)

□

**Example 4**
The next example shows that there are place invariant properties that cannot be derived from place invariants. The reason is initial states do not play a role in place invariants and therefore they are not always sufficiently sophisticated. In figure 19.4 an actor model with complete and total processors is displayed. The Petri filter is used again. The flow function for this case is displayed in table 19.4. Hence, the flow balance gives $w(a) = w(b)$ and $-2 \times w(a) = 0$: the only solution is $w(a) = w(b) = 0$. So there is no non-trivial place invariant. However, it is clear that if there is only one token in the system in the initial state, then there will always be one. So this property is invariant!

Table 19.4. *Flow matrix for example 4*

| $N$ | $p$ | $q$ | $r$ |
|-----|-----|-----|-----|
| $a$ | $-1$ | $1$ | $-2$ |
| $b$ | $1$ | $-1$ | $0$ |

☐

Next we consider the case of the identity filter. Here, we have to consider with the firing rules. If the processor relations are specified by a schema, it is in general not easy to characterize the set of all firing rules and therefore the flow function. However, if the schema for the processor relation has the following *canonical form*, there is a "natural" way to express the flow function.

**Definition 19.7** A schema with signature $x_1 : T_1, \ldots, x_n : T_n$ is in *canonical form* if there is a type $T$ and a set of functions $\{f_i \mid i \in \{1, \ldots, n\}\}$ such that

- $\forall i \in \{1, \ldots, n\} : f_i : T \Rightarrow T_i$.
- The predicate of the schema is of the form

$$\exists x : T \bullet x_1 = f_1(x) \ \wedge \ \ldots \ \wedge \ x_n = f_n(x).$$

The variable $x$ is called the *firing variable*.
☐

An example of such a schema $s$ is as follows.

---
$s$ ─────────────────────────────────────

$a : \mathbf{N}$
$b : \mathbf{N}$
$c : \mathbf{N}$

─────

$\exists x : \mathbf{N} \times \mathbf{N} \bullet$
$a = \pi_1(x) \ \wedge \ b = \pi_2(x) \ \wedge \ c = \pi_1(x) + \pi_2(x)$

─────────────────────────────────────

If a processor is complete and functional it is always possible to transform its schema into canonical form. To verify this consider a processor with input connectors $x_1, \ldots, x_m$ and output connectors $y_1, \ldots, y_n$. The functionality of the processor implies the existence of functions $f_j$ for each output connector $y_j$ such that

$$y_j = f_j(x_1, \ldots, x_m).$$

Hence, if we introduce a variable $z$ with the Cartesian product of all the types of the input and output connectors as its type (denoted by $T$), then the predicate of the schema becomes

$\exists\, z \in T\bullet$

$$\forall\, i \in \{1, \ldots, m\} \bullet x_i = \pi_i(z) \;\wedge\; \forall\, j \in \{1, \ldots, n\} \bullet y_j = f_j(x_1, \ldots, x_m).$$

The converse is not true, i.e. there are canonical schemas for processors that are not functional. For processors with a canonical schema we may rewrite the equation that defines a place invariant. We will assume that there is at most one connection between each processor and each place.

**Theorem 19.9** Consider a processor $p$ with connectors $x_1, \ldots, x_n$ and a processor schema in canonical form with predicate

$$\exists\, x : T \bullet x_1 = f_1(x) \;\wedge\; \ldots \;\wedge\; x_n = f_n(x).$$

Further, assume that processors have at most one connector with a place, i.e.

$$\forall\, l \in L : \#\{x \in C \mid M_p(x) = l\} \leq 1.$$

Then:

(i) Each value of the firing variable $x$ determines a unique equivalence class of firing rules in $R_p$.

(ii) The flow balance can be written in the form

$\forall\, x \in T:$

$$\sum_{l \in \bullet p} w(l, f_l(x)) = \sum_{l \in p\bullet} w(l, f_l(x)).$$

Here we have used the following notational convention for $i \in \{1, \ldots, n\}$: $f_l = f_i$ if and only if $M_p(x_i) = l$.

*Proof* Note that for each $x \in T$ all connector values in the processor schema are determined by $x_i = f_i(x)$ ($i \in \{1, \ldots, n\}$). Hence any corresponding firing rule $r$ satisfies

$$\pi_2(r(x_i)) = f_i(x) \;\; (i \in \{1, \ldots, n\}).$$

So each $x$ uniquely determines (by definition 19.3) an equivalence class of firing rules. (Note that the connector names are used as variables in the schema and also as arguments for the firing rules, which are functions.)

To verify the second assertion note that, since each processor has at most one connection with a place

(i) $N(l, v, p, r) = 1$ if and only if $f_l(x) = v$ for some $x$ that corresponds to $r$ and $l \in p\bullet$,

(ii) $N(l, v, p, r) = -1$ if and only if $f_l(x) = v$ for some $x$ that corresponds to $r$ and $l \in \bullet p$,

(iii) $N(l, v, p, r) = 0$, otherwise.

Hence we may rewrite the flow balance

$$\forall r \in R_p : \sum_{l \in L, v \in V} w(l, v) \times N(l, v, p, r) = 0$$

as

$$\forall x \in T : \sum_{l \in p\bullet} w(l, f_l(x)) - \sum_{l \in \bullet p} w(l, f_l(x)) = 0.$$

$\square$

If we define functions $w_l$ for $l \in L$ by $dom(w_l) = V$ and $w_l(v) = w(l, v)$ we can write the flow balance as

$$\forall x \in T : \sum_{l \in \bullet p} w_l(f_l(x)) = \sum_{l \in p\bullet} w_l(f_l(x)).$$

So the place invariants are sets of functions now and the flow balance is a *functional equation*, i.e. an equation with a function as the unknown. We consider an example.

**Example 5**

In figure 19.5 a very simple elevator system is displayed. Place $a$ contains the cages of the elevator that are at rest and place $b$ the moving cages of the elevator. A cage may contain at most one person. The values of the tokens in these places are natural numbers; the value of a token in $a$ denotes the level at which the elevator is waiting and the value of the token in $b$ denotes the level towards which the elevator is moving. Places $c$ and $d$ contain transport requests of the form $(x, y)$ where $x$ and $y$ are natural numbers denoting that somebody wants to move from level $x$ to level $y$. In $d$ are the active requests and in $c$ the requests of persons that have made a move and are otherwise occupied on the level at which they have arrived: it is assumed that every person that makes a move from level $x$ to level $y$ will eventually make the inverse move from $y$ to $x$. Processors $p$ and $r$ consume one token and produce a new one with the same value (i.e. the same complex). However, the time stamps of the new tokens have a delay with respect

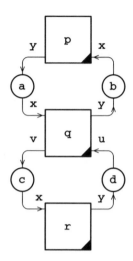

Fig. 19.5. Example 5.

to their event time; this delay reflects both the transportation time and the sojourn time on a level. We do not consider the time stamps further. Processor $q$ takes a request from place $d$, say $(x, y)$, and looks for a token in $a$ with value $x$; it then consumes these tokens and produces a token for $b$ with value $y$ and a token for $c$ with value $(y, x)$. Note that $q$ has a precondition: the value of the token consumed from $a$ should have the same value as the first component of the token consumed from $d$, so $q$ is not total. However, all processors are complete. In this case the identity filter is used. The set $V$ can be represented as $\mathbb{N} \cup (\mathbb{N} \times \mathbb{N})$, although this is not an allowed type. The schemas for the processors in canonical form are as follows:

$$p := [x : \mathbb{N},\, y : \mathbb{N} \mid \exists z : \mathbb{N} \bullet y = z \,\wedge\, x = z],$$
$$q := [x : \mathbb{N},\, y : \mathbb{N},\, u : \mathbb{N} \times \mathbb{N},\, v : \mathbb{N} \times \mathbb{N} \mid \exists z : \mathbb{N} \times \mathbb{N} \bullet$$
$$x = \pi_1(z) \,\wedge\, y = \pi_2(z) \,\wedge\, u = z \,\wedge\, v = (\pi_2(z), \pi_1(z))],$$
$$r := [x : \mathbb{N} \times \mathbb{N},\, y : \mathbb{N} \times \mathbb{N} \mid \exists z : \mathbb{N} \times \mathbb{N} \bullet x = z \,\wedge\, y = z].$$

The flow balances for the three processors are respectively (for firing variable $z$),

$$\forall z \in \mathbb{N} : w(a, z) - w(b, z) = 0,$$
$$\forall z \in \mathbb{N} \times \mathbb{N} :$$
$$-w(a, \pi_1(z)) + w(b, \pi_2(z)) - w(d, z) + w(c, (\pi_2(z), \pi_1(z))) = 0,$$
$$\forall z \in \mathbb{N} \times \mathbb{N} : w(d, z) - w(c, z) = 0.$$

There are several solutions for $w$; for instance,

$$\forall l \in L,\, v \in V : w(l, v) = 1$$

is a solution. This solution gives the following place invariant property, for $z \in \mathbb{N} \times \mathbb{N}$,

$$\sum_{z \in \mathbb{N} \times \mathbb{N}} m_s(a, \pi_1(z)) + m_s(b, \pi_2(z)) + m_s(c, z) + m_s(d, z) = \text{constant},$$

for all reachable states $s$. This can be rewritten as

$$\sum_{x \in \mathbb{N}, \, y \in \mathbb{N}} m_s(a, x) + m_s(b, x) + m_s(c, (x, y)) + m_s(d, (x, y)) = \text{constant}.$$

The interpretation of this property is straightforward: the number of tokens in all reachable states is constant.

Another solution of the flow balance is

$$\forall z \in \mathbb{N}:$$
$$w(a, z) = w(b, z) = 0 \, \wedge \, \forall z \in \mathbb{N} \times \mathbb{N}: w(c, z) = w(d, z) = 1.$$

This gives the place invariant property

$$\sum_{x \in \mathbb{N}, \, y \in \mathbb{N}} m_s(c, (x, y)) + m_s(d, (x, y)) = \text{constant},$$

which means that the number of tokens in places $c$ and $d$ is constant. Similarly, $\forall z \in \mathbb{N}: w(a, z) = w(b, z) = 1 \, \wedge \, \forall z \in \mathbb{N} \times \mathbb{N}: w(c, z) = w(d, z) = 0$ is a solution which means that the number of tokens in $a$ and $b$ is constant.

A more interesting solution is

$$\forall z \in \mathbb{N}: w(a, z) = w(b, z) = -2 \times z$$

$$\wedge$$

$$\forall z \in \mathbb{N} \times \mathbb{N}: w(c, z) = w(d, z) = \pi_1(z) - \pi_2(z).$$

It is easy to verify for the three flow balances that this is indeed a solution. The corresponding place invariant property is that

$$\sum_{x \in \mathbb{N}} -2x \times (m_s(a, x) + m_s(b, x))$$

$$+$$

$$\sum_{x, y \in \mathbb{N}} (x - y) \times (m_s(c, (x, y)) + m_s(d, (x, y)))$$

is constant. The meaning of this equation is that the difference between twice the total value of the tokens in places $a$ and $b$ and the total difference of the first and second components of the tokens in places $c$ and $d$ is constant. To verify this we note that the firing of processors $p$ and $r$ has no influence on this difference and that the firing of processor $q$ with $(x, y)$ as firing mode changes the total value of $a$ and $b$ by $y - x$ and the total value of the differences in the first and second components of $c$ and $d$ by $2 \times (y - x)$.

□

This example demonstrates that it is not particularly easy to give a useful meaning to a place invariant. Therefore, it is often more fruitful to guess a place invariant property and to check it with the flow balance. For other filters no specific techniques are known.

## 19.2 Computational aspects

Next, we consider the computational aspects of the place invariants in the case of actor models with only complete processors and the Petri filter. In the examples we have seen that finding place invariant properties is solving linear equations. The equation we need to consider is $N^T w = 0$. The number of columns is $\#(L)$ and the number of rows is $\#(P)$. If $\#(P) > \#(L)$ there are linearly dependent rows and therefore we may reduce $N^T$ by deleting some rows (i.e. processors!), without loss of information, i.e. the reduced equation has exactly the same solutions as the original one. Therefore, we may assume without loss of generality that $\#(P) \leq \#(L)$ and that the rows are independent.

The only property from *linear algebra* that we need is the following.

**Lemma 19.3** Let a matrix equation of the form $Bx = 0$ be given, where

- $B$ is a matrix with $p$ rows and $l$ columns,
- $l \geq p$,
- $p$ is the number of independent rows of $B$,
- $x$ is a vector of $l$ unknown variables.

Then there is a suitable rearrangement of the rows and columns of $B$, and a matrix $A$ with $p$ rows and $l - p$ columns, such that for all $x$ and for all $i \in \{1, \ldots, p\}$

$$x(i) + \sum_{j=1}^{l-p} A(i,j) \times x(j + p) = 0 \qquad (*)$$

Or, in matrix notation

$$[I, A]x = 0,$$

where $I$ is a $p \times p$ -unit matrix and $[I, A]$ is the matrix obtained by the concatenation of $I$ and $A$. If the entries $B$ are integers then every solution can be multiplied by a natural number such that it becomes an integer solution.

The matrix $A$ can be found by the well-known pivoting process and rearrangement of rows and columns of the matrix $B$. Note that $x = 0$ is always a solution. That there is an integer solution follows from the fact that if all entries of $B$ are integer, then $A$ has only rational entries (because of the pivoting process which involves only arithmetical operations). By multiplying both sides of $(*)$ by the greatest denominator we obtain an integer solution.

The equation $(*)$ is called the *transformed equation* of $Bx = 0$. Note that we may choose variables $x(p+1), \ldots, x(l)$ freely, the others are then determined.

**Theorem 19.10** Let an actor model with complete processors and the Petri filter be given. Let $P$ be the set of processors, with $\#(P) = p$, $L$ the set of places, with $\#(L) = l$ and $N$ the flow matrix. The places and the processors are given numbers in $\{1, \ldots, l\}$ and $\{1, \ldots, p\}$ respectively. Let the transformed equation of $N^T x = 0$ be (after rearranging the numbers of places and processors, if necessary), for $i \in \{1, \ldots, p\}$,

$$x(i) + \sum_{j=1}^{l-p} A(i,j) \times x(j+p) = 0.$$

Further, let $W$ be the set of functions $w_k \in \{1, \ldots, l\} \to \mathbb{Z}$, with $k \in \{1, \ldots, l-p\}$, such that

$$\forall\, i \in \{1, \ldots, p\} : w_k(i) = -A(i,k),$$
$$w_k(k+p) = 1,$$
$$w_k(i) = 0 \text{ for } i \in \{p+1, \ldots, l\}\backslash\{k+p\}.$$

Then the following hold:

- The functions $w$ are place invariants.
- They are mutually independent.
- Every place invariant is a linear combination of them.

In other words $W$ is a *base* for the linear space of place invariants.

*Proof* It is obvious that the place invariants in $W$ are independent, since only function $w_k$ has the property that $w_k(k+p) \neq 0$. To show that each function $w_k$ is a place invariant note that, by definition, for $i \in \{1, \ldots, p\}$, $w_k(i) = -A(i,k)$ and

$$\sum_{j=1}^{l-p} A(i,j) \times w_k(j+p) = A(i,k).$$

Hence

$$w_k(i) + \sum_{j=1}^{l-p} A(i,j) \times w_k(j+p) = 0,$$

which is, according to lemma 19.3, equivalent to

$$N^T w = 0.$$

Hence $w$ is a place invariant. Finally we have to verify that each place invariant is a linear combination of the place invariants of $W$. Let $v$ be an arbitrary place invariant. Let $z$ be defined by: $z(k) = v(p+k)$ for $k \in \{1, \ldots, l-p\}$. Then we will show, for $i \in \{1, \ldots, l\}$, that

$$v(i) = \sum_{k=1}^{l-p} z(k) \times w_k(i).$$

We distinguish two cases.

(i) Let $i \in \{p+1, \ldots, l\}$; then, by the definition of $w_k$,

$$\sum_{k=1}^{l-p} z(k) \times w_k(i) = z(i-p) = v(i),$$

(remember that $w_k(k+p) = 1$).

(ii) Let $i \in \{1, \ldots, p\}$; then, by the definition of $w_k$,

$$\sum_{k=1}^{l-p} z(k) \times w_k(i) = \sum_{k=1}^{l-p} -A(i,k) \times z(k) = \sum_{k=1}^{l-p} -A(i,k) \times v(p+k) = v(i),$$

since $v$ is a place invariant.

This proves the theorem.                                                      □

Thus, we have found a method of computing a base in the space of place invariants. However, this base is rather arbitrary. Invariants with only non-negative weights are often easier to interpret than place invariants with arbitrary weights. In example 2 we have shown that there are cases where all invariants have positive and negative weights, so it is not always possible to restrict ourselves to place invariants with non-negative weights. Nevertheless, we give a method of computing a special class of such invariants, if they exist. These place invariants are called *minimal support invariants*.

**Definition 19.8** Let an actor model with complete processors and the Petri filter be given. The *support* of a non-negative place invariant $w$ is the set of places whose weights are positive, i.e. $\| w \| = \{l \in L \mid w(l) > 0\}$.

Further, let $w$ be a non-negative and non-zero place invariant (i.e. $w > 0$ which means that $\forall\, l \in L : w(l) \geq 0$ and $\exists\, l \in L : w(l) \neq 0$). The invariant $w$ is called a *minimal support invariant* if and only if there are no non-negative non-zero place invariants that have a support which is a "real" subset of the support of $w$.
□

If $w$ is a minimal support invariant then every other invariant $w'$ has a support that is not a (real) subset of the support of $w$ ($\| w' \| \not\subseteq \| w \|$). In the remainder of this section we will assume that the support of an invariant $w$ contains at least one element, i.e. $w > 0$. Note that the invariant $w$ with $\forall\, l \in L : w(l) = 0$ is the only non-negative invariant without support.

Minimal support invariants satisfy a number of interesting properties.

**Lemma 19.4** Let an actor model with complete processors and the Petri filter be given. Then the following assertions hold.

   (i) Every non-negative invariant is a linear combination of minimal support invariants with positive coefficients.

  (ii) Two minimal support invariants with the same support are linearly dependent.

*Proof* For assertion (i), suppose that $w$ is a non-negative invariant. We have to prove that $w$ is a linear combination of minimal support invariants with positive coefficients.

Clearly, a minimal support invariant is also a linear combination of minimal support invariants.

If $w$ is not a minimal support invariant then there exists a non-negative place invariant $w'$ such that $\| w' \| \subseteq \| w \|$. We define

$$\lambda = min_{l \in \|w'\|}\ \frac{w(l)}{w'(l)}.$$

For all $n$, $w(n) - \lambda \times w'(n) \geq 0$ and there exists $\mu > 0$ such that $w''(n) = \mu(w(n) - \lambda \times w'(n))$ and for any $l \in L$: $w''(l) \in \mathbf{N}$. Note that $w''$ is a non-negative invariant and $w$ is a (positive) linear combination of $w'$ and $w''$. Repeat this process with $w'$ and $w''$ until $w$ is expressed as a minimal support invariant. It is easy to see that the process terminates (the support becomes smaller). In this way we can decompose $w$ into a linear combination of minimal support invariants with positive coefficients.

For assertion (ii), suppose $w$ and $w'$ are two minimal support invariants and $\| w \| = \| w' \|$. Define $\lambda$ as above. Again there exists a $\mu > 0$ such that, for all $n$ $w''(n) = \mu(w(n) - \lambda \times w'(n))$ and, for any $l \in L$, $w''(l) \in \mathbf{N}$. If $\| w'' \| = \emptyset$ then

$w$ is the linear combination of $w'$, otherwise, the support of $w''$ is a real subset of $w$, since $w''$ is zero for a minimizing $l$ and therefore, $w$ is not a minimal support invariant. $\qquad\square$

Note that if $w$ is a minimal support invariant then, for each $k \geq 1$, $k \times w$ is also a minimal support invariant. A minimal support invariant $w$ is called *elementary* if and only if every minimal support invariant $w'$ having the same support satisfies $\forall l \in L : w(l) \leq w'(l)$. Note that (by the second assertion of lemma 19.4) there is for every minimal support invariant $w'$ precisely one elementary minimal support invariant $w$ and a $k \geq 1$ such that $w' = k \times w$.

Because of these properties there are efficient algorithms for calculating minimal support invariants. To illustrate this we describe one of them. The algorithm given below starts from the matrix $[I_l, N]$, where $\#(L) = l$, $I_l$ is the identity matrix with $l$ rows and columns, and $N$ is the flow matrix. The matrix is modified by replacing rows with linear combinations of these rows. The matrix $[D^i, A^i]$ is the result of the $i$th iteration of the algorithm. The algorithm terminates when $D^i$ contains all minimal support invariants of the net represented by $N$. It will be shown that the matrix equation

$$[D^i, N] = A^i$$

is invariant during the computation and that finally $A^p = 0$ (the matrix consisting of zeros only).

## Algorithm

Let an actor model with complete processors and the Petri filter be given. The set of places and the set of processors are enumerated as follows: $L = \{1, .., l\}$ and $P = \{1, .., p\}$. Furthermore, let $N$ be the flow matrix obtained after rearranging the places and processors. The algorithm is then as follows:

$A := N; \quad D := I_l; \quad i := 1;$
**while** $i \leq p$
**do**

    (i) Append to $[D, A]$ every row $y = (d_1, .., d_l, a_1, .., a_p)$ that satisfies the following:

        (a) $y$ can be constructed as a non-negative linear combination of two rows in $[D, A]$;
        (b) $a_i = 0$;
        (c) $y$ is elementary (i.e. the coefficients are as small as possible);

    (ii) Remove all rows $y = (d_1, .., d_l, a_1, .., a_p)$ with $a_i \neq 0$;
    (iii) $i := i + 1;$

**od**
(Here := denotes the assignment and **while...do...od** the repetition.)

**Theorem 19.11** The algorithm generates all the minimal support invariants of the actor model represented by $N$. These invariants are given by the final matrix $D$.

*Proof* Let $[D^i, A^i]$ be the matrix after the $i$th iteration. We will prove (by induction) that $D^i$ contains all minimal support invariants of the net *without* the processors $\{i+1, i+2, .., p\}$. (This net will be denoted by $N^i$.) To do so we will also prove that every row $y_j = (d_1, .., d_l, a_1, .., a_p)$ of the matrix $[D^i, A^i]$ is such that

$$\forall k \in \{1, .., p\} : \sum_{g=1}^{l} d_g \times N_{gk} = a_k \qquad (*)$$

In other words the $j$th row of $A^i$, $A^i_j$, represents the "effect" of each processor on the invariant in the $j$th row of $D^i$, $D^i_j$, i.e. for every $1 \le k \le p$, if processor $k$ fires, then the weighted token sum (the weights are given by $D^i_j$) changes with $A^i_{jk}$.

Now we will prove (by induction) that these properties hold for all $i$.

1. Initially $D^0 = I_l$ and $A^0 = N$. Let $y_j = (d_1, .., d_l, a_1, .., a_p)$ be the $j$th row of $[D^0, A^0]$. Note that $d_g$ is equal to 1 if $g = j$; otherwise $d_g$ is zero. It is easy to verify that $D^0$ contains all (elementary) minimal support invariants of the net without processors ($N^0$) and that equation $(*)$ holds for $i = 0$.

2. Assume that $D^i$ contains all minimal support invariants of $N^i$ and equation $(*)$ holds for $[D^i, A^i]$.

First we show that equation $(*)$ also holds for $i + 1$. Every new row in $[D^{i+1}, A^{i+1}]$ is a positive linear combination of two rows of $[D^i, A^i]$. It easy to verify that if two rows $y$ and $y'$ satisfy $(*)$ then row $(k_1 \times y) + (k_2 \times y')$ also satisfies $(*)$. Hence $(*)$ holds for $[D^{i+1}, A^{i+1}]$.

Every invariant of $N^{i+1}$ is an invariant of $N^i$. Every non-negative invariant is equal to a positive linear combination of minimal support invariants (*see* lemma 19.4). Hence, every non-negative invariant of $N^{i+1}$ is a positive linear combination of the invariants represented by $D^i$.

Any invariant of $N^{i+1}$ that is the positive linear combination of more than two invariants of $D^i$ is not a minimal support invariant nor can it be generated by taking the positive linear combination of only two invariants of $D^i$ that annuls the $(l+i+1)$th column. To verify this note that (a) two minimal support invariants are linearly dependent if their supports are the same (*see* lemma 19.4), and that (b) if a linear combination of more than two invariants makes the $(l+i+1)$th column zero, then this linear combination uses two invariants: one with a positive

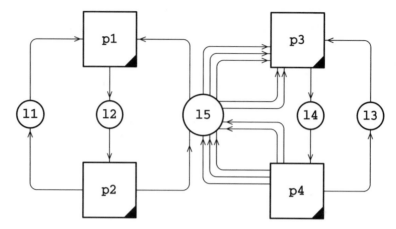

Fig. 19.6. The readers and writers system.

$(l+i+1)$th column and one with a negative $(l+i+1)$th column. Therefore we can use these two rows to generate an invariant with the same support or with a smaller support.

Hence it suffices to consider the linear combinations described in the algorithm.

Next the algorithm removes all rows where the $(l+i+1)$th column is not equal to zero. As a result $D^{i+1}$ contains all minimal support invariants of $N^{i+1}$. Induction shows that $D^p$ contains all the minimal support invariants.  □

To illustrate the algorithm we present an example.

### Example 6
Consider the actor shown in figure 19.6. This actor has only complete processors and represents a resource (represented by place $l_5$) shared by five readers and two writers. A read process is represented by a token in $l_1$ (waiting) or $l_2$ (reading). A write process is represented by a token in $l_3$ (waiting) or $l_4$ (writing). Initially place $l_5$ contains five tokens; thus it is guaranteed that if a write process is operational, then all the other processes are waiting. We will prove this by calculating the minimal support invariants. The matrix $[D^0, A^0]$ is as given in the following table.

| $l_1$ | $l_2$ | $l_3$ | $l_4$ | $l_5$ | $p_1$ | $p_2$ | $p_3$ | $p_4$ |
|---|---|---|---|---|---|---|---|---|
| 1 | 0 | 0 | 0 | 0 | −1 | 1 | 0 | 0 |
| 0 | 1 | 0 | 0 | 0 | 1 | −1 | 0 | 0 |
| 0 | 0 | 1 | 0 | 0 | 0 | 0 | −1 | 1 |
| 0 | 0 | 0 | 1 | 0 | 0 | 0 | 1 | −1 |
| 0 | 0 | 0 | 0 | 1 | −1 | 1 | −5 | 5 |

During the first iteration we add rows for processor $p_1$, as shown at the bottom of the next table, and we delete the rows where the $p_1$-entry is not equal to zero (these rows are marked with an asterisk in the next table).

| $l_1$ | $l_2$ | $l_3$ | $l_4$ | $l_5$ | $p_1$ | $p_2$ | $p_3$ | $p_4$ | |
|---|---|---|---|---|---|---|---|---|---|
| 1 | 0 | 0 | 0 | 0 | $-1$ | 1 | 0 | 0 | * |
| 0 | 1 | 0 | 0 | 0 | 1 | $-1$ | 0 | 0 | * |
| 0 | 0 | 1 | 0 | 0 | 0 | 0 | $-1$ | 1 | |
| 0 | 0 | 0 | 1 | 0 | 0 | 0 | 1 | $-1$ | |
| 0 | 0 | 0 | 0 | 1 | $-1$ | 1 | $-5$ | 5 | * |
| 1 | 1 | 0 | 0 | 0 | 0 | 0 | 0 | 0 | |
| 0 | 1 | 0 | 0 | 1 | 0 | 0 | $-5$ | 5 | |

We thus obtain the first iteration $[D^1, A^1]$ by deleting all rows in the table above for which the $p_1$-entry is not equal to zero. The next iteration of the algorithm (add processor $p_2$) does not alter the matrix. If we iterate for processor $p_3$, then we obtain the matrix $[D^3, A^3]$ by deleting the rows marked with an asteriks in the table below:

| $l_1$ | $l_2$ | $l_3$ | $l_4$ | $l_5$ | $p_1$ | $p_2$ | $p_3$ | $p_4$ | |
|---|---|---|---|---|---|---|---|---|---|
| 0 | 0 | 1 | 0 | 0 | 0 | 0 | $-1$ | 1 | * |
| 0 | 0 | 0 | 1 | 0 | 0 | 0 | 1 | $-1$ | * |
| 1 | 1 | 0 | 0 | 0 | 0 | 0 | 0 | 0 | |
| 0 | 1 | 0 | 0 | 1 | 0 | 0 | $-5$ | 5 | * |
| 0 | 0 | 1 | 1 | 0 | 0 | 0 | 0 | 0 | |
| 0 | 1 | 0 | 5 | 1 | 0 | 0 | 0 | 0 | |

The addition of $p_4$ does not alter the matrix, i.e. $[D^4, A^4]$ looks as follows:

| $l_1$ | $l_2$ | $l_3$ | $l_4$ | $l_5$ | $p_1$ | $p_2$ | $p_3$ | $p_4$ |
|---|---|---|---|---|---|---|---|---|
| 1 | 1 | 0 | 0 | 0 | 0 | 0 | 0 | 0 |
| 0 | 0 | 1 | 1 | 0 | 0 | 0 | 0 | 0 |
| 0 | 1 | 0 | 5 | 1 | 0 | 0 | 0 | 0 |

There are three minimal support invariants, the corresponding place invariant properties are as follows:

$$m_s(l_1) + m_s(l_2) = 5,$$
$$m_s(l_3) + m_s(l_4) = 2,$$
$$m_s(l_2) + 5 \times m_s(l_4) + m_s(l_5) = 5.$$

The last property guarantees that if a write process is operational all the other processes are waiting. The two other invariants state that the number of read and write processes is constant.

□

For larger nets the algorithm often generates, in addition, invariants that do not have a minimal support. There are two ways to deal with this problem: eliminate the non-minimal support invariants *after* applying the algorithm or eliminate the non-minimal support invariants the moment they are generated. It is quite easy to remove the non-minimal support invariants from the final matrix $D^p$. However, it is more efficient to remove the non-minimal support invariants immediately.

### 19.3  Transition invariants

Besides the place invariants there is another kind of invariant, called a *transition invariant*. A *transition invariant property* concerns *firing sequences*. It says that a system returns to a state with the marking of the initial state, if a certain firing sequence occurs.

**Definition 19.9**  A *firing sequence* of an actor model is a sequence of the form:

$$\langle (p_1, r_1), \ldots, (p_n, r_n) \rangle,$$

where $p_i \in P$ and $r_i \in R_{p_i}$ for $i \in \{1, \ldots, n\}$.

□

A firing sequence and an initial event determine a trace of the same length as the firing sequence.

Transition invariants play a less important role in applications than place invariants. We consider again filters and their corresponding markings. First we introduce formally the concept of a transition invariant.

**Definition 19.10**  Let an actor model with filter $f$ and filter set $V$ be given. A *transition invariant* $w$ is a function such that:

- $w \in K \to \mathbb{N}$, where $K = \{(p, r) \mid p \in P \wedge r \in R_p\}$,
- $\forall l \in L, v \in V : \sum_{(p,r) \in K} w(p, r) \times N(l, v, p, r) = 0.$

This set of equations is called the *transition balance*.

□

Here we have assumed that the time domain $T$ is countable (for instance $\mathbb{Q}$), in order to guarantee that the summation over the firing rules is restricted to a countable set. There are several properties of transition invariants that are similar to properties of place invariants, for example the following trivial result.

**Theorem 19.12** Let $w_1$ and $w_2$ be transition invariants for some actor model and some filter. For all $a,\ b \in \mathbf{N}$,

$$a \times w_1 + b \times w_2$$

is also a transition invariant.

The next theorem is the main result.

**Theorem 19.13** Let an actor model with filter $f$ with filter set $V$ be given. Further, let $w$ be a transition invariant for this model and let $s$ be the initial state. For all firing sequences such that each firing rule $r$ of processor $p$ executes exactly $w(p, r)$ times and that the final state is $s'$, the following property holds:

$$\forall l \in L, v \in V : m_s(l, v) = m_{s'}(l, v).$$

*Proof* Let

$$\langle (p_1, r_1), \dots, (p_n, r_n) \rangle$$

be a firing rule in which processor $p$ executes exactly $w(p, r)$ times and let $s$ be the initial state and $s'$ the final state. For all $l \in L$ and $v \in V$, in a way similar to that in the proof of theorem 19.2, we have

$$m_s(l, v) + N(l, v, p_0, r_0) + \dots + N(l, v, p_n, r_n) = m_{s'}(l, v).$$

Since addition is associative and commutative we may rewrite this as

$$m_s(l, v) + \sum_{(p,r) \in K} w(p, r) \times N(l, v, p, r) = m_{s'}(l, v).$$

$\square$

A transition invariant is called *realizable* if there is a firing sequence that generates an autonomous trace. Note that transition invariants have only non-negative values, because a processor cannot "fire back". For actor models with only complete processors and the Petri filter, we can find the transition invariants by elementary linear algebra techniques, as for the place invariants. As an example we consider the train control case, example 3. (Here we use for the Petri filter the shorthand of definition 19.2 and write $w(p)$ for $w(p, r)$.)

**Example 3, continued**

We recall the flow matrix $N$. We have to solve the transition balance (in matrix for $m$):

$$Nw = 0.$$

This gives the following two equations: $w(p) = w(r)$ and $w(p) = w(q)$. Hence the values of $w$ should be the same for all processes. So the system returns to its initial marking every time it occurs that all processors have fired the same number of times. Note that in this example, with the given initial state, such a trace is possible, this is however not guaranteed in general.

□

The weakness of transition invariants is that they are not necessarily realizable. Even live actor models do not guarantee that transition invariants are realizable. (The construction of a counter-example is an exercise.) There are cases in which it is not allowable for a system to return to its initial marking. If it is proved that there is no transition invariant then we have proved that there is no such trace. So we can use transition invariants to exclude certain behavior.

In the next example we consider the identity filter for the elevator case.

**Example 5, continued**

We recall the processor specifications for the elevator system. The flow function has the properties given below. We consider the firing variables instead of the firing rules. For the firing variables $x, y \in \mathbb{N}$,

$$N(a, x, p, x) = 1,$$
$$N(a, x, q, (x, y)) = -1,$$
$$N(b, x, p, x) = -1,$$
$$N(b, y, q, (x, y)) = 1,$$
$$N(c, (y, x), q, (x, y)) = 1,$$
$$N(c, (x, y), r, (x, y)) = -1,$$
$$N(d, (x, y), q, (x, y)) = -1,$$
$$N(d, (x, y), r, (x, y)) = 1.$$

The transition balance

$$\sum_{(p',r')\in K} w(p', r') \times N(l, v, p', r') = 0$$

gives for each place the following equations for $x, y \in \mathbb{N}$:

$$a : \sum_{x \in \mathbb{N}}(w(p, x) - \sum_{y \in \mathbb{N}} w(q, (x, y))) = 0,$$
$$b : \sum_{x \in \mathbb{N}}(-w(p, x) + \sum_{y \in \mathbb{N}} w(q, (y, x))) = 0,$$
$$c : \sum_{x, y \in \mathbb{N}}(w(q, (y, x)) - w(r, (x, y))) = 0,$$
$$d : \sum_{x, y \in \mathbb{N}}(-w(q, (x, y)) + w(r, (x, y))) = 0.$$

Hence

$$w(q, (x, y)) = w(q, (y, x)) = w(r, (x, y)) = w(r, (y, x)),$$

and therefore

$$w(p, x) = \sum_{y \in \mathbb{N}} w(q, (x, y))$$

is an example of transition invariant. So for each sequence of firings we can check whether the sequence agrees with the transition invariant. A firing sequence brings the system back to its initial marking, if every firing is allowed and if the sequence has the same number of firings of $q$ and $r$, both with an equal number of consumptions of $(x, y)$ and $(y, x)$. Further, $p$ has to fire for each $x$ for which $q$ fires with some $(x, y)$. For example,

$(p, 5), (q, (4, 5)), (r, (5, 3)), (p, 4), (r, (4, 5)), (q, (5, 3)), (p, 3)(q, (5, 4)),$
$(q, (3, 5)), (r, (3, 5)), (r, (5, 4)), (p, 5)$ is such a sequence.

□


The computational aspects of transition invariants are similar to those for the place invariants. For the Petri filter we can use linear algebra and for the general case the only technique is *trial and error*. Again let $p = \#(P)$ and $l = \#(L)$. Now $p$ is the number of unknown variables. If $l \leq p$ there may be more than one solution and then we may use theorem 19.10 to find a base of transition invariants. Note that the differences from the case of place invariants are that there we used the transpose of $N$, while here we use $N$ itself, and that we are looking for non-negative solutions only.

# 20

# Occurrence graph

Many questions about the behavior of an actor model can be formulated such as: "Is it possible to reach a state with a certain property?" and: "Will a state with a certain property always be reached?" Often these *reachability* questions concern the avoidance of *unsafe* or *unwanted* states. For example, is it possible to reach a state in which vehicles from orthogonal directions may pass a crossing at the same time in a traffic control system? Some of these questions can be formulated as place invariants, for instance if the initial state is "safe" then every reachable state should be safe. Reachability of desired states is also a question, for example the reachability in a production system of states where all orders of a certain age are fulfilled.

Many questions about *protocols* for communication between actors can also be expressed as reachability questions. A protocol describes the order in which two or more actors exchange tokens of certain kinds. In many cases it is possible to modify an actor model by adding places and processors such that a disturbance of the order of token exchange leads to the occurrence of tokens in the extra places. So the question whether a protocol is incorrect can be expressed in terms of the reachability of states where there is at least one token in an extra place. The *occurrence graph* contains all this information.

**Definition 20.1** Let an actor model with initial state $s_0$ be given. The *occurrence graph* is a graph with the states that are reachable from $s_0$ as nodes, denoted by $St_0$, and a set of edges

$$E \subseteq St_0 \times St_0,$$

such that

$$(s, s') \in E \Leftrightarrow (s, s') \in Tr.$$

□

Note that in most cases the occurrence graph is infinite and dependent on the initial state. Therefore we will not be able to compute this graph completely and so it will not be possible to verify properties that require inspection of the whole occurrence graph. However, *negative* answers may be found in the occurrence graph, i.e. *counter-examples* for questions that require inspection of the whole graph. For example if we can find one reachable state in the traffic system where vehicles in orthogonal directions are allowed to pass a crossing at the same time, then we know that the desired property does not hold. One cause of the infiniteness of the occurrence graph is that the identities of new tokens differ from the identities of old ones. Another reason is that the time stamps of new tokens are in most cases larger than those of old ones.

To compute an occurrence graph in part, there are several approaches: *depth-first search*, *breadth-first search* and a mixture of these two. In the first case all nodes on a trace are computed and if the trace ends the next trace is computed. In the second case all nodes that are reachable from the initial node in $n$ steps are computed before those that are reachable in $n + 1$ steps. It is clear that the depth-first approach can only be carried out in pure form if all traces end in a deadlock. There are several techniques for making the computation of part of an occurrence graph more efficient but they will not covered in this book.

If all processors are *functional* then the number of edges leaving a state is finite, because there are only finitely many combinations of input tokens that may cause a transition. If there are non-functional processors then the number of edges leaving a state can be infinite, so then a breadth-first search is not possible.

In practice it is normal to compute and store a few hundred thousand states or markings for inspection. Instead of computing all successor nodes of a given node it makes sense to compute only a few of them, for instance a fixed number $k$. This makes it possible to inspect the (filtered) occurrence graph to a greater depth, if we have a fixed amount of computing time and storage space available. When we compute for each node only one successor we are *simulating* the model. Then we still can find interesting results as will be shown later.

We can compute a finite tree instead of the infinite occurrence graph. This finite tree is called the *coverability tree* and it contains much (but not all) information of the occurrence graph.

**Definition 20.2** Let an actor model with initial state $s_0$, filter $f$ and finite filter set $V$ be given. The *coverability tree* has nodes in the set $Q' = L \times V \to \mathbb{N} \cup \{\infty\}$. The tree is constructed as follows.

(i) The root is the marking of $s_0$ under $f$ and is denoted by $m_0$.

(ii) Node $m$ is a leaf node if

$$\forall p \in P : \forall r \in R_p : \exists l \in L, v \in V : m(l, v) < N^-(l, v, p, r),$$

(i.e. each processor is disabled).

(iii) A node $m$ is also a leaf node if there is a node $m'$ on the trace from $m_0$ to $m$ such that $m = m'$.

(iv) If $m$ is not a leaf node, then $m'$ is a successor node and $(m, m')$ is an edge if and only if $\exists p \in P : \exists r \in R_p :$

$$\forall l \in L, v \in V : m(l, v) \geq N^-(l, v, p, r) \ \wedge \ m'(l, v) = c(l, v)$$

where

- $\forall l \in L, v \in V : c(l, v) = \infty,$ if $: \exists a \in A : a(l, v) < b(l, v),$
  $\qquad\qquad = b(l, v),$ otherwise,
- $\forall l \in L, v \in V : b(l, v) = m(l, v) + N(l, v, p, r),$
- $A$ is the set of nodes $a$ on the trace from $m_0$ to $m$ such that

$$\forall l \in L, v \in V : a(l, v) \leq b(l, v).$$

$\square$

So, the nodes are markings possibly with infinitely many tokens per place. Here we have used the following conventions for $\infty$:

$$\forall n \in \mathbf{N} : n < \infty,$$
$$\forall n \in \mathbf{N} : \infty + n = \infty \ \wedge \ \infty - n = \infty.$$

In example 7 we consider an example of a coverability tree.

There exists an edge $(m, m')$ in the coverability tree if there is a transition possible from states with marking $m$ to states with marking $b$ such that either $m'(l, v) = b(l, v)$ or $m'(l, v) = \infty$. The last situation occurs if there is a marking $a$ on some trace from $m_0$ to $m$ such that $a$ is at most $b$ and $a(l, v) < b(l, v)$. If the filter set is finite, the number of edges leaving a node in the coverability tree are finite. From now on we assume the filter set is finite.

**Lemma 20.1** Let an actor model with filter $f$, finite filter set $V$, initial marking $s_0$ and flow function $N$ be given. The number of edges leaving a node in the coverability tree is finite.

*Proof* Consider, for $p \in P$ and $r \in R_p$, the functions

$$\{((l, v), N(l, v, p, r)) \mid l \in L \ \wedge \ v \in V\}.$$

Because $L$ and $V$ are finite and the values of $N(l, v, p, r)$ are natural numbers, bounded by the structure of the flat net model, there are only finitely many of these functions. It follows from the definition of the coverability tree that the number of edges in each node is at most equal to the number of these functions.

□

As we will prove, a coverability tree is finite (if the filter set of the filter is finite). Therefore the coverability tree is easy to compute by the four rules of definition 20.2. First, we demonstrate an important property of sequences of finite functions with extended natural values, i.e. natural values or $\infty$. It will be used in the theorem that follows.

**Lemma 20.2** Let $A$ be a finite set, let $B = A \to \mathbb{N} \cup \{\infty\}$ and for $b \in B^+$ (i.e. a finite or infinite sequence) and $i \in dom(b)$, let

$$q(b, i) = (\forall j \in dom(b) : j < i \Rightarrow \exists a \in A : b_j(a) > b_i(a)).$$

Further, let

$$\tilde{B} = \{b \in B^+ \mid \forall i \in \mathbb{N}, a \in A : b_i(a) = \infty \Rightarrow b_{i+1}(a) = \infty\}.$$

Then

$$\forall b \in \tilde{B} : \{i \in dom(b) \mid q(b, i)\} \text{ is finite.}$$

*Proof* We use induction with the cardinality of $A$. Let $\#(A) = 1$. Let $A = \{a_0\}$, let $b \in B^+$ and let $\langle b_{i_0}, \ldots, b_{i_n} \rangle$ be a finite sub-sequence of $b$ such that $\forall l \in \{0, \ldots, n\} : q(b, i_l)$. Then, clearly

$$b_{i_0}(a_0) > b_{i_1}(a_0) > \ldots > b_{i_n}(a_0) \geq 0.$$

Hence $b_{i_n}(a_0) \leq b_{i_0}(a_0) - n$ and therefore $n \leq b_{i_0}(a_0)$. So all sub-sequences of $b$ that satisfy $q$ are finite.

Assume the assertion is true for all $A$ with $\#(A) < k$.
Let $\#(A) = k$. Let $b \in \tilde{B}$ and let $Q = \{i \in dom(b) \mid q(b, i)\}$ be infinite. We will show that this leads to a contradiction. Fix $a_0 \in A$. Since $Q$ is infinite there is an infinite sub-sequence $\langle b_{i_0}, b_{i_1}, \ldots \rangle$ of $b$ such that

- $\forall n \in \mathbb{N} : i_n \in Q$,
- $b_{i_0}(a_0) \leq b_{i_1}(a_0), \ldots$.

To verify this, consider first the case where $b_i(a_0) = \infty$ for some $i \in \mathbb{N}$. Then the value $\infty$ occurs infinitely often in the sequence

$$\langle b_{i_0}(a_0), b_{i_1}(a_0), \ldots \rangle$$

and we can take the sub-sequence consisting of $\infty$ only. For the other case note that the set $\{b_i(a_0) \mid i \in dom(b)\}$ is either finite or infinite. In the first case there

is a value that occurs infinitely many times and so we can find an infinite sub-
sequence with this value and in the second case we can even find an increasing
sub-sequence.

Clearly $\langle b_{i_0}, b_{i_1}, \ldots \rangle$ is an element of $\tilde{B}$ that can be represented as $\langle \tilde{b}_0, \tilde{b}_1, \ldots \rangle$.
Further, we have $\forall n \in dom(\tilde{b}) : q(\tilde{b}, n)$. Because of the second property of the
sub-sequence we have for, all $i \in dom(\tilde{b})$:

$$\forall j \in dom(\tilde{b}) : j < i \Rightarrow \exists a \in A \backslash \{a_0\} : \tilde{b}_j(a) > \tilde{b}_i(a).$$

Let $b^*$ be $\tilde{b}$ but with $A$ replaced by $A_0 = A \backslash \{a_0\}$. Then

$$\{n \in dom(b^*) \mid q(b^*, n)\}$$

is infinite which is a contradiction since $\#(A_0) = k - 1$. Hence $Q$ is finite, which
proves the assertion.                                                          □

**Theorem 20.1** Let an actor model with filter $f$, finite filter set $V$ and initial
state $s_0$ be given. Let $m_0$ be the marking of $s_0$ with respect to $f$. Then the
coverability tree is finite.

*Proof* We first show that every trace starting in $m_0$ has only a finite number of
nodes.

Let $m = \langle m_0, m_1, \ldots \rangle$ be a trace in the tree. Apply lemma 20.2 with $A = L \times V$.
Then for only finitely many $i \in \mathbb{N}$ we have $q(m, i)$. Hence for all but a finite
number of $i \in \mathbb{N}$ we have $\neg q(m, i)$ or

$$\exists j \in \mathbb{N} : j < i \wedge \forall l \in L, v \in V : m_j(l, v) \leq m_i(l, v).$$

So for all but a finite number of $i \in \mathbb{N}$ we have either $m_i = m_j$ or, by the
definition of the coverability tree, $m_i > m_j$ (i.e. for all pairs $(l, v) \in L \times V$ we
have $m_i(l, v) \geq m_j(l, v)$ and for at least one pair $(l, v)$ we have $m_i(l, v) = \infty$).
By the construction of the coverability tree we know that there cannot be more
than two identical nodes on a trace and also the number of nodes $i$ for which
there is a $j$ such that $m_j < m_i$ is finite because $m_i$ attains the value $\infty$ for at
least one pair $(l, v)$ more. (Note that $L \times V$ is finite.) So every trace is finite.

Next we show that the number of markings reachable from $m_0$ is finite. Suppose
the contrary: infinitely many nodes are reachable from $m_0$. Then we can construct
an infinite trace starting at $m_0$. Remember that every node is a starting point
of only a finite number of edges (*see* lemma 20.1). Consider $m_0$. From this node
start finitely many edges. At least one of the edges leads to a node from which
infinitely many nodes are reachable. Choose one of these as the next node. We
use induction. Suppose we have constructed a trace of length $n$ and that at
least one of the edges starting in the last node of this trace has infinitely many

reachable nodes. Then we can extend the trace with one of these nodes. Hence we can construct an infinite trace. This is a contradiction. □

In the following theorem we establish an important property of the coverability tree. It says that if a state $s$ with marking $m$ is reachable from the initial state then there is a node $m'$ in the coverability tree with the property that $m' \geq m$ (i.e. $\forall l \in L, v \in V : m'(l, v) \geq m(l, v)$).

**Theorem 20.2** Let an actor model with filter $f$, finite filter set $V$ and an initial state $s_0$ be given. Let $m_{s_0}$ be the marking of $s_0$ with respect to $f$. Then, for every reachable state $s$ with marking $m_s$ there is a marking $m$ in the coverability tree with $m \geq m_s$.

*Proof* We use induction. If $s = s_0$ then $m_{s_0} \leq m_0$ and then the theorem holds. Assume the theorem holds for all states that are reachable in $n$ steps from the initial state. Let $s$ be reachable in $n$ steps and let a firing assignment $\{(p, r)\}$ be applicable in $s$ and let application of this assignment give state $s'$. By the induction hypothesis we have a node $m$ in the coverability tree such that $m \geq m_s$. Since

$$in(p, r) \subseteq s$$

we have

$$\forall l \in L, v \in V : m_s(l, v) \geq N^-(l, v, p, r).$$

Hence

$$\forall l \in L, v \in V : m(l, v) \geq N^-(l, v, p, r)$$

and therefore there is a node $m'$ in the coverability tree with

$$\forall l \in L, v \in V : m'(l, v) \geq m(l, v) + N(l, v, p, r) = m_{s'}(l, r).$$

(Note that it is possible that we can choose $m' = m$.) □

So, if we can express a property in terms of the markings of the coverability tree, and if these markings are not reachable in the coverability tree, then states with the corresponding property are not reachable either.

In general we cannot be sure that if there is an edge in the coverability tree then there is also a possible transition. However, if all processors are *total* this is the case.

**Theorem 20.3** Let an actor model with its coverability tree be given. If all processors are total then for each node in the coverability tree there is at least one edge that corresponds to a legal transition in the underlying actor model.

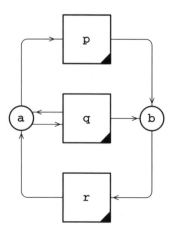

Fig. 20.1. Example 7

The proof is an exercise.

We conclude this section with an example.

### Example 7

In figure 20.1 an actor model is displayed. We assume that all processors are complete and the Petri filter is used. The coverability tree is presented in table 20.1. A pair of numbers $(a, b)$ denotes the amount of tokens in places $a$ and $b$

Table 20.1. *Coverability tree for example 7.*

| $(2,0)$ | $(1,1)$ | $(0,2)$ | $[1,1]$ | | |
|---|---|---|---|---|---|
| | | $(1,\infty)$ | $(0,\infty)$ | | |
| | | | $[1,\infty]$ | | |
| | | | $(\infty,\infty)$ | $[\infty,\infty]$ | |
| | | $[2,0]$ | | | |
| | $(2,\infty)$ | $(1,\infty)$ | $(0,\infty)$ | $(\infty,\infty)$ | $[\infty,\infty]$ |
| | | | $[1,\infty]$ | | |
| | | | $(\infty,\infty)$ | $[\infty,\infty]$ | |
| | | $[2,\infty]$ | | | |
| | | $(\infty,\infty)$ | $[\infty,\infty]$ | | |

respectively . If a pair is represented as $[a, b]$ it is a leaf node. The traces are represented from left to right. So $(2,0)$ is the root and its direct successors are $(1,1)$ and $(2,\infty)$. The branches are made by processor firings in the order $p, q, r$.

☐

The example shows that coverability trees can be big and that the only way to construct and inspect a coverability tree of a realistic example is by means of a computer. It also shows there is much repetition because we often expand the same node more than once. Therefore it is more efficient to develop an acyclic graph instead of a tree. We will omit this modification because it is rather technical.

# 21

# Time analysis

In chapter 19 we considered only the (filtered) values of tokens. In this chapter we focus on the time stamps of the tokens. Questions that can be answered by observation of the time stamps only concern, for example, the arrival times of tokens in certain places and, in particular, the arrival time of the first token in a certain place. Examples of such questions are: "What is the throughput time of products in a factory?" and: "What is the response time of an information system?". Here we ignore the values and the identities of the tokens.

Of course we could use the occurrence graph to answer these questions but this graph is very large and contains many details that are not relevant for the analysis of time. Therefore we choose another approach: we will consider not all the possible states but *equivalence classes* of them. (Note that markings are also equivalence classes of states.) In fact we will develop a new actor model, called the *interval-timed actor model*, in which the time stamps of tokens are replaced by *time intervals* instead of time points. The processor relation of this model will also be characterized by time intervals. The relationship between the original actor model and the interval-timed actor model is that the first one is *similar* to the second one, so for each trace of the original model there is a similar trace of the interval-timed model. Hence for each state that is reachable in the original model an equivalent state in the interval-timed model is reachable. The systems engineer has to specify the similarity relation: first a filter is specified (usually the Petri filter) and secondly the *delay intervals* are specified for each output connector of each processor. So we assume that the delays specified per processor, are only dependent on the output connector and not on the values of the consumed tokens. The delay intervals should be *correct*, i.e. all tokens produced by a processor in the original model should have delays that fit into the corresponding delay interval.

The first step is the definition of the interval-timed actor model. The main difference is that we have to define a calculus for time intervals.

**Definition 21.1** Let $TT = \{t \in \mathbb{R} \times \mathbb{R} \mid \pi_1(t) \le \pi_2(t) \wedge \pi_1(t) \ge 0\}$. Let $a, b \in TT$, $A \subseteq TT$ and $i \in \{1, 2\}$. The functions $+$, $max_i$, $min_i$ $(i \in \{1, 2\})$, $\le$, $\ge$ and $\cap$ are defined via the following statements:

$$a + b = (\pi_1(a) + \pi_1(b), \pi_2(a) + \pi_2(b)),$$
$$nmax_i(A) = max\{\pi_i(a) \mid a \in A\},$$
$$nmin_i(A) = min\{\pi_i(a) \mid a \in A\},$$
$$a \le b \Leftrightarrow \exists c \in TT : a + c = b,$$
$$a \ge b \Leftrightarrow \exists c \in TT : b + c = a,$$
$$a \cap b = \{x \in \mathbb{R} \mid max_1(\{a, b\}) \le x \le min_2(\{a, b\})\}).$$

□

Note that if $a, b \in TT$ and $a \le b$ then $\pi_1(a) \le \pi_1(b) \wedge \pi_2(a) \le \pi_2(b)$. But the reverse is not true. So $(3, 5) \le (4, 6)$ holds but not $(3, 5) \le (5, 6)$, because $c = (2, 1) \notin TT$. Further, note that we represent intervals by their begin and end point.. Next we define the interval-timed actor model. (Here we use the definitions of the actor framework intensively.) There are two main differences from the original actor model: the time is replaced by time intervals and in the firing rules these time intervals play a different role: the time intervals belonging to the input connectors do not play a role at all and the time intervals belonging to the output connectors have to be interpreted as *delays* (interval delays to be precise). So we switch from *absolute* time in the original processor relations to *relative* time in the interval-timed processor relations.

**Definition 21.2** An *interval-timed actor model* is an actor model as defined in definition 11.3 and in definition 11.6 with the following modifications.

- Model modifications:
    (i) the time domain $T \subseteq TT$ is such that $\forall a, b \in T : a + b \in T$, with $TT$ and the functions defined as in definition 21.1,
    (ii) the firing rules do not have to satisfy requirement (iii) in definition 11.3.

- Transition relation modifications (*see* definition 11.6):
    (i) $tim(f) = (max_1(A), max_2(A))$, where $A = \{\pi_3(x) \mid x \in In(f)\}$;
    (ii) $time(s) = (min_1(B), min_2(B))$, where
        $B = \{tim(f) \mid f \in FA \wedge In(f) \subseteq s\}$;
    (iii) a firing assignment $f$ is applicable in state $s$ if and only if it satisfies requirements (i) and (ii) and $time(s) \cap tim(f) \ne \emptyset$;

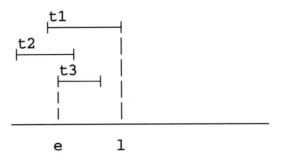

Fig. 21.1. Time intervals of three tokens.

(iv) $(s, s') \in Tr \Leftrightarrow s' = (s \setminus In(f)) \cup D(Out(f), time(s))$,
where $D$ is defined by

$$D(Y, x) =$$
$$\{(i, v, t, l) \mid \exists d \in TT : t = x + d \ \wedge \ (i, v, d, l) \in Y\}.$$

The state space is defined as in definition 11.4.
□

In order to clarify some consequences of the time intervals of tokens we consider the following example.

### Example 8
In figure 21.1 the time intervals of three tokens in a state $s$ are displayed. Assume these tokens can be consumed by one processor $p$ in one event. The time points $e$ and $l$ mark the earliest and latest possible times at which $p$ can execute. Hence

$$e = max\{\pi_1(t_1), \pi_1(t_2), \pi_1(t_3)\}$$

and

$$l = max\{\pi_2(t_1), \pi_2(t_2), \pi_2(t_3)\}.$$

The *enabling interval* of $p$ is equal to $[e, l]$. If $p$ is the only processor in a firing assignment $f$ (i.e. $dom(f) = \{p\}$), we have $time(f) = (e, l)$.

In figure 21.2 the enabling time intervals of three processors are displayed. Suppose no other processor is enabled, i.e. no other processor has enough tokens of the right values in their input places. The *transition time* of the system will be within the interval $[e, l]$, because no transition can fire before $e$ and since we assume systems to be eager, processor 3 will execute before time point $l$. Hence

$$e = min\{\pi_1(p_1), \pi_1(p_2), \pi_1(p_3)\},$$

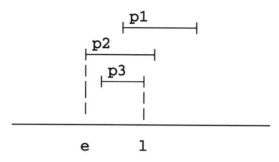

Fig. 21.2. Enabling intervals of three processors.

and

$$l = min\{\pi_2(p_1), \pi_2(p_2), \pi_2(p_3)\}.$$

If there are three firing assignments $f_1$, $f_2$ and $f_3$ with $dom(f_i) = \{p_i\}$, then

$$time(s) = (min\{min_1(tim(f_1)), min_1(tim(f_2)), min_1(tim(f_3))\},$$
$$min\{min_2(tim(f_1)), min_2(tim(f_2)), min_2(tim(f_3))\}).$$

Hence $time(s) = (e, l)$.
□

In the same way as in part II we can prove that all autonomous traces are *monotonous* with respect to the modified ordering relations. Many other properties of actor models hold also for the interval-timed model. (We do not give proofs here.)

The next step is the introduction of a similarity relation between the original model and the interval-timed model.

**Definition 21.3** Let $A$ be an actor model and $B$ an interval-timed actor model with the same flat net model. Let $g$ be a function from the object universe $OU_A$ to the object universe $OU_B$. Let $(s_A, t_A)$ and $(s_B, t_B)$ be events of $A$ and $B$, respectively. The *similarity relation* $C$ is defined as follows:

$$((s_A, t_A), (s_B, t_B)) \in C \Leftrightarrow$$
$$dom(s_A) = dom(s_B) \wedge$$
$$(\forall i \in dom(s_A):$$
$$g(\pi_1(s_A(i))) = \pi_1(s_B(i)) \wedge$$
$$\pi_1(\pi_2(s_B(i))) \le \pi_2(s_A(i)) \le \pi_2(\pi_2(s_B(i))) \wedge$$
$$\pi_3(s_A(i)) = \pi_3(s_B(i))) \wedge$$
$$\pi_1(t_B) \le t_A \le \pi_2(t_B).$$

$\square$

Hence two events are similar if and only if all the following hold:

- their states have tokens with the same identities (we call them *corresponding* tokens) (this assumption can be weakened);
- a token of $A$ has the same filtered value (with filter $g$) as the corresponding token in $B$;
- corresponding tokens reside in the same place;
- the time stamps of tokens of $A$ belong to the time intervals of the corresponding tokens in $B$;
- the event time of $A$ fits into the event interval of $B$.

**Theorem 21.1** Let $A$ be an actor model and $B$ an interval-timed actor model with the same flat net model. Let $g$ and $C$ be defined as in definition 21.3. Let there be a bijective mapping for each $p \in P$: $\phi_p \in R_{A,p} \rightarrow R_{B,p}$ such that

$\forall p \in P : \forall r \in R_{A,p} : r' = \phi_p(r)$ and

   (i) $dom(r) = dom(r')$,
   (ii) $\forall x \in dom(r) : \pi_1(r(x)) = \pi_1(r'(x)) \wedge g(\pi_2(r(x))) = \pi_2(r'(x))$,
   (iii) $\forall x \in dom(r) \cap O(p)$ :

$$\pi_3(r(x)) - max\{\pi_3(r(y)) \mid y \in dom(r) \cap I(p)\} \in \pi_3(r'(x)).$$

Then, for each pair of initial states $(s_A, s_B)$, such that $((s_A, 0), (s_B, (0, 0))) \in C$, system $A$ is *similar* to system $B$, i.e. $A \sim_C B$.

*Proof* It is sufficient to show that if two (not necessarily initial) states $s_A$ and $s_B$, and two times $t_A \le time(s_A)$ and $t_B \le time(s_B)$, satisfy $((s_A, t_A), (s_B, t_B)) \in C$ then for all firing assignments $f_A$ that are applicable in $s_A$ there is an applicable firing assignment $f_B$ in $s_B$ such that

$$((s'_A, time(s_A)), (s'_B, time(s_B))) \in C,$$

where

$$s'_A = (s_A \setminus In(f_A)) \cup Out(f_A),$$
$$s'_B = (s_B \setminus In(f_B)) \cup D(Out(f_B), time(s_B)).$$

To verify this let an applicable firing assignment $f_A$ be given. Let $f_B$ satisfy $\forall p \in P : f_B(p) = \phi_p(f_A(p))$. Fix some $p \in P$ and let $r = f_A(p)$ and $r' = f_B(p)$. Then $r$ and $r'$ satisfy the properties 1 to 3 of the theorem. First we check whether $f_B$ is applicable, i.e. $time(s_B) \cap tim(f_B) \neq \emptyset$. Suppose this is not true. Then there is another firing assignment $f'_B$ such that $time(s_B) \cap tim(f'_B) \neq \emptyset$ and

$$\pi_2(tim(f'_B)) < \pi_1(tim(f_B)),$$

because of the properties of *time* and *tim*. However, then there is a firing assignment $f'_A$ for model $A$ that consumes the corresponding tokens of $f'_B$. (Note that $In(f'_A)$ and $In(f'_B)$ posses only corresponding tokens and the same holds for $In(f_A)$ and $In(f_B)$.) So we have

$$tim(f'_A) \leq \pi_2(tim(f'_B)) < \pi_1(tim(f_B)) \leq tim(f_A).$$

Hence $f_A$ is not applicable because it does not satisfy requirement (iii) of definition 11.6. This is a contradiction and therefore $f_B$ is applicable in $s_B$. In a similar way we can show that $time(s_A) \in time(s_B)$.

Next we show that $((s'_A, time(s_A)), (s'_B, time(s_B))) \in C$. The correspondence of tokens in $s_A \setminus In(f_A)$ with tokens in $s_B \setminus In(f_B)$ follows from the assumption that $(s_A, t_A)$ and $(s_B, t_B)$ are similar. Note that (by the eagerness assumption) for all $p \in dom(f_A)$ and $r = f_A(p)$ we have

$$time(s_A) = max\{\pi_3(r(y)) \mid y \in dom(r) \cap I(p)\}.$$

Hence we may substitute $time(s_A)$ in the third requirement of $\phi_p$.

Therefore for all $(i, x) \in Out(f_A)$ there is exactly one $(i, y) \in Out(f_B)$ such that

$$g(\pi_1(x)) = \pi_1(y) \wedge \pi_1(\pi_2(y)) \leq \pi_2(x) - time(s_A) \leq \pi_2(\pi_2(y))$$

and since $time(s_A) \in time(s_B)$ we have

$$\pi_2(x) \in \pi_2(y) + time(s_B).$$

(Note that $(i, x)$ and $(i, y)$ are tokens.) This proves the assertion. □

The importance of this theorem is that for each autonomous trace of an actor model there is a similar trace of the corresponding interval-timed actor model. Hence if a state is reachable in the original model it is also reachable in the interval-timed model. This approach has much resemblance to the coverability

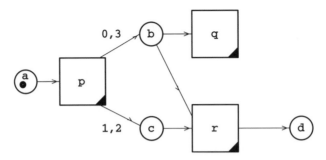

Fig. 21.3. No bisimilarity.

tree method, because for all traces in the original actor model there is a corresponding trace in the coverability tree.

It is a pity that we cannot prove that the two models $A$ and $B$ are bisimilar. The following counter-example shows why not.

**Example 9**

In figure 21.3 an interval-timed actor model $B$ is displayed. All processors are complete and the object universe is a singleton. The labels (0,3) and (1,2) denote the delay intervals. Suppose there is only one token in the initial state $s_0$ in place $a$ with time interval [1,2], so that $time(s_0) = (1,2)$. The next state $s_1$ is reached by execution of processor $p$. This state has only two tokens, in places $b$ and $c$ and with time intervals [1,4] and [2,5] respectively. It is easy to verify that there are two possible firing assignments: one in which $q$ executes and one in which $r$ executes, we call them $f_1$ and $f_2$ respectively. The values of the functions $tim$ and $time$ are as follows:

$$tim(f_1) = (1,2) + (0,3) = (1,5),$$
$$tim(f_2) = (1,2) + (1,2) = (2,4),$$
$$time(s_1) = (1,4).$$

Since $tim(f_i) \cap time(s_1) \neq \emptyset$, $i \in \{1,2\}$, both firing assignments are applicable and so there is a next state $s_2$ that is reached by executing processor $r$. In $s_2$ there will be a token in place $d$.

Now we consider the corresponding original actor model $A$ having the same flat net model and initial state $s'_0$ with only one (corresponding) token in $a$. This has a time stamp $x$ that satisfies $1 \leq x \leq 2$. Further, let the tokens sent to $b$ and $c$ have delays 1 and 2 respectively. Then the (unique) next state $s'_1$ will have two tokens in places $b$ and $c$ with time stamps $x+1$ and $x+2$ respectively. Hence the only possible next state is reached by the execution of processor $q$ and therefore there will never be a token in place $d$.

It is clear that the models $A$ and $B$ satisfy the conditions of theorem 21.1 and so $A \sim_C B$; however, $B \sim_C A$ does not hold. ($C$ is defined as in the former theorem.) The reason is that requirement (iii) of the transition relation (definition 11.6) in the original actor model is stronger than the corresponding requirement in the interval-timed actor model (definition 21.2).

□

We will apply theorem 21.1 to the simpler situation where the function $g$ is the Petri filter, i.e. $OU_B$ is a singleton. Further, we assume that all processors are complete and total. In this case a (partial) occurrence graph of model $B$ is easy to compute.

**Definition 21.4** Let an actor model $A$ with only complete, functional and total processors be given. There are two functions *low* and *up* given that satisfy

(i) $dom(low) = dom(up) = \{(p, x) \mid p \in P \land x \in O(p)\}$,

(ii) $\forall (p, x) \in dom(up) : 0 \leq low(p, x) \leq up(p, x)$,

(iii) $\forall p \in P : \forall r \in R_{A,p} : \forall x \in dom(r) \cap O(p) :$
$$\pi_3(r(x)) - max\{\pi_3(r(y)) \mid y \in dom(r) \cap I(p)\} \in$$
$$(low(p, x), up(p, x)).$$

Model $A$ is called a *delay model*. The *corresponding model* $B$ is defined as in the former theorem, but with the additional requirements that

(i) $OU_B$ is a singleton,

(ii) $\forall p \in P : \forall r \in R_{B,p} : \forall x \in dom(r) \cap O(p) :$

$$\pi_3(r(x)) = (low(p, x), up(p, x)).$$

□

So the processor relation of a delay model has upper and lower bounds on the delays and these delays are only dependent on the output connector and not on the firing rules. As we have seen in example 9, the calculation of the next states in the corresponding model is very simple: only the times of the tokens count and these times are determined by adding $(low(p, x), up(p, x))$ to the interval of the transition time ($time(s)$) if processor $p$ fires and if we have to calculate the time interval of the token sent via connector $x$.

Since the processors are total and complete in the delay model and since the values do not play a role in the corresponding model, the computation of successor nodes in the occurrence graph of the corresponding model is relatively easy. Because the states of the corresponding model are equivalence classes containing large numbers of states of the delay model, transformation to the corresponding model gives an essential reduction of the state space.

Interesting questions to be asked concern the arrival times of tokens in places that were empty in the initial state. These questions can be answered for a delay model by inspecting the occurrence graph of the corresponding model.
We first define what we mean by earliest and latest arrival time.

**Definition 21.5** Let an interval-timed actor model and an initial state $s$ be given. Let $\Pi(s)$ be the set of autonomous traces (i.e. sequences of states) starting in $s$. Then the *earliest arrival time* in place $l$, denoted by $eat(s, l)$, and the *latest arrival time* in $l$, denoted by $lat(s, l)$, satisfy respectively

$$eat(s, l) = inf\{a_1(\sigma, l) \mid \sigma \in \Pi(s)\},$$
$$lat(s, l) = sup\{a_2(\sigma, l) \mid \sigma \in \Pi(s)\},$$

where, for $i \in \{1, 2\}$,

$$a_i(\sigma, l) = min_i\{\pi_2(\sigma_n(j)) \mid n \in dom(\sigma) \wedge j \in dom(\sigma_n) \wedge \pi_3(\sigma_n(j)) = l\}.$$

(We have to use here *inf* and *sup* instead of *min* and *max* because the latter two do not have to exist.)
□

Note that $a_1(\sigma, l)$ is the earliest arrival time of a token in place $l$ on trace $\sigma$. The term "latest arrival time" is a bit misleading; it is in fact the *maximal earliest arrival time*. It is not difficult to generalize these concepts to the arrival of the $n$th token in a place. (This is an exercise.) The concepts *eat* and *lat* are also defined for the original actor model if we delete the subscripts $i$ in the *min* function and in $a_i$. In the next theorem we formulate the relationship between the arrival times in the two models.

**Theorem 21.2** Let a delay model $A$ and a corresponding model $B$ be given. Let $s_A$ and $s_B$ be the initial states and let $((s_A, 0), (s_B, (0, 0))) \in C$ where $C$ is given in definition 21.3 . Then, for all $l \in L$,

$$eat_A(s_A, l) \geq eat_B(s_B, l),$$
$$lat_A(s_A, l) \leq lat_B(s_B, l).$$

(The subscripts refer as usual to the models.)

*Proof* By theorem 21.1 there is for each trace of model $A$ a similar trace of model $B$. Fix $l \in L$. Consider the first inequality. Suppose $eat_A(s_A, l)$ is finite (if not, it can immediately be seen that the first inequality holds). If there is a trace $\sigma_A$ such that $a(\sigma_A, l) = eat_A(s_A, l)$ then there is a similar trace $\sigma_B$ and, further, the time stamps of the tokens in states of $\sigma_A$ have time stamps in the intervals of the corresponding tokens in states of $\sigma_B$; so we have the first inequality. If there is not such a trace then there is for each $\epsilon > 0$ a trace $\sigma_A$ with $a(\sigma_A, l) < eat_A(s_A, l) + \epsilon$. So there is a similar trace $\sigma_B$ for the corresponding model with

$$eat_B(s_B, l) \leq a_1(\sigma_B, l) \leq a(\sigma_A, l) < eat_A(s_A, l) + \epsilon.$$

This holds for all $\epsilon > 0$ so the first inequality is true.

Next consider the second inequality. We distinguish two cases. In the first, we assume that $lat_A(s_A, l)$ is infinite. This means that there is for each $K \in \mathbb{R}$ a trace $\sigma_A$ such that $a(\sigma_A, l) > K$; thus, there is a similar trace $\sigma_B$ with $a_2(\sigma_B) > K$. Hence in this case we have also $lat_B(s_B, l) = \infty$. In the case where $lat_A(s_A, l)$ is finite the proof is similar to that for the first inequality. □

This theorem can be applied by computing a part of the occurrence graph of the corresponding model; the earliest and latest arrival times in this graph are bounds for the corresponding values in the original model.

We conclude this chapter with another method of time analysis for a specially structured actor model. This method is in fact a generalization of the well-known *critical path method* for bipartite acyclic graphs. We assume that we have a *conflict free* delay model and that no processor has more than one input connector attached to the same place. Note that an *activity network* (*see* chapter 14) is a special case of such a model. For this case we have the following algorithm.

## Algorithm for conflict free delay models

There are in fact two almost identical algorithms: one for computing $eat(s, l)$ and another for computing $lat(s, l)$ for an initial state $s$ and all places $l$. We use the corresponding model. We will give each place a time point as *label*. In the first algorithm the label denotes the earliest arrival time of the first token in this place, found so far. In the second algorithm it denotes the latest arrival time of the first token. Finally we combine these two labels to obtain a time interval as a label for each place, denoting the earliest and latest arrival time for the first token in a place. We give only the first algorithm in detail.

We distinguish two kinds of labels: *tentative* and *permanent* labels. At the start all labels are tentative and for initial state $s$ and place $l$ are equal to

$$min_1\{\pi_2(s(i)) \mid i \in dom(s) \wedge \pi_3(s(i)) = l\}.$$

(The minimum over the empty set is $\infty$.) At the end the labels are permanent and are equal to $eat(s, l)$. The only properties of the processor relation used are the bounding functions *low* and *up* defined in definition 21.4.

In the algorithm we are updating the function $d$ by $d \in L \to \mathbb{R}$. In each stage of the computing process the label of place $l$ is $d(l)$. Further we update two sets of places: $L_t$, the tentatively labeled places and $L_p$, the permanently labeled places. The steps of the algorithm are as follows.

Assign a tentative label to all places, i.e. $L_t = L$ and $L_p = \emptyset$.
For each place $l$ make the label equal to

$$min_1\{\pi_2(s(i)) \mid i \in dom(s) \ \wedge \ \pi_3(s(i)) = l\}.$$

**while** there is a place with a label in $L_t$ different from $\infty$
**do**

    (i) Select a place $l$ with the smallest tentative label and move this place from the set $L_t$ to the set $L_p$.

    (ii) Search for all processors $p$ with the following property: $l$ is an input place and all input places of $p$ are in $L_p$ (i.e. $p \in l\bullet \ \wedge \ \bullet p \subseteq L_p$).

    (iii) For each of these processors $p$ consider all output places $k$ with a tentative label (i.e. $k \in L_t \cap p\bullet$).
If $d(k) > d(l) + low(p, k)$ then set $d(k) := d(l) + low(p, k)$.

**od**

In the second algorithm the function *low* is replaced by *up* and we use $min_2$ instead of $min_1$ in the initialization of $d$.

The correctness of these algorithms is asserted in the following theorem.

**Theorem 21.3** Consider a conflict free delay model $A$, having at most one input connector attached to any one place, and a corresponding model $B$. Assume that the model is *livelock free*. Let $s \in St$ be the initial state. Then the above algorithms terminate and the final values of $d(l)$ are $eat(s, l)$ for the first algorithm and $lat(s, l)$ for the second (for all $l \in L$).

*Proof* We give only a sketch of the proof for the first algorithm. Consider the following four *invariants* of the computational process:

    (i) $L_t \cup L_p = L \ \wedge \ L_t \cap L_p = \emptyset$,
    (ii) $\forall k \in L_p, \ l \in L_t : d(k) \leq d(l)$,
    (iii) $\forall l \in L_p : d(l) = eat(s, l)$,
    (iv) $\forall l \in L_t : d(l) = min\{a, b\}$, where

$$a = min_1\{\pi_2(s(i)) \mid i \in dom(s) \ \wedge \ \pi_3(s(i)) = l\},$$
$$b = min\{max\{d(m) \mid m \in \bullet p\} + low(p, l) \mid p \in P \ \wedge \ \bullet p \subseteq L_p\}.$$

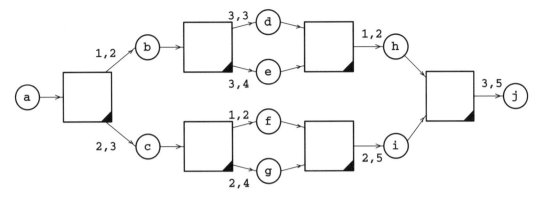

Fig. 21.4. Time analysis in an activity network

It is easy to verify that these invariants are valid at the initial stage of the algorithm and that 1, 2 and 4 are valid at every stage. The only difficulty is the verification of invariant 3 for subsequent stages. For this we have to show that for the new permanent place $l$ the new value $d(l)$ equals $eat(s, l)$. We use structural induction. Consider a place $l \in L_t$ with minimal $d$ value. Note that, by the induction hypothesis;

$$b = min\{max\{eat(s, m) \mid m \in \bullet p\} + low(p, l) \mid p \in P \ \wedge \ \bullet p \subseteq L_p\}.$$

It is sufficient to consider processors with only permanent input places in this expression since the others cannot execute earlier because of invariant 2. A processor will fire as soon as possible. Therefore $b$ is equal to the smallest possible event time for which a token is produced for $l$. (Here we have used the properties that the model is conflict free and that there is only one input connector to each place. We have also used the property that the model is livelock-free, because without this property we are not sure that $b$ is ever reached.)

The algorithm terminates because the number of places in $L_t$ decreases in each step. □

We conclude this section with an example of the last algorithm.

**Example 10**

Consider the interval-timed activity network displayed in figure 21.4. In the initial state there is only one token in $a$ with time interval [0,2]. All the delay intervals are attached to the output connectors of the processors. The $eat$ and $lat$ values are displayed in table 21.1.

Note that the algorithm is also applicable if there are several tokens in each

Table 21.1. *The eat and lat values for example 10*

| place | a | b | c | d | e | f | g | h | i | j |
|-------|---|---|---|---|---|---|---|----|----|----|
| eat | 0 | 1 | 2 | 4 | 4 | 3 | 4 | 5 | 6 | 9 |
| lat | 2 | 4 | 5 | 7 | 8 | 7 | 9 | 10 | 14 | 19 |

place in the initial state, or if there are cycles in the network, or if two processors share an output place.

□

# 22

# Simulation

The term "simulation" is used for a variety of techniques for analyzing models. We give only a survey of simulation techniques. (For more details see the section "References and further reading" at the end of part IV.) A main characteristic of simulation is that one trace of a system is computed. A trace is called a *run* in simulation terminology. For statistical reasons one often repeats this computation several times to determine averages over these traces. To compute a trace one has to choose a next event in the case where there is more than one possible next state. (Note that most systems have some non-determinism, for instance because the environment is part of a closed system and environments are usually non-deterministic.) One approach for the random selection of this choice is the use of a so-called *(pseudo) random number generator* (this will be explained below). Another approach is to let a person select the next state in an interactive way. So the non-determinism in an actor model is "solved" by means of random or human selection or by a combination of both methods. Simulation can be considered as performing an *experiment* with a model of a system. As in all empirical sciences the set-up of an experiment has to be done carefully in order to be able to draw conclusions from the experiments.

We can never be sure that a certain property that does not occur on the computed trace(s) will not occur in any of the possible traces. However, if in one of the simulation runs a property does occur then we are sure that the property can occur, so that if the property considered is an error then simulation is a good method to find this error. In particular, if persons are involved in simulation experiments they might find unwanted properties that were not excluded in the requirements. This happens frequently because (potential) users of a system are often not able to formulate all requirements of a system, but can easily find properties they do not want, in an executable model of a system. Note that an executable model of an information system can be considered as a *prototype* of that system. Therefore simulation and prototyping are closely related techniques.

If a particular property does not occur on a careful designed set of traces, then we still can make *statistical assertions* about this property. There are many interesting statistical assertions concerning distributions of *random variables* of a model. An example of a random variable is the arrival interval of messages in a system. Statistical assertions are derived by **two** kinds of procedure:

(i) hypothesis testing,
(ii) parameter estimation.

An example of the first kind is the assertion that a property will not occur on an arbitrary trace of a certain length. An example of the second kind is that the expected number of occurrences of a property on an arbitrary trace is equal to some value. In neither case are we sure and therefore we have to give a *measure* for the possible error. The theory of statistical inference is needed to give statistical assertions. This is beyond the scope of this book and the reader is referred to the bibliography for references to text books on these topics. In the rest of this chapter we will use as little statistical theory as possible though we will assume that the basic notions of statistics are known. (Statistical terms are printed in italics but they are not defined here.)

There are six important topics in simulation:

(i) data collection,
(ii) parameter estimation,
(iii) generation of random numbers,
(iv) design of runs,
(v) variance reduction,
(vi) model validation.

We will cover them all in a necessarily superficial way.

**Data collection**

If we have constructed an executable model of a system then we can run it with or without interaction with a person. Running a system is only interesting if we learn something from it and this means that we have to collect data from the trace we are computing. The data we collect depends on the questions we want to answer. Often a tool that can execute a model has built-in facilities for data collection, but if not then the systems engineer has to model his own *data collection system* as an extension of the model of the system under consideration. It is most likely that the data collection system will never be constructed in reality, since it is only meant for simulation experiments, but in principle it is

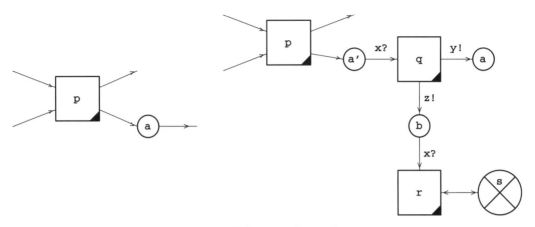

Fig. 22.1. Collecting data tokens.

possible to realize it. There is an important principle of data collection: "Collect data as close as possible to its source". In our framework, processors create tokens and so the principle prescribes that we have to collect data as close as possible to the processor that creates the data. We assume that the data we want to collect is already available in the values of produced tokens. If not, we have to modify our original model. So we need the values of tokens also for data collection and therefore we have to copy these values in new tokens, called *data tokens*, that did not play a role in the original model. There are two approaches to copying these values: one is to modify the processor that produces the tokens with the interesting values in such a way that it will have extra output connectors for the data tokens and the other approach is to intercept the output tokens by means of extra processors that only copy the value of tokens in the original model and that send these tokens to the data collecting system. In figure 22.1 we display on the left the part of an actor model for which we want to collect the values of the tokens produced for place $a$. On the right we see the data collecting processor $q$ and an extra place $a'$. Note that we have to modify the actor model in order to observe it! Processor $q$ is generic, i.e. we only have to define it once and it can be used in all cases where the type variable is properly instantiated. Its schema is displayed in table 22.1.

The processing of the data objects is discussed below.

**Parameter estimation**

The data objects we collect represent samples of random variables in the system we are modeling, for example the queuing time of a request. The data objects are used to estimate parameters that characterize the probability distributions

Table 22.1. *Schema for processor q.*

| $q$ |
| --- |
| $x? : \$$ |
| $y! : \$$ |
| $z! : \$$ |
| $y! = x? \ \land \ z! = x?$ |

of these random variables. So we are often not interested in the collected values themselves but the estimates computed from them. Typical examples of these estimates are: the *frequency distribution* of the collected data objects, or, if the random variables are numbers, their *mean* and *variance*. These quantities can easily be accumulated in a store of the data collecting system. Processor $r$ in figure 22.1 performs these accumulations. If $r$ has to compute the frequency distribution then its schema is presented in table 22.2. If the type of the value

Table 22.2. *Schema for processor r(1).*

| $r$ |
| --- |
| $x? : \$$ |
| $s, s' : \mathbb{F}(\$ \times \mathbb{N})$ |
| $dom(s') = ins(x?, dom(s))$ |
| $s'(x?) = s(x?) + 1 \ \land \ \forall x : \$ \bullet x \neq x? \Rightarrow s'(x) = s(x)$ |

of the tokens in $a$ is $\mathbb{Q}$ and if we want to estimate the mean and variance of the distribution of the tokens arriving in $a$, the schema of $r$ is as displayed in table 22.3. Here we assume that the tokens arriving in $a$ can be considered as *independent samples*.

(Note that we did not declare the shorthand for the components of $s$ and $s'$.) In the initial state store $s$ has value $(0, 0, 0)$. It is easy to verify that after the $n$th update of the store $s$ its second and third component have the following values:

$$\frac{1}{n} \sum_{i=1}^{n} x_i, \quad \frac{1}{n-1} \sum_{i=1}^{n} (x_i - \bar{x}_n)^2,$$

respectively, where $x_i$ is the value of the $i$th input token and $\bar{x}_n$ the average of the first $n$ values. These values are *unbiased estimates* for the mean and variance of the distribution of the token values in $a$.

Instead of the estimation of parameters of probability distributions of random

Table 22.3. *Schema for processor* $r(2)$

| $r$ |
|---|
| $x? : \$$ |
| $s, s' : \mathbb{N} \times \mathbb{Q} \times \mathbb{Q}$ |
| $s = (n, \mu, \sigma) \ \wedge \ s' = (n', \mu', \sigma')$ |
| $n > 0$ |
| $n' = n + 1$ |
| $\mu' = \frac{1}{n+1}(n \times \mu + x?)$ |
| $\sigma' = \frac{n-1}{n}\sigma + \frac{1}{n+1}(\mu - x?)^2$ |

variables we are often interested in estimating the parameters of a function $f$ that satisfies:

$$Y_n = f(x_{1,n}, \dots, x_{m,n}) + E_n,$$

where $n$ denotes the $n$th occurrence of an event, the $x_{i,n}$-values are "input" parameters, $Y_n$ is the observed "output" and $E_n$ is a random disturbance. The function $f$ is, for instance, a polynomial with unknown coefficients. The technique for solving this problem is called *regression analysis*.

### Random number generation

The most commonly used method for generating random numbers with a *uniform distribution* is called the *congruential method*. The formula for producing a sequence of samples of *independent uniformly distributed random variables* is

$$x_{n+1} = (a \times x_n + b) \ mod \ m,$$

where $a$, $b$ and $m$ are parameters of type $\mathbb{N}$. For $m$ one usually selects a value of the form

$$m = 2^k - 1.$$

(A typical example is $a = 16807$, $b = 0$, $m = 2^{31} - 1$.) Note that the values are not "real" samples of random variables, but they cannot be distinguished from such samples by statistical methods. Useful features of the congruential methods are that the values can be computed very fast and that they are reproducible. In figure 22.2 processor $p$ produces random values in place $b$. (All processors are complete, total and functional.) Any of the processors $q$, $r$ and $t$ can get a random value from $b$; after it has taken one it sends a token to $a$ in order to activate $p$ to produce a new value. In the initial state there is one token with a random value in $b$. In store $s$ there is a token with a value $x_n$, the $n$th value of

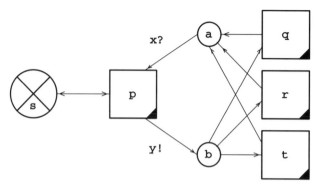

Fig. 22.2. Random number generator.

the congruential sequence. The values produced for $b$ are

$$\frac{x_n}{m-1},$$

because we use the uniform distribution on $[0, 1)]$.

If we need random values from a distribution other than the uniform distribution, we can use the *inverse transformation method* to transform values from the
congruential sequence into values of the desired distribution. Let $F$ be the *cumulative distribution function* of the distribution (over the rational numbers) from
which we need random values. This function is non-decreasing and *continuous
from the right* and satisfies:

$$\forall x \in \mathbf{Q} : P[X \leq x] = F(x),$$

where $X$ is a random variable and $P$ is the probability. Let $F^{-1}$ be defined by

$$F^{-1}(y) = inf\{x \in \mathbf{Q} \mid F(x) \geq y\}.$$

Then clearly $F^{-1}$ is non-decreasing and it can be proven that

$$\forall x, y \in \mathbf{Q} : F^{-1}(y) \leq x \Leftrightarrow y \leq F(x).$$

Let $U$ be a random variable with uniform distribution on $[0, 1]$; then $F^{-1}(U)$ has
cumulative distribution $F$ because:

$$P[F^{-1}(U) \leq x] = P[U \leq F(x)] = F(x).$$

(The last equality is a direct consequence of the definition of the uniform distribution.) In figure 22.3 a cumulative distribution function is displayed. For the
values $y_1$ and $y_2$ the values of $F^{-1}$ are displayed as well. So, the algorithm for
computing a sequence of independent samples from a given distribution $F$ starts
with the computation of a congruential sequence; the values then are divided by

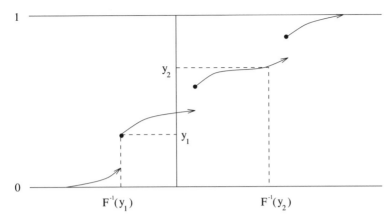

Fig. 22.3. Inverse transformation method.

$m - 1$ and transformed according to $F^{-1}$. An example of $F$ for which the inverse can be computed analytically is the cumulative distribution function of the *exponential distribution*: $F(x) = 1 - e^{-\lambda x}$. For this case: $F^{-1}(y) = -\frac{1}{\lambda} ln(1 - y)$.

## Design of runs

The next problem we have to solve if we are performing simulation experiments is determination of the length of a trace or the *run length*. A very pragmatic solution to this problem is to let the simulation run for a period of time that is convincing for the persons who have to make decisions on the basis of the simulation experiments. For instance, if the model describes a factory then simulation of a year of operation could give enough information for the decision makers because such a period could be long enough to see all relevant phenomena. Of course, this simulated year might, by chance, be a very successful or an extremely bad year, from which we might draw mistaken conclusions. A more sophisticated approach is based on statistics again. The run length depends on the precision we want. When we are estimating parameters we often construct a *confidence interval*. This interval depends on the number of observations we have made during a run and so we can compute the number of observations required to obtain a given confidence interval. In that case we do not specify the run length itself but the number of observations that has to be in the run.

An important problem is that, for most statistical analysis techniques, independent observations of a probability distribution are required and observations on one trace are often dependent. Therefore it is important to look for *regeneration states* on a trace. These states have the property that the observations in subsequent states are independent of the previous observations. In a queuing system, for instance, each state where the queues become empty is a regeneration state. Then we base our computations on the aggregated observations between consecutive regeneration states on the trace and these aggregates are independent observations. Also, the run length is determined by the number of regeneration points on the trace.

In most cases we do not consider only one trace but compute several traces. Then we have to decide how to allocate the computing time: a few long runs or many short ones. If regeneration points are rare we need more runs.

### Variance reduction

When we are estimating mean values we use averages as estimates. For instance if $X_1, \ldots, X_n$ are identically distributed random variables then

$$\frac{1}{n} \sum_{i=1}^{n} X_i$$

is an (the best) estimator for $\mu_X$, the mean of the distribution. The estimation error (that occurs as the confidence interval for the estimate) depends on the variance of the estimator (for some $i \in \{1, \ldots, n\}$):

$$\sigma^2 \left( \frac{1}{n} \sum_{i=1}^{n} X_i \right) = \frac{1}{n} \sigma^2(X_i).$$

(Note that this variance tends to 0 if $n$ tends to $\infty$.) There are at least two important methods to reduce this variance. One method is called the *control variates technique*. It can be applied if we have additional identically distributed random variables $Y_1, \ldots, Y_n$, with known mean value $\mu_Y$, and if we know that $X_i$ and $Y_i$ are *negatively correlated*. We can exploit this fact by using

$$\frac{1}{n} \sum_{i=1}^{n} (X_i + \alpha \times (Y_i - \mu_Y))$$

as an estimator, which has the same mean $\mu_X$ but a smaller variance owing to the fact that

$$\sigma^2 \left( \frac{1}{n} \sum_{i=1}^{n} (X_i + \alpha \times (Y_i - \mu_Y)) \right) = \frac{1}{n} (\sigma^2(X_i) + \alpha^2 \times \sigma^2(Y_i)),$$

where $\alpha$ is a parameter. With the right choice of $\alpha$ it is possible to reduce the variance of this estimator to

$$\frac{1}{n} \sigma^2(X_i) \times (1 - \rho^2),$$

where $\rho$ is the *correlation coefficient* of $X_i$ and $Y_i$.

Sometimes we can exploit the fact that we are able to choose the runs rather than being completely dependent on "nature" as we are in real-world experiments. The next variance-reduction method, called the *antithetic variates technique*, is based on this observation. Instead of taking two runs with independent random samples we make the second run dependent on the first one, in such a way that the corresponding variables have a negative correlation. Let the random variables $X_1, \ldots, X_n$ of the first run be constructed of $n$ independent uniformly distributed random variables $U_1, \ldots, U_n$ such that, for $i \in \{1, \ldots, n\}$, $X_i = F^{-1}(U_i)$, where $F$ is a cumulative distribution function. The next run is computed with $Y_1, \ldots, Y_n$ where $Y_i = F^{-1}(1 - U_i)$. Now we have a negative correlation between $X_i$ and $Y_i$, which implies that the *covariance* $cov(X_i, Y_i)$ is negative. Note that $X_i$ and $Y_i$ have the same distribution and let $\mu$ be their mean. The estimator for $\mu$ is

$$\frac{1}{2n} \sum_{i=1}^{n} (X_i + Y_i),$$

and the variance of this estimator is

$$\frac{1}{2n} (\sigma^2(X_i) + cov(X_i, Y_i)),$$

which is smaller than the variance in the independent case.

## Model validation

One of the main problems of simulation is to determine whether a model is a faithful description of the real system so that properties of the model are also properties of the real system. If the model is used as a design then there is no possibility for validation other than interactive simulation with persons who have an idea of the system in mind. However, if there is a real system, then we can check whether simulated traces correspond to *historical traces* of the real system. So, we collect historical data from the real system and use these data in our model. Then we compare *performance indicators* in the real system with the corresponding indicators in the model. (An example of a performance indicator is the mean of the waiting-time distribution.) If we use historical data for all random variables then the simulation model and the real system should have identical performance indicators. Often we first have to estimate some parameters from the real system to be used in the model. These parameters should be estimated from historical data that is not used in the simulation runs in which the model and the real system are compared.

Suppose we have established that the model is a faithful description of the real system, then we can modify the model and use the results of simulations to explore the behavior of the real system after the modifications.

# 23

# References and exercises for part IV

The *place* and *transition invariants* for classical Petri nets, and therefore for actor models with only complete processors and the Petri filter, were first published in [Lautenbach, 1975]. A survey is offered in [Sifakis, 1977]. In [Reisig, 1985; Peterson, 1981] all relevant details can be found. For colored nets K. Jensen has generalized the ideas of place and transition invariants, *see* [Jensen, 1992] and [Reisig, 1985]. For a survey of the computational aspects *see* [Colom and Silva, 1991]. The algorithm for finding minimal support invariants is due to [Martinez and Silva, 1982]. The necessary background in linear algebra can be found in [Gelbaum, 1989].

The *coverability tree*, also called the *reachability tree*, was first discribed in [Karp and Miller, 1969]. We have followed the approach of [Reisig, 1985] and [Reisig, 1987]. Another approach can be found in [Jantzen and Valk, 1980]. For colored nets, i.e. filters other than the Petri filter, coverability trees are treated in [Finkel, 1990] and [Jensen, 1992].

The *analysis of time* is based on [van der Aalst, 1992]. Several papers on performance analysis can be found in [IEEE, 1989; IEEE, 1991]. In [Berthomieu and Menasche, 1983; Berthomieu and Diaz, 1991] time analysis is, as here, based on interval timing. For the analysis of *cycle times* in Petri nets *see* [Murata, 1989; Ramamoorthy and Ho, 1980] and [Sifakis, 1977].

For *simulation methods* there are many good books. The statistical aspects are covered in [Ross, 1990] and [Kleijnen and Groenendaal, 1992]. For other simulation techniques *see* [Shannon, 1975; Zeigler, 1976].

## Exercises for part IV

(1)     Consider the simple railroad system of exercise 4 at the end of part III and show that the system behaves correctly.

- Compute the place invariants.
- Compute the transition invariants.
- Compute the coverability tree.

(2)    Consider the railroad station displayed in figure 14.6 and figure 14.7.

- Compute the place invariants.
- Formulate criteria for the system to behave safely.
- Show, using the place invariants, that the system is safe.

(3)    Prove that the number of tokens in an actor model with state machine structure and complete processors is always constant.

(4)    Determine the occurrence graph for the classical Petri net of the ball game of exercise 5 at the end of part I.

(5)    Consider an arbitrary actor model. Modify this model by *duplicating* all processors, i.e. for each processor an identical processor is added that has the same connections as the original. Show that both models have the same place invariants.

(6)    Prove theorem 19.4.

(7)    Show that the union of dead sets is a dead set and that the union of traps is a trap.

(8)    Prove theorem 19.6.

(9)    Construct an actor model in which all processors are live and for which a transition invariant is not realizable.

(10)   Prove theorem theorem 20.3.

(11)   Give a definition of the maximal and minimal earliest arrival times of the $n$th token in a place.

(12)   Consider a classical Petri net with flow matrix given by

|       | $t_1$ | $t_2$ | $t_3$ | $t_4$ | $t_5$ | $t_6$ |
|-------|-------|-------|-------|-------|-------|-------|
| $l_1$ | $-1$  | $1$   |       |       |       |       |
| $l_2$ | $1$   | $-1$  | $-1$  | $1$   |       |       |
| $l_3$ |       |       | $1$   | $-1$  | $-1$  | $1$   |
| $l_4$ |       |       |       |       | $1$   | $-1$  |
| $l_5$ |       | $-1$  |       |       |       | $1$   |
| $l_6$ | $1$   |       |       |       | $-1$  |       |

Let there be only one token, in place $l_1$, in the initial state.

- Compute the transition invariants.
- Prove that all processors are live.
- Determine the unrealizable transition invariants.

(This example is taken from [Reisig, 1985].)

(13)     Consider an actor model with complete processors and the Petri filter and with flow matrix as follows:

|        | $t_1$ | $t_2$ | $t_3$ | $t_4$ | $t_5$ | $t_6$ |
|--------|-------|-------|-------|-------|-------|-------|
| $l_1$  | $-1$  |       |       |       |       | $1$   |
| $l_2$  | $1$   | $-1$  |       |       | $1$   |       |
| $l_3$  |       | $1$   | $-1$  |       |       |       |
| $l_4$  |       |       | $1$   | $-1$  |       |       |
| $l_5$  |       |       |       | $1$   | $-1$  | $-1$  |

Characterize the transition invariants of this model.

# Part V

# Specification language

# 24

# Introduction

We specify systems by defining simplex and complex classes on the one hand, and actors on the other hand. For these simplex and complex classes we have already introduced a graphical language to define their important parts; however, we have not, as yet, given a language to define the values and value types for attributes. Similarly, we have introduced a graphical language to define the net model of an actor, but we do not yet have a language to define the processor relations. The specification language will be used to fill these gaps.

We want to have a specification language of high *expressive comfort*, which means that it is relatively easy to express the concepts we need in a formal way. Since we have chosen to use mathematical concepts to model systems and since we aim to develop precise, well-defined models of systems, it seems natural to choose the *language of mathematics* for our purpose. However, there is no such thing. To give a formal definition of such a language is very difficult and may be impossible. Therefore, we define a subset of the mathematical language formally. The main restrictions we make are that we do not allow function-valued functions and that all sets are finite. (As a consequence we do not have, for example, the limit concept.)

In modeling systems we often want our models to be *executable*, which means that a computer can simulate the behavior of a system, given a model of it. So the language should at least have an executable subset.

Another desired feature of the specification language is that it should have a *static type system*. This means that all expressions we define in the language have a *type* and that it is possible to verify the assigned types without evaluation of expressions. (So the types can be verified at *compile* time instead of *run* time.) Many errors can be detected in an early stage by type checking.

At first sight one may think that *imperative programming* languages like Pascal or C could satisfy our need. They certainly have enough *expressive power*, which means that every concept we possibly need can be expressed in such a language. (In particular every computable function can be expressed in such a language.) However, the *expressive comfort* in these languages is too low and they lack a powerful type system. A typical weakness of imperative languages is the *assignment statement*, which enables one variable to have two different values in the same expression. Therefore the semantics and verification of expressions is difficult.

Logical languages like Prolog and functional languages like ML are better candidates, specifically if, like ML, they have a type system. However, they still do not have the expressive comfort of the usual mathematical notations.
*Algebraic specification* languages like Act One and Obj are also quite good candidates, but *model-oriented specification* languages like Z and VDM are more suitable for our purpose because they allow explicit modeling of data structures.

Our specification language is a subset of Z and we shall give *type rules* and *semantics*. (The name of the language, Z, is a mark of honor to Zermelo, who was one of the pioneers of the axiomatic foundation of set theory.) A subset of our language is *constructive* and is in fact a *typed lambda calculus*. Specifications in the constructive subset are called *executable specifications*. Our language is *extendable* because we do not limit the number of primitive types and primitive functions. So, a systems engineer may add his own primitives.

The term *specification language* is normally used for languages that specify data structures and functions or relations on them and not for languages that express complete system models. Therefore we shall also use the term in this sense. Together with the *graphical languages* that define simplex and complex classes and actors, they form a complete *modeling language*.

There are three important approaches to the formal foundation of mathematics, based on *set theory, predicate logic* and *lambda calculus*. In the approach based on lambda calculus every mathematical concept is expressed as a lambda expression. In set theory every concept is considered to be a set. Using the symbol $\emptyset$ for the empty set, commas and set brackets only, one is able to represent all finite sets. For instance, the natural numbers can be represented as follows: $0 = \emptyset, 1 = \{\emptyset\}, 2 = \{\emptyset, \{\emptyset\}\}$ and an arbitrary natural number is represented by $n = \{0, 1, \dots, n-1\}$ (where each natural number $n$ should be replaced by its representation).

To express functions, one needs pairs of elements. Suppose $a$ and $b$ are mathematical values represented as sets; then we can represent the pair $(a, b)$ as $\{\{a\}, \{a, b\}\}$. (Note that it is possible to deduce which element is the first and which is the second element.)

We use a mixture of the three approaches, which may be called a *typed set theory.* Instead of using only sets we use other mathematical constructs such as vectors, sequences and tuples, as well. Our construction starts with an arbitrary (but finite) number of primitive sets (called *basic types*) and a fixed set of *constructors*. Everything mathematical concept that can be constructed in this way is called a *finite mathematical value* or, in brief, a *value*. (In fact all values can be represented as finite sets as we have seen above.) Note that simplexes and complexes are also values, in this sense! Besides finite mathematical values we have *types* which are (finite or infinite) sets of these values and *functions* that map values of one type onto values of another type. Note that functions are not values!

The semantics of our language will be expressed in untyped set theory and predicate logic. Because this *meta-language* and the specification language are very close, we use the same symbols for semantics and syntax. From the context it will be clear which we mean. In chapter 25 we consider the mathematical notions we need. In chapter 26 we treat the syntax of the *constructive* part of the language and its mapping to the semantic notions. Here we define types, values and functions that can be executed. In chapter 27 we define the *declarative* part of the language, introducing predicates, function declarations, schemas and finally scripts. In chapter 28 we consider some methods for the construction of functions. In chapter 29 we give some methods for the definition of complex classes and processor relations.

# 25

# Semantic concepts

In this chapter we introduce the *semantic concepts* of the language, in particular the notions of *values*, *types* and *functions*. (So the only syntax in this chapter belongs to the meta-language.) We start with values and types.

## 25.1 Values and types

The mathematical concepts that we consider belong to specific sets called *types*. The elements of types are called *finite mathematical values* or simply *values*. We postulate the existence of *basic types*.

**Definition 25.1** A *basic type* is a finite or countable set. The elements of these sets are called *constants*. The set of basic types $\mathcal{B}$ is finite and contains at least

- $\varnothing$, the *empty* type,
- $\mathbb{B}$ the type of *truth values*, i.e. $\mathbb{B} = \{true, false\}$,
- $\mathbb{N}$, $\mathbb{Z}$ and $\mathbb{Q}$, the types consisting of the *natural*, *integer* and *rational* numbers. (Note $0 \in \mathbb{N}$.)

The basic types are mutually disjoint. The set of all constants is denoted by $C$, i.e. $C = \bigcup \mathcal{B}$.

□

All values are constructed from finitely many constants and therefore they are called "finite mathematical values". At first sight it might look strange that we assume $\mathbb{N}$, $\mathbb{Z}$ and $\mathbb{Q}$ to be mutually disjoint. There is good reason to make this assumption: we can then construct $\mathbb{Z}$ from $\mathbb{N}$ and $\mathbb{Q}$ from $\mathbb{Z}$. In these constructions an integer is an equivalence class of pairs of naturals and a rational is an equivalence class of pairs of integers: for example $-5$ is the equivalence class of all pairs of naturals $(x, y)$ such that $x + 5 = y$. So according to this construction the types really are disjoint. However, there are isomorphisms that embed $\mathbb{N}$ and $\mathbb{Z}$ into $\mathbb{Q}$. The values in $\mathbb{N}$ are denoted by $\{0, 1, 2, \ldots\}$, the values in $\mathbb{Z}$ as those in $\mathbb{N}$ but with a sign (for example $+3$ and $-3$), and the values in $\mathbb{Q}$ as pairs separated by $/$ and with a sign (for example $+3/4$). This notation is the same as that used in the specification language in the next chapter.

At first sight $\emptyset$ as a type seems to be useless because it does not contain values. There is, however, a type constructor ($\mathbb{F}$) that can build on $\emptyset$ to obtain types that contain values.

Next, we introduce *value constructors* to construct new values out of constants and one special value $\perp$ that does not belong to the basic types. It has the particular meaning of "unknown" or "non-existent". The value $\perp$ is used in the following cases:

- to express that a processor does not consume a token from a certain input connector;
- to express that a function is not defined for a certain argument;
- in three-valued logic, where there is besides *true* and *false* a third value *unknown*.

**Definition 25.2** All constants and $\perp$ are values.
We consider four *value constructors*.

(i) *Set constructor*:
If, for $n \geq 0$, $b_1, \ldots \ldots, b_n$ are values then

$$\{b_1, \ldots, b_n\}$$

is also a value, called a *set* although it is always a finite set, because the set constructor forms finite sets of values. In particular $\{\}$ is also a value, called the *empty set*.

(ii) *Vector constructor*:
If, for $n \geq 2$, $b_1, \ldots \ldots, b_n$ are values, then

$$(b_1, \ldots, b_n)$$

is also a value, called a *vector*. A vector of two elements is called a *pair*.

(iii) *Sequence constructor*:
If, for $n \geq 0$, $b_1 \ldots, b_n$ are values, then

$$\langle b_1, \ldots, b_n \rangle$$

is also a value called a *sequence*. In particular $\langle\,\rangle$ is a value, called the *empty sequence*.

(iv) *Tuple constructor*:

Tuples are constructed with the use of *attributes*. Therefore we postulate the existence of a countable set of *attributes* L, which is disjoint with all basic types and does not contain $\perp$.

If, for $n \geq 0$, $b_1, \ldots, b_n$ are values and $\ell_1, \ldots, \ell_n$ are different *attributes* then

$$\{\ell_1 \mapsto b_1, \ldots, \ell_n \mapsto b_n\}$$

is a value, called a *tuple*. The elements $l \mapsto b$ of a tuple are called *components*. In particular $\{\}$ denotes the *empty tuple* (which is the same as the empty set).

□

Note that $\varnothing$ and $\{\}$ are different concepts: the first is a type while the second is a value.

A sequence only differs, at this moment, from a vector by the kind of brackets used. Later, when we introduce types, we will see the "real" difference between vectors and sequences. A tuple is, in fact, a set of pairs; the first component of a pair is an attribute. Since the attributes are unique it is in fact a function. We use a different notation for the pairs in a tuple to distinguish them from "normal" pairs, because the first element of these pairs is an attribute instead of a value.

The set of all possible values that can be formed from the constants and $\perp$ by finite application of the value constructors is called the *free value universe*. For example

$$(3, \perp, \perp, \langle 4, 5, 6 \rangle)$$

and

$$\{a \mapsto 3, b \mapsto \perp, c \mapsto (4, 5, 6)\}$$

are values. Note that all values are made of *finitely* many constants, which explains why values are called *finite mathematical values*.

The equality function, denoted by $=$, will be seen to have the property that two sets with the same elements but with a different representation are equal. (Note that we consider $=$ to be a Boolean-valued function with two arguments when represented in infix notation.) For instance $\{1, 2, 3, 3\} = \{3, 2, 1\}$ is *true*. (Note that $\{1, 2, 3, 3\}$ is a well-formed set here.) Similarly two tuples are equal if they have the same components; for instance,

$$\{a \mapsto 2, b \mapsto 3\} = \{b \mapsto 3, a \mapsto 2\}$$

is true. However, two vectors are equal if and only if they have identical representations, so

$$(1, 2, 3, 3) = (3, 2, 1)$$

is false. Tuples are important for expressive comfort; their components can be retrieved by specifying a attribute, whereas we have to compute the position of an element in a vector in order to retrieve it.

**Definition 25.3** Let $\mathcal{B}$ be a non-empty finite set of basic types. The set $FU$, called the *free value universe*, is the smallest set such that

- $\perp \in FU$,
- $C \subseteq FU$,
- $FU$ is closed under the four value constructors.

□

This set contains too many values. For instance the value $\{3, true, (1, false)\}$ is not a value we want to consider, since for a set to be itself a value it should contain only values of the same type. Analogously to value constructors we define *type constructors*. Remember, a type is just a set of values.

**Definition 25.4** The four *type constructors* are as follows.

(i) *Set type constructor*:
   If $T$ is a type then

$$\mathbb{F}(T)$$

   denotes the type of all finite sets of values of T and is called a *set type*.
(ii) *Product type constructor*:
   If $T_1, \ldots, T_n$, for $n \geq 2$, are types then

$$(T_1 \times \ldots \times T_n)$$

   denotes the type of all vectors $(t_1, \ldots, t_n)$, where $t_i \in T_i$ for $i \in \{1, \ldots, n\}$, and is called a *product type*.
(iii) *Sequence type constructor*:
   If $T$ is a type then

$$T^*$$

   is the type of all finite sequences of values of type $T$.
(iv) *Tuple type constructor*:
   If $T_1, \ldots, T_n$ are types and $\ell_1, \ldots, \ell_n$ are distinct attributes, then

$$[\ell_1 : T_1, \ldots, \ell_n : T_n]$$

is the type of all tuples $\{\ell_1 \mapsto t_1, \ldots, \ell_n \mapsto t_n\}$ where $t_i \in T_i$ for $i \in \{1, \ldots, n\}$.

□

Two values of type $T^*$ may therefore have different length but their elements will be all of the same type.

Note that two tuple types are equal if they have the same set of attributes and, for each attribute, the same type. For notational convenience we usually leave out the top-level parentheses in a product type; so we write $A \times B \times C$ instead of $(A \times B \times C)$. Note that

$$A \times (B \times C) \neq A \times B \times C.$$

Next we introduce the *type universe TU* and the universe of allowed values $U$. (Note that the notion of a tuple in the specification language differs from the tuple we used to define frameworks!)

**Definition 25.5** Let $\mathcal{B}$ be a non-empty, finite set of basic types. The set $TU$, called the *typeuniverse*, is the smallest set such that

- $\forall B \in \mathcal{B} : B_\perp \in TU$, where $B_\perp = B \cup \{\perp\}$,
- $TU$ is closed under the four type constructors.

The *value universe* $U$ satisfies

$$U = \{x \mid \exists\, T \in TU : x \in T\}$$

□

Note that it is not excluded that a value from $U$ belongs to more than one type.

**Theorem 25.1** All elements of the value universe are in the free value universe, i.e. $U \subseteq FU$.

*Proof* First note that (by definition) all constants and $\perp$ belong to $U$. If $x \in U$ then there is a type $\tilde{T}$ such that $x \in \tilde{T}$. We use structural induction to show that $\tilde{T} \subseteq FU$. Let $T, T_1, \ldots, T_n$ belong to $TU$ and let them be subsets of $FU$. Assume $\tilde{T} = \mathbb{F}(T)$. Then $\tilde{T} \subseteq FU$ since all elements of $\tilde{T}$ are finite sets of elements of $FU$. Next, assume that $\tilde{T} = T_1 \times \ldots \times T_n$. Then it is also a subset of $FU$ because all elements of $\tilde{T}$ are vectors formed by elements of $FU$. The other cases are similar.                                                                                         □

**Theorem 25.2** All types in the type universe are countable.

*Proof* We use structural induction. First note that, by definition all basic types, extended with $\perp$, are countable.

– Assume that type $T$ is countable. So $T$ is isomorphic with $\mathbb{N}$. Consider $\mathbb{F}(T)$. Each element of $\mathbb{F}(T)$ can be represented as an infinite sequence of 0's and 1's: its $n$th element is a 1 if and only if the $n$th element of $T$ (according to the isomorphism) is in the set. Hence every element of $\mathbb{F}(T)$ has finitely many 1's and so it represents a natural number in binary notation. So $\mathbb{F}(T)$ is also isomorphic to the set of natural numbers, and therefore countable.

– Assume that $T_1, \ldots, T_k$ are countable types. Consider $T_1 \times \ldots \times T_k$. This set is isomorphic with the set $\mathbb{N}^k$, because each $T_i$ is isomorphic with $\mathbb{N}$. It is *countable* because for each natural number $m$ the set of vectors $(n_1, \ldots, n_k)$ with $n_1 + \ldots + n_k = m$ is finite, and therefore we can count them (first the set with $m = 0$, then $m = 1$ etc.).

– Assume $T$ is countable, so that it is isomorphic with $\mathbb{N} \backslash \{0\}$. Consider $T^*$. This set is isomorphic with the set of all finite sequences of natural numbers (unequal to zero). For each $k \in \mathbb{N}$ the number of sequences with sum $k$ is finite. Therefore we can count them.

– Assume that $T_1, \ldots, T_k$ are countable types and that $\ell_1, \ldots, \ell_k$ are distinct attributes. Then $[\ell_1 : T_1, \ldots, \ell_k : T_k]$ is isomorphic with $T_1 \times \ldots \times T_k$ and therefore it is countable.

So we conclude that all $T \in TU$ are countable. □

**Theorem 25.3** The sets $U$ and $FU$ are countable.

*Proof* The proof is an exercise. □

Next we assume that every basic type has total ordering, denoted by $\leq$. We will see how this ordering induces an ordering for every type.

**Definition 25.6** Let $\leq$ be an ordering on every basic type. By induction we extend $\leq$ to every type in $TU$ according to the procedure given below. The ordering $\leq$ is called the *lexicographical* ordering. (Let $x < y$ be an abbreviation for $x \leq y \wedge x \neq y$.)

(i) $\forall c \in C : \bot \leq c$.
(ii) If $T$ is already ordered by $\leq$ then we extend $\leq$ to $\mathbb{F}(T)$ as follows: let $\{a_1, \ldots, a_m\}, \{b_1, \ldots, b_n\} \in \mathbb{F}(T)$ be such that

– $\forall i \in \{1, \ldots, m-1\} : a_i < a_{i+1}$,
– $\forall i \in \{1, \ldots, n-1\} : b_i < b_{i+1}$;

then

$$\{a_1, \ldots, a_m\} \leq \{b_1, \ldots, b_n\}$$

if and only if one of the following conditions holds:

$$\exists\, k \in \{1,\ldots, min(m,n)\} : (\forall\, i \in \{1,\ldots, k-1\} : a_i = b_i) \wedge a_k < b_k;$$

$$m \leq n \wedge \forall\, i \in \{1,\ldots, m\} : a_i = b_i.$$

If $p, q \in \mathbb{F}(T)$ do not satisfy (a) and (b), we can find equivalent elements $\tilde{p}, \tilde{q} \in \mathbb{F}(T)$, i.e. $\tilde{p} = p$ and $\tilde{q} = q$, such that $\tilde{p}$ and $\tilde{q}$ do satisfy (a) and (b). Then we define $p \leq q$ if and only if $\tilde{p} \leq \tilde{q}$.

(iii) If $T_1, \ldots, T_n$ are already ordered by $\leq$ then we extend $\leq$ to $T_1 \times \ldots \times T_n$ as follows: let

$$(a_1, \ldots, a_n), (b_1, \ldots, b_n) \in T_1 \times \ldots \times T_n;$$

then

$$(a_1, \ldots, a_n) \leq (b_1, \ldots b_n)$$

if and only if one of the following conditions holds:

$$\exists\, k \in \{1,\ldots, n\} : (\forall\, i \in \{1,\ldots, k-1\} : a_i = b_i) \wedge a_k < b_k;$$
$$\forall\, k \in \{1,\ldots, n\} : a_k = b_k.$$

(iv) If $T$ has already been ordered then we extend $\leq$ to $T^*$ as we did for $\mathbb{F}(T)$.

(v) If $\ell_1, \ldots, \ell_n$ are distinct attributes and $T_1, \ldots, T_n$ are types already ordered by $\leq$ then we extend $\leq$ to $[\ell_1 : T_1, \ldots, \ell_n : T_n]$ as follows:

 – introduce an ordering (also denoted by $\leq$) on the attribute set $L$;
 – map each tuple to a vector in $T_{\ell_{i_1}} \times \ldots \times T_{\ell_{i_n}}$ where $\ell_{i_1} \leq \ldots \leq \ell_{i_n}$, and call this map $f$;
 – two tuples $x$ and $y$ satisfy $x \leq y$ if and only if $f(x) \leq f(y)$. (The last ordering is defined above.)

□

In fact, as will be seen, the relation $\leq$ is not an ordering on tuples and sets but on the *equivalent classes* with respect to the equality function of tuples and sets!

**Theorem 25.4** For all $T \in TU$, $\leq$ is an ordering relation on T.

*Proof* By structural induction the proof is an immediate consequence of definition 25.6. □

Note that sets can be represented in a *normal form*, which is the representation of a set where the elements are arranged in ascending order and duplicates are left out. The normal forms are representatives of equivalence classes. Similarly we introduce an equivalence relation on tuple types and use it to define a *normal form* for tuple types.

We also introduce another type constructor called *join*, denoted by $\bowtie$.

**Definition 25.7** Let $[k_1 : S_1, \ldots, k_m : S_m]$ and $[\ell_1 : T_1, \ldots, \ell_n : T_n]$ be two tuple types. They are called *equivalent* if and only if

(i) $m = n$,
(ii) there is a permutation $(i_1, \ldots, i_n)$ of $(1, \ldots, n)$ such that
$$\forall j \in \{1, \ldots, n\} : k_j = \ell_{i_j} \wedge S_j = T_{i_j}.$$

Two tuples are *equivalent* if and only if they have the same components, but maybe in a different order.

Tuple types are called *compatible* if and only if

$$\forall i \in \{1, \ldots m\}, j \in \{1, \ldots, n\} : k_i = \ell_j \Rightarrow S_i = T_j.$$

If they are compatible their *join* is denoted by

$$[k_1 : S_1, \ldots, k_m : S_m] \bowtie [\ell_1 : T_1, \ldots, \ell_n : T_n]$$

and is equal to the set of all tuples

$$\{k_1 \mapsto s_1, \ldots, k_m \mapsto s_m\} \cup \{\ell_1 \mapsto t_1, \ldots, \ell_n \mapsto t_n\}$$

such that

$$\forall i \in \{1, \ldots, m\}, j \in \{1, \ldots, n\} : k_i = \ell_j \Rightarrow s_i = t_j.$$

□

Note that $\bowtie$ is similar to $\times$, since we can write

$$[k_1 : S_1] \bowtie \ldots \bowtie [k_m : S_m]$$

instead of

$$[k_1 : S_1, \ldots, k_m : S_m].$$

Also note that any tuple type $T$ is compatible with $\varnothing$ and that

$$T \bowtie \varnothing = T.$$

We assume there is an ordering on the set of attributes $L$ and we say that a tuple type with attributes in ascending order is in *normal form*. For example, if $k \leq \ell$ then the second tuple type of

$$[\ell : T, k : S] \text{ and } [k : S, \ell : T]$$

is the normal form of the first one. Similarly we say that a tuple is in normal form if its attributes are in ascending order.

Note that we have values that do not contain any constants, for example

$$(\langle\rangle), (\{\}), \{\}, \{\{\}\}, \{\langle\rangle\}, \langle\{\}\rangle, (\{\perp\}, \langle\rangle), (\perp).$$

They are examples of *singular values*.

**Definition 25.8**  A *simple singular value* is a value that does not contain a constant. A *singular value* is a simple singular value or a value that contains a simple singular value. All other values are called *regular values*.

□

Singular values may belong to more than one type, for example $\{a \mapsto 3, b \mapsto \{\}\}$ belongs to $[a : \mathbb{N}, b : \mathbb{F}(A)]$ as well as to $[a : \mathbb{N}, b : \mathbb{F}(A \times A)]$, for some type $A$. However, regular values have a unique type.

**Theorem 25.5**  Regular values have a unique type.

*Proof*  We will show that two types $T_1$ and $T_2$ have only singular values in common, which is equivalent to the assertion of the theorem.

Suppose $T_1$ and $T_2$ are different basic types extended by $\perp$. Then $\perp$ is their only common value, because basic types are disjoint by definition. If $T_1$ and $T_2$ are types of different structure, i.e. they belong syntactically to different categories (the categories are set type, product type, sequence type and tuple type), then it is easy to verify that they have no regular values in common. The only difficulty occurs with tuples and sets, because they have the same brackets. However, the only common value is $\{\}$, which is singular.

Now assume that $T_1 = \mathbb{F}(A)$ and $T_2 = \mathbb{F}(B)$ and that $A$ and $B$ have no regular value in common. Suppose now that $\{a_1, \ldots, a_n\}$ is a regular value and that it belongs to $T_1 \cap T_2$. Then at least one of the elements $a_1, \ldots, a_n$ is a regular value and this value should belong to $A$ and $B$. This is a contradiction.

Next consider $T_1 = A_1 \times \ldots \times A_n$ and $T_2 = B_1 \times \ldots \times B_n$, where $A_i$ and $B_i$ have no regular value in common, for all $i \in \{1, \ldots, n\}$. Suppose that now $T_1$ and $T_2$ have a regular value in common, say $(c_1, \ldots, c_n)$. Then, for at least one $i$ the value $c_i$ is a regular value and should occur in $A_i$ and $B_i$, which is a contradiction.

The same arguments apply to the other two cases for which $T_1$ and $T_2$ belong to the same syntactical category. (The proof of the other cases is an exercise.)

□

Hence there exists a function, *type*, that assigns to regular values the type to which it belongs.

## 25.2 Functions

We have defined a universe $U$ of values; however, we have not yet defined *functions* on this universe. The set of all total functions $UF$ is called the *function universe*, i.e.

$$UF = U \rightarrow U.$$

Almost all functions in which we are interested are defined as *partial* functions. For example, the function *pick* is only defined for sets and not for sequences. In order to make all functions total, we define them as $\perp$ outside their *meaningful domain*. So we assume all functions to be total on $U$.

Each function has a *name* and a *graph*. Recall that the graph of a function is a set of pairs such that the first elements of these pairs are unique. Note that a function may have an infinite graph, so a graph of a function is not in general a value.

We will represent function application using parentheses so that $f$ applied to $a$ is represented by $f(a)$. A function of more than one variable, for example $a$ and $b$, is in fact a function on a vector, namely $(a, b)$, which can be considered as one variable. If we apply a function to a vector we use only one set of parentheses, writing $f(a, b)$ instead of the more precise notation $f((a, b))$.

Although types are countable sets, $UF$ is *uncountable*! To verify this, take the set of functions $\mathbb{N} \rightarrow \mathbb{B}$. Since $\mathbb{B}$ is isomorphic with the set $\{0, 1\}$, the set of functions $\mathbb{N} \rightarrow \mathbb{B}$ is isomorphic with all real numbers in the interval $[0, 1]$, which is an uncountable set. (To understand this note that each element of $\mathbb{N} \rightarrow \mathbb{B}$ can be considered as a binary fraction.) However, in specifications we will only use countably many functions: those that can be defined in our language, which only has countable many sentences. The functions we will use are *constructed* from a given, countable set of *primitive functions*, using *abstraction* and *recursion* (*see* chapter 26).

There may be more than one defined function for the same graph. Also, since each defined function may have its own name, we may have two functions with different names but with the same graph. Therefore two functions are identical if and only if they have the same name and the same graph. (Note, however, that we will not define equality for functions in the specification language, because equality of function graphs is undecidable.) This fact allows us to use the same name for functions having different graphs. This phenomenon is called *overloading* and is often used in mathematics. For instance the function "+" is used for the addition of natural numbers but also for the addition of complex numbers and for the addition of vectors in some vector space. The signatures of the functions with the same names have to be different and in each expression in which the function name is used, only one signature have to be correct.

Since we are not interested in all values in the free universe, we are not interested in all functions either. We will use the types to characterize the "interesting" functions. These functions have meaningful domains that are types or unions of types. The notion of a *signature* is important here.

**Definition 25.9** A *signature* of a function in $UF$ is a set of pairs of types, i.e. a signature is an element of $\mathbb{P}(TU \times TU)$. For $f \in FU$ we denote the signature by $sign(f)$.
□

We will consider two kinds of functions, *monomorphic* and *polymorphic*.

**Definition 25.10** A *monomorphic* function $f \in UF$ has a signature that is a singleton $\{(T, S)\}$ such that

$$\forall\, u \in T : f(u) \in S \vee f(u) = \bot \wedge \forall\, u \in U \backslash T : f(u) = \bot.$$

The type $T$ is called the *domain type* of $f$, and type $S$ the *range type*.
□

So a monomorphic function has one type as meaningful domain. Polymorphic functions have a meaningful domain that consists of several types.

**Definition 25.11** A *polymorphic* function $f$ has a signature $sign(f)$ with at least two elements such that, $\forall\, u \in U$,

(i)   $(\forall (T \times S) \in sign(f) : u \notin T) \Rightarrow f(u) = \bot,$
(ii)  $\forall (T \times S) \in sign(f) : u \in T \Rightarrow (f(u) \in S \vee f(u) = \bot),$
(iii) $\forall (T_1 \times S_1), (T_2 \times S_2) \in sign(f) :$

$$u \in T_1 \cap T_2 \Rightarrow f(u) \in S_1 \times S_2 \vee f(u) = \bot.$$

□

The (meaningful) domain of a polymorphic function $f$ is

$$\bigcup \{\pi_1(x) \mid x \in sign(f)\}$$

and the range is

$$\bigcup \{\pi_2(x) \mid x \in sign(f)\}.$$

An example of a polymorphic function is *union*, which assigns to two sets of values of the same type a set of values of that type. Its signature is

$$\{(\mathbb{F}(x) \times \mathbb{F}(x), \mathbb{F}(x)) \mid x \in TU\}.$$

Note that an "overloaded" function name can be considered as the name of one polymorphic function. However, in the specification language we make a distinction between overloaded function names and polymorphic functions: an overloaded name has several different signatures assigned to it, while a polymorphic function name has only one signature with type variables in it.

Next, we make another distinction, between strict and non-strict functions. A *strict* function evaluates to $\perp$ if it is applied to a singular value. A function that does not is called *non-strict*. An example of a strict function is $+$, since $3 + \perp$ equals $\perp$. An example of a non-strict function is the *selection* function discussed below. An important subset of the non-strict functions is formed by the *lazy functions*. A function with more than one argument (i.e. a function on vectors) is called *lazy* when its function value is already determined when some of the variables are bound by values. If, for example,

$$\forall\, x, y : f(3, x) = f(3, y)$$

then the function value is determined by the first argument and we do not have to evaluate the second one. In particular, $f(3, \perp)$ will have the same value. Lazy functions are important in recursive definitions because there we are not able to evaluate all the arguments. The selection function is the most important lazy function.

In our specification language we have some *primitive functions*, i.e. functions that are not defined in the language but for which we know only the name, the signature and the graph. The graph is known only in implicit form, which means that we assume that there is a "retrieval mechanism" that delivers the function value if we give the argument. Primitive functions are therefore defined in the meta-language. They are defined informally in part I and formally in appendix C. Two primitive functions are defined here, because they are very important: the *equality* function $(=)$ and the *selection* function *if.then.else.fi*. We use them in infix notation. The function $=$ compares two values and if they are (syntactically) identical or if they are equivalent (in the case of sets or tuples) then the function value is *true*, or else *false*. The function is lazy, since $\perp = \perp$ is true, $x = \perp$ is false and $\perp = x$ is false for any $x \neq \perp$.

An application of the selection function reads

$$if\ a\ then\ b\ else\ c\ fi.$$

If $a$ is *true* then the function value is equal to the value of $b$, otherwise, to the value of $c$. The function is lazy: if $a$ is *true* then $c$ may be $\perp$ and if $a$ is *false* then $b$ may be $\perp$. If $a$ is $\perp$ then the function evaluates to $\perp$.

There are in principle countably many primitive functions because of the *projection functions* $(\pi_i, \Pi_{i,j,\dots})$. For each attribute (set) there is another projection function. We have chosen this approach rather than the introduction of *attribute (set) variables*, since this would require another kind of lambda construction in which there are functions with two kinds of variables: value variables and attribute variables. Using tools it is easy to generate the projection functions we need.

New functions are defined from primitive functions and previously defined functions by means of syntactical constructs that are defined in the next chapter.

# 26

# Constructive part of the language

In this chapter we give the syntax for defining types, values and functions and map the syntactical constructs onto the semantic notions. This part of the language is the *constructive* or *executable* subset of the language. In the next chapter we shall introduce the non-constructive part. As noted before, our syntax will be close to the syntax of the meta-language. We start with the *meta-syntax*, i.e. the syntax we use to define the syntax of the specification language. It is a form of extended BNF (Backus Naur Form.).

**Definition 26.1** The *meta-syntax* follows these rules.

- (i) The definition sign for non-terminals is ::=.
- (ii) Any part of a syntax in <u>underlined</u> typeface is to be taken specifically, i.e. according to a specific definition.
- (iii) Any part between braces may be repeated. So, '$a$ ::= $\{b\}$' is shorthand for '$a$ := $b \mid b\,a$'.
- (iv) Any part between square brackets may be omitted. So, '$a$ ::= $[b]c$' is shorthand for '$a$ ::= $bc \mid c$'.
- (v) Any part between triangular brackets may be repeated; each repetition must be preceded by a comma. So, '$< a >$' is shorthand for '$a[\{,a\}]$'.
- (vi) The syntax for identifiers, digits and characters is not further elaborated.

□

We define in fact a *family* of languages. Each language is characterized by a so-called *syntax base* and the syntax rules. (Some components of the syntax base are needed in subsequent chapters only.)

**Definition 26.2** A *syntax base* is a 8-tuple of sets of names

$$(L, C, TV, V, VN, FN, TN, SN)$$

where

> (i)    $L$ is a set of attributes,
> (ii)   $C$ is a set of constants,
> (iii)  $TV$ is a set of type variables,
> (iv)   $V$ is a set of value variables,
> (v)    $VN$ is a set of value names,
> (vi)   $FN$ is a set of function names,
> (vii)  $TN$ is a set of type names,
> (viii) $SN$ is a set of schema names.

Here, the set $TN$ contains at least the names of the basic types, i.e. at least $\varnothing$, $\mathbb{N}$, $\mathbb{Z}$, $\mathbb{Q}$ and $\mathbb{B}$. The sets $TV$ and $TN$ are disjoint and $TV = \{\$, \$_1, \$_2, \ldots\}$. The sets $V$ and $VN$ are disjoint. The sets $L$ and $V$ satisfy $L \cap V \neq \varnothing$.

□

We assume in the rest of this part that a syntax base is given. The mapping of expressions onto their semantics is performed by an *evaluation function* $\epsilon$. So $\epsilon$ maps expressions to values, types or functions. Not all expressions have semantics: only expressions without *free variables* (this notion will be explained later). We will distinguish the expressions in the specification language from expressions in the meta-language by using $[\![\,]\!]$ brackets for functions that have expressions as domain, for example $\epsilon[\![E]\!]$. Type expressions have the following syntax.

**Definition 26.3** The syntax of *type expressions* and *type definitions* is as follows.

$$
\begin{aligned}
\textit{type expression}::=&\textit{type name} \mid \textit{type variable} \mid \textit{set type} \mid \\
&\textit{product type} \mid \textit{sequence type} \mid \textit{tuple type} \\
\textit{set type} \qquad ::=&\mathbb{F}\,(\textit{type expression}) \\
\textit{product type} \quad ::=&(\textit{type expression} \times \textit{product list}) \\
\textit{product list} \quad ::=&\textit{type expression} \mid \textit{type expression} \times \textit{product list} \\
\textit{sequence type} ::=&\textit{type expression}^{*} \\
\textit{tuple type} \qquad ::=&\textit{type variable} \mid [\langle \textit{attribute} : \textit{type expression}\rangle] \mid \\
&\textit{tuple type} \bowtie \textit{tuple type} \\
\textit{type definition} ::=&\textit{type name} := \textit{type expression} \\
\textit{attribute} \in & L \\
\textit{type name} \in & TN \\
\textit{type variable} \in & TV
\end{aligned}
$$

The set of all type expressions without type variable is denoted by $TE$.

□

In a subexpression, of the form $\$_1 \bowtie \$_2$, of a type expression we know that $\$_1$ and $\$_2$ have to be replaced by *compatible* tuple types only.

The semantics of type expressions is straightforward, since the metalanguage and the specification language are so close. For the semantics, i.e. the range of $\epsilon$, we use the same symbols as for the specification language. The semantics of type expressions and type definitions is defined formally in the next definition. Note that "type" is a semantic notion and "type expression" is a syntactic notion. In expressions of the form $\epsilon[\![\mathbf{N}]\!] = \mathbf{N}$ the symbol $\mathbf{N}$ is just a name on the left-hand side but is the set of natural numbers on the right-hand side.

**Definition 26.4** The *evaluation function* $\epsilon$, applied to type expressions without type variables, satisfies the following rules, in which all capitals denote type expressions without type variables and with known evaluations.

(i) If $T$ is a basic type then $\epsilon[\![T]\!] = T$.

(ii) $\epsilon[\![\mathbf{F}(T)]\!] = \mathbf{F}(\epsilon[\![T]\!])$.

(iii) $\epsilon[\![(T_1 \times \ldots \times T_n)]\!] = (\epsilon[\![T_1]\!] \times \ldots \times \epsilon[\![T_n]\!])$.

(iv) $\epsilon[\![T^*]\!] = \epsilon[\![T]\!]^*$.

(v) $\epsilon[\![[l_1 : T_1, \ldots, l_n : T_n]]\!] = [l_1 : \epsilon[\![T_1]\!], \ldots, l_n : \epsilon[\![T_n]\!]]$.

(vi) $\epsilon[\![[l_1 : T_1, \ldots, l_n : T_n] \bowtie [k_1 : S_1, \ldots, k_m : S_m]]\!] = [a_1 : \epsilon[\![P_1]\!], \ldots, a_r : \epsilon[\![P_r]\!]]$ if and only if

- $\forall i, j : l_i = k_j \Rightarrow \epsilon[\![T_i]\!] = \epsilon[\![S_j]\!]$,
- $\{a_1, \ldots, a_n\} = \{l_1, \ldots, l_n\} \cup \{k_1, \ldots, k_m\}$,
- if $a_i = l_j$ then $P_i = T_j$ and if $a_i = k_j$ then $P_i = S_j$.

(vii) The semantics of a defined type name is equal to the semantics of the defining expression.

□

Note that $TE$ is the syntactical equivalent of the type universe $TU$. Next, we consider the definition of values. We define them by means of *terms* or *value expressions*. The value constructors, given for the meta-language in definition 25.2, are already in syntactical form; we will use them here too. With value constructors we are able to define values by constructing them *explicitly*, which means writing down their representation. However, we often need to define values *implicitly* by some expression that indicates how the value should be constructed. For instance, if we want to define the set of all prime numbers that are elements of some given (finite) set $s$ of type $\mathbf{F}(\mathbf{N})$ we do not want to construct this set explicitly. This would require us to check all elements of $s$ to see whether they are prime; however, we want to define this set by an expression of the form

$$\{x : s \mid prime\,(x)\}$$

where *prime* is a Boolean-valued function that attains the value *true* if and only if its argument is a prime number. (How we construct or specify these functions will be explained later.) We call such an expression a *set term*. Here, we assume that we have such a collection of functions given by their names, for example, primitive functions. Note that *s* in the expression is a *set value* and not a type! Therefore we are sure that the expression denotes a finite value and not an infinite set, such as

$$\{x : \mathbb{N} \mid prime\,(x)\}.$$

Another expression found by the use of this set constructor is

$$\{x : prod\,(s, t) \mid \pi_2(x) = \pi_1(x) \times \pi_1(x)\}$$

which denotes, in meta-language,

$$\{(y, z) \mid y \in s \wedge z \in t \wedge z = y^2\}.$$

Here *s* and *t* are of the type $\mathbb{F}(\mathbb{N})$, *prod* is a function that forms the Cartesian product from two finite sets and "×" denotes multiplication. (These functions can be constructed from the primitive functions.) The set constructed above represents, in fact, a finite function with a domain that is a subset of *s* and a range that is a subset of *t*. Of course, it is a value itself with type $\mathbb{F}(\mathbb{N} \times \mathbb{N})$. Finite functions or *maps* are very useful in specifications and therefore it is important to have a convenient notation. The construction above is cumbersome, because we have to define explicitly the set that is to contain the range of the map. Therefore we will introduce another syntactical construct to express maps. The same map is expressed, using this construct, by ($s \in \mathbb{F}(\mathbb{N})$):

$$(x : s \mid x \times x).$$

This construct is called a *map term* and is formally a *typed lambda expression*.

Now, we have come across two constructs that define values implicitly, set term and map term. There is a third one: *function application*. We have seen that, in the examples above, *prime*(3) evaluates to the Boolean value *true* and $4 \times 5$ to the number 20. There is also a fourth construct that uses the value constructors for terms (instead of constants and $\bot$).

**Definition 26.5** The syntax of *terms* is as follows:

| | |
|---|---|
| *term* | ::= *value variable* \| *value name* \| *constant* \| <br> (*term*) \| *value construction* \| *application* \| <br> *set term* \| *map term* |
| *value construction* | ::= *set construction* \| *vector construction* \| <br> *sequence construction* \| *tuple construction* |
| *set construction* | ::= {⟨*term*⟩} \| {} |
| *vector construction* | ::= (⟨*term*⟩) |
| *sequence construction* | ::= ⟨⟨*term*⟩⟩ \| ⟨⟩ |
| *tuple construction* | ::= {⟨*attribute*↦*term*⟩} \| {} |
| *application* | ::= *function name* (*term*) |
| *set term* | ::= { *value variable* : *domain* \| *term*} |
| *map term* | ::= (*value variable*: *domain* \| *term*) |
| *domain* | ::= *set construction* \| *set term* |
| *value definition* | ::=*value name* ≔ *term* : *type expression* |
| *value variable* ∈ *V* | |
| *value name* ∈ *VN* | |
| *constant* ∈ *C* ∪ {⊥} | |
| *function name* ∈ *FN* | |

The type expression in the value definition may not contain type variables.
□

Note that there is for each *value* an identical *value construction* in the language. Therefore all values are terms! A value definition gives a name to a term, such that the name can be used as abbreviation for the term. Not all terms generated by the syntax are allowed. First of all the terms used should be *well-typed*. Typing of terms is defined using a *typing function* $\tau$ defined below. For instance, in a set term the term on the right-hand side of the bar should be of the Boolean type, as is *prime* in our example above.

In order to be able to define the *typing function* $\tau$ and the *evaluation* of terms, i.e. $\epsilon$ for terms, we need the notion of *scope*.

**Definition 26.6** In set terms and map terms the term on the right-hand side of the bar is called the *scope*. An occurrence of a variable in a set or map term is said to be *bound* if it appears on the left of the colon or if it appears in the term to the right of the bar and is the same as a variable occurring on the left of the colon.

If set or map terms are nested, a bound variable on the right-hand side of the bar is bound by the first set or map term which has this variable on the left-hand side of the colon and which is encountered if we go from this variable to the left. The occurrence of a non-bound variable is called a *free-variable* occurrence. □

Consider for example the set term

$$\{x : \{1, 2, 3, 4, 5, 6, \} \mid x \in rng((x : \{1, 2, 3\} \mid x \times x))\}.$$

The first $x$ and second $x$ are bound by the set term, the third, fourth and fifth $x$'s by the map term. (Here $\in$ and $rng$ are defined functions; they can be found in the toolkit (*see* appendix C). We consider only the semantics of terms without free variables. Hence terms with free variables have semantics with respect to some *context* in which these free variables are bound.

The function $\tau$ assigns to terms a type and to $\epsilon$ a value only when the term does not have free variables. We will assume that all free variables in a term differ from bound variables occurring in the term. This can be accomplished by a proper renaming of bound variables. This process is sometimes called *standardizing* and terms that are standardized are called *standard terms*.

We use the *substitution* of variables by values. This is denoted by sub- and superscripts. For example

$$b_e^x$$

is the term derived from the term $b$ by *substituting* each free occurrence of $x$ by the term $e$. Where we have a simultaneous substitution of variables $x_1, \ldots, x_n$ by terms $e_1, \ldots, e_n$ we write

$$b_{(e_1, \ldots, e_n)}^{(x_1, \ldots, x_n)}.$$

**Definition 26.7** The *type function* $\tau$ assigns to *well-typed* terms a type according to the following rules.

Regular values are well-typed; if $t$ is a regular value then

$$\tau[\![t]\!] = type[\![t]\!],$$

where *type* is the function that assigns to constants their type (see theorem 25.5). Let $t, t_1, \ldots, t_n$ be a well-typed term.

- Consider a value name $n$ that is defined in an expression of the form $n := t : T$; then $\tau[\![n]\!] = \epsilon[\![T]\!]$.
- The type of a constant is the unique basic type to which it belongs.
- $\tau[\![(t)]\!] = \tau[\![t]\!]$.
- $\tau[\![\{t_1, \ldots, t_n\}]\!] = \mathbb{F}(\tau[\![t_1]\!])$ provided that $\tau[\![t_i]\!] = \tau[\![t_1]\!]$ for $i \in \{2, \ldots, n\}$.
- $\tau[\![(t_1, \ldots, t_n)]\!] = \tau[\![t_1]\!] \times \ldots \times \tau[\![t_n]\!]$.
- $\tau[\![\langle t_1, \ldots, t_n \rangle]\!] = (\tau[\![t_1]\!])^*$ provided that $\tau[\![t_i]\!] = \tau[\![t_1]\!]$ for $i \in \{2, \ldots, n\}$.

- $\tau[\![\{\ell_1 \mapsto t_1, \ldots, \ell_n \mapsto t_n\}]\!] = [\ell_1 : \tau[\![t_1]\!], \ldots, \ell_n : \tau[\![t_n]\!]]$ provided that $\ell_1, \ldots, \ell_n$ are distinct.
- Consider an application of the form $f(t)$ and let $f$ have signature $sign(f)$; then
$$\forall (A, B) \in sign(f) : \tau[\![t]\!] = A \Rightarrow \tau[\![f(t)]\!] = B.$$
- $\tau[\![\{x : a \mid b\}]\!] = \tau[\![a]\!]$ if there is a type $T$ such that $\tau[\![a]\!] = \mathbb{F}(T)$ and if for some value $e$ of type $T$: $\tau[\![b_e^x]\!] = \mathbb{B}$.
- $\tau[\![(x : a \mid b)]\!] = \mathbb{F}(T \times S)$, where $T$ is a type such that $\tau[\![a]\!] = \mathbb{F}(T)$ and $S$ is a type such that $\tau[\![b_e^x]\!] = S$ for some value $e$ of type $T$.
- A value definition of the form $n := t : T$ is well-typed if and only if $\tau[\![t]\!] = \epsilon[\![T]\!]$.

If a type can be derived by these rules, the term to which it applies is well-typed; otherwise, it is not well-typed.

$\square$

Definition 26.7 is in fact a type checking algorithm. Note that the type of a map term is a set of pairs, without the restriction that the first of each pair is unique.

In rule 8 we assume that $f$ might be polymorphic, in which there would be more than one domain type. Note that singular values are *polymorphic*. For instance

$$\{(\{\}, \langle\{\}\rangle)\}$$

belongs to

$$\mathbb{F}(\mathbb{F}(T) \times \mathbb{F}(S)^*)$$

for all types $T$ and $S$.

One could extend the domain of $\tau$ to singular values by extending its range to sets of types, so that $\tau$ applied to singular values would return a set of types instead of one type. Such a set of types can be represented by a type expression with type variables. We do not follow this approach here, to keep the type checking simple; in consequence, our type checking is not as powerful as it could be, because we do not type singular values.

Next we will see how to map terms without free variables to values. This is determined by the evaluation function $\epsilon$. Here we assume that for each function name $f$, the graph of $f$ can be consulted. This means that we must be able to decide whether, for two values $a$ and $b$,

$$(a, b) \in graph(f).$$

Later we will see how this problem can be solved, at least in many practical cases.

**Definition 26.8** The *evaluation function* $\epsilon$ maps terms to values according to the following rules.

If $t$ is a value then $\epsilon[\![t]\!] = t$.

Let $t, t_1, \ldots, t_n$ be terms from which the value is known.

- If $t$ is a constant, then $\epsilon[\![t]\!] = t$.
- If $n$ is a value name defined by $n := t : T$, then $\epsilon[\![n]\!] = \epsilon[\![t]\!]$.
- $\epsilon[\![(t)]\!] = \epsilon[\![t]\!]$.
- $\epsilon[\![\{t_1, \ldots, t_n\}]\!] = \{\epsilon[\![t_1]\!], \ldots, \epsilon[\![t_n]\!]\}$ (in fact its normal form).
- $\epsilon[\![(t_1, \ldots, t_n)]\!] = (\epsilon[\![t_1]\!], \ldots, \epsilon[\![t_n]\!])$.
- $\epsilon[\![\langle t_1, \ldots, t_n\rangle]\!] = \langle \epsilon[\![t_1]\!], \ldots, \epsilon[\![t_n]\!]\rangle$.
- $\epsilon[\![\{\ell_1 \mapsto t_1, \ldots, \ell_n \mapsto t_n\}]\!] = \{\ell_1 \mapsto \epsilon[\![t_1]\!], \ldots, \ell_n \mapsto \epsilon[\![t_n]\!]\}$ (in fact its normal form).
- Let $t$ be an application of the form $f(a)$; then $\epsilon[\![f(a)]\!] = b$ if and only if $(\epsilon[\![a]\!], b) \in graph(f)$.
- Let $t$ be a set term of the form $\{x : a \mid b\}$ then (expressed in the meta-language)

$$\epsilon[\![t]\!] = \{y \mid y \in \epsilon[\![a]\!] \wedge \epsilon[\![b_y^x]\!] = true\}.$$

- If $t$ is a map term of the form $(x : a \mid b)$ then, in the meta-language,

$$\epsilon[\![t]\!] = \{(y, z) \mid y \in \epsilon[\![a]\!] \wedge \epsilon[\![b_y^x]\!] = z\}.$$

□

Most of these rules are obvious: they are exactly what we intuitively mean by language constructs. Note that we require, for the evaluations of function applications of the form $f(a)$, that $\epsilon[\![a]\!]$ has to be known before we can determine $\epsilon[\![f(a)]\!]$. This is called *applicative order reduction* in lambda calculus or function programming languages. We will make one exception to this rule for lazy functions: for them we assume that "sufficient" arguments are evaluated. In particular to accommodate *recursion* the selection function *if.then.else.fi* is "lazily" evaluated. This means that to evaluate the term

$$if\, x\ then\ y\ else\ z\ fi$$

we evaluate $x$ first and then evaluate $y$ only if $\epsilon(x) = true$ and $z$ only if $\epsilon(x) = false$.

We have introduced terms to construct values in an implicit way. One of the main constructions is made by function application. However, we have given only a very limited set of primitive functions. In principle we "possess" all functions in *UF* but we are only able to use them if we can characterize them by a finite *description.* We use two mechanisms, *(lambda) abstraction* and *recursion*, to define new functions from primitive or previously defined functions.

*Abstraction* is the well-known way in which we define functions in mathematics. For instance (in meta-language)

$$f(x) = a \, sin(x) + b \, cos^2(x)$$

is a definition of $f$ by giving a term and indicating which name has to be considered as variable (in this case $x$). In (untyped) lambda calculus this definition is of the form

$$f = \lambda x \bullet (a sin(x) + b cos^2(x))$$

An example of abstraction in our languages is

$$+(x, y) := (x - (0 - y))$$

which is the addition function constructed from the function "$-$" and the constant 0. We may apply this function (in infix notation) as $3 + 5$, which evaluates to 8.

*Recursion* is the construction of a function by an *explicit equation*, which means that it is an abstraction with *self-reference*. For instance, a recursive equation for the union of sets is

$$union(x, y) = if \; x = \{\} \; then \; y \; else \; ins \; (pick(x), union(rest(x), y)) \; fi.$$

The equation is called "explicit" because the value we want to define is given explicitly on the left-hand side of the equation. An example of an implicit equation is

$$f(x)^2 + f(y)^2 = c.$$

In general it is not certain that an explicit equation has precisely one solution; it may have many solutions or no solution at all.

Consider for instance the recursive equation

$$f(x) = -f(x+1)$$

with $x \in \mathbf{Z}$, which has the solution

$$f(x) = (-1)^x c \; for \; any \; c \in \mathbf{Z}.$$

The next recursive definitions have no solution at all ($x \in \mathbf{N}$):

$$f(x) = f(x) + 1,$$

$$f(x) = f(x+1) + 1.$$

Now that we have defined functions by abstraction of variables from terms, we will give the syntax of function definitions. Each definition ends with the specification of the *signature* of the function. For polymorphic functions we use type variables.

**Definition 26.9** The syntax of *function definitions* is as follows:

> *function definition*::=*function name*($\langle variable \rangle$) := *term* : *signature*
> *signature* ::=*type expression* $\Rightarrow$ *type expression*
> *function name* $\in$ *FN*
> *variable* $\in$ *V*

$\square$

In signatures the domain and range types are separated by the $\Rightarrow$ sign. If a type variable occurs, the signature is a set of pairs that belongs to a polymorphic function. If no type variable occurs, the signature is a singleton and belongs to a monomorphic function. Note that a value definition can be considered as a function definition without a domain. Formally the semantics of a signature is defined by the following definition.

**Definition 26.10** Let a *signature* $T \Rightarrow S$ be given, where $T$ and $S$ are type expressions. If neither $T$ nor $S$ contain type variables, then the semantics of this signature is

$$\epsilon[\![ T \Rightarrow S ]\!] = \{(\epsilon[\![ T ]\!], \epsilon[\![ S ]\!])\}.$$

If $T$ or $T$ and $S$ contain type variables $\$_1, \ldots, \$_n$, then

$$\epsilon[\![ T \Rightarrow S ]\!] =$$
$$\{(\epsilon[\![ A ]\!], \epsilon[\![ B ]\!]) \mid \exists A_1, \ldots, A_n \in TE : A = T^{(\$_1,\ldots,\$_n)}_{(A_1,\ldots,A_n)} \wedge B = S^{(\$_1,\ldots,\$_n)}_{(A_1,\ldots,A_n)}\}.$$

If subexpressions of the form $\$_1 \bowtie \$_2$ occur, then $\$_1$ and $\$_2$ may be replaced by compatible tuple types only.

$\square$

Hence, all simultaneous substitutions of occurrences of the type variables by "proper" types determine the signature of a function.

We only allow recursion for each function construction, so we do not allow for instance that function $f$ is defined using applications of a function $g$ that is defined using applications of $f$. This is not a real restriction since we may transform these two *mutually recursive* equations into one recursive equation, as follows. Let

$$f(x) := term_1 : A \Rightarrow T,$$
$$g(y) := term_2 : B \Rightarrow S.$$

We define a function $h$ such that: $h(x, y) = (f(x), g(y))$. Choose $a$ and $b$ such that $f(a)$ and $g(b)$ can be computed without evaluation of applications of $f$ and $g$, and that for all $x$ and $y$,

$$f(x) = \pi_1(h(x, b)) \text{ and } g(y) = \pi_2(h(a, y)).$$

Then the definition of $h$ becomes

$$h(x, y) := (term_1', term_2') : A \times B \Rightarrow T \times S,$$

where in $term_i'$ we have $term_i$ but with each occurrence of the form $f(E)$ replaced by $\pi_1(h(E, b))$ and each occurrence of the form $g(E)$ by $\pi_2(h(a, E))$ for expressions $E$.

It is important that the definitions of $f$ and $g$ can be derived from the definition of $h$. ( So $h(x, y) = (\pi_1(h(x, y)), \pi_2(h(x, y)))$ is not a good one.) As an example consider

$$f(x) = \text{if } x = a \text{ then } c \text{ else } l(x, g(d)) \text{ fi},$$

$$g(y) = \text{if } y = b \text{ then } e \text{ else } k(y, f(y)) \text{ fi}.$$

Then we obtain

$$h(x, y) =$$
$$\text{if } (x, y) = (a, b) \text{ then } (c, e) \text{ else } (l(x, \pi_2(h(a, c))), k(y, \pi_1(h(y, b)))) \text{ fi}.$$

To give the semantics of a *function definition* we consider, as for terms, the type rules and evaluation rules. We start by defining when a function definition is *correctly typed*, i.e. when it has a correct signature. Remember that we consider a function of more than one variable as a function on a product type.

**Definition 26.11** A function definition of the form

$$f(x_1, \ldots, x_n) := t : E_1 \times \ldots \times E_n \Rightarrow E_0$$

where $t$ is a term and $E_0, \ldots, E_n$ are type expressions with, possibly, type variables $\$_1, \ldots, \$_m$ in the signature, and with no other free variables in $t$ then $x_1, \ldots, x_n$ is *well-typed* if and only if all the following hold.

(i) All type variables in $E_0$ also occur in at least one of the type expressions $E_1, \ldots, E_n$.

(ii) For all substitutions of the type variables by type expressions without type variables $A_1, \ldots, A_n$, the expressions

$$B_i = (E_i)^{(\$_1,\ldots,\$_n)}_{(A_1,\ldots,A_n)} \quad (i \in \{0, \ldots, n\})$$

are correct type expressions.

(iii) For all substitutions of the value variables $x_1, \ldots, x_n$ by regular values $e_1, \ldots, e_n$ such that $e_i$ is of type $B_i$ $(i \in \{1, \ldots, n\})$, the value

$$b = t^{(x_1,\ldots,x_n)}_{(e_1,\ldots,e_n)}$$

has to satisfy these conditions:

(a) if $b$ does not contain applications of $f$: $\tau[\![b]\!] = \epsilon[\![B_0]\!]$;

(b) if $b$ contains applications of $f$ of the form $f(c_1, \ldots, c_n)$ then this expression should be given the type $\epsilon[\![B_0]\!]$ first.

□

Note that we do not give an algorithm here, but only a definition of correctly typed function constructions. To see how an algorithm could work we give an example. Consider the recursive definition of *union* again. Let $A$ be an arbitrary, non-empty type and let $e_1$ and $e_2$ be values of type $\mathbb{F}(A)$. Consider

$$\tau[\![union(e_1, e_2)]\!] = \\ \tau[\![\textit{if } e_1 = \{\} \textit{ then } e_2 \textit{ else } ins(pick(e_1),\ union(rest(e_1),\ e_2))\textit{fi}]\!].$$

We derive the type of this term by a reversed procedure (i.e. bottom-up).

- $\tau[\![e_2]\!] = \mathbb{F}(A)$ ( by assumption).
- $\tau[\![rest(e_1)]\!] = \mathbb{F}(A)$ (since *rest* is polymorphic).
- $\tau[\![union(rest(e_1),\ e_2)]\!] = \mathbb{F}(A)$ (by the signature of *union* ).
- $\tau[\![pick(e_1)]\!] = A$ (by the polymorphism of *pick*).
- $\tau[\![ins(pick(e_1),\ union(rest(e_1),\ e_2))]\!] = \mathbb{F}(A)$ ( by definition of *ins*).
- $\tau[\![e_2]\!] = \mathbb{F}(A)$ (given).
- $\tau[\![e_1 = \{\}]\!] = \mathbb{B}$ (by definition of $=$).
- Hence the original term has type $\mathbb{F}(A)$, as it fits the signature of *if.then.else.fi*.

Next we define how the graph of a constructed function is determined.

**Definition 26.12** A function construction of the form

$$f(x_1, \ldots, x_n) := t : E_1 \times \ldots \times E_n \Rightarrow E_0$$

determines the *graph* of $f$ in the following way:

- if the definition is not recursive, then

$$graph(f) = \{((e_1, \ldots, e_n), \epsilon[\![t^{(x_1,\ldots,x_n)}_{(e_1,\ldots,e_n)}]\!]) \mid (e_1, \ldots, e_n) \in U\};$$

- if the definition is recursive, then $f$ is a solution of the equation with unknown graph $g$:

$$g = \{((e_1, \ldots, e_n), \epsilon_g[\![t^{(x_1,\ldots,x_n)}_{(e_1,\ldots,e_n)}]\!]) \mid (e_1, \ldots, e_n) \in U\},$$

where $\epsilon_g$ is the evaluation function $\epsilon$ modified in such a way that every evaluation of the form $\epsilon[\![f(e_1, \ldots, e_n)]\!]$ is replaced by $c$ if and only if $(e_1, \ldots, e_n), c) \in graph(g)$.

$\square$

Note that we have not specified which function should be chosen, in case there are more solutions to the equation in $g$. In chapter 28 we will see which one we recommend the reader to choose.

Another way to define the graph of $f$ is by means of a $\lambda$-expression. Define a function $F$ as follows:

$$F = \lambda g \bullet \lambda x_1, \ldots, x_n \bullet t^f_g$$

and let the function $f$ be a fixed point of $F$, i.e. $F(f) = f$. (Note that here we mix specification language and meta-language.)

As an application of the primitive functions we consider the logical functions $\vee$, $\wedge$, $\Rightarrow$ and $\neg$ which can be constructed from these primitives. In part I we gave the standard definitions for these functions. Here we give them for the *three-valued logic* with *truth values* in $\mathbb{B}_\perp$ (i.e. *true*, *false* and $\perp$). We will use them in the next chapter.

We start with $\Rightarrow$, it satisfies the equation

$$x \Rightarrow y := if \; x = \perp \; then$$
$$\qquad if \; y \; then \; true \; else \perp fi$$
$$\qquad else$$
$$\qquad if \; x \; then \; y \; else \; true \; fi$$
$$\qquad fi : \mathbb{B} \times \mathbb{B} \Rightarrow \mathbb{B}.$$

(Note the different meanings of $\Rightarrow$.)
This gives the following truth table for $\Rightarrow$:

| $\Rightarrow$ | | | $y$ | |
|---|---|---|---|---|
| | | *true* | *false* | $\perp$ |
| | *true* | *true* | *false* | $\perp$ |
| $x$ | *false* | *true* | *true* | *true* |
| | $\perp$ | *true* | $\perp$ | $\perp$ |

With this function we can define the other logical functions in a well-known way:

$$\neg x \quad := x \Rightarrow false : \mathbb{B} \Rightarrow \mathbb{B},$$
$$x \vee y := \neg x \Rightarrow y : \mathbb{B} \times \mathbb{B} \Rightarrow \mathbb{B},$$
$$x \wedge y := \neg(\neg x \vee \neg y) : \mathbb{B} \times \mathbb{B} \Rightarrow \mathbb{B}.$$

The truth tables for these functions can be derived easily, for example

| $\vee$ | | | $y$ | |
|---|---|---|---|---|
| | | *true* | *false* | $\perp$ |
| | *true* | *true* | *true* | *true* |
| $x$ | *false* | *true* | *false* | $\perp$ |
| | $\perp$ | *true* | $\perp$ | $\perp$ |

In this way we define in the language all other functions we need. Often we want functions to be strict. If we have defined a function, for example $f : \$_1 \Rightarrow \$_2$, that is non-strict and we want to make it strict we simply define

$$\tilde{f}(x) := if \ x = \perp \ then \ \perp \ else \ f(x) \ fi : \$_1 \Rightarrow \$_2.$$

(In examples we often "forget" this modification, because it makes the specification less readable.)

# 27

# Declarative part of the language

In the foregoing chapters we have introduced the *constructive* part of the specification language: finite mathematical values and function definitions. Specifying systems in this way is on the one hand useful; we obtain constructs that can be evaluated by a machine, so we can *simulate* the systems we define. The only problem is recursive constructions, where we have to find a solution (see the next chapter). On the other hand, the *expressive comfort* is limited. In this chapter we introduce *declarative expressions* that cannot be executed. They are meant for the systems engineer who has to transform them into constructive expressions. Consider for instance the construction of the function *union* that we have seen before. A more natural and better understandable specification is:

- name : *union*

- signature : $\mathbb{F}(T) \times \mathbb{F}(T) \Rightarrow \mathbb{F}(T)$

- predicate : $\forall\, x,\, y\, :\, \mathbb{F}(T) \bullet \forall z : T \bullet z \in union(x, y) \Leftrightarrow z \in x \lor z \in y$

This is an example of a *function declaration*; this concept will be defined later. We see here a *predicate* that involves quantification over a type. Up to now we have only considered quantification over sets which involves the set term and the map term. The Boolean functions *forall* and *exists* are examples (*see* appendix C). Note that, in general, such a quantification over a type is not computable, i.e. there is no algorithm for it. However, for expressive comfort we will introduce them.

Another reason for the introduction of predicates and quantification over types is that we wish to introduce *restricted tuple types*, which are called *schemas*. We have seen examples of schemas in part I. Schemas are used for the specification of complex classes and processor relations.

## 27.1 Predicates and function declarations

A *predicate* generalizes the concept of a Boolean type term.

**Definition 27.1** Given a syntax base and the syntax defined so far, *predicates* are defined as follows:

$$predicate ::= bool \mid \neg \, predicate \mid (predicate \,\, \underline{\theta} \,\, predicate) \mid$$
$$quantor \,\, \langle variable \rangle \underline{:} \,\, domain \bullet predicate$$

$$domain \,\, ::= type \,\, expression$$
$$bool \quad ::= Boolean \,\, term$$
$$\theta \in \{\vee, \wedge, \Rightarrow\}$$
$$quantor \in \{\forall, \exists\}$$
$$variable \in V$$

A Boolean term is a term with type $\mathbb{B}$.
The functions $\neg$, $\vee$, $\wedge$ and $\Rightarrow$ are defined in chapter 26.
□

The quantors ($\forall$ and $\exists$) have scope rules defined as in definition 26.6. Predicates without free variables have semantics: the function $\epsilon$ assigns one of the values *true*, *false* or $\bot$ to them. Therefore they can be used as Boolean values.

   To define which predicates are *well-typed* we proceed along the same lines as we did for function construction.

**Definition 27.2** Predicates without free (value) variables are *well-typed* if the following rules hold.
Consider first the case without type variables:

 - If $p$ is a Boolean term then $\epsilon[\![p]\!] = \mathbb{B}$;
 - If $p$ is a well-typed predicate then

$$\forall \, x_1, \ldots, x_n \,\, : \,\, T \bullet p$$

   and

$$\exists \, x_1, \ldots, x_n \,\, : \,\, T \bullet p$$

   are well-typed if and only if $x_1, \ldots, x_n$ are the only free variables of predicate $p$ and, for all values $e_1, \ldots, e_n$ of type $T$, $p^{(x_1,\ldots,x_n)}_{(e_1,\ldots,e_n)}$ is well-typed.

If any domain contains type variables, these rules apply for all substitutions of these type variables by type expressions without type variables.
□

The semantics of predicates in the case of no free variables and no type variables is given below. We extend the evaluation function $\epsilon$ defined in definition 26.8 to predicates.

**Definition 27.3** Predicates without free value variables and without type variables are *evaluated* according to the following rules. Assume predicate $p$ is well-typed.

(i) If predicate $p$ is a Boolean term then $\epsilon(p)$ is already defined.

(ii) $\epsilon[\![\neg p]\!] = \epsilon[\![\neg]\!](\epsilon[\![p]\!])$.

(iii) For a predicate of the form $p\ \theta\ q$ where $\theta \in \{\vee, \wedge, \Rightarrow\}$,

$$\epsilon[\![p\ \theta\ q]\!] = \epsilon[\![p]\!]\ \epsilon[\![\theta]\!]\ \epsilon[\![q]\!].$$

(iv) If $p$ is a predicate of the form

$$\forall\, x_1, \ldots, x_n : T \bullet q$$

then

- $\epsilon(p)$ is *true* if for all values $e_1, \ldots, e_n$ of type $T$: $\epsilon[\![q_{(e_1,\ldots,e_n)}^{(x_1,\ldots,x_n)}]\!] = true$,
- $\epsilon(p)$ is *false* if there is at least one vector $\langle e_1, \ldots, e_n \rangle$ of type $T^*$ such that $\epsilon[\![q_{(e_1,\ldots,e_n)}^{(x_1,\ldots,x_n)}]\!] = false$,
- $\epsilon(p) = \bot$, in all other cases.

(v) If $p$ is a predicate of the form

$$\exists\, x_1, \ldots, x_n : T \bullet q$$

then

- $\epsilon(p)$ is *true* if there is at least one vector $\langle e_1, \ldots, e_n \rangle$ of type $T^*$ such that $\epsilon[\![q_{(e_1,\ldots,e_n)}^{(x_1,\ldots,x_n)}]\!] = true$,
- $\epsilon(p)$ is *false* if for all values $e_1, \ldots, e_n$ of type $T$: $\epsilon[\![q_{(e_1,\ldots,e_n)}^{(x_1,\ldots,x_n)}]\!] = false$,
- $\epsilon(p) = \bot$, in all other cases.

□

We apply predicates to *function declarations*. We have seen how useful it is to have another mechanism to describe a function in addition to the function definition.

**Definition 27.4** The syntax of a *function declaration*, given a syntax base and the syntax introduced so far, is

$$function\ declaration\ ::=\ function\ name\ ::\ signature\ ::\ predicate$$

□

We have to define *well-typed* in this context and what the *meaning* of a well-typed function declaration is. This is done in the following definitions.

**Definition 27.5**   A function declaration is *well-typed* if and only if all the following hold.

(i) The predicate is well-typed.

(ii) The predicate does not contain free (value) variables.

(iii) The type variables in the predicate also occur in the signature.

(iv) The signature is well-typed (i.e. all type variables occur at least in the domain type).

$\square$

**Definition 27.6**   The meaning of a well-typed function declaration of the form

$$f :: D \Rightarrow R :: p$$

where $D$ and $R$ are type expressions, possibly with type variables $\$_1, \ldots, \$_n$, is the set of all (mono- or polymorphic) functions $g$ such that:

– $sign(g) = \{(\epsilon[\![D_{(T_1,\ldots,T_n)}^{(\$_1,\ldots,\$_n)}]\!], \epsilon[\![R_{(T_1,\ldots,T_n)}^{(\$_1,\ldots,\$_n)}]\!]) \mid T_1, \ldots, T_n \in TE\}.$

– for all suitable type expressions $T_1, \ldots, T_n \in TE$

$$\epsilon[\![p_{(g,T_1,\ldots,T_n)}^{(f,\$_1,\ldots,\$_n)}]\!] = true.$$

(Note that $g$ is used as a function name and that it is assumed that $graph(g)$ is known and that $TE$ is the set of type expressions without type variables.)

$\square$

So the meaning of a function declaration is the set of all functions that fit into its signature and have the property expressed by the predicate.

Note that this set may be empty, as in this example:

$$f :: \mathbb{N} \Rightarrow \mathbb{B} :: \quad \forall x : \mathbb{N} \bullet (3 \times (x \ div \ 3) = x \Rightarrow f(x) = true)$$

$$\wedge$$

$$(5 \times (x \ div \ 5) = x \Rightarrow f(x) = false).$$

It is impossible to give a function definition for this function because to do so we would have to indicate explicitly for each argument a unique value and, for all multiples of 15, we have here two different values. It may also happen that a function declaration denotes a set with many elements, for instance

$$f :: \mathbb{N} :: \quad \forall x : \mathbb{N} \bullet f(x) \leq f(x+1).$$

It is the task of the systems engineer to prove that there is at least one function in the set. If there is more than one function the systems engineer leaves the choice to a constructor of the system.

## 27.2 Schemas and scripts

Schemas play an important role in models because they are used to define complex classes on the one hand and processor relations for processors on the other hand. The complexes can be represented as *tuples* belonging to a schema and the firing rules of processor relations are represented by tuples of the schema that belongs to the processor. The schemas for processor relations may contain type variables to express that we have a *generic* processor definition that can be used in different locations in an actor model with respectively different type substitutions. Because schemas are so important there is a set of *operators* on schemas that enable us to construct a schema stepwise out of simpler schemas. The syntax of schemas is given in the next definition.

**Definition 27.7** Given a syntax base, a *schema* has the following syntax:

$$schema \qquad ::= [schema\ signature \mid predicate]$$
$$schema\ signature ::= \langle\ variable : type\ expression \rangle$$
$$variable \in V \cap L$$

All free variables of the predicate have to occur in the schema signature as well.
□

Note that we use here the fact that *attributes* may also be *variables*. Their meaning varies depending on their role in an expression. The semantics of a schema is defined below.

**Definition 27.8** Consider a schema of the form

$$[x_1 : T_1, \ldots, x_n : T_n \mid p].$$

Then

$$\epsilon[[x_1 : T_1, \ldots, x_n : T_n \mid p]] =$$
$$\{z : \epsilon[[x_1 : T_1, \ldots, x_n : T_n]] \mid \epsilon[p_{(\pi_1(z),\ldots,\pi_n(z))}^{(x_1,\ldots,x_n)}]\}.$$

The value $z$ belongs only to the set, if the predicate evaluates to *true*. (So if it is $\perp$ then $z$ does not belong to the set.) The set of all schemas without type variables is called the *schema universe* and is denoted by $SU$ .
□

So a schema is in fact a *restricted set of tuples*.

**Definition 27.9**  A schema without type variables, of the form

$$[x_1 : T_1, \ldots, x_n : T_n \mid p]$$

is *well-typed* if, for all values $e_1, \ldots, e_n$ of types $T_1, \ldots, T_n$ respectively, the predicates

$$p_{(e_1,\ldots,e_n)}^{(x_1,\ldots,x_n)}$$

are well-typed.

   If there are type variables involved, the assertion should hold for all possible substitutions of the type variables by type expressions without type variables.
□

Next we introduce schema expressions and schema definitions. Afterwards we give some examples that illustrate the use of these expressions. This part of the language incorporates most of the *schema calculus* of $Z$.

**Definition 27.10**  A *schema expression* and a *schema definition* have the following syntax:

$$
\begin{aligned}
\textit{schema expression} ::= &\textit{schema} \mid (\textit{schema expression}) \mid \\
&\textit{schema name}(\langle \textit{ type expression } \rangle) \mid \\
&\neg \textit{schema expression} \mid \\
&\textit{schema expression } \theta \textit{ schema expression} \mid \\
&\textit{schema expression} \backslash (\langle \textit{ variable} \rangle) \mid \\
&\textit{schema expression} \upharpoonright (\langle variable \rangle) \mid \\
&\textit{quantor variable} \mid \\
&\textit{predicate} \bullet \textit{schema expression} \\
\textit{schema definition} ::= &\textit{schema name } [(\langle \textit{type variable} \rangle)] := \\
&\qquad\qquad\qquad\qquad\qquad \textit{schema expression}
\end{aligned}
$$

$\theta \in \{\vee, \wedge, \Rightarrow\}$
*quantor* $\in \{\forall, \exists\}$
*variable* $\in V \cap L$

The following conditions must hold:

(i)  The variables to the left of the symbols $\backslash$ and $\upharpoonright$ must occur in the schema signatures of the schema expression.

(ii)  The variable behind a quantor should appear in a signature of the schema expression with the same type expression, and the predicate should have no free variables or type variables.

(iii) The schema expression in a schema definition may contain type variables; however, these type variables must appear also on the left hand side of the "$:=$" symbol.

(iv) Schema definitions may not be recursive.

□

A schema expression, in the case where there are no type variables, determines a schema. For all these expressions we will define the semantics below. A schema definition with type variables defines a *schema-valued function* over a Cartesian product of *TE*.

For example,

$$h(\$) := [x : \$, y : \mathbb{F}(\$) \mid x \in y]$$

defines a *function* $h$. For every $T \in TE$ the function value $h(T)$ is obtained by substituting $T$ for $\$$. If there are no type variables on the right-hand side of a schema definition, then the schema name is not allowed to have type variables, in which case it is used as a shorthand for a schema expression such as type definition. The requirement that schema definitions are not recursive means that the schema name on the left-hand side is not allowed to occur on the right-hand side.

In order to define the semantics of schema expressions and schema definitions we introduce a *syntactical transformation function* that maps schema expressions to schemas; this function is called $\delta$. So, the semantics of a schema expression is in fact the *composition* of $\epsilon$ and $\delta$: first we transform a schema expression into a schema ($\delta$) and then we apply the evaluation function ($\epsilon$).

**Definition 27.11** The semantics of a schema expression without type variables is given by the function $\delta$. Let $s$ be a schema expression.

- If $s$ is a schema then $\delta[\![s]\!] = s$.
- $\delta[\![(s)]\!] = s$.
- $\delta[\![\neg[x_1 : T_1, \ldots, x_n : T_n \mid p]]\!] = \delta[\![[x_1 : T_1, \ldots, x_n : T_n \mid \neg p]]\!]$.
- $\delta[\![[x_1 : T_1, \ldots, x_n : T_n \mid p] \; \theta \; [y_1 : S_1, \ldots, y_m : S_m \mid q]]\!] =$

$$[z_1 : R_1, \ldots, z_\ell : R_\ell \mid p \; \theta \; q],$$

where

- $\theta \in \{\vee, \wedge, \Rightarrow\}$,
- $\forall \, i, j : x_i = y_j \Rightarrow T_i = S_j$,
- $\{z_1, \ldots, z_\ell\} = \{x_1, \ldots, x_n\} \cup \{y_1, \ldots, y_m\}$,
- $\forall \, i, j, k : z_k = x_i \Rightarrow R_k = T_i \wedge z_k = y_j \Rightarrow R_k = S_j$.

- If $n \geq m$: $\delta[\![x_1 : T_1, \ldots, x_n : T_n \mid p] \setminus (x_1, \ldots, x_m)]\!] =$

$$[x_{m+1} : T_{m+1}, \ldots, x_n : T_n \mid \exists x_1 : T_1 \bullet \ldots \exists x_m : T_m \bullet p].$$

- If $n \geq m$: $\delta[\![x_1 : T_1, \ldots, x_n : T_n \mid p] \upharpoonright (x_1, \ldots, x_m)]\!] =$

$$[x_1 : T_1, \ldots, x_m : T_m \mid \exists x_{m+1} : T_{m+1} \bullet \ldots \exists x_n : T_n \bullet p\}.$$

- $\delta[\![\forall x_1 : T \mid q \bullet [x_1 : T_1, \ldots, x_n : T_n \mid p]]\!] =$

$$[x_2 : T_2, \ldots, x_n : T_n \mid \forall x_1 : T \bullet q \Rightarrow p].$$

- $\delta[\![\exists x_1 : T \mid q \bullet [x_1 : T_1, \ldots, x_n : T_n \mid p]]\!] =$

$$[x_2 : T_2, \ldots, x_n : T_n \mid \exists x_1 : T \bullet q \wedge p].$$

Variables may be rearranged first. The semantics of schemas is given in definition 27.8.

□

**Definition 27.12** The *semantics* of a *schema definition* of the form

$$f(\$_1, \ldots, \$_n) := s$$

(where $n \geq 0$) is a function, also denoted by $f$, such that

$$f \in TE^n \rightarrow SU,$$

where $TE$ is the set of all type expressions without free variables and $SU$ is the schema universe and where, for $T_1, \ldots, T_n \in TE$,

$$f(T_1, \ldots, T_n) = \delta[\![s_{(T_1, \ldots, T_n)}^{(\$_1, \ldots, \$_n)}]\!]$$

if the right-hand side is defined.

□

We introduce the concept of *equality* for schema expressions.

**Definition 27.13** Two schema expressions $s_1$ and $s_2$ are said to be *equal*, (notation $s_1 = s_2$) if and only if

(i) $\epsilon[\![\delta[\![s_1]\!]]\!]$ and $\epsilon[\![\delta[\![s_2]\!]]\!]$ are defined,

(ii) $\epsilon[\![\delta[\![s_1]\!]]\!] = \epsilon[\![\delta[\![s_2]\!]]\!]$.

□

We will elucidate these definitions with some examples. Consider the schema definitions

$$s_1 := [x : \mathbf{N}, y : \mathbf{N} \mid x \leq y],$$
$$s_2 := [y : \mathbf{N}, z : \mathbf{N} \mid y \leq z],$$
$$s_3 := [x : \mathbf{N}, y : \mathbf{N}, z : \mathbf{N} \mid x + z = y].$$

Obviously,

$\{x \mapsto 1, y \mapsto 3\}$ belongs to $s_1$ and $\{x \mapsto 1, y \mapsto 2, z \mapsto 1\}$ to $s_3$,

$s_1 \wedge s_2 = [x : \mathbf{N}, y : \mathbf{N}, z : \mathbf{N} \mid x \leq y \wedge y \leq z]$,

$s_1 \Rightarrow s_2 = [x : \mathbf{N}, y : \mathbf{N}, z : \mathbf{N} \mid x \leq y \Rightarrow y \leq z]$,

$\{x \mapsto 1, y \mapsto 0, z \mapsto 0\}$ belongs to $s_1 \Rightarrow s_2$,

$\{x \mapsto 1, y \mapsto 3, z \mapsto 4\}$ belongs to $s_1 \wedge s_2$,

$s_3 \backslash (z) = [x : \mathbf{N}, y : \mathbf{N} \mid \exists z : \mathbf{N} \bullet x + z = y]$,

$s_3 \backslash (z) = s_1$ (by the properties of natural numbers),

$s_3 \upharpoonright (z) = [z : \mathbf{N} \mid \exists x : \mathbf{N} \bullet \exists y : \mathbf{N} \bullet x + z = y]$,

$\forall z : \mathbf{N} \mid z \bmod 2 = 0 \bullet s_2 = [y : \mathbf{N} \mid \forall z : \mathbf{N} \bullet z \bmod 2 = 0 \Rightarrow y \leq z]$
$\qquad\qquad\qquad\qquad = [y : \mathbf{N} \mid y = 0]$(by the properties of N),

$\exists z : \mathbf{N} \mid true \bullet s_3 = [x : \mathbf{N}, y : \mathbf{N} \mid \exists z : \mathbf{N} \bullet x + z = y] = s_1$.

Note that a schema with the predicate *true* is in fact a tuple type, i.e.

$$[x_1 : T_1, \ldots, x_n : T_n \mid true] = [x_1 : T_1, \ldots, x_n : T_n].$$

As a consequence we have

$$[x_1 : T_1, \ldots, x_n : T_n \mid true] \wedge [y_1 : S_1, \ldots, y_n : S_n \mid true] =$$
$$[x_1 : T_1, \ldots, x_n : T_n] \bowtie [y_1 : S_1, \ldots, y_n : S_n].$$

Another property is:

$$\exists x : T \mid p \bullet [x : T, y_1 : S_1, \ldots, y_n : S_n \mid q] =$$
$$([x : T \mid p] \wedge [x : T, y_1 : S_1, \ldots, y_n : S_n \mid q]) \backslash (x).$$

(The proof is an exercise.) These properties show that our language is redundant, but that is a consequence of the wish to have greater expressive comfort.

Next we introduce *scripts*. A script is a coherent set of definitions and declarations.

We have required several times that we do not allow recursion in type definitions, schema definitions and function specifications. For function constructions we allow a limited form of recursion.

To formalize what we mean, we will require that all definitions and declarations in a script can be given a *rank* (i.e. a natural number) such that all names used in this definition or declaration have a definition or declaration with a lower rank. For function definitions we make an exception: they may use names with equal rank also (i.e. the name of the definition may be used in the definition). This means that we use this principle: *define before use*, with an exception for function construction. In the next definition we give the syntax of a script.

**Definition 27.14** A *script* has the following *syntax*:

$$script ::= line \mid line \ ;\ script$$
$$line \quad ::= type\ definition \mid value\ definition \mid$$
$$function\ definition \mid function\ declaration \mid$$
$$schema\ definition$$

such that there is a function that assigns a natural number $n$ to every line $\ell$ with the property that every name occurring in the definition part of the line is itself defined in a line with a number which is smaller than or equal to $n$ if the line is a function definition and which is smaller than $n$ otherwise.

□

In the table format of the language we allow any kind of definition in a *schema body*, i.e. the part where the predicate is written. A definition in a schema body is considered to be *local* to that schema.

# 28

# Methods for function construction

We address four problems: the *correctness* of recursive constructions; *finding* them; *transforming* them into easier-to-handle constructions; the *transformation* of function *declarations* into *constructions*. The only difficult part of function construction is recursion; therefore we focus on that aspect here. In some cases the systems engineer will declare a function first, then transform this declaration into a construction and finally transform this construction into an *algorithm*. This is the longest path. It is also possible to start with a construction and that it turns out that this construction can be executed sufficiently fast.

## 28.1 Correctness of recursive constructions

As already mentioned, a recursive construction is the definition of a function by means of an *explicit equation*. In order to have a *correct* recursive construction we have to answer three questions.

**Existence:** is there a solution?

**Unicity:** is there only one solution and if there are more which one should we choose?

**Computability:** is the solution computable, i.e. is there an algorithm to compute for an arbitrary argument the corresponding function value?

Note that the first question is undecidable, so there is no algorithm to solve this problem.

In order to answer these questions we introduce first another view on recursive equations. Consider for example the recursive equation

$$union(x, y) :=$$
$$\text{if } x = \{\} \text{ then } y \text{ else } ins \, (pick(x), union(rest(x), y)) \text{ fi} :$$
$$\mathbb{F}\$ \times \mathbb{F}\$ \Rightarrow \mathbb{F}\$.$$

Another view on this equation is that the term that defines the function *union* specifies a function in $UF = U \to U$, the function universe with *union* as argument. In lambda calculus this function can be expressed as

$$\lambda f \bullet \lambda x, y \bullet \text{if } x = \{\} \text{ then } y \text{ else } ins \; (pick(x), f(rest(x), y)) \; \text{fi}.$$

(Note that we do not allow such functions in the specification language, but they are allowed in the meta-language.) We call this function the *recursion operator* of the equation. Then we may rephrase the problem as: find a solution of the equation for $f$ with recursion operator $F$:

$$f = F(f).$$

So *union* is a *fix point* of $F$ and therefore

$$f = F(f) = F^2(f) = \ldots = F^n(f).$$

It is in many cases possible, for some argument $x$, to compute $f(x)$ by *iterated application* of $F$, i.e. by $F^n(f)(x)$. It turns out that we can compute $F^n(f)(x)$ *without* knowing $f$. As an example consider the multiplication function *mult*:

$$mult \; (x, y) := \text{if } x = 0 \text{ then } 0 \text{ else } y + mult \; (x - 1, y) \text{ fi} : \mathbb{N} \times \mathbb{N} \Rightarrow \mathbb{N}$$

For example, take $x = 2$, $y = 5$; then, iterated application of $(mult(2, 5))$ works as follows:

$$
\begin{aligned}
mult \; (2, 5) & = \text{if } 2 = 0 \text{ then } 0 \text{ else } 5 + mult(1, 5) \text{fi} \\
& = 5 + mult \; (1, 5) \\
& = 5 + (\text{if } 1 = 0 \text{ then } 0 \text{ else } 5 + mult(0, 5) \text{fi}) \\
& = 5 + 5 + mult(0, 5) \\
& = 5 + 5 + (\text{if } 0 = 0 \text{ then } 0 \text{ else } mult(-1, 5) \text{fi}) \\
& = 10
\end{aligned}
$$

Note that $mult(-1, 5)$ does not have to be evaluated: it would have given $\bot$, since $-1$ is not in $\mathbb{N}$.

Next we consider the *method of successive approximations*, which is a general method for solving fix point equations. In the rest of this section we do not consider signatures of function definitions and we will identify graphs of functions with their names.

We start with the definition of some technical concepts.

**Definition 28.1**

(i) A *partial ordering* on $UF$ is defined by

$$\forall f, g \in UF : f \subseteq g \Leftrightarrow \forall x \in U : f(x) = g(x) \vee f(x) = \bot.$$

(ii) Let $\langle f_0, f_1, \ldots \rangle$ be a sequence of functions in $UF$. The sequence is called *monotonous* if and only if

$$\forall n \in \mathbf{N} : f_n \subseteq f_{n+1}.$$

(iii) The *limit* of a monotonous sequence, denoted by $lim_{n \in \mathbf{N}} f_n$, is given by:

$$(lim_{n \in \mathbf{N}} f_n)(x) = \bot, \text{ if } \forall n \in \mathbf{N} : f_n(x) = \bot,$$
$$= f_k(x), \text{ for some } k \text{ such that } f_k(x) \neq \bot.$$

(Hence for all $k$: $f_k \subseteq lim_{n \in \mathbf{N}} f_n$.)

(iv) A function $F \in UF \rightarrow UF$ is called *monotonous* if and only if

$$\forall f, g \in dom(F) : f \subseteq g \Rightarrow F(f) \subseteq F(g).$$

(v) A function $F \in UF \rightarrow UF$ is called *stable* if and only if, for all monotonous sequences $\langle f_0, f_1, \ldots \rangle$,

$$F(lim_{n \in \mathbf{N}} f_n) \subseteq lim_{n \in \mathbf{N}} F(f_n).$$

$\square$

The method of successive approximations constructs a monotonous sequence of functions $\langle f_0, f_1, \ldots \rangle$ such that the limit is the fix point of the recursive equation.

**Theorem 28.1** Let $F \in UF \twoheadrightarrow UF$ be *monotonous* and *stable* and let the sequence $\langle f_0, f_1, \ldots \rangle$ satisfy

(i) $\forall x \in U : f_0(x) = \bot$,
(ii) $\forall n \in \mathbf{N} : f_{n+1} = F(f_n)$.

Then $f^* = lim_{n \in \mathbf{N}} f_n$ has the property

$$f^* = F(f^*).$$

The components of the sequence are called *successive approximations*.

*Proof* From the monotonicity of $F$ we derive by induction that $\forall n \in \mathbf{N} : f_n \subseteq f_{n+1}$. Note that $f_0 \subseteq f_1$. Assume $f_n \subseteq f_{n+1}$. Then $f_{n+1} = F(f_n) \subseteq F(f_{n+1}) = f_{n+2}$. So the sequence is monotonous and for all $k \in \mathbf{N}$ we have $f_k \subseteq f^*$. Hence

$$f_k \subseteq f_{k+1} = F(f_k) \subseteq F(f^*)$$

and so

$$f^* \subseteq F(f^*).$$

From the stability of $F$ we derive: $F(f^*) \subseteq lim_{n \in \mathbf{N}} F(f_n)$.
Since $lim_{n \in \mathbf{N}} f_n = lim_{n \in \mathbf{N} \setminus \{0\}} f_n$ and $F(f_n) = f_{n+1}$ we have

$$F(f^*) \subseteq f^*.$$

Combining these statements gives the desired result. $\qquad \Box$

The approach of solving a recursive equation by means of such a sequence is called the *method of successive approximations*. Note that we do not compute these functions completely (which is impossible) but that we compute them for sufficiently many arguments in order to compute the value of the fix point function for one given argument.

We call the method of successive approximations *applicable* for a recursive equation if the recursion operator $F$ is monotonous and stable.

**Theorem 28.2**   Under the conditions of theorem 28.1, the solution $f^*$ is the *smallest* solution of the equation in the sense that if $g$ is another fix point of $F$ then $f^* \subseteq g$.

*Proof*   We prove this by induction. Of course, $f_0 \subseteq g$. Assume that $f_n \subseteq g$. Since $F$ is monotonous we have $F(f_n) \subseteq F(g)$. Because $g$ is a fix point and by the definition of $f_{n+1}$, we have $f_{n+1} \subseteq g$. Hence $\forall n \in \mathbf{N} : f_n \subseteq g$ and therefore $f^* \subseteq g$. $\qquad \Box$

There is a good reason to take the least fix point $f^*$ always because all other solutions $g$ have the property that

$$\forall x : f^*(x) \neq \bot \Rightarrow f^*(x) = g(x),$$

so $f^*$ is the only "sure" solution. The next theorem shows that $f^*$ is "reached" by successive approximations in finitely many steps, for each argument.

**Theorem 28.3**   Under the conditions of theorem 28.1 we have

$$\forall x \in U : \exists n \in \mathbf{N} : f^*(x) = F^n(f_0)(x).$$

*Proof*   The proof is an immediate consequence of $f_n = F^n(f_0)$ and the definition of the limit. $\qquad \Box$

So, if the method of successive approximations is applicable we can compute the function value of the least fix point by *iterated application* of the recursion operator. We will apply this result to an important special case, *linear recursive functions*. Here we give a *sufficient* condition for applicability.

**Theorem 28.4** Consider the equation for a *linear recursive function*:

$$f(x) := if \ b(x) \ then \ a(x) \ else \ h(x, f(g(x))) \ fi$$

where $a$, $b$, $h$, $g$ are strict functions. Then the method of successive approximations is *applicable*.

*Proof* Let $F$ be the recursion operator of the equation. First we show the *monotonicity* of $F$. Let $p$ and $q$ be functions such that $p \subseteq q$ and let $x \neq \perp$ be given. If $F(p)(x) = \perp$ then nothing has to be proven; otherwise, either $b(x) = true$ or $p(g(x)) \neq \perp$ (we use the strictness of $h$). In the latter case $p(g(x)) = q(g(x))$, since $p \subseteq q$. So in both cases we have $F(p)(x) = F(g)(x)$, which proves the monotonicity of $F$.

The next step is to verify the *stability*. Let $\langle s_0, s_1, \ldots \rangle$ be a monotonous sequence and $s^* = lim_{n \in \mathbb{N}} s_n$. If $F(s^*)(x) = \perp$ nothing has to be proven, otherwise either $b(x) = true$ or $s^*(g(x)) \neq \perp$. In the first case $F(s^*)(x) = F(s_n)(x) = a(x)$ (for all $n \in \mathbb{N}$). In the latter case there is an $n \in \mathbb{N}$ such that $s_n(g(x)) \neq \perp$, since the sequence is monotonous. Hence, since $s_n \subseteq s^*$ we have $s^*(g(x)) = s_n(g(x))$ and so $F(s^*)(x) = F(s_n)(x)$.

So, we have shown that

$$\forall x \in U : F(s^*)(x) \neq \perp \Rightarrow \exists n \in \mathbb{N} : F(s^*)(x) = F(s_n)(x)$$

and hence $F(s^*) \subseteq lim_{n \in \mathbb{N}} F(s_n)$. □

For this case we can derive a more detailed result.

**Theorem 28.5** Let $F$ be defined as in theorem 28.1 and let $f^*$ be the least fix point of $F$. If for some $x \in U$ the following properties hold,

$$b(x) = b(g(x)) = \ldots = b(g^{n-1}(x)) = false \ \wedge \ b(g^n(x)) = true,$$

then

$$f^*(x) = h(x, h(g(x)), \ldots, h(g^{n-1}(x), a(g^n(x))) \ldots))$$

and, for $k > n$, $F^k(f_0)(x) = f^*(x)$.

*Proof* Since $b(x) = false$ we have

$$f^*(x) = F(f^*)(x) = h(x, f^*(g(x))).$$

By iterated application we obtain

$$f^*(x) = F(f^*)(x) = h(x, h(g(x)), \ldots, h(g^{n-1}(x), f^*(g^n(x))) \ldots)) \quad (*)$$

Since $b(g^n(x)) = true$ we have $f^*(g^n(x)) = a(g^n(x))$. If we substitute this in $(*)$ we obtain the first assertion.

Similarly,

$$f_{n+1}(x) = h(x, h(g(x), \ldots, h(g^{n-1}(x), f_1(g^n(x))) \ldots)).$$

Since $b(g^n(x)) = true$ we have $f_1(g^n(x)) = a(g^n(x))$. So, $f_{n+1}(x) = F^{n+1}(f_0) = f^*(x)$.                                                                                      □

Note that we used the laziness of *if.then.else.fi* here. Next we consider a class of recursive equations for which there is always a solution that can be obtained by one of the methods discussed above. The functions defined in this way are called *primitive recursive functions*. They are very important because most of the functions we encounter in practice are primitive recursive (*see* appendix C).

**Definition 28.2**  A function construction is *primitive recursive* if it is of the form

$$f(x, y) := if \ x = 0 \ then \ a(x, y) \ else \ h(x, y, f(x - 1, y)) \ fi$$

where $a$ and $h$ are given strict functions and the type of $x$ is $\mathbb{N}$.
□

Primitive recursive functions satisfy the conditions of theorem 28.4. To verify this let $b(z) := (\pi_1(z) = 0)$, $z = (x, y)$ and $g(z) := (\pi_1(z) - 1, \pi_2(z))$. Then we may transform the equation for $f$ as:

$$f(z) := if \ b(z) \ then \ a(z) \ else \ h(z, f(g(z))) \ fi.$$

**Theorem 28.6**  Consider a primitive recursive equation in $f$ as defined above. This recursive equation has a *unique solution*.

*Proof* Let $f$ and $g$ be two solutions. Fix some $y$. Clearly $f(0, y) = a(0, y) = g(0, y)$. Assume, for some $n \in \mathbb{N}$, that $f(n, y) = g(n, y)$. Then

$$f(n + 1, y) = h(n + 1, y, f(n, y)) = h(n + 1, y, g(n, y)) = g(n + 1, y).$$

Hence, we have shown by induction that there is at most one solution. By iterated application we obtain

$$f(n, y) = h(n, y, h(n - 1, y, \ldots, h(1, y, a(0, y)))).$$

□

There are many applications of this theorem. For instance, according to the theorem the multiplication function *mult* has a unique solution. There are different syntactical forms of the theorems in this section; for example, the functions *a*, *b*, *h* and *g* could have been given by their defining terms instead of by an application.

## 28.2 Derivation of recursive constructions

One of the major problems of constructive specifications is to find a correct and easily understood recursive construction for a function *f*. In many cases we can use the following approach.

(i) Determine the signature $S \Rightarrow T$ of the function *f*.
(ii) Determine a subset *B* of *S*, so that *B* is a value of type $\mathbb{F}(S)$, on which the function is known (note that *B* is often given in the form of a Boolean function on *b* with signature $S \Rightarrow \mathbb{B}$).
(iii) Determine a function *a* with the same signature as *f* that coincides with *f* on *B*: $\forall x \in B : f(x) = a(x)$.
(iv) Determine a set-valued function *R* with signature $S \Rightarrow \mathbb{F}(S)$ and with the meaning that the value $f(x)$ can be expressed by means of the values $f(y)$ for $y \in R(x)$, where $x \notin B$.
(v) Determine a function *h* that tells how to compute $f(x)$ from the values given by $R(x)$: $f(x) = h(x, \{(y, f(y)) \mid y \in R(x)\})$.
(vi) Create an equation of the form

$$f(x) := \textit{if } x \in B \textit{ then } a(x) \textit{ else } h(x, \{(y, f(y)) \mid y \in R(x)\}) \textit{fi}.$$

Note that this equation is not an expression in the language, but a *template* for such expressions.

This method is very similar to the technique called *dynamic programming* and to the technique for constructing *differential equations* to describe physical phenomena.

We will illustrate these steps with some examples. The first example is the well-known the Fibonacci sequence. The function *fib* computes the *n*th value of this sequence. Carrying out the above steps gives the following.

(i) The signature of *fib* is $\mathbb{N} \Rightarrow \mathbb{N}$, so $S = \mathbb{N}$,
(ii) $B = \{0, 1\}$,
(iii) $\forall x \in B : \textit{fib}(x) = 1$,
(iv) $\forall x \in S : R(x) = \{x - 1, x - 2\}$,
(v) $h(x, \{(y, \textit{fib}(y)) \mid y \in R(x)\}) = \textit{fib}(x - 1) + \textit{fib}(x - 2)$.

So we thus obtain, in the specification language,

$$f(x) := \text{if } x = 0 \lor x = 1 \text{ then } 1 \text{ else } fib(x-1) + fib(x-2) \text{ fi} : \mathbb{N} \Rightarrow \mathbb{N}.$$

The next example is the construction of a function $f$ that assigns to each node the length of a *shortest path in a graph* to some specific node $b$. We again carry out the recursive procedure and obtain the following.

(i) The signature of $f$ is $S \Rightarrow \mathbb{Q}$, where $S$ is some type that contains all the *nodes*,

(ii) $B = \{b\}$,

(iii) $f(b) = 0$,

(iv) $R$ is a function that assigns to each node a set of nodes, so its signature is $S \Rightarrow \mathbb{F}(S)$; in fact $R$ determines the *edges* of the graph,

(v) $h(x, \{(y, f(y)) \mid y \in R(x)\}) = min((y : R(x) \mid d(x,y) + f(y)))$ where $d$ is the distance function with signature $S \times S \Rightarrow \mathbb{Q}$ and where *min* is a function with signature $\mathbb{F}(\$ \times \mathbb{Q}) \Rightarrow \mathbb{Q}$ that determines the minimum of the range of a binary relation (see *fmax* in appendix C).

We thus obtain, in the specification language,

$$f(x) := \text{if } x = b \text{ then } 0 \text{ else } min((y : R(x) \mid d(x,y) + f(y))) \text{fi} : S \Rightarrow \mathbb{Q}.$$

Note that we need to verify several conditions to guarantee that this definition is correct, such as: for each node there is a finite path to $b$; the range of $d$ contains only non-negative values. A proof that iteration terminates is required. This example is a typical case of dynamic programming.

The method does not work in every case. Consider for instance the *Ackermann function*, defined by

$$\begin{aligned}
A(x,y) := \quad &\text{if } x = 0 \text{ then } y + 1 \\
&\text{else if } y = 0 \text{ then } A(x-1, 1) \\
&\qquad \text{else } A(x-1, A(x, y-1)) \\
&\quad \text{fi} \\
&\text{fi}.
\end{aligned}$$

Here we see that $R(x, y)$ includes $(x-1, 1)$ and also $(x-1, A(x, y-1))$, which is dependent on $A$. However, this function is a pathological case.

Our last example is a classical problem of numerical analysis. We are looking for a root of an equation of the form $f(x) = 0$ where $f$ is a given function with signature $\mathbb{Q} \Rightarrow \mathbb{Q}$. Suppose that we have already found an approximation to the root, i.e. a value $x$ such that $f(x)$ is close to 0. We use the well-known *Newton-Raphson method* to solve the problem. Based on two domain values $y$ and $z$ that

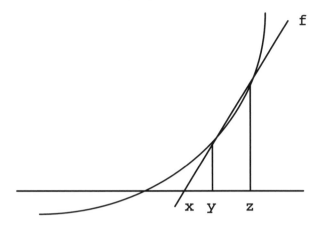

Fig. 28.1. Newton-Raphson method.

can be considered as successive approximations to the unknown $x$, we can derive a better approximation to $x$ using the equation

$$\frac{f(z) - f(y)}{z - y} = \frac{f(y)}{y - x};$$

see figure 28.1. We follow the steps again using the function *root* that will determine an approximation to the root.

(i) The signature of *root* is $\mathbb{Q} \times \mathbb{Q} \Rightarrow \mathbb{Q}$,
(ii) $B$ is determined by the absolute value of the function value of the approximation $B = \{(y, z) \mid z = abs(f(y)) \ \wedge \ z < \epsilon\}$, where $\epsilon$ is some given non-negative number and *abs* gives the absolute value of its arguments,
(iii) $a$ is defined by $a(y, z) = y$, the last computed approximation of the root,
(iv) $R$ is given by $R(y, z) = \{(y - (z - y) \times \frac{f(y)}{f(z) - f(y)}, y)\}$,
(v) $h$ is simply found: $h(y, z) = (y - (z - y) \times \frac{f(y)}{f(z) - f(y)}, y)$.

We thus obtain, in the specification language

$$root(y, z) :=$$

$$if \ abs(y - z) < \epsilon \ then \ y \ else \ root\left(y - (z - y) \times \frac{f(y)}{f(z) - f(y)}, y\right) \ fi.$$

A proof of the correctness of this construction requires the verification of some conditions for $f$ (the Lipschitz condition, for instance); this is, however, beyond the scope of this book.

We call functions for which the set $R(x)$ never contains more than one element *linear recursive functions*. Most of the examples that we have met belong to this class. In fact they reduce to the special case we have considered before, i.e. they are of the form

$$f(x) := \text{if } b(x) \text{ then } a(x) \text{ else } h(x, f(g(x))) \text{ fi}.$$

Here $g(x)$ is the unique element of $R(x)$. An important subclass of the linear recursive functions is the class of *tail recursive functions*. They are characterized by the fact that

$$h(x, f(g(x))) = f(g(x)).$$

Next we consider the problem of transforming constructions into easier ones. Tail recursive functions are important because they can be computed relatively fast by *repetition* instead of iterated application. By "repetition" we mean the loop construction of imperative programming languages. If we have a tail recursive function construction of the form

$$f(x) := \text{if } b(x) \text{ then } a(x) \text{ else } f(g(x)) \text{ fi}$$

then the following imperative program will compute $f$:

$$\text{while } \neg b(x) \text{ do } x \leftarrow g(x) \text{ od } ; \ x \leftarrow a(x)$$

If the precondition of this repetition is $x = x_0$ then the postcondition is $x = f(x_0)$. (Note that "$\leftarrow$" denotes the assignment statement and ";" the composition operator.) In general it is not possible to transform the construction of a linear recursive function into tail recursion; however, if $h$ has some special properties it is possible. The next theorem gives sufficient conditions. (We consider the type information afterwards.)

**Theorem 28.7** Let a linear recursive construct of the form

$$f(x) := \text{if } b(x) \text{ then } a(x) \text{ else } h(k(x), f(g(x))) \text{ fi}$$

be given. Suppose that the following are satisfied:

(i) $b$, $a$, $h$, $k$ and $g$ are strict functions;
(ii) there is a *unit* element $e$ such that $\forall y : h(e, y) = y$;
(iii) $h$ is *associative*, i.e. $\forall x, y, z : h(x, h(y, z)) = h(h(x, y), z)$.

Then we have

$$\forall x : f(x) = r(e, x),$$

where $r$ is defined by

$$r(y, x) := \text{if } b(x) \text{ then } h(y, a(x)) \text{ else } r(h(y, k(x)), g(x)) \text{ fi}.$$

(Note that $r$ is a tail recursive function.)

*Proof* We show by induction that for all relevant $x$ and $y$

$$r_n(y, x) = h(y, f_n(x)),$$

where the index $n$ refers to the $n$th approximation according to the method of successive approximations. Clearly, for $n = 0$ the equation holds because both sides are $\bot$. Assume the equality holds for $n$. Consider $r_{n+1}(y, x)$. If $b(x) = \bot$ the assertion holds, so there remain two cases: either $b(x) = true$ or $b(x) = false$. In the first case we have $r_{n+1}(y, x) = h(y, a(x))$ and also $f_{n+1}(x) = a(x)$; hence the equation holds. In the second case we have, by the induction hypothesis,

$$r_{n+1}(y, x) = r_n(h(y, k(x)), g(x)) = h(h(y, k(x)), f_n(g(x))).$$

On the other hand,

$$f_{n+1}(x) = h(k(x), f_n(g(x)))$$

and therefore

$$h(y, f_{n+1}(x)) = h(y, h(k(x), f_n(g(x))));$$

the associativity of $h$ gives the assertion. □

Note that, notwithstanding the function $k$ in the construction, this is an example of the special case we considered before. Here we used $k$ because we had to decompose $h$ a little. The types involved are as follows:

$f, a, k : \$_1 \Rightarrow \$_2,$
$b : \$_1 \Rightarrow \mathbb{B},$
$g : \$_1 \Rightarrow \$_1,$
$h : \$_2 \times \$_2 \Rightarrow \$_2,$
$r : \$_2 \times \$_1 \Rightarrow \$_2.$

The term "associativity" becomes clearer if the function $h$ is represented in infix notation. Finally note that this transformation can be carried out automatically. We illustrate this transformation using the *factorial function*, defined by

$$fac(x) := if\ x = 0\ then\ 1\ else\ x \times fac(x - 1)\ fi : \mathbb{Q} \Rightarrow \mathbb{Q}.$$

The tail recursive equivalent is

$$r(y, x) := if\ x = 0\ then\ y\ else\ r(y \times x, x - 1)\ fi : \mathbb{Q} \times \mathbb{Q} \Rightarrow \mathbb{Q}.$$

Note that $h(x, y) = x \times y$, $k(x) = x$ and that $g(x) = x - 1$ in this case. Clearly $h$ is associative and 1 is the unit element.

Transformation to tail recursion is not restricted to linear recursive constructions. Consider for example the following solution for the Fibonacci sequence:

$$Fib(n, x, y) := \quad \text{if } n = 1 \text{ then } y$$
$$\text{else} \quad \text{if } n = 2 \text{ then } x$$
$$\text{else} \, Fib(n - 1, x + y, x) \, fi$$
$$fi : \mathbb{N} \times \mathbb{N} \times \mathbb{N} \Rightarrow \mathbb{N}$$

This function is easy to transform into an imperative program having one repetition.

The last problem we consider is the transformation of a function declaration into a construction. There are very few methods for doing this. It is more of an art than a science and often requires background knowledge, for instance in the form of theorems. Consider for instance the following specification of the function *root* that was constructed above:

$$root :: \mathbb{Q} \times \mathbb{Q} \Rightarrow \mathbb{Q} :: \forall x : \mathbb{Q} \bullet \forall y : \mathbb{Q} \bullet$$

$$root(x, y) = x \Leftrightarrow abs(f(x)) < \epsilon.$$

There is no way to derive the construction given above from this specification. Thus, sometimes a construction is the best specification we can give. Consider for instance the function *fac*. Informally we would specify this by the construction

$$fac(x) = 1 \times 2 \times \ldots \times x.$$

If we try to formalize this we will obtain

$$fac(x) = x \times fac(x - 1)$$

in the case $x \neq 0$, which is almost the construction.

Next we consider again the specification of the function *union*.

$$union :: \mathbb{F}(\$) \times \mathbb{F}(\$) \Rightarrow \mathbb{F}(\$) :: \forall x : \mathbb{F}(\$) \bullet \forall y : \mathbb{F}(\$) \bullet$$

$$\forall z : \$ \bullet z \in union(x, y) \Leftrightarrow z \in x \lor z \in y.$$

To derive a construction from this specification we have to infer that, for $x$ and $y$ of type $\mathbb{F}(\$)$;

(i) *union* is associative, i.e. $union(union(x, y), z) = union(x, union(y, z))$,
(ii) $union(\emptyset, y) = y$,
(iii) $union(\{a\}, y) = ins(a, y)$,
(iv) $ins(pick(x), rest(x)) = x$.

The first two properties are easy to prove, while the other two require some knowledge of the primitive functions *ins*, *pick* and *rest*. Now we are able to rewrite *union*$(x, y)$, in the case $x \neq \emptyset$, as follows:

$$
\begin{aligned}
union(x, y) &= union(ins(pick(x), rest(x)), y) \\
&= union(union(\{pick(x)\}, rest(x)), y) \\
&= union(\{pick(x)\}, union(rest(x), y)) \\
&= ins(pick(x), union(rest(x), y)).
\end{aligned}
$$

Here we used the properties in the following order: 4, 3, 1 and 3. From this we derive the well-known construction

$$
union(x, y) := if\ x = \{\}\ then\ y\ else\ ins(pick(x), union(rest(x), y))\ fi.
$$

(We have left out the signature; it was given above.) This example illustrates that *term rewriting* is a good technique for deriving properties that can be used in a function construction.

# 29

# Specification methods

The specification of an actor model requires that all the complex classes should be mapped to a value type and that for each processor a schema is defined. In this chapter we give some methods of finding suitable value types for complex classes and schemas for processors.

## 29.1 Value types for complex classes

Remember that sometimes a complex class is rather trivial, for instance, if the complex class contains only one simplex class and satisfies the (only possible) tree constraint. In that case the complex class will have the type of the simplex class. For simplex classes we are free to choose a value type and in many cases we define a basic type for them, sometimes one of the standard basic types such as $\mathbb{N}$, $\mathbb{Q}$ or $\mathbb{B}$ and sometimes some new basic types. In the latter case we could also have some new primitive functions. However in most cases we do not introduce new primitive functions for new basic types, which means that we can compare two values only by means of the equality function ($=$) and that we may perform set operations on them.

There are various ways of representing a complex class by a value type. The constraints and the functions we will apply to the complexes influence our choice. There is, however, one *standard construction* for representing a complex class by a *schema*. This construction is studied first; afterwards we will exploit the constraints to obtain representations that are easier to use in functions and processor relations.

Consider a complex class having name $c$ having simplex classes having names $s_1, \ldots, s_n$ and relationships having names $r_1, \ldots, r_m$. Assume that the simplex classes are given by (defined) types having names $S_1, \ldots, S_n$ respectively. Then the complex class $c$ is represented by the following schema:

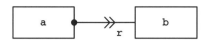

Fig. 29.1. A simple complex class.

$$[s_1 : \mathbb{F}(S_1), \ldots, s_n : \mathbb{F}(S_n),$$
$$r_1 : \mathbb{F}(S_{DM(r_1)} \times S_{RG(r_n)}), \ldots, r_m : \mathbb{F}(S_{DM(r_m)} \times S_{RG(r_m)}) \mid$$
$$r_1 \subseteq prod(s_{DM(r_1)}, s_{RG(r_1)}), \ldots, r_m \subseteq prod(s_{DM(r_m)}, s_{RG(r_m)})].$$

Note that the subscripts *DM* and *RG* of the variables do not belong to the language, so that this is a mixture of meta-language and specification language. (The subscripts denote a permutation of $1, \ldots, n$.) In this definition we have used the function *prod* that assigns to two sets their Cartesian product. Note that we have a type constructor for forming of the Cartesian product of types but no function yet to do the same for sets. The construction of *prod* can be found in appendix C.

It is easy to verify that this value type is a correct representation of the function *com* defined in part II. If we have other constraints we can add them to the predicate part of the schema. In chapter 15 we have already used the specification language to express constraints. There we considered every simplex class as a basic type, as we do here. Consider the simple complex class $C$ displayed in figure 29.1. Then we have the following schema definition for $C$:

$$C := [a : \mathbb{F}(A), b : \mathbb{F}(B), r : \mathbb{F}(A \times B) \mid r \subseteq prod(a, b)].$$

For each relationship $r$ we can define functions as we did in chapter 15. Then we define

$$r(x) := setapply(r, x) : \ A \Rightarrow \mathbb{F}(B).$$

(Note that we are overloading the name $r$.) If we want to express a cardinality constraint for $r$, for instance that $r$ is functional and surjective, then we add to the predicate of the schema $C$

$$\forall x : A \bullet x \in a \Rightarrow size(r(x)) = 1.$$

This is a non-executable expression! However, we can always transform it into an executable one since the domain of quantification is finite. The executable form of this constraint is

$$forall((x : a \mid size(r(x)) = 1),$$

where the function *forall* is defined in appendix C. There is no need for an executable form of a constraint if we can *prove* that the constraint is invariant for
all transitions of the actor. However, if we cannot prove this, then we use the
constraint as part of a *postcondition* in a processor relation, and then its executability might be essential. (Note that the invariance of the constraint is then
fulfilled in a trivial way, namely by allowing only transitions that keep the constraint valid.) In most cases we will not *test* a constraint in a processor relation
completely and so there is no need for executability.

There is one important case where testing of a constraint is necessary, that
where tokens from an outside source enter the system and it is not guaranteed
that these tokens are correct. Then we may use the constraint as a *precondition* in
a processor relation. Note that the standard constraints can be transformed into
predicates or executable expressions automatically. Since we now have a standard
construction for all complex classes, we are able to express for all characteristic
modeling problems of chapter 15 a suitable value type. However, sometimes the
constraints allow us to find a value type, that is actually more convenient.

There are several constraints that can be exploited to obtain simpler representations than the standard type of representation for a complex class. In all these
cases it is easy to find the one-to-one transformations that map the instances of
the schemas to the corresponding complexes.

First we consider the case where we have a relationship that is *total* and *surjective*. In this case we do not have to represent the simplex classes separately
in the schema. Suppose, in the example of figure 29.1, relationship $r$ is total and
surjective. Then the schema can be reduced to one without predicate (i.e. a tuple
type):

$$C := [r : \mathbb{F}(A \times B)]$$

because the simplexes in a complex of class $C$ can be derived from $r$. So, if we
want to refer within the schema's predicate to the simplexes of class $A$ and $B$
then we use $dom(r)$ and $rng(r)$ respectively in a schema with $r$ as attribute.

The second case we consider is a *domain key constraint*, formed by *total* and
*functional* relationships. Consider the complex class $D$ displayed in figure 29.2.
Since relationships $r$ and $q$ form a key, we can define the complex class $D$ by

$$D := [a : \mathbb{F}(B \times C), b : \mathbb{F}(B), c : \mathbb{F}(C) \mid a \subseteq prod(b, c)].$$

The relationships are here implicit.

The next case concerns a *tree constraint* with some *total, functional and surjective* relationships. (Note that this kind of structure often occurs in practice.)
In figure 29.3, we display a complex class $E$ having $a$ as root simplex class. A

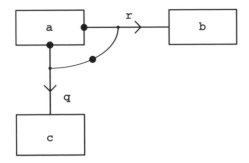

Fig. 29.2. Exploitation of a key constraint

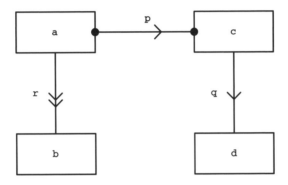

Fig. 29.3. Exploitation of tree constraint.

schema definition is:

$$E := [a : A, c : C, d : D, b : \mathbb{F}(B)].$$

(Note that this just a tuple type.) So the relationships are all implicit here and again we do not have to worry about the constraints. If there were two or more relationships between the simplex classes, the schema definition would have the relationship names as attributes as well.

In the final case we consider *inheritance constraints* in combination with *exclusion constraints*. In figure 29.4 we display a complex class $S$ as an example. In addition to the previously mentioned constraints we assume that a tree constraint holds with *person* as root. A schema definition for $S$ is:

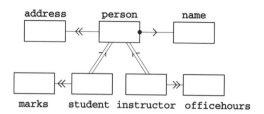

Fig. 29.4. Exploitation of inheritance

$$S := [p : person, a : \mathbb{F}(address), n : name, m : \mathbb{F}(marks),$$
$$\quad o : \mathbb{F}(officehours), k : kind \mid$$
$$\quad k \in \{'student', 'instructor'\} \ \wedge \ k =' student' \Rightarrow o = \{\} \ \wedge$$
$$\quad k =' instructor' \Rightarrow m = \{\}].$$

So we have not represented the simplex classes *student* and *instructor* directly but have used another attribute to make the distinction between the two kinds of persons. This "trick" is, at the level of object modeling, not recommended because it would introduce constraints that involve specific simplexes; however, at this level of specification it might be handy, because it gives a simple schema definition.

We conclude this section with the representation of the *relational data model* in the specification language. In chapter 15 we have seen how we can represent our object model in several other frameworks, for instance the relational data model. These transformations are useful if the systems engineer wants to continue the specification process in another framework. However, the type system of our specification language has schemas that can be considered as a generalization of the relations of the relational data model. Therefore it should be easy to express a relational model in schemas. If we combine this transformation with the transformation from an object model into a relational model then we have another "standard" type for complex classes (note that we restrict ourselves to one complex class, which might be considered as a universal complex class). Consider again the relational schema studied in section 15.3:

| relation | attribute | domain | key |
|----------|-----------|--------|-----|
| $r_1$ | $a_1$ | $A_1$ | n |
|  | $a_2$ | $A_1$ | y |
|  | $a_3$ | $A_2$ | y |
| $r_2$ | $a_4$ | $A_2$ | y |
|  | $a_5$ | $A_3$ | y |
|  | $a_6$ | $A_3$ | n |
| $r_3$ | $a_7$ | $A_3$ | y |
|  | $a_8$ | $A_4$ | y |
|  | $a_9$ | $A_4$ | n |

(Note the difference in the sense of the language between a "relational schema" and a "schema".) A schema for this relational model is defined in two steps: first we define tuple types for each table and afterwards we define a schema $D$ for the whole database. Note that we have to take care of the key constraints.

$$R_1 := [a_1 : A_1, a_2 : A_1, a_3 : A_2],$$
$$R_2 := [a_4 : A_2, a_5 : A_3, a_6 : A_3],$$
$$R_3 := [a_7 : A_3, a_8 : A_4, a_9 : A_4],$$
$$D := [r_1 : \mathbb{F}(R_1), r_2 : \mathbb{F}(R_2), r_3 : \mathbb{F}(R_3) \mid$$
$$\forall x : R_1, y : R_1 \bullet (x \in r_1 \;\wedge\; y \in r_1 \;\wedge$$
$$\pi_{a_2}(x) = \pi_{a_2}(y) \;\wedge\; \pi_{a_3}(x) = \pi_{a_3}(y)) \Rightarrow x = y \;\wedge$$
$$\forall x : R_2, y : R_2 \bullet (x \in r_2 \;\wedge\; y \in r_2 \;\wedge$$
$$\pi_{a_4}(x) = \pi_{a_4}(y) \;\wedge\; \pi_{a_5}(x) = \pi_{a_5}(y)) \Rightarrow x = y \;\wedge$$
$$\forall x : R_3, y : R_3 \bullet (x \in r_3 \;\wedge\; y \in r_3 \;\wedge$$
$$\pi_{a_7}(x) = \pi_{a_7}(y) \;\wedge\; \pi_{a_8}(x) = \pi_{a_8}(y)) \Rightarrow x = y].$$

For other data models similar representations can be found. In particular we can express the nested relational model directly in the specification language. (This is an exercise.)

Queries for a relational model can be expressed in the *relational algebra*. The relational algebra has the following operators:

*projection, selection, rename, join, union* and *set difference*.

We show here how these operators can be "simulated" in the specification language. Consider a relation $r$ that belongs to a tuple type with at least $a$ as attribute, so that

$$r : \mathbb{F}([a : \$_1] \bowtie \$_2).$$

Operator *projection* should be defined for each attribute list; for example the projection on attribute $a$ is

$$Pa(r) :=$$
$$rng((x : r \mid \pi_a(x)) : \mathbb{F}([a : \$_1] \bowtie \$_2) \Rightarrow \mathbb{F}(\$_1).$$

Operator *selection* selects tuples with certain values, for example the selection on attribute $a$ that should have value $x$ is ($x$ is a variable):

$$Sel(r, x) :=$$
$$\{y : r \mid \pi_a(y) = x\} : \mathbb{F}([a : \$_1] \bowtie \$_2) \times \$_1 \Rightarrow \mathbb{F}([a : \$_1] \bowtie \$_2).$$

Operator *rename* only changes attribute names. For example, let

$$r : \mathbb{F}([a : \$_1, \ b : \$_2]) \text{ and}$$
$$Rbc(r) := rng((x : r \mid \{a \mapsto \pi_a(x), c \mapsto \pi_b(x)\})) :$$
$$\mathbb{F}([a : \$_1, \ b : \$_2]) \Rightarrow \mathbb{F}([a : \$_1, \ c : \$_2]).$$

These functions are specific, i.e. they have to be defined for each query. The other operators are *generic* functions, i.e. they are defined for arbitrary relations.

For operator *join* we need an auxiliary function, *semijoin*:

$$semijoin(x, y) :=$$
$$\textit{if } x \oplus pick(y) = pick(y) \oplus x \textit{ then } ins(x \oplus pick(y), semijoin(x, rest(y)))$$
$$\textit{else } semijoin(x, rest(y))$$
$$fi : \$_1 \times \mathbb{F}(\$_2) \Rightarrow \mathbb{F}(\$_1 \bowtie \$_2).$$

Operator *join* is then defined by:

$$join(x, y) :=$$
$$\textit{if } x = \{\} \textit{ then } \{\}$$
$$\textit{else } ins(semijoin(pick(x), y), join(rest(x), y))$$
$$fi : \mathbb{F}(\$_1) \times \mathbb{F}(\$_2) \Rightarrow \mathbb{F}(\$_1 \bowtie \$_2).$$

Operator *union* has already been defined.
Operator *set difference* is defined by

$$setdif(x, y) := \{z : x \mid \neg(z \in y)\} : \mathbb{F}(\$) \times \mathbb{F}(\$) \Rightarrow \mathbb{F}(\$).$$

Thus the relational algebra is incorporated into the specification language.

## 29.2 Specification of processors

The final piece in the puzzle is the specification of processors. We use schemas to specify them. We will address the following problems:

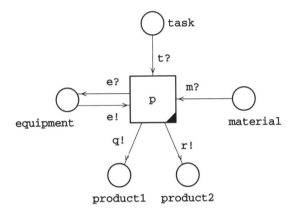

Fig. 29.5. Production system

- How does a schema defines a processor relation?
- How do we deal with token identity and time stamps?
- How can we use the processor characteristics?
- How do we deal with pre- and postconditions?

We will answer these questions using a simple example of a processor. In figure 29.5 we display this processor, which is executing tasks. A task defines a product. There are four kinds of task and so there are four kinds of product (1, 2, 3 and 4). Only two kinds of task (3 and 4) require equipment, while all tasks require materials. There are two kinds of equipment ($A$ and $B$) and there are also two kinds of material ($C$ and $D$). The four kinds of product are to be sent to two different places: products 1 and 3 are sent to one place and the other products to the other place. In table 29.1 below we give an informal description of the processor relation: We will give a schema for this processor. According

Table 29.1. *Informal description of the processor relation*

| t? | e? | m? | e! | q! | r! |
|----|----|----|----|----|----|
| 1 | $\perp$ | $C$ | $\perp$ | 1 | $\perp$ |
| 2 | $\perp$ | $D$ | $\perp$ | $\perp$ | 2 |
| 3 | $A$ | $C$ | $A$ | 3 | $\perp$ |
| 4 | $B$ | $D$ | $B$ | $\perp$ | 4 |

to the definition of the actor model a processor relation $R_p$ for processor $p$ is a set of functions with domains that are subsets of the set of input and output connectors. The function values are triples consisting of an *identity*, a *value* and a *time stamp*. We will represent these triples as different variables in the schema. (We sometimes mix up the terms "connector" and "variable" in the schema that represents the processor relation.) For each connector $c$ we have in principle three variables in the schema representing a processor relation: $c$, $c_i$ and $c_t$. The first one denotes the *value* of the token that is consumed or produced via connector $c$, the second one denotes the *identity* of the token and the third its *time stamp*. We also use decorations to distinguish the input and output connectors, "?" and "!" respectively for channels and "" for the output to a store.

If a variable equals $\bot$ for some tuple that belongs to the schema, it will denote that no token passes during the firing of the corresponding connector (i.e. the connector with the same name). So here we give the symbol $\bot$ a specific interpretation. This interpretation fully agrees with the fact that no token should pass a connector if the connector does not appear in the domain of the firing rule. Recall that if the predicate of a schema evaluates to $\bot$, then the tuple does not belong to the schema and therefore not to the processor relation (see definition 27.8). Consider the following example (in which we do not consider identities and time stamps):

$$[a? : \mathbb{N}, b? : \mathbb{N}, c! : \mathbb{N} \mid a? \le 5 \ \wedge \ c! = 2 \times a?].$$

So $b?$ is free: it may be either $\bot$ or some natural number. This is a form of non-determinism we seldom want, because it is not determined whether the processor will consume a token from connector $b?$ or not. If we want to exclude this, we have to add, for instance, $b? \ne \bot$ in the predicate of the schema definition. Suppose now that the predicate were to be extended by a conjunct:

$$b? = \frac{60}{a?}.$$

In this case it would also be unclear whether a token via connector $b?$ should be consumed or not, because if $a? = 0$ then $b? = \bot$ and in all other cases ($a?$ is 1, 2, 3, 4 or 5) $b?$ is properly defined.

In general it is undecidable whether a token will be consumed or produced for a connector or not, because it depends on the evaluation of an arbitrary function. An example that shows the role of $\bot$ in a schema is a modification of the example above:

$$[a? : \mathbb{N}, b? : \mathbb{N}, c! : \mathbb{N} \mid a? = \bot \ \wedge \ b? = \bot \ \wedge \ c! = \bot].$$

This schema denotes a set of exactly one tuple:

$$\{a \mapsto \bot, b \mapsto \bot, c \mapsto \bot\},$$

however this tuple means that there is neither consumption nor production of tokens, so it is an incorrect definition of a processor relation, because the domain of the (only) firing rule in the processor relation is empty!

To be safe, it is wise to specify the consumption/production properties of a processor explicitly; for example

$$x? \neq \perp \ \wedge \ y? \neq \perp \ \wedge \ (z! = \perp \vee w! = \perp)$$

for an input complete processor with two input and two output connectors that gives output to one connector at most.

Next we consider the time stamps and identities in the processor relation and give a schema for the example of figure 29.5. For the variables representing the identity and time stamp of a token we have the following types, $ID$ and $TIME$, where $ID = \mathbb{N}^*$ and $TIME = \mathbb{Q}$. (Remember that we may use sequences of natural numbers as representations for token identities and that the parent function $F$ assigns to an identity its parent by deleting the last element of the identity.) We do not allow that the identity and time variable are defined if the corresponding value variable is undefined, i.e. $\perp$. The schema definition for the example of figure 29.5 is displayed in figure 29.6. The function $f$ defines for task $t?$ the production time. The type $CHAR$ is the basic type of characters. The function $max$ should be defined in a way that ignores $\perp$. (The definition of $\neq$ is obvious.) The example of figure 29.5 shows that it is cumbersome to specify the time stamps and identities in this way, particularly if we do not need to use the identities or the time stamps. Therefore we recommend dividing the specification into two schemas: one dealing with the values only and one schema for the identities and the time stamps. If the identities or time stamps play no role, then the last schema can be generated automatically. In our example we would then have a schema $P_{val}$ and a schema $P_{id-time}$ and the total schema would become:

$$P := P_{val} \ \wedge \ P_{id-time}.$$

Schema $P_{val}$ has six variables, namely only the variables that deal with values and the first four predicates. Schema $P_{id-time}$ has 16 variables: the variables that deal with time stamps and identities and the value variables that are used to determine them, further it has the last five predicates. We call $P_{id-time}$ the *auxiliary* schema of $P_{val}$, which is called the *main* schema. Schema $P_{val}$ is displayed in figure 29.7.

As we have seen in this example, in many cases we determine the time stamp of output tokens by means of a *delay* with respect to the transition time. The transition time is always available as the maximum of the time stamps of the consumed tokens. Instead of specifying the time stamps of the produced tokens

Fig. 29.6. Schema definition for the example of the production system

$$
\begin{array}{l}
\hline
\quad P \\
\hline
t? : \mathbb{N} \\
e? : CHAR \\
m? : CHAR \\
e! : CHAR \\
q! : \mathbb{N} \\
r! : \mathbb{N} \\
t_i?, e_i?, e_i!, m_i?, q_i!, r_i! : ID \\
t_t?, e_t?, e_t!, m_t?, q_i!, r_i! : TIME \\
\hline
\end{array}
$$

if $t? = 1 \ \wedge \ e? = \perp \ \wedge \ m? = 'C'$ then $e! = r! = \perp \ \wedge \ q! = 1$
else
if $t? = 2 \ \wedge \ e? = \perp \ \wedge \ m? = 'D'$ then $e! = q! = \perp \ \wedge \ r! = 2$
else
if $t? = 3 \ \wedge \ e? = 'A' \ \wedge \ m? = 'C'$ then $e! = 'A' \ \wedge \ q! = 3 \ \wedge \ r! = \perp$
else
if $t? = 4 \ \wedge \ e? = 'B' \ \wedge \ m? = 'D'$ then $e! = 'B' \ \wedge \ q! = \perp \ \wedge \ r! = 4$
else true fi fi fi fi
$h := max(\{t_t?, e_t?, m_t?\}) + f(t?) : \mathbb{Q}$
if $e! \neq \perp$ then $F(e_i!) = t_i? \ \wedge \ e_t! = h$ else $e_i! = e_t! = \perp$ fi
if $q! \neq \perp$ then $F(q_i!) = t_i? \ \wedge \ q_t! = h$ else $q_i! = q_t! = \perp$ fi
if $r! \neq \perp$ then $F(r_i!) = t_i? \ \wedge \ r_t! = h$ else $r_i! = r_t! = \perp$ fi
$q_i! \neq \perp \Rightarrow q_i! \neq e_i!$
$r_i! \neq \perp \Rightarrow r_i! \neq e_i!$

Fig. 29.7. Main schema $P_{val}$ for the example of the production system

$$
\begin{array}{l}
\hline
\quad P_{val} \\
\hline
t? : \mathbb{N} \\
e? : CHAR \\
m? : CHAR \\
e! : CHAR \\
q! : \mathbb{N} \\
r! : \mathbb{N} \\
\hline
\end{array}
$$

if $t? = 1 \ \wedge \ e? = \perp \ \wedge \ m? = 'C'$ then $e! = r! = \perp \ \wedge \ q! = 1$
else
if $t? = 2 \ \wedge \ e? = \perp \ \wedge \ m? = 'D'$ then $e! = q! = \perp \ \wedge \ r! = 2$
else
if $t? = 3 \ \wedge \ e? = 'A' \ \wedge \ m? = 'C'$ then $e! = 'A' \ \wedge \ q! = 3 \ \wedge \ r! = \perp$
else
if $t? = 4 \ \wedge \ e? = 'B' \ \wedge \ m? = 'D'$ then $e! = 'B' \ \wedge \ q! = \perp \ \wedge \ r! = 4$
else true fi fi fi fi

in the auxiliary schema, we write in the main schema an expression of the form

$$x_t! = Trans\,Time + delay,$$

where $x!$ is an output variable, $Trans\,Time$ is a value equal to the maximum of the time stamps of the consumed tokens and $delay$ is a term that evaluates to a non-negative element of $\mathbb{Q}$. So we introduce in an underhand way a *time variable* $Trans\,Time$ into the main schema. It is easy to transform such a "polluted" main schema into a correct one by transferring this predicate to the auxiliary schema in the right form.

The choice of the input token that was used for identification of the output tokens was rather arbitrary, in the example above. The only thing that counts is that there really is an input token for the connector.

There are cases in which it is important to use the identities of tokens also in the *values* of tokens. Sometimes a simplex in the complex of a token represents an identity, for example an order number or a transaction identity. In these cases it is very convenient that we have always available a source of new identities, namely the token identities. Then we may give an output variable $y!$ an identity as value provided that it has *ID* as type. Formally this requires a quite complex predicate which includes $F(y!) = x_i?$ as a conjunct and in which $x_i?$ is the input token that is used for the generation of new identities. The rest of the predicate states that all other children of $x_i?$, either used as the identity of an output token or as a value, should be different. It is not difficult to express this, but it can be generated automatically. Therefore we introduce another keyword like $Trans\,Time$ above, namely *New*, and use it as follows:

$$y! = New.$$

A specification with these two keywords in it can be transformed into a "correct" one.

If we use identities as values then we can do more than just comparing them by means of $=$ and $\neq$. It is sometimes interesting to check whether one identity is a prefix of another or whether they have a common prefix. These questions arise in *object oriented modeling*.

Next we consider the *processor characteristics*. The processor in the example above is neither input nor output *complete*, which is easy to verify by the occurrence of $\perp$ in the schema. The processor is not *total* either, since there are several combinations of values of input tokens for which there is no firing rule. However, the processor is *functional*. Functionality also includes that if a processor can fire with for example $n$ specific input tokens then it cannot fire with more tokens, these $n$ being included. For a complete and functional processor we can find a function that determines the processor relation. Consider for example a processor with input connectors $a?$, $b?$ and $c?$ and output connectors $x!$ and $y!$. Then there should be a function $f$ such that

$$x! = \pi_1(f(a?, b?, c?)) \ \wedge \ y! = \pi_2(f(a?, b?, c?)).$$

In general the predicate in the main schema of a processor relation has the following format:

$\quad$ if $\ p_1(x_1?, \ldots, x_m?)\ $ then $\ q_1(x_1?, \ldots, x_m?, y_1!, \ldots, y_n!)\ $ else

$\quad \ldots \ldots \ldots$

$\quad$ if $\ p_k(x_1?, \ldots, x_m?)\ $ then $\ q_k(x_1?, \ldots, x_m?, y_1!, \ldots, y_n!)\ $ else false

$\quad$ fi $\ldots$ fi.

Here the Boolean functions $p_1, \ldots, p_k$ are the preconditions and the Boolean functions $q_1, \ldots, q_k$ are the postconditions.

If at least one precondition evaluates to *true* for an input variable equal to $\bot$, then the processor is not input complete. If the processor relation is functional, the postconditions can be transformed into the following form:

$$q_i(x_1?, \ldots, x_m?, y_1!, \ldots, y_n!) =$$

$$y_1! = f_{i,1}(x_1?, \ldots, x_m?) \ \wedge \ \ldots \ \wedge \ y_n! = f_{i,n}(x_1?, \ldots, x_m?).$$

In that case the processor specification is *executable*.

# 30

# References and exercises for part V

The *specification language* is very close to the language Z. The main difference is that we do not consider a function signature as a type. Further our language has a constructive (and therefore executable) subset, i.e. it is a *functional language*. The main literature for Z is [Spivey, 1987] for the semantics, [Spivey, 1989] for the language and the toolkit, and [Wordsworth, 1992; Hayes, 1987; Woodcock and Loomes, 1988] for the specification methodology, including the verification of properties. The language Z is close to the language of VDM, *see* [Jones, 1990; Andrews and Ince, 1991]. In the VDM literature stepwise refinement and verification is emphasized.

An important aspect of specification is the recursive definition of functions, which is the key issue of *functional programming*. Good books on functional programming are: [Glaser *et al.*, 1984], [Meyer, 1990] and [Wilkstrom, 1987]. A good reference for *type theory* in combination with functional programming is [Thompson, 1991]. Type systems with tuple types usually adopt Cardelli's method for polymorphy (*see* [Cardelli and Wegner, 1985]). We do not need this approach because we have the $\bowtie$ operator for types. Functional languages are based on *lambda calculus* and the main reference is [Barendregt, 1984]. For set theory and predicate logic *see* [Enderton, 1972], [Enderton, 1977].

## Exercises for part V

(1)  Prove theorem 25.3.

(2)  Prove the remaining cases of theorem 25.5.

(3)  Prove the following equality in schema calculus:

$$\exists\, x : T \mid p \bullet [x : T, y_1 : S_1, \ldots, y_n : S_n \mid q] =$$
$$([x : T \mid p] \wedge [x : T, y_1 : S_1, \ldots, y_n : S_n \mid q])\backslash(x)$$

371

(4)      Give type definitions to represent the nested relational model in the specification language.

(5)      Prove that the function *dom* (*see* appendix C) satisfies the declaration

$$\text{signature } dom : \mathbb{F}(\$_1 \times \$_2) \Rightarrow \mathbb{F}(\$_1)$$
$$\text{predicate } \forall f : \mathbb{F}(\$_1 \times \$_2) \bullet \forall x : \$_1 \bullet \exists y : \$_2 \bullet$$
$$(x, y) \Leftrightarrow x \in dom(f).$$

(6)      Give a declaration and a definition for a function *update* that assigns to a binary relation $f$ with signature $\mathbb{F}(\$_1 \times \$_2)$ and two elements $x \in \$_1$ and $y \in \$_2$ a new binary relation $r'$, which contains the pair $(x, y)$ and satisfies

$$\forall v : \$_1 \bullet \forall w : \$_2 \bullet x \neq v \Rightarrow ((v, w) \in r \Leftrightarrow (v, w) \in r')$$

$$\wedge$$

$$\forall w : \$_1 \bullet (x, w) \in r' \Rightarrow w = y.$$

Prove that the result of the function *update* is a functional binary relation if it is applied to a functional binary relation.

(7)      Give a declaration and a definition of the function *In* that assigns to two integers $k$ and $l$ the set of all integers $i$ that satisfy $k \leq i \leq l$.

(8)      Give a definition for the function *reverse* that computes the reverse of a sequence.

(9)      Give a definition for the function *length* that computes the length of a sequence.

(10)      Give a definition for the function *setrange* that computes the set of all values occurring in a sequence.

(11)      Give more efficient constructions for the functions *forall* and *exists* defined in the toolkit.

(12)      Give a declaration and a definition for a function that assigns to an arbitrary singular value a suitable type expression. (Hint: represent a singular value and a type expression as a sequence.)

(13)      Give declarations and definitions of two functions that compute respectively the union and the intersection, of the elements of a set of sets.

(14)      Give declarations and definitions for two functions that compute the mean and standard deviation of a frequency distribution, i.e. the arguments are of the type $\mathbb{F}(\mathbb{Q} \times \mathbb{N})$ and have unique first components.

(15)      Consider the Car Rental Company of exercise 6 in part III again. The rental prices are based on the following rules. There are three types of cars: compact, midsize and fullsize. The rental price of a car is a *basic*

*day price* (depending on the type of car) multiplied by a *daily discount (factor)* for the length of the rental period and by the number of days of the rental. Further, a *drop off charge* has to be paid if the car is delivered by the client to another station of CRC. The drop off charge is equal to the basic day price if the car is returned to a station not further away than 1000 km and two times the basic day price if it is delivered at a farther station.

There are three exceptions to this rule.

(a) If the car is rented for a longer period (i.e. longer than 15 days) and it is not a compact car, then the drop off charge for long distance stations (i.e. more than 1000 km away) is only one basic day price.

(b) If a fullsize car is rented for at least 6 days, but no longer than 15 days, then the drop off charge for long distance is also only one basic day price.

(c) If a fullsize car is rented for at least 16 days and it is returned to a station not further away than 1000 km, no drop off charge has to be paid.

There is no *daily discount* if a car is rented for less than 6 days. If a compact car is rented for a period longer than 5 days and shorter than 16 days, the daily discount is 10% if the car is returned to the rental station, 5% if it is returned to another station not further than 1000 km and there is no discount if it is returned to a station further than 1000 km.

If a compact car is rented for a long period (longer than 15 days), then the discount is 20% if the car is returned to the rental station, 10% if it is returned to another station not further away than 1000 km and 5% if it is returned to a station further away than 1000 km.

For midsize and fullsize cars rented for a period longer than 5 days and at most less than 15 days, the discount is 20% if the car is returned to the rental station, 15% if it is returned to another station not further away than 1000 km and 10% in case it is returned to a station further than 1000 km. For for fullsize cars that are rented for more than 15 days the discounts for a rental period of between 6 and 16 days are increased by 15% and for midsize cars by 10%.

The basic daily price of a compact car is $30, of a midsize car $50 and of a fullsize car $70.

Give a specification for the processor that computes the rental price.

(All the functions in the toolkit can be considered as exercises as well.)

# Glossary

In this glossary the most important terminology of the book is collected. Not included are terms referring to modeling problems (such as "broadcasting") and standard mathematical concepts (such as "function").

**active objects:** objects in the context of object oriented methods. They are called o-objects in this book.

**activity network:** an actor model in which each place is connected to exactly two processors; to one as input place and to the other as output place. It is a special kind of conflict free net.

**actor:** an active component of a system. Its activity consists of the consumption and production of (passive) objects called tokens. In terms of Petri nets an actor is a (possibly open) sub-net. An actor can be decomposed, unless it is a processor; the latter is also known as an *elementary actor*.

**actor framework:** the framework in which actors are formalized.

**actor model** : an element of the actor framework. Formally it consists of a flat net model, an object model, a processor relation and some auxiliary sets and functions.

**antithetic variates technique:** a method for reducing the variance of an estimator in simulation experiments (*see also* the control variates technique).

**applicative order reduction:** the strategy of evaluating all arguments of a function before the function value is evaluated. (For lazy functions there is another strategy.)

**association simplex class:** a simplex class with the property that all relationship classes with it as domain class form a minimal key constraint provided that it is not a range class for other simplex classes.

**attribute:** a label for a value in a tuple, tuple type, schema or framework. In the relational data model "attribute" has the same meaning.

**attribute domain:** the value type associated with an attribute in the relational data model.

**attribute simplex class:** a simplex class that is not the domain class of any relationship class.

**automated systems:** discrete dynamic system consisting of a physical system and an automated information system that controls it.

**autonomous behavior:** the set of all traces of a system that can be produced by the transition law of the system.

**autonomous trace:** a trace of the autonomous behavior of a system. An autonomous trace is called *maximal* if it is infinite or if it is a deadlock.

**automaton:** a finite state machine.

**basic type:** a given set with finite or countably many elements. Typical examples of basic types are the sets of natural, integer and rational numbers, Boolean values and Ascii characters. The values of basic types are called *constants*.

**bisimilar:** *see* similarity

**bounded net:** an actor model with the property that the maximal number of tokens in each reachable state is bounded. For example $k$-*bounded* means that the maximal number of tokens is less or equal to $k$ in each reachable state. A 1-bounded net is called a *safe net*.

**business system::** a discrete dynamic system in which tokens or objects have an economic value. The total value of the consumed tokens should be less or equal to the total value of the produced tokens, in each transition of a processor.

**canonical form of a processor relation:** a schema for the processor relation in which there is a variable such that each firing rule corresponds to one value of this variable. This variable is called the *firing variable*.

**cardinality constraint:** a relationship constraint that restricts the number of relationships in which a simplex is involved. There are four kinds: totality, functionality, injectivity and surjectivity.

**channel:** a place that may contain an arbitrary number of tokens. It is used to model communication by means of the exchange of tokens.

**class model:** a 7-tuple consisting of the names of simplex classes, relationship classes, complex classes and standard constraints. It is part of an object model.

**classical Petri net:** a timeless and valueless actor model. It is in fact a Petri net in its original form (*see also* Petri net).

**closed actor:** an actor without connectors.

**completeness:** a processor characteristic which states that a processor always consumes tokens via all its input connectors (*input completeness*) or produces via all its output connectors (*output completeness*). A processor that is both input and output complete is simply called *complete*.

**complex** or **complex object:** an object composed of simplexes and relationships between simplexes. Complexes are the "molecules" of a model.

**complex class:** the set of all complexes of a certain kind, i.e. complexes having the same structure.

**conceptual model:** *see* model

**conflict free net:** an actor model whose flat net model has the property that each place is an input place for at most one processor. A conflict free net is a special kind of free choice net.

**congruential method:** a method for generating (pseudo) random numbers.

**connector:** a link from an actor to either a place or a connector of a containing actor.

**constant:** a value of a basic type.

**constraint:** a restriction on a set. A *dynamic* constraint is a restriction on the autonomous behavior of a system. A *static* constraint is either a restriction on a state space, which is called a *global* constraint, or a restriction on a complex class, which is called a *local* constraint.

**construction model:** a model of a system that can be used as a blueprint for the system.

**constructor:** an operator for building values out of given values or types out of given types, called a *value* constructor or a *type* constructor respectively. Typical value constructors are: set constructor, row constructor, sequence constructor and tuple constructor. For types there are similar constructors. Values are syntactically defined by means of terms.

**consumption function:** *see* flow function

**context actor:** an actor that represents an environment. It will usually not be decomposed and in simulation experiments is replaced by some random mechanism.

**context diagram:** a graphical representation of a part of a hierarchical net model showing context actors.

**control variates technique:** a method for reducing the variance of estimators in simulation experiments (*see also* antithetic variates technique).

**coverability tree of an actor model:** a tree with marking-like functions as nodes. These functions give a natural number or $\infty$ to each pair consisting of a place and a filter value. An edge between two nodes means that there is a possible transition. The tree is finite and contains information on the reachability of states with a certain marking: for each reachable state with marking $m$ there is a node $n$ in the coverability tree with $n \geq m$, component-wise.

**data oriented approach:** a guideline to develop an actor model, which starts with an object model.

**dead set:** a set of places such that all processors producing for these places, also consume from these places. In the Petri net literature such a set is usually called a *deadlock* (*see also* deadlock and trap).

**deadlock:** a (finite) trace without subsequent events, according to the transition law. There is also another meaning: *see* dead set.

**discrete dynamic systems:** a system the state of which changes over time but in each finite time interval the number of state changes is at most countably infinite. A (conceptual) model of a discrete dynamic system is a *transition system*.

**domain class:** the left-hand side of a relationship class, i.e. all relationships of this class have simplexes from this simplex class as left element. In simplex diagrams it is the tail of the arrow that represents the relationship class.

**domain type:** the domain of a monomorphic function.

**eagerness:** a property of transition systems; it means that an event with minimal event time is always chosen (if this is possible).

**eager autonomous behavior:** the set of all eager traces produced by the transition law of a system.

**earliest arrival time:** *see* interval-timed actor model

**elementary actor:** another term for a processor.

**entity-relationship data model:** an object framework that is closely related to the object framework of this book.

**entity simplex class:** any simplex class that is neither an attribute simplex class nor an association simplex class.

**equivalent firing rules:** firing rules with the same values or complexes for each connector.

**evaluation function $\epsilon$:** a function that maps language expressions to their semantics: i.e. type expressions to types, value expressions to values, function expressions to functions and schema expressions to sets of tuples.

**event:** the occurrence of a state transition to another or the same state. It is formally defined as a pair consisting of a state and the time point at which the state is entered, the *event time*. An event caused by the transition law is called an *internal* event and an event caused by some external influence is called an *external* event.

**event set:** the set of all possible events of a transition system.

**event time:** *see* event

**exclusion constraint:** a relationship constraint that forbids a simplex to be related to simplexes in different simplex classes. There are *domain* and *range* exclusion constraints. An exclusion constraint is determined by a set of relationships having a common domain or range class.

**executable model:** a complete actor model in which each place has a type and each processor has a schema without quantors.

**executable specification:** an executable model.

**filter:** a function that assigns to all complexes in an object universe a value in a *filter set*. The *Petri filter* gives all complexes the same value. The *identity filter* gives all complexes their own value. Filters are used to identify tokens.

**finite mathematical value** *see* value

**finite-state machine** or **automaton:** an abstract machine that can be defined as a finite-state machine net.

**firing assignment:** a function that assigns to processors a firing rule for execution. A firing rule is called *applicable* if it could cause a legal transition.

**firing rule:** an element (or tuple) of a processor relation. A firing rule relates consumed and produced tokens when the processor executes or *fires* with this rule. An element of a firing rule consists of an identity, a complex (or value) and a time stamp.

**firing sequence:** a finite sequence of pairs of a processor and a firing rule for this processor. A firing sequence and an initial event determine a trace of the same length.

**firing variable** *see* canonical form

**flat net model:** a 6-tuple that defines the graphical structure of an actor model without non-elementary actors, i.e. the names of places, processors, connectors and their relations. A flat net model is a special kind of hierarchical net model.

**flow balance:** a set of equations, one for each firing rule of a processor, in which the weighted sum of the flow function over the places and the filter values is equal to zero (see transition balance).

**flow function:** a function that assigns to a 4-tuple consisting of a place, a filter value, a processor and a firing rule, the balance of the produced and consumed tokens in that place with that filter value. It is the balance if the processor executes this firing rule. The similar function that only counts the produced tokens is called the *production function* and the similar function that only counts the consumed tokens is called the *consumption function*.

**flow matrix:** a representation of a flow function for the case of a Petri filter. It is a matrix with a column for each processor and a row for each place whose entries are the balance of the number of tokens in that place, if the processor executes.

**formalism:** a pair consisting of a language and a mathematical framework; the semantics of the language are expressed in the mathematical framework. In other literature a formalism often has a third component: an *inference mechanism*, to make deductions of the formulas of the language.

**framework** or **mathematical framework:** this is formally defined as a set of functions with a common domain. The domain values are called *attributes*. Each function in a framework is called a model. A framework is used to define a kind of model. In the book three frameworks are considered: the *transition systems framework*, the *object framework* and the *actor framework*.

**free choice net:** an actor model in whose flat net model every place is either an input place for only one processor, or it is the input place for more than one processors each of which has only this input place. There are several kinds of free choice nets: conflict free nets, state machine nets and activity networks.

**free constraint** *see* standard constraint

**free value universe:** the set of all values that can be formed out of the constants and ⊥, by application of the value constructors. This set also contains values that we do not want to consider (*see* value universe).

**function universe:** the set of all functions from the value universe to itself.

**functional data model:** an object framework. An object model in this framework is called a *functional object model*. It is in fact an object model with the property that all relationship classes satisfy the functionality constraint. This framework is also called the *irreducible data model*.

**functional dependence:** a kind of constraint in the relational data model. It is similar to a key constraint of the object framework.

**functional model:** an abstract description of a system that captures the behavior of the system.

**functionality:** this has two meanings, one for cardinality constraints and one for processor characteristics. A relationship is called *functional* if at most one simplex of the range class is associated with each simplex of the domain class. (In each instance the relation is a, possibly partial, function.) A processor relation is called *functional* if the produced tokens are functionally dependent on the consumed tokens, i.e. the processor behaves deterministically.

**global constraint:** a constraint for states of a system. The other constraints, called *local* constraints restrict complexes only.

**graph of a function:** the set of pairs of which the function consists. Often a function is considered to be the same as its graph. Sometimes a function is considered as a pair consisting of a name and a graph. In the latter case two different functions can have the same graph and two functions with the same name can have different graphs.

**hierarchical net model:** a 10-tuple that defines a graphical representation of an actor model including non-elementary actors (*see also* flat net model). A hierarchical net model determines precisely one flat net model.

**identity filter** *see* filter

**induced transition system:** the transition system that is defined by an actor model.

**information system:** a discrete dynamic system in which all tokens carry complexes that represent information. An information system is always part of another discrete dynamic system, called the target system, and it has the task of supporting the control of that system.

**inheritance constraint:** a standard constraint that relates simplexes of different classes in such a way that one can be considered as a specialization of the other, which means that the specialized one "inherits" the properties (i.e. the relationships) of the other. An inheritance constraint is determined by a set of inheritance relationships.

**inheritance relationship:** a relationship that is total, functional and injective.

**initial event:** the first event of a system, i.e. the event that brings the system "alive".

**injectivity:** a cardinality constraint requiring that each simplex of the domain simplex class is related to at most one simplex of the range class of a relationship.

**instance:** an element of a set; the term is used for elements of classes, types and frameworks. The instances are called objects, values and models, respectively.

**instance model:** the part of an object model that determines the sets of all possible simplexes and complexes, in particular the functions *sim* and *com*.

**intelligent information system:** an information system that incorporates knowledge and that supports persons with creative work such as designing, planning and diagnosis.

**inter-organizational information system:** an information system that supports the business communications between two or more autonomous organizations.

**interval-timed actor model:** a kind of actor model in which all time stamps are replaced by *time intervals*. The meaning of the time interval of a token is that the token arrives in a place during the time interval. The model is used to derive upper and lower bounds on arrival times of tokens in (ordinary) actor models. In particular the *earliest* and *latest* arrival times of tokens are determined using the interval-timed actor model.

**invariance properties:** properties of the behavior of an actor model. Two important invariance properties are *place invariants* and *transition invariants*.

**inverse transformation method:** a method to generate samples from an arbitrary probability distribution.

**key constraint:** a relationship constraint that requires that simplexes are uniquely determined in each instance by their relationships. There are two kinds of key constraint: *domain* and *range* key constraints. A key constraint is determined by a set of relationship classes with a common domain or range class.

**latest arrival time:** *see* interval-timed actor model

**lazy function:** a non-strict function with more than one argument and with the property that the function value is already determined if some of the arguments are bound by values. Function applications can be evaluated by first evaluating sufficient, but not necessarily all, arguments.

**life cycle:** the interval of the time domain in which a system or an o-object is existent.

**liveness:** a property of processors in which all finite autonomous traces can be extended to at least one autonomous trace for which the processor executes after the given prefix.

**livelock:** a system exhibiting this phenomenon is making infinitely many transitions in finite time.

**local constraint:** a constraint working on a complex class. (*see also* global constraint.)

**map** or **mapping:** a function with a finite domain. In the specification language it is considered as a value, while other functions are not considered as values.

**marking:** one function that assigns to a state another function that gives for each place and each filter value the number of tokens in that place with that value.

**maximal autonomous behavior:** the set of all maximal autonomous traces of a system.

**maximal exclusion constraint:** an exclusion constraint that does not contain a proper subset that itself forms an exclusion constraint.

**m-complex class:** a complex class used in the object oriented approach. The m-complexes are considered as *messages* that are sent from one o-object to another.

**measurement actor:** an actor that is not part of the real system. Its role is to collect and analyze information over the real system. Measurement actors only play a role in simulation experiments.

**memoryless a transition law:** any event depends only on the previous event and not on the rest of the history.

**method:** this has two meanings, first a way of working in systems engineering, second, an operation performed by an o-object, which is called an *o-object method*. A method in the first sense is either a *guideline* or a *technique*.

**method of successive approximations:** a computational method for determining a recursive function by iterated application of the recursion operator (*see also* recursion operator).

**minimal key constraint:** a key constraint that does not have a proper subset of relationship classes that itself forms a key constraint.

**minimal support invariant:** a non-negative place invariant such that no other non-negative place invariant has a smaller *support*, i.e. it is a set of places where the weight is positive.

**model:** a system that has so much similarity with another system (here called a "target system") that conclusions drawn from the model are also valid for the target system. The model should be easier to analyze than the target system. We distinguish *conceptual* or *abstract* models, *executable* models and *physical* models. The first kind exists only on paper or in the mind. The second kind is a computer program that simulates the modeled system. The third kind of model is beyond the scope of this book. Formally, an abstract model is an element of a framework.

**modeling:** the activity of constructing models.

**modeling language:** a language for expressing models.

**monitoring information system:** an information system that *records* events of its target system to maintain an up-to-date image of the state of the target system, *triggers* the target system if the recorded state of the target system satisfies some condition and produces *reports* of the state of the target system.

**monomorphic function:** a function with a specific type as domain and another specific type as range (*see also* polymorphic functions).

**monotonous transition system:** a transition system with a transition law such that for all finite traces any event has an event time greater than or equal to the event time of the previous event of the trace.

**nested relational data model:** an object framework. It is a generalization of the relational data model in which attribute values may be relations themselves. A model in this framework is determined by a (nested relational) schema and a set of instances.

**normal form of a set:** a representation of a set in which all elements are arranged in ascending order.

**o-actor:** the actor that represents the life cycle of an o-object. Its flat net model has the structure of a state machine net.

**o-complex class:** the complex class of an o-object. Each o-object is represented by one o-complex.

**o-object:** this refers to the concept of "object" in the sense of object oriented design methods. An o-object is a subsystem with active and passive components. The active component is an o-actor and the passive components are o-complexes.

**o-object class:** a triple consisting of an o-complex class, an o-actor and a set of m-complex classes (one class for each message type).

**o-object method:** another term for the processor inside an o-actor.

**object:** a term for a passive component of a system. We distinguish simple objects or simplexes, complex objects or complexes and tokens, which are "containers" for complexes.

**object framework:** the framework in which simplexes, relationships and complexes are formalized.

**object life cycle:** the structure of an actor used as an o-actor.

**object model:** an element of an object framework. It consists of a class model, an instance model and a set of constraints. Another term for object model is *data model*.

**object oriented approach:** a guideline to develop actor models, which uses the object oriented paradigm of o-objects.

**object oriented data model:** a framework for data models. (The object framework of this book satisfies many but not all requirements of an object oriented data model.)

**object universe:** the set of all complexes of an object model.

**occurrence graph:** a graph the nodes of which are the states that can be reached from a set of initial nodes. There is an edge between two nodes if there is a transition from the first to the second node (i.e. state).

**office information system:** an information system that supports the work of persons in offices by the routine processing of information.

**open actor:** an actor with a non-empty set of (input or output) connectors.

**overloading:** the phenomenon whereby one name is used for two or more functions with different domains.

**path:** a (partial) function from a time domain to the state space of a system. The graph of it is called a *state-time diagram*.

**parent function:** a function that assigns to an identifier the identifier from which it is derived. Parent functions are used to create identities for tokens.

**partial function:** a function that is not defined for all its domain values.

**Petri filter** *see* filter

**Petri net:** an actor-like model without hierarchy, in which tokens do not have identities, complexes or time stamps. The framework of classical Petri nets is the origin of the actor framework and several other frameworks (*see also* classical Petri net).

**place invariant:** a function that assigns to a pair consisting of a place and a filter value a natural number as *weight*. The weight function has to satisfy the flow balance. If all weights are non-negative it is called a *non-negative place invariant* and if all weights are positive it is called a *positive place invariant*. A set of place invariants is called *independent* if no element of the set is a linear combination of other elements of the set (*see also* place invariant property).

**place invariant property:** a behavioral property that states that all reachable states have the same weighted marking (*see also* place invariant).

**polymorphic function:** a function with more than one domain and range type. Domain-range pairs are defined by means of type expressions containing type variables (*see also* signature).

**predicate:** a Boolean function.

**prefix of a sequence:** the sequence that is obtained by deleting all elements after some point in the sequence.

**prefix-closed:** this describes a set of sequences such that for all sequences in the set the prefixes also belong to the set.

**primary key:** a set of attributes in a relational schema belonging to the relational data model. These attributes identify the tuples in a relational instance.

**process oriented approach:** a guideline to develop an actor model, which starts with a hierarchical net model.

**processor:** an elementary or "atomic" actor, one that cannot be decomposed.

**processor characteristics:** these are the properties of processors. These properties are often determined before the processor relation is fully specified. The processor characteristics are: totality, functionality and (input and output) completeness.

**processor relation:** a relation that relates consumed tokens to produced tokens in one execution of a processor. The elements of a processor relation are called *firing rules*.

**production function:** *see* flow function

**prototype:** an executable model of an information system.

**range class:** the right-hand side of a relationship class (*see also* domain class).

**range type:** the range of a monomorphic function.

**reachable state:** a state that can be reached from an initial state by the autonomous behavior of a system, i.e. the state occurs in some event of an autonomous trace.

**recursion operator:** a function, determined by a recursive equation, with the function universe as domain and range. The function defined by the recursive equation is a fix point of the recursion operator.

**recursive function:** a function defined by an equation in which the function is the unknown. (Note that the term is confusing because it is a characteristic of the definition of the function and not of the function itself.) There are special kinds of recursive functions, *linear recursive functions* and *primitive recursive functions*, and special methods for computing them.

**referential integrity:** a kind of constraint in the relational data model, similar to surjectivity in the object framework of this book.

**regular value** *see* singular value

**relational data model:** an object framework. A model in this framework is called a *relational model* and it consists of a relational schema and a set of relational instances.

**relationship:** a pair of simplexes with a label, the latter being the relationship class.

**relationship class:** the name for all relationships of a certain kind.

**relationship constraint:** one of the standard constraints. There are three kinds of relationship constraint: cardinality, key and exclusion constraints (*see also* the latter).

**root simplex** *see* tree constraint

**safe net** *see* bounded net

**schema:** a restricted tuple type, i.e. a set of tuples that satisfy some predicate. So a schema is a set of functions having the same set of attributes as domain and satisfying some predicate. Schemas are used to define processor relations or state spaces. In the *relational data model* the term schema is used differently. There it has the meaning of a class model and the function *sim* of an instance model.

**schema operator:** an operator that assigns to one or two schemas a new schema. Such operators are used to define schemas in a bottom-up approach.

**schema universe:** the set of all schemas without type variables.

**script:** a complete specification. It consists of type definitions, value definitions, function definitions (and declarations) and schema definitions.

**serializability:** the property that an event in which two or more processors execute can be split into two or more events which have the same final state, if these events occur in sequence.

**signature:** this has two, related, meanings, a syntactical and a semantic meaning. The syntactical meaning of signature refers to a pair of type expressions that may contain type variables: the first component determines the domain type and the second one the range type of a function. The semantic meaning of signature is a finite set of pairs of types. The semantics of a signature according to the first meaning is a signature according to the second meaning.

**similarity:** the property that one transition system mimics the behavior of another transition system with respect to some binary relation over the event sets of the systems. (The binary relation identifies events of the two systems.) When two transition systems are similar to each other with respect to one binary relation over the event sets, the systems are called *bisimilar*.

**simple singular value** *see* singular value

**simplex** or **simple object:** the smallest kind of (passive) object that is considered. They are the "atoms" of a model. Simplexes represent concrete or abstract entities in the real world, or units of information.

**simplex class:** the set of all simplexes of a certain kind.

**simplex diagram:** a graphical representation of the simplex and the relationship classes of a class model, together with the standard constraints.

**simulation:** the computation of one or more (finite) traces of a system. If there is more than one possible next event, the choice is often made by means of a *random number generator*. Simulation can be considered as experimenting with an executable model of a system.

**singular value:** a *simple singular value* or a value that contains a simple singular value. A simple singular value is a value that does not contain a constant. All other values are called *regular values*.

**specification:** a term used in narrow and in broad sense: in narrow sense it is a definition of a value type or a processor relation and in broad sense it is a synonym for "model".

**standard constraint:** a constraint with a graphical representation in a simplex diagram. It has to be specified in an early stage of the modeling process. There are three kinds of standard constraint: relationship constraints, inheritance constraints and tree constraints. A non-standard constraint is called a *free constraint*.

**state:** the status, stage or configuration in which a system is at some moment in time.

**state space:** the set of all possible states in which a system might be.

**state machine net:** an actor model whose flat net model has the property that each processor has precisely one input place and one output place. It models a *finite-state machine* and it is a special kind of free choice net.

**state trace** *see* trace

**state-time diagram:** the graph of a path, i.e. of a function that gives the state of a system for the moments in the time domain of the system.

**store:** a special place that always contains one token that is always available, i.e. the token's time stamp is never later than the actual time.

**strict function:** a function that evaluates to $\perp$ for all singular values. All other functions are called *non-strict* (*see also* lazy function).

**strongly memoryless transition law:** any event depends only on the previous state.

**suffix-closed:** a set of sequences such that if an infinite sequence belongs to the set then all its (finite) prefixes are in the set.

**surjectivity:** a cardinality constraint that requires that each simplex of the range class is related to at least one simplex of the domain class of a relationship.

**syntax base:** an 8-tuple containing name sets. Each syntax base determines another specification language.

**system:** a term used for a discrete dynamic system or a conceptual model of it, i.e. a transition system. (An actor model specifies a transition system.)

**system composition:** the integration of two systems into one new system. The composition of actor models involves the composition of flat net models and of object models.

**terms:** syntactical entities to define values. There are four kinds of term: *value construction*, the syntactical counterpart of a value constructor, set restriction (called *set term*), function application (called *application*) and map construction (called *map term*).

**time domain:** the set of moments at which we observe a system.

**time stamp:** the attribute of a token that denotes the time from which the token is available for consumption by a processor.

**timed colored Petri nets:** another name for actor models, expressing that actor models are extensions of classical Petri nets.

**timeless actor model:** an actor model in which all time stamps of tokens are equal to zero.

**token:** a container or carrier for a complex. It has a unique identity, a time stamp and a place where the token resides.

**token identity** *see* token

**totality:** this has two meanings, one for cardinality constraints and one for processor characteristics. A relationship class is called *total* if all simplexes in the domain simplex class of the relationship are related to at least one simplex in the range simplex class. A processor is called *total* if there is no precondition for the execution of the processor, i.e. if the processor will consume each combination of offered tokens.

**trace:** a finite or infinite sequence of events. The sequence of projections onto the state of the events of a trace, is called a *state trace*, or simply *trace*.

**transition balance:** a set of equations, one per combination of a place and a filter value, such that the weighted sum of the flow function over the firing rules of the processors equals zero (*see also* flow balance).

**transition invariant:** a weight function that assigns to firing rules of processors a natural number as weight. A transition invariant has to satisfy the transition balance. It is used in a transition invariant property.

**transition invariant property:** is a behavioral property that states that a system returns to a state with the original marking if a certain firing sequence occurs (*see also* transition invariant).

**transition law:** a set-valued function that assigns to a finite trace the set of all possible *next* events. A *deterministic* transition law has at most one next event for each finite trace.

**transition law relation:** a binary relation over the event set of a transition system. It is used to characterize a memoryless transition law. (*see also* transition relation.)

**transition relation:** a binary relation over the states of a transition system. It is used to characterize a strongly memoryless transition law (*see also* transition law relation).

**transition system:** a pair consisting of an event set and a transition law. A transition system is a (conceptual) model of a discrete dynamic system.

**transition time:** the time of the earliest possible event in a state, according to the transition law of the system.

**trap:** a set of places with the property that all processors that consume tokens from these places also produce for these places (*see also* dead set).

**tree constraint:** a standard constraint for complex classes that requires all simplexes in a complex from a class so constrained are connected by a path of relationships to one specific simplex in the complex, called the *root simplex*.

**tuple:** a row, each element of which is labeled by an attribute. Formulated differently, a function with an attribute set as domain (*see also* tuple type).

**tuple join:** a constructor for compatible tuple types (It is the same constructor as the "join" in the relation algebra).

**tuple type:** the set of all tuples with the same domain. Two tuple types are called *equivalent* if they only differ in the order of their attributes. They are called *compatible* if they have the same types for the same attributes.

**type:** the set of all (finite mathematical) values with the same structure. There are some given basic types and countably many constructed types.

**type checking:** the activity of checking the correctness of the definitions and use of types in a script. There are two ways of type checking: *static type checking* and *dynamic type checking*. The first kind is performed on a script without evaluation of expressions, while the second kind needs expression evaluation.

**type expression:** an expression that determines one or more types.

**type function $\tau$:** this assigns to well-typed terms a type.

**type variable:** a syntactical entity that may be replaced by any type in each type expression.

**type universe:** the set of all types.

**universal complex class:** the complex class formed by all simplex classes and all relationship classes of one (actor) model.

**validation:** the activity of checking whether a system has certain properties by means of simulation experiments. In particular if the properties are formulated informally, as for requirements, validation is all that can be done.

**value universe:** the set of all values that belong to some type. It is a subset of the free value universe.

**valueless actor model:** an actor model with only one object class and only one object.

**values or finite mathematical values:** this is constructed from a given set of constants. Each value is built from finitely many constants.

**verification:** the activity of checking whether a system has certain properties, by means of a formal proof.

# Appendix A
# Mathematical notions

In this text, mathematics and, in particular mathematical logic has been used to define and analyze the frameworks and as the *meta-language* for the specification language. The mathematical notations are very similar to the specification language. The basic notions used belong to *set theory*, *predicate calculus* and *lambda calculus*.

Let $A$, $A_1, \ldots, A_n$, $B$ and $C$ be *sets* and $a$, $a_1, \ldots, a_n$ be *elements*.

## Sets

- $\emptyset$, $\mathbb{N}$, $\mathbb{Z}$, $\mathbb{Q}$, $\mathbb{R}$ and $\mathbb{B}$ denote special sets, the natural numbers ($0 \in \mathbb{N}$), the integers, the rational numbers, the real numbers and the set of Boolean values (*true* and *false*) respectively. These sets are mutually disjoint.
- $a \in A$ is *true* if and only if $a$ is an *element* of $A$.
- $A \subseteq B$ is *true* if and only if $A$ is a *subset* of $B$, i.e. if and only if all elements of $A$ are also elements of $B$.
- $A \cup B$ is the *union* of $A$ and $B$, i.e. the set of elements that belong to $A$ or $B$.
- $A \cap B$ is the *intersection* of $A$ and $B$, i.e. the set of elements that belong to $A$ and $B$.
- $A \backslash B$ is the *difference* of $A$ and $B$, i.e. the set of all elements of $A$ that do not belong to $B$.
- An *enumerated* set is denoted by $\{a_1, \ldots, a_n\}$, where $a_1, \ldots a_n$ are elements.
- $\#(A)$ is the *cardinality* of $A$, i.e. the number of elements in $A$ (this number can be $\infty$).

## Constructed sets

- $\mathbb{P}(A)$ is the *power set* of $A$, i.e. the set of all subsets of $A$.
- $\mathbb{F}(A)$ is the *finite power set* of $A$, i.e. the set of all finite subsets of $A$.

- $A^*$ is the set of all *sequences* of elements of $A$, including the *empty sequence* $\epsilon$; these are denoted by $\langle a_1, \ldots, a_n \rangle$.
- $A_1 \times \ldots \times A_n$ is called a *Cartesian product* and is the set of all *vectors* $(a_1, \ldots, a_n)$ such that $a_i \in A_i$; vectors of two elements are called *pairs*.
- $[b_1 : A_1, \ldots, b_n : A_n]$ is called a *tuple type* and is the set of all *tuples* of the form $\{b_1 \mapsto a_1, \ldots, b_n \mapsto a_n\}$ where $b_1, \ldots, b_n$ are different elements of a set $B$, they are called *attributes* in this role. For all $i$ it must hold that $a_i \in A_i$. Formally there is no difference between a tuple and set of *pairs* $\{(b_1, a_1), \ldots, (b_n, a_n)\}$.

There are two other constructions for sets: set comprehension and the generalized Cartesian product. They are defined after the introduction of some other notions.

## Functions

- A *function* is a set of pairs such that the first elements of the pairs are unique (note that a tuple is also a function).
- The *domain* of a function $f$ is the set of first elements of the pairs that belong to the function; it is denoted by $dom(f)$.
- The *range* of a function $f$ is the set of all second elements of the pairs that belong to the function; it is denoted by $rng(f)$.
- $A \nrightarrow B$ is the set of all functions $f$ with $dom(f) \subseteq A$ and $rng(f) \subseteq B$; the elements of $A \nrightarrow B$ are called *partial functions*.
- $A \rightarrow B$ is the set of all functions $f \in A \nrightarrow B$ with $dom(f) = A$.
- Let $f \in A \nrightarrow B$; then $f \upharpoonright C$ is the *restriction* of $f$ to $C$, i.e. the set of all pairs of $f$ such that the first element belongs to $C$.
- If $a \in dom(f)$ then $f(a)$ is the element in $rng(f)$ such that $(a, f(a)) \in f$; $f(a)$ is called the *application* of $f$ to $a$.
- For functions on a Cartesian product applications are sometimes represented by subscripts so that, for example, $f(a, b)$ becomes $f_a(b)$ and $f(a, b, c)$ becomes $f_{a,b}(c)$.
- If $f \in A \nrightarrow (B \nrightarrow C)$ then $f$ is a *function-valued* function. There is then an equivalent function $\tilde{f} \in (A \times B) \nrightarrow C$ such that, for all $a$ and $b$, $f(a)(b) = \tilde{f}(a, b)$; $\tilde{f}$ is called the *curried version* of $f$.
- If $F$ is a *set-valued* function (i.e. the range elements are sets) then $\Pi(F)$ is the *generalized Cartesian product*, i.e. the set of all functions $f$ such that $dom(f) = dom(F)$ and, for all $x \in dom(F)$, $f(x) \in F(x)$.
- The *inverse* of a function $f \in A \nrightarrow B$ is a set-valued function $f^{-1}$ such that, for $b \in B$, $f^{-1}(b)$ is the set of all elements of $a \in A$ such that $f(a) = b$.
- A function $f \in A \nrightarrow B$ is called *injective* if, for all $a$, $b$ in $dom(f)$ with $a \neq b$, $f(a) \neq f(b)$.

- A function $f \in A \twoheadrightarrow B$ is called *surjective* if $rng(f) = B$.
- A function $f \in A \twoheadrightarrow B$ is called *bijective* if it is injective and surjective.
- A function $f \in A \twoheadrightarrow B$ is called *total* if $dom(f) = A$ (so that $f \in A \to B$).

## Predicates

- Functions $f \in A \twoheadrightarrow \mathbb{B}$ are called *Boolean functions* or *predicates*.
- If $a$ and $b$ are Boolean values then $\neg a$, $a \wedge b$, $a \vee b$, $a \Rightarrow B$ are also Boolean values, denoting *negation*, *conjunction*, *disjunction* and *implication* respectively.
- For a predicate $p \in A \twoheadrightarrow \mathbb{B}$ the *universal* and *existential quantification* over the set $A$ are denoted by $\forall\, x \in A : p(x)$ and $\exists\, x \in A : p(x)$ respectively.
- If $p$ is a predicate then $\{x \in A \mid p(x)\}$ is the set of all elements $a$ of $A$ for which $p(a)$ evaluates to *true*; if the notation $\{x \mid p(x)\}$ is used this means that $A$ has to be replaced by $dom(p)$; this notation is called *set comprehension*.

## Ordering

- A *partial ordering* on a set $A$, denoted by the symbol $\leq$, is a predicate in $A \times A \twoheadrightarrow \mathbb{B}$ ( denoted in infix notation, i.e. we write $a \leq b$ instead of $\leq (a, b)$) such that

    - $a \leq a$, for all $a \in A$ (*reflexivity*),
    - if $a \leq b$ and $b \leq a$ then $a = b$ (*antisymmetry*),
    - if $a \leq b$ and $b \leq c$ then $a \leq c$ (*transitivity*).

    A partial ordering $\leq$ on $A$ is called a *total ordering* if the domain of $\leq$ is $A \times A$.
- If B has a partial ordering and $A \subseteq B$ then $b$ is $sup(A)$, called the *supremum* or the *least upper bound* of $A$ with respect to $B$ if, for all $a \in A$, $a \leq b$ and if for each other element $c \in B$ with this property it holds that $b \leq c$. (It can be proved that $sup$ is unique.)
- Similarly, $b$ is $inf(A)$, called the *infimum* or the *greatest lower bound* of $A$ with respect to $B$ if, for all $a \in A$, $b \leq a$ and if for each other element $c \in B$ with this property it holds that $c \leq b$.

### Lambda calculus

Lambda calculus is a formalism that is used in this book to define functions. It has its own language and rules for deriving new expressions from given expressions. First we define this language.

- There is a set of *variables* and a set of *constants*; they are disjoint.
- Each variable and each constant is an expression.
- If $E_1$ and $E_2$ are expressions then $E_1(E_2)$ is an expression, called the *application* of $E_1$ to $E_2$.

– If $x$ is a variable and $E$ an expression then $(\lambda x \bullet E)$ is an expression, called an *abstraction* or a *lambda expression*.

For expressions we have the following *rewrite rules*. Let $x$ and $y$ be variables and $E$ an expression. (We use "=" to indicate that two expressions can be obtained from each other by applying a rewrite rule.)

**α-conversion:** $(\lambda x \bullet E) = (\lambda y \bullet E_y^x)$, where $E_y^x$ denotes the expression $E$ but with each occurrence of $x$ replaced by $y$. Here we assume that $y$ does not occur (as a free variable) in $E$ (*see* part V for a definition of the "free occurrence" of a variable).

**β-reduction:** $(\lambda x \bullet E)(y) = E_y^x$.

**η-reduction:** $(\lambda x \bullet E(x)) = E$.

A rewriting step is called a *reduction* if the number of $\lambda$'s has decreased. An expression that cannot be reduced is called a *normal form*. The (first) Church-Rosser theorem states that an expression can be reduced to at most one normal form. If all normal forms can be *evaluated*, i.e. have a value, then all expressions with a normal form take the value of their normal form. As an example we consider

$$(\lambda x \bullet f(g(x))$$

where $f$ and $g$ are constants that denote given functions. Then the lambda expression denotes the function $\{(a, f(g(a))) \mid a \in dom(g)\}$, if $rng(g) \subseteq dom(f)$. In general if $x$ is the only variable in $E$ then the lambda expression $(\lambda x \bullet E)$ denotes the function consisting of all pairs $(a, E_a^x)$. If it is not clear from the context which elements $a$ we have to consider we write $\lambda x \in A \bullet E$, to specify that we have to consider all elements of $A$ for which the expression $E$ can be evaluated. This is an expression in *typed lambda calculus* because all variables have a domain or type. This is the lambda calculus we use in the specification language. The variables in an expression may be place holders for functions, for example $(\lambda y \bullet y(a))$ denotes the function that assigns to an arbitrary function $y$ the function value for argument $a$ ($a$ is a constant here). An example of reduction is the following

$$(\lambda y \bullet (\lambda x \bullet y(x)))(a) \overset{(1)}{=} (\lambda x \bullet a(x)) \overset{(2)}{=} a$$

in which step (1) is β-reduction and step (2) is η-reduction.

## Principle of structural induction

Structural induction is a generalization of induction over the natural numbers.

Suppose we have a finite set of rules to construct objects out of given objects and that we have a finite set of atomic objects (i.e. objects that are not constructed out of others). If we have to show that a property holds for all objects then:

(i) we have to show that all atomic objects have the property,

(ii) assuming that all components of an arbitrary object have the property we have to prove that the object has the property.

If we take the natural numbers as objects and the construction rule is "addition by one" then the principle of structural induction says that we have to prove the property for 0 and under the assumption that it holds for $n$ we have to show that it holds for $n + 1$.

# Appendix B
## Syntax summary

### Meta-syntax

- The definition sign for non-terminals is ::=.
- Any part of a syntax in <u>underlined</u> typeface is to be taken literally.
- Any part between braces may be repeated. So "$a$ ::= $\{b\}$" is shorthand for "$a$ ::= $b \mid b\,a$".
- Any part between square brackets may be omitted. So "$a$ ::= $[b]c$" is shorthand for "$a$ ::= $bc \mid c$".
- Any part between triangular brackets may be repeated; each repetition must be preceded by a comma ",". So "$< a >$" is shorthand for "$a[\{\underline{,}\,a\}]$".
- The syntax for identifiers, digits and characters is not further elaborated.

### Syntax base

The syntax base is denoted as follows:

$$(L, C, TV, V, VN, FN, TN, SN)$$

where

$L$ is the set of attributes,
$C$ is the set of constants,
$TV$ is the set of type variables,
$V$ is the set of value variables,
$VN$ is the set of value names,
$FN$ is the set of function names,
$TN$ is the set of type names,
$SN$ is the set of schema names.

The set $TN$ contains the names of the basic types, i.e. at least $\varnothing$, $\mathbf{N}$, $\mathbf{Z}$, $\mathbf{Q}$ and $\mathbf{B}$. The sets $TV$ and $TN$ are disjoint and $TV = \{\$, \$_1, \$_2, \ldots\}$.

The sets $V$ and $VN$ are disjoint. The sets $L$ and $V$ satisfy $L$ and $V$ are not disjoint. The syntactical variables that range over these sets are:

$$constant \in C \cup \{\bot\}$$
$$variable \in V$$
$$attribute \in L$$
$$a.variable \in V \cap L$$
$$value\ name \in VN$$
$$type\ variable \in TV$$
$$type\ name \in TN$$
$$function\ name \in FN$$
$$quantor \in \{\forall, \exists\}$$
$$\theta \in \{\vee,\ \wedge,\ \Rightarrow\}$$

## Type expressions and type definitions

*type expression* ::=
  *type name* | *type variable* | *set type* |
  *product type* | *sequence type* | *tuple type*
*set type* ::= $\mathbb{F}$ (*type expression*)
*product type* ::= (*type expression* $\times$ *product list*)
*product list* ::= *type expression* | *type expression*$\times$*product list*
*sequence type* ::= *type expression*$^*$
*tuple type* ::=
  *type variable* | [$\langle$*attribute* : *type expression*$\rangle$] |
  *tuple type* $\bowtie$ *tuple type*
*type definition* ::= *type name* :=*type expression*

## Terms

*term* ::=
  *variable* | *value name* | *constant* | (*term*) |
  *value construction* | *application* | *set term* |
  *map term*
*value construction* ::=
  *set construction* | *vector construction* |
  *sequence construction* | *tuple construction*
*set construction* ::= $\{\langle$*term*$\rangle\}$ | $\{\}$
*vector construction* ::= ($\langle$*term*$\rangle$)
*sequence construction* ::= $\langle\langle$*term*$\rangle\rangle$ | $\langle\rangle$
*tuple construction* ::= $\{\langle$*attribute* $\mapsto$ *term*$\rangle\}$ | $\{\}$
*application* ::= *function name* (*term*)
*set term* ::= { *value variable* : *domain* | *term*}

*map term* ::= ⟨*value variable*: *domain* | *term*⟩
*domain* ::= *set construction* | *set term*
*value definition* ::= *value name* :≡ *term* : *type expression*

## Function definition

*function definition* ::=
  *function name*(⟨*variable*⟩) :≡ *term* : *signature*,
*signature* ::= *type expression* ⇒ *type expression*.

## Predicates

*predicate* ::= *bool* | ¬ *predicate* | (*predicate* θ *predicate*) |
  *quantor* ⟨*variable*⟩: *domain* • *predicate*
*domain* ::= *type expression*
*bool* ::= *Boolean term*
θ ∈ {∨, ∧ , ⇒}
*quantor* ∈ {∀, ∃}
*variable* ∈ V

A Boolean term is a term with type 𝔹.

## Function declaration

*function declaration* ::= *function name* :: *signature* :: *predicate*

## Schema

*schema* ::= [*schema signature* | *predicate*]
*schema signature* ::= ⟨ *a.variable* : *type expression*⟩

## Schema expression

*schema expression* ::=
  *schema* | (*schema expression* ) |
  *schema name*(⟨ *type expression* ⟩) |
  ¬ *schema expression* |
  *schema expression* θ *schema expression* |
  *schema expression*\ (⟨ *a.variable*⟩) |
  *schema expression*↾ (⟨*a.variable*⟩) |
  *quantor* *a.variable* | *predicate* • *schema expression*
*schema definition* ::=
  *schema name* [(⟨*type variable*⟩)] :≡ *schema expression*

The following conditions should hold.

– The variables (a.variable) left of the symbols \ and ↾ should occur in the schema signatures of the schema expression.
– The variable immediately following of a quantor should appear in a signature of the schema expression with the same type expression, and the predicate should have no free variables or type variables.
– The schema expression in a schema definition may contain type variables; however, these type variables must appear also on the left hand-side of the ":=" symbol.
– Schema definitions may not be recursive.

## Script

> *script* ::= *line* | *line*; *script*
> *line* ::= *type definition* | *value definition* |
>   *function definition* | *function declaration* |
>   *schema definition*

There must be a function that assigns a natural number $n$ to every line $\ell$, with the property that every name occurring in the definition part of the line is defined itself in a line with a number smaller than or equal to $n$ if the line is a function definition and in a line with a number smaller than $n$ otherwise.

# Appendix C

# Toolkit

The functions are grouped by their kind. They are presented in the following format:

- the "user" name (for example "equality"),
- symbolic name and signature (for example $=: \$_1 \times \$_2 \Rightarrow \mathbb{B}$)
-     (i) infix or prefix; this indicates how we use the function (for example in infix notation "$=$" is used as $a = b$, while in prefix notation we have $= (a, b)$)
  - (ii) strict or non-strict; in the latter case we have to modify the definition sometimes to guarantee this, for example if $f$ is defined but not yet strict, then we modify its definition by

$$\tilde{f}(x) := \text{ if } x = \bot \text{ then } \bot \text{ else } f(x) \text{ } fi$$

  - (iii) primitive or derived; in the first case the function is defined in the meta-language and in the second case in the specification language
- definition of the function without signature; if a function name is overloaded there are several definitions
- auxiliary definitions, if necessary

**General functions**

  (1) **equality**

-    $= : \$_1 \times \$_2 \Rightarrow \mathbb{B}$
- infix / non-strict / primitive
- this function compares two values and if they are identical or equivalent (in case of sets and tuples) then the function value is *true*, else, it is *false*.

  $\bot = \bot$ is true $\wedge \; \forall x \in U : x \neq \bot \Rightarrow x = \bot$ is false.

Note that if "=" is applied to values of different types it will always be *false*.

(2) **selection**

- *if .then.else.fi* : $\mathbb{B} \times \$ \times \$ \Rightarrow \$$
- infix / non-strict and lazy / primitive
- *if a then b else c fi*,
  if *a* is *true* then the function value is equal to *b*, else, to *c*;
  the function is lazy: if *a* is *true* then *c* may be $\perp$ and if *a* is *false* then *b* may be $\perp$;
  if *a* is $\perp$ then the function value is $\perp$

**Numerical functions**

(3) **subtraction**

- $- := \mathbb{Z} \times \mathbb{Z} \Rightarrow \mathbb{Z}$
  $- := \mathbb{Q} \times \mathbb{Q} \Rightarrow \mathbb{Q}$
- infix / strict / primitive
- the meaning is the well-known subtraction

(4) **integer division**

- *div* : $\mathbb{N} \times \mathbb{N} \Rightarrow \mathbb{N}$
  *div* : $\mathbb{Z} \times \mathbb{Z} \Rightarrow \mathbb{Z}$
- infix / strict/ primitive
- the meaning of *a div b* is the maximum number of *b*'s contained in *a*, division by 0 gives $\perp$

(5) **rational division**

- $\div$ : $\mathbb{Q} \times \mathbb{Q} \Rightarrow \mathbb{Q}$
- infix / strict / primitive
- this is the well-known division for rational numbers; division by 0 gives $\perp$

(6) **truncation to integer**

- *truncint* : $\mathbb{Q} \Rightarrow \mathbb{Z}$
- prefix / strict / primitive
- $truncint(x) = max\{y \in \mathbb{Z} \mid y \le x\}$

(7) **truncation to natural**

- $truncnat : \ \mathbb{Z} \Rightarrow \mathbb{N}$
  $truncnat : \ \mathbb{Q} \Rightarrow \mathbb{N}$
- prefix / strict / primitive
- if $x \in \mathbb{Z}$ and $x \geq 0$ then: $truncnat(x) = x$,
  if $x < 0$ then $truncnat(x) = 0$,
  else $truncnat(x) = max\{y \in \mathbb{N} \mid y \leq x\}$

(8) **conversion to integer**

- $toint : \ \mathbb{N} \Rightarrow \mathbb{Z}$
- prefix / strict / primitive
- $toint(x) = +x$

(9) **conversion to rational**

- $torat : \ \mathbb{N} \Rightarrow \mathbb{Q}$
- prefix / strict / primitive
- $torat(x) = +x/1$

(10) **addition**

- $+ : \ \mathbb{N} \times \mathbb{N} \Rightarrow \mathbb{N}$
  $+ : \ \mathbb{Z} \times \mathbb{Z} \Rightarrow \mathbb{Z}$
  $+ : \ \mathbb{Q} \times \mathbb{Q} \Rightarrow \mathbb{Q}$
- infix / strict / derived
- $x + y := truncnat(toint(x) - ((+0) - toint(y)))$, for the first function,
  $x + y := x - (0 - y)$ for the second function and
  $x + y := x - ((+0/1) - y)$ for the third function

(11) **multiplication**

- $\times : \ \mathbb{N} \times \mathbb{N} \Rightarrow \mathbb{N}$
  $\times : \ \mathbb{Z} \times \mathbb{Z} \Rightarrow \mathbb{Z}$
  $\times : \ \mathbb{Q} \times \mathbb{Q} \Rightarrow \mathbb{Q}$
- infix / strict / derived
- $x \times y := truncnat(torat(x) \div ((+1/1) \div torat(y)))$ for the first function,
  $x \times y := truncint(torat(x) \div ((+1/1) \div torat(y)))$ for the second function
  and
  $x \times y := x \div ((+1/1) \div y)$, for the last function

(12) **modulo**

- $mod : \mathbb{N} \times \mathbb{N} \Rightarrow \mathbb{N}$
  $mod : \mathbb{Z} \times \mathbb{Z} \Rightarrow \mathbb{Z}$
- infix / strict / derived
- $x \ mod \ y := x - y \times (x \ div \ y)$

(13) **power**

- $\uparrow := \mathbb{Q} \times \mathbb{N} \Rightarrow \mathbb{Q}$
- infix / strict / derived
- $x \uparrow n := \text{ if } n = 0 \text{ then } (+1/1) \text{ else } x \times x \uparrow (n-1) \text{ fi}$

(14) **less than**

- $<: \mathbb{N} \times \mathbb{N} \Rightarrow \mathbb{B}$
  $<: \mathbb{Z} \times \mathbb{Z} \Rightarrow \mathbb{B}$
  $<: \mathbb{Q} \times \mathbb{Q} \Rightarrow \mathbb{B}$
- infix / strict / primitive
- these are the well-known comparison functions

(15) **less than or equal to**

- $\leq: \mathbb{N} \times \mathbb{N} \Rightarrow \mathbb{B}$
  $\leq: \mathbb{Z} \times \mathbb{Z} \Rightarrow \mathbb{B}$
  $\leq: \mathbb{Q} \times \mathbb{Q} \Rightarrow \mathbb{B}$
- infix / strict / derived
- $x \leq y := \text{ if } x = y \text{ then } true \text{ else}$
  $\qquad\qquad\qquad \text{if } x < y \text{ then } true \text{ else } false \text{ fi}$
  $\qquad\quad \text{fi}$

(16) **greater than**

- $>: \mathbb{N} \times \mathbb{N} \Rightarrow \mathbb{B}$
  $>: \mathbb{Z} \times \mathbb{Z} \Rightarrow \mathbb{B}$
  $>: \mathbb{Q} \times \mathbb{Q} \Rightarrow \mathbb{B}$
- infix / strict / derived
- $x > y := y < x$

(17) **greater than or equal to**

- $\geq: \mathbb{N} \times \mathbb{N} \Rightarrow \mathbb{B}$
  $\geq: \mathbb{Z} \times \mathbb{Z} \Rightarrow \mathbb{B}$
  $\geq: \mathbb{Q} \times \mathbb{Q} \Rightarrow \mathbb{B}$
- infix / strict / derived
- $x \geq y := y \leq x$

(18) **maximum**

- $max : \mathbb{N} \times \mathbb{N} \Rightarrow \mathbb{N}$
- infix / strict / derived
- $x \; max \; y := \text{ if } x \leq y \text{ then } y \text{ else } x \text{ fi}$

(19) **minimum**

- $min : \mathbb{N} \times \mathbb{N} \Rightarrow \mathbb{N}$
- infix / strict / derived
- $x \ min \ y := \ if \ x \geq \ y \ then \ y \ else \ x \ fi$

(20) **summation**

- $sum : \mathbb{F}(\$ \times \mathbb{Q}) \Rightarrow \mathbb{Q}$
- prefix / strict / derived
- $sum(f) := \ if \ f = \{\} \ then \ 0$
  $$else \ \pi_2(pick(f)) + sum(rest(f)) \ fi$$

**Boolean functions**

(21) **implication**

- $\Rightarrow: \mathbb{B} \times \mathbb{B} \Rightarrow \mathbb{B}$
- infix / non-strict / derived
- $x \Rightarrow y := \ if \ x = \perp \ then$
  $$if \ y \ then \ true \ else \ \perp fi$$
  $$else$$
  $$if \ x \ then \ y \ else \ true \ fi$$
  $$fi$$

(22) **negation**

- $\neg : \mathbb{B} \Rightarrow \mathbb{B}$
- prefix / non-strict / derived
- $\neg x := x \Rightarrow false$

(23) **or**

- $\vee : \mathbb{B} \times \mathbb{B} \Rightarrow \mathbb{B}$
- infix / non-strict / derived
- $x \vee y := \neg x \Rightarrow y$

(24) **and**

- $\wedge : \mathbb{B} \times \mathbb{B} \Rightarrow \mathbb{B}$
- infix / non-strict / derived
- $x \wedge y := \neg(\neg x \vee \neg y)$

(25) **universal quantification**

- $forall : \mathbb{F}(\$ \times \mathbb{B}) \Rightarrow \mathbb{B}$
- prefix / strict / derived
- $forall(f) := \ if \ f = \{\} \ then \ true$
  $$else \ \pi_2(pick(f)) \wedge forall(rest(f)) \ fi$$

(26) **existential quantification**

- $exists : \mathbb{F}(\$ \times \mathbb{B}) \Rightarrow \mathbb{B}$
- infix / strict / derived
- $exists(f) :=$ *if* $f = \{\}$ *then false*
  *else* $\pi_2(pick(f)) \vee exists(rest(f))$ *fi*

## Set functions

(27) **insertion**

- $ins : \$ \times \mathbb{F}(\$) \Rightarrow \mathbb{F}(\$)$
- prefix / strict / primitive
- the function satisfies the equation $ins(a, b) = \{a\} \cup b$

(28) **choice function**

- $pick : \mathbb{F}(\$) \Rightarrow \$$
- prefix / strict / primitive
- the function satisfies $pick(x) \in x$ and $pick(\{\}) = \bot$

(29) **rest of set**

- $rest : \mathbb{F}(\$) \Rightarrow \mathbb{F}(\$)$
- prefix / strict / primitive
- the function satisfies $rest(x) = x \backslash \{pick(x)\}$ and $rest(\{\}) = \bot$

(30) **element of**

- $\in: \$ \times \mathbb{F}(\$) \Rightarrow \mathbb{B}$
- infix / strict / derived
- $x \in y :=$ *if* $y = \{\}$ *then false else*
  *if* $x = pick(y)$ *then true else*
  $x \in rest(y)$
  *fi*
  *fi*

(31) **subset**

- $\subseteq : \mathbb{F}(\$) \times \mathbb{F}(\$) \Rightarrow \mathbb{B}$
- infix / strict / derived
- $x \subseteq y := forall(z : x \mid z \in y)$

(32) **union**

- $\cup : \mathbb{F}(\$) \times \mathbb{F}(\$) \Rightarrow \mathbb{F}(\$)$
- infix / strict / derived
- $x \cup y :=$ *if* $x = \{\}$ *then* $y$ *else* $ins(pick(x), rest(x) \cup y)$ *fi*

(33) **intersection**

- $\cap := \mathbb{F}(\$) \times \mathbb{F}(\$) \Rightarrow \mathbb{F}(\$)$
- infix / strict / derived
- $x \cap y := \{z : x \mid z \in y\}$

(34) **set difference**

- $\setminus : \mathbb{F}(\$) \times \mathbb{F}(\$) \Rightarrow \mathbb{F}(\$)$
- infix / strict / derived
- $x \setminus y := \{z : x \mid \neg(z \in y)\}$

(35) **size**

- $size : \mathbb{F}(\$) \Rightarrow \mathbb{N}$
- prefix / strict / derived
- $size\,(x) := \ if\ x = \{\}\ then\ 0\ else\ 1\ +\ size\,(rest\,(x)\,)\ fi$

## Sequence functions

(36) **concatenation**

- $cat : \$^* \times \$ \Rightarrow \$^*$
- prefix / strict / primitive
- let $a = \langle a_1, \ldots, a_m \rangle \in \$^*$ and $c \in \$$; then
  $cat(a, c) = \langle a_1, \ldots, a_m, c \rangle$

(37) **head of the vector**

- $head : \$^* \Rightarrow \$$
- prefix / strict / primitive
- let $a = \langle a_1, \ldots, a_m \rangle \in \$^*$; then
  $head(a) = a_1$

(38) **tail of the vector**

- $tail : \$^* \Rightarrow \$^*$
- prefix / strict / primitive
- let $a = \langle a_1, \ldots, a_m \rangle \in \$^*$; then
  $tail(a) = \langle a_2, \ldots, a_m \rangle$

## Vector functions

(39) **projection on one index**

- $\pi_n : \$_1 \times \ldots \times \$_m \Rightarrow \$_n,$
  for each $n, m \in \mathbb{N} \setminus \{0\}$ with $m \geq n$ we have such a function
- prefix / non-strict / primitive
- for $x = (a_1, a_2, \ldots, a_n, \ldots)$ we have $\pi_n(x) = a_n$

## (40) **projection on a set of indices**

- $\Pi_{(i_1,\ldots,i_k)} : \$_1 \times \ldots \times \$_n \Rightarrow \$_{i_1} \times \ldots \times \$_{i_k}$,
  for each vector $(i_1,\ldots,i_k)$ and $n \in \mathbb{N}$ we have such a function, provided
  that the vector is ascending and $n \geq k$
- prefix / non-strict / primitive
- for $x = (a_1, a_2, \ldots, a_n, \ldots)$ we have
  $\Pi_{(i_1,\ldots,i_k)}(x) = (a_{i_1} \ldots, a_{i_k})$

## (41) **Cartesian product**

- $prod : \mathbb{F}(\$_1) \times \mathbb{F}(\$_2) \Rightarrow \mathbb{F}(\$_1 \times \$_2)$
- infix / strict / derived
- $prod(a, b) :=$
  if $a = \{\}$ then $\{\}$
  else $iprod((pick(a), b) \cup prod(rest(a), b))$ fi
- auxiliary function:
  $iprod(x, b) :=$
  if $b = \{\}$ then $\{\}$
  else $ins((x, pick(b)), iprod(x, rest(b)))$
  fi $: \$_1 \times \mathbb{F}(\$_2) \Rightarrow \mathbb{F}(\$_1 \times \$_2)$

# Tuple functions

## (42) **projection on one attribute**

- $\pi_\ell : [\ell : \$_1] \bowtie \$_2 \Rightarrow \$_1$,
  for each attribute $\ell \in L$ there is such a function
- prefix / non-strict / primitive
- for $x = \{\ell \mapsto a, \ldots\}$ we have $\pi_\ell(x) = a$

## (43) **projection on a set of attributes**

- $\Pi_{(l_1,\ldots,l_k)} : [l_1 : \$_1, \ldots, l_k : \$_k] \bowtie \$ \Rightarrow [l_1 : \$_1, \ldots, l_k : \$_k]$
- prefix / non-strict / primitive
- for $x = \{\ell_1 \mapsto a_1, \ldots\}$ we have
  $\Pi_{(l_{i_1},\ldots,l_{i_k})}(x) = \{\ell_{i_1} \mapsto a_{i_1}, \ldots, \ell_{i_k} \mapsto a_{i_k}\}$,
  provided that $\{\ell_{i_1}, \ldots, \ell_{i_k}\} \subseteq \{\ell_1, \ldots\}$

(44) **tuple update**

- $\oplus : \$_1 \times \$_2 \Rightarrow \$_1 \bowtie \$_2$
- infix / non-strict / primitive
- $\{k_1 \mapsto a_1, \ldots, k_m \mapsto a_m\} \oplus \{l_1 \mapsto b_1, \ldots, l_n \mapsto b_n\} = \{r_1 \mapsto c_1, \ldots, r_p \mapsto c_p\}$, where $\{k_1, \ldots, k_m\} \cup \{l_1, \ldots, l_n\} = \{r_1, \ldots, r_p\}$
  and

$$\forall i, j : (r_i = l_j \Rightarrow c_i = b_j) \wedge$$
$$(r_i = k_j \wedge \neg \exists t : r_i = l_t) \Rightarrow c_i = a_j$$

(45) **join**

- $join : \mathbb{F}(\$_1) \times \mathbb{F}(\$_2) \Rightarrow \mathbb{F}(\$_1 \bowtie \$_2)$
- prefix / strict / derived
- $join(x, y) :=$
      *if* $x = \{\}$ *then* $\{\}$
      *else* $ins(semijoin(pick(x), y), join(rest(x), y))$ *fi*
- auxiliary function:
  $semijoin(x, y) :=$
  *if* $x \oplus pick(y) = pick(y) \oplus x$ *then*
      $ins(x \oplus pick(y), semijoin(x, rest(y)))$
  *else* $semijoin(x, rest(y))$ *fi* :
  $\$_1 \times \mathbb{F}(\$_2) \Rightarrow \mathbb{F}(\$_1 \bowtie \$_2)$

**Functions on binary relations**

(46) **domain**

- $dom : \mathbb{F}(\$_1 \times \$_2) \Rightarrow \mathbb{F}(\$_1)$
- prefix / strict / derived
- $dom(f) :=$
      *if* $f = \{\}$ *then* $\{\}$ *else* $ins(\pi_1(pick(f)), dom(rest(f)))$ *fi*

(47) **range**

- $rng : \mathbb{F}(\$_1 \times \$_2) \Rightarrow \mathbb{F}(\$_2)$
- prefix / strict / derived
- $rng(f) :=$
      *if* $f = \{\}$ *then* $\{\}$ *else* $ins(\pi_2(pick(f)), rng(rest(f)))$ *fi*

(48) **maximum of a relation**

- $fmax : \mathbb{F}(\$ \times \mathbb{Q}) \Rightarrow \mathbb{Q}$
- prefix / strict / derived
- $fmax(f) :=$
      *if* $f = \{\}$ *then* $0$ *else* $\pi_2(pick(f))$ *max* $fmax(rest(f))$

(49) **set apply**

- $setapply :: \mathbb{F}(\$_1 \times \$_2) \times \$_1 \Rightarrow \mathbb{F}(\$_2)$
- prefix / strict / derived
- $setapply(f, x) := \{y : rng(f) \mid (x, y) \in f\}$

(50) **apply for mappings**

- $. : \mathbb{F}(\$_1 \times \$_2) \times \$_1 \Rightarrow \$_2$
- infix / strict / derived
- $f.x := pick(setapply(f, x))$

(51) **inverse**

- $inv : \mathbb{F}(\$_1 \times \$_2) \Rightarrow \mathbb{F}(\$_2 \times \$_1)$
- prefix / strict / derived
- $inv(f) := \{z : prod(rng(f), dom(f)) \mid (\pi_2(z), \pi_1(z)) \in f\}$

# Bibliography

[Abrial, 1974] J.R. Abrial. Data semantics. In *Data Base Management*, pages 1–59. North-Holland, 1974.

[Aerts *et al.*, 1992] A.T.M. Aerts, P.M.E. de Bra, and K.M. van Hee. Transforming functional database schemes to relational representations. In *Specification of Database Systems*. Workshops in Computing Series, Springer-Verlag, 1992.

[Agha, 1986] G.A. Agha. *ACTORS, A Model of Concurrent Computation in Distributed Systems*. MIT Press, 1986.

[Ajmone Marsan *et al.*, 1985] M. Ajmone Marsan, G. Bablo, A. Bobbio, G. Chiola, G. Conte, and A. Cumani. On Petri nets with stochastic timing. In *IEEE Proceedings of the International Workshop on Timed Petri Nets*, pages 80–87, Torino, Italy, 1985.

[Andrews and Ince, 1991] D. Andrews and D. Ince. *Practical Formal Methods with VDM*. McGraw-Hill International, 1991.

[Atkinson *et al.*, 1989] M. Atkinson, F. Bancilhon, D. DeWitt, K. Dittrich, D. Maier, and S. Zdonik. The object-oriented database system manifesto. In *Proceedings of the First International Conference on Deductive and Object-Oriented Databases*, pages 40–57, Kyoto, Japan, 1989.

[Bachman, 1969] C.W. Bachman. Data structure diagrams. *Data Base 1*, 2, 1969.

[Baeten and Weijland, 1990] J.C.M. Baeten and W.P. Weijland. *Process Algebra*, volume 18 of *Cambridge Tracts in Theoretical Computer Science*. Cambridge University Press, 1990.

[Barendregt, 1984] H.P. Barendregt. *The Lambda Calculus - Its Syntax and Semantics*. Studies in Logic and Foundations of Mathematics. North-Holland, 1984.

[Berthomieu and Diaz, 1991] B. Berthomieu and M. Diaz. Modelling and verification of time dependent systems using timed Petri nets. *IEEE Transactions on Software Engineering*, 17(3):259–273, March 1991.

[Berthomieu and Menasche, 1983] B. Berthomieu and M. Menasche. An enumerative approach for analyzing time Petri nets. In R.E.A. Mason, editor, *IFIP Information Processing*, volume 83, pages 41–46. Elsevier Science Publishers, 1983.

[Boardman, 1990] J. Boardman. *Systems Engineering: An Introduction*. Prentice-Hall, 1990.

[Boehm, 1981] B.W. Boehm. *Software Engineering Economics*. Prentice-Hall, 1981.

[Booch, 1991] G. Booch. *Object Oriented Design*. Benjamin Cummings, 1991.

[Brauer, 1980] W. Brauer. *Net Theory and Applications: Proceedings of Advanced Course on General Net Theory, Processes and Systems*, volume 84 of *Lecture Notes in Computer Science*. Springer-Verlag, 1980.

[Brodie *et al.*, 1984] M.L. Brodie, J. Mylopoulos, and J. Schmidt. *On Conceptual Modelling: Perspective from Artificial Intelligence Databases*. Springer-Verlag, 1984.

[Buneman and Frankel, 1979] O.P. Buneman and R.E. Frankel. FQL - a functional query language. In *International Conference on the Management of Data*. ACM Sigmod, 1979.

[Cardelli and Wegner, 1985] L. Cardelli and P. Wegner. On understanding types, data abstraction and polymorphism. *ACM Computing Surveys*, 17(4), December 1985.

[Ceri and Pelagatti, 1984] S. Ceri and G. Pelagatti. *Distributed Databases: Principles and Systems*. McGraw-Hill, 1984.

[Checkland, 1981] P. Checkland. *Systems Thinking, Systems Practice*. John Wiley and Sons Ltd., 1981.

[Chen, 1976] P.P. Chen. The entity-relationship model: Towards a unified view of data. *ACM Transactions on Database Systems*, 1:9–36, January 1976.

[Coad and Yourdon, 1990] P. Coad and E. Yourdon. *Object-Oriented Analysis*. Prentice-Hall, 1990.

[Codd, 1970] E.F. Codd. A relational model of data for large shared data banks. *Communications of the ACM*, 13:377–387, 1970.

[Cohen *et al.*, 1986] B. Cohen, W.T. Harwood, and M.I. Jackson. *The Specification of Complex Systems*. Addison-Wesley, 1986.

[Colom and Silva, 1991] J.M. Colom and M. Silva. Convex geometry and semiflows in P/T nets, a comparative study of algorithms for computation of minimal p-semiflows. In G. Rozenberg, editor, *Advances in Petri Nets 1990*, volume 483 of *Lecture Notes in Computer Science*, pages 79–112. Springer-Verlag, 1991.

[Dahl *et al.*, 1970] O.J. Dahl, B. Myhrhaug, and K. Nygaard. Simula 67 common base language. Technical Report S-22, Norwegian Computing Center, 1970.

[Date, 1990a] C.J. Date. *An Introduction to Database Systems: Volume I*. Addison-Wesley, 5th edition, 1990.

[Date, 1990b] C.J. Date. *An Introduction to Database Systems: Volume II*. Addison-Wesley, 5th edition, 1990.

[David and Alla, 1989] R. David and H. Alla. *Du Grafcet aux Réseaux de Petri*. Hermes-Paris, 1989.

[David and Alla, 1990] R. David and H. Alla. Autonomous and timed continuous Petri nets. In *Proceedings of 11th International Conference on Applications and Theory of Petri Nets*, Paris, France, 1990.

[Davis and Olson, 1985] G.B. Davis and M.H. Olson. *Management*. McGraw-Hill, 2th edition, 1985.

[De Nicola, 1987] R. De Nicola. Extensional equivalences for transition systems. *Acta Informatica*, 24:211–237, 1987.

[Di Giovanni and Iachini, 1990] R. Di Giovanni and P.L. Iachini. HOOD and Z for the development of complex software systems. In D. Bjorner and C.A.R. Hoare, editors, *VDM'90, VDM and Z - Formal Methods of Software Development*, volume 428 of *Lecture Notes in Computer Science*. Springer-Verlag, 1990.

[Dijkstra, 1968] E.W. Dijkstra. Co-operating sequential processes. In F. Genuys, editor, *Programming Languages*. Academic Press, 1968.

[Enderton, 1972] H.B. Enderton. *A mathematical introduction to logic*. Academic Press, London, 1972.

[Enderton, 1977] H.B. Enderton. *Elements of Set Theory*. Academic Press, 1977.

[Falkenberg and Lindgreen, 1989] E.D. Falkenberg and P. Lindgreen, editors. *Informa-*

*tion System Concepts: An In-depth Analysis*, IFIP TC8 Working Conference, Namur, Belgium, 1989. Elsevier Science Publishers.

[Finkel, 1990] A. Finkel. A minimal coverability graph for Petri nets. In *Proceedings of the 11th International Conference on Applications and Theory of Petri nets*, Paris, 1990.

[Galbraith, 1973] J. Galbraith. *Designing Complex Organizations*. Addisson-Wesley, Reading MA, 1973.

[Gelbaum, 1989] B. Gelbaum. *Linear algebra: basics, practice and theory*. North-Holland, Amsterdam, 1989.

[Genrich and Lautenbach, 1979] H.J. Genrich and K. Lautenbach. The analysis of distributed systems by means of predicate/transition-nets. In G. Kahn, editor, *Semantics of Concurrent Compilation*, volume 70 of *Lecture Notes in Computer Science*, pages 123–146. Springer-Verlag, 1979.

[Genrich and Lautenbach, 1981] H.J. Genrich and K. Lautenbach. System modelling with high level Petri nets. *Theoretical Computer Science*, 13:109–136, 1981.

[Genrich, 1987] H.J. Genrich. Predicate/transition-nets. In W. Brauer, W. Reisig, and G. Rozenberg, editors, *Advances in Petri Nets 1986 Part I: Petri Nets, Central Models and their Properties*, volume 254 of *Lecture Notes in Computer Science*, pages 207–247. Springer-Verlag, 1987.

[Glaser *et al.*, 1984] H. Glaser, C. Hankin, and D. Till. *Principles of Functional Programming*. Prentice-Hall International, 1984.

[Goldberg and Robson, 1983] A. Goldberg and D. Robson. *Smalltalk-80: The Language and its Implementation*. Addison-Wesley, 1983.

[Gyssens *et al.*, 1990] M. Gyssens, J. Paredaens, and D. van Gucht. A graph-oriented object database model. In *Principles of Database Systems*, 1990.

[Hammer and McLeod, 1981] M. Hammer and D. McLeod. Data description with SDM: a semantic database model. *ACM Transactions on Database Systems*, 6(3), 1981.

[Hayes, 1987] I. Hayes, editor. *Specification Case Studies*. Prentice-Hall, 1987.

[Hennessy, 1988] M. Hennessy. *Algebraic Theory of Processes*. The MIT Press, Cambridge, MA, 1988.

[Hesselink, 1988] W.H. Hesselink. Deadlock and fairness in morphisms of transition systems. *Theoretical Computer Science*, 59:235–257, 1988.

[Hoare, 1985] C.A.R. Hoare. *Communicating Sequential Processes*. Prentice-Hall, 1985.

[Hopcroft and Ullmann, 1979] J.E. Hopcroft and J.D. Ullmann. *Introduction to Automata Theory, Languages and Computation*. Addison-Wesley, 1979.

[Hull and King, 1987] R. Hull and R. King. Semantic database modelling: Survey, applications, and research issues. *ACM Computing Surveys*, 19(3), March 1987.

[IEEE, 1989] IEEE, editor. *Petri Nets and Performance Models*. Computer Society Press, 1989.

[IEEE, 1991] IEEE, editor. *Petri Nets and Performance Models*. IEEE Computer Society Press, 1991.

[Jackson, 1983] M. Jackson. *System Development*. Prentice-Hall International, 1983.

[Jantzen and Valk, 1980] M. Jantzen and R. Valk. Formal properties of place-transition nets. In W. Brauer, editor, *Net Theory and Applications*, volume 84 of *Lecture Notes in Computer Science*. Springer-Verlag, 1980.

[Jensen, 1990] K. Jensen. Coloured Petri nets: a high level language for system design and analysis. In G. Rozenberg, editor, *Advances in Petri Nets 1990*, volume 483 of *Lecture Notes in Computer Science*, pages 342–416. Springer-Verlag, 1990.

[Jensen, 1992] K. Jensen. *Coloured Petri Nets: Basic Concepts, Analysis Methods and*

*Practical Use.* EATC Monographs on Theoretical Computer Science. Springer-Verlag, 1992.

[Jones, 1990] C.B. Jones. *Systematic Software Development using VDM.* Prentice-Hall, 1990.

[Karp and Miller, 1969] R.M. Karp and R.E. Miller. Parallel program schemata. *Journal of Computer and System Sciences*, 3:147–195, 1969.

[Kleijnen and Groenendaal, 1992] J.P.C. Kleijnen and W. van Groenendaal. *Simulation: a Statistical Perspective.* John Wiley, 1992.

[Lautenbach, 1975] K. Lautenbach. Liveness in Petri nets. Technical report, Gesellschaft für Mathematik und Datenverarbeitung, (GMD), Bonn, 1975. GMD-ISF 75-02-1.

[Lewis and Papadimitriou, 1981] H.R. Lewis and Papadimitriou. *Elements of the Theory of Computing.* Prentice-Hall, 1981.

[Lundeberg *et al.*, 1981] M. Lundeberg, G. Goldkuhl, and A. Nilsson. *Information Systems Development - A Systematic Approach.* Prentice-Hall, 1981.

[Lyytinen, 1987] K. Lyytinen. Different perspectives on information systems: Problems and solutions. *ACM Computing Surveys*, 19(1), March 1987.

[Marca and McGowan, 1988] D.A. Marca and C.L. McGowan. *SADT : Structured Analysis and Design Technique.* McGraw-Hill, 1988.

[Martinez and Silva, 1982] J. Martinez and M. Silva. A simple and fast algorithm to obtain all invariants of a generalised Petri net. In C. Girault and W. Reisig, editors, *Application and Theory of Petri Nets: Selected Papers from the First and the Second European Workshop*, volume 52 of *Informatik Fachberichte*, pages 301–310. Springer-Verlag, 1982.

[Mazurkiewicz, 1984] A. Mazurkiewicz. Traces, histories, graphs: instances of a process monoid. In *Mathematical Foundations of Computer Science*, volume 176 of *Lecture Notes in Computer Science*, pages 115–133. Springer-Verlag, 1984.

[Meyer, 1988] B. Meyer. *Object Oriented Software Construction.* Prentice-Hall, 1988.

[Meyer, 1990] B. Meyer. *Introduction to the Theory of Programming Languages.* Prentice-Hall, 1990.

[Milner, 1980] R. Milner. *A Calculus of Communicating Systems*, volume 92 of *Lecture Notes in Computer Science.* Springer-Verlag, 1980.

[Mintzberg, 1979] H.. Mintzberg. *The Structuring of Organisations.* Prentice-Hall, 1979.

[Murata, 1989] T. Murata. Petri nets: Properties, analysis and applications. *Proceedings of the IEEE*, 77(4):541–580, April 1989.

[Nijssen and Halpin, 1989] G.M. Nijssen and T.A. Halpin. *Conceptual Schema and Relational Database Design: A Fact Oriented Approach.* Prentice-Hall, 1989.

[Olderog, 1991] E.R. Olderog. *Nets, terms and formulas: three views of concurrent processes and their relationships.* Cambridge University Press, Cambridge, 1991.

[Ören *et al.*, 1984] T.I. Ören, B.P. Zeigler, and M.S. Elzas. *Simulation and Model-based Methodologies: An Integrated Perspective*, volume 10 of *Nato ASI-series F: Computer and Systems Science.* Springer-Verlag, 1984.

[Paredaens *et al.*, 1989] J. Paredaens, P. de Bra, M. Gijssens, and D. van Gucht. *The structure of the Relational Data Model.* EATC Monographs on Theoretical Computer Science. Springer-Verlag, 1989.

[Parent and Spaccapietra, 1985] S. Parent and S. Spaccapietra. An algebra for a general entity-relationship model. *IEEE Transactions on Software Engineering*, 11(7), 1985.

[Park, 1981] D.M.R. Park. Concurrency and automata on infinite sequences. In Peter Deussen, editor, *Proceedings of the fifth GI conference*, volume 104 of *Lecture Notes in Computer Science*, pages 167–183. Springer-Verlag, 1981.

[Peterson, 1980] J.L. Peterson. A note on coloured Petri nets. *Information Processing Letters*, 11(1):40–43, August 1980.

[Peterson, 1981] J.L. Peterson. *Petri Net Theory and the Modeling of Systems*. Prentice-Hall, 1981.

[Petri, 1962] C.A. Petri. *Kommunikation mit Automaten*. PhD thesis, Institut für Instrumentelle Mathematik, Bonn, Germany, 1962.

[Petri, 1980] C.A. Petri. Introduction to general net theory. In W. Brauer, editor, *Net Theory and Applications : Proceedings of the Advanced Course on General Net Theory, Processes and Systems*, volume 84 of *Lecture Notes in Computer Science*, pages 1–20. Springer-Verlag, 1980.

[Pless and Plünnecke, 1980] E. Pless and H. Plünnecke. *A Bibliography of Net Theory*, volume 80-05 of *ISF-Report*. Gesellschaft fur Mathematik und Datenverarbeitung Bonn, 2nd edition, 1980.

[Pnueli, 1977] A. Pnueli. The temporal logic of programs. In *Proceedings of the 18th IEEE Annual Symposium on the Foundations of Computer Science*, pages 46–57. IEEE Computer Society Press, 1977.

[Pressman, 1987] R.S. Pressman. *Software Engineering - A Practitioner's Approach*. McGraw-Hill, 2nd edition, 1987.

[Ramamoorthy and Ho, 1980] C.V. Ramamoorthy and G.S. Ho. Performance evaluation of asynchronous concurrent systems using Petri nets. *IEEE Transactions on Software Engineering*, 6(5):440–449, September 1980.

[Reed and Roscoe, 1988] G.M. Reed and A.W. Roscoe. A timed model for communicating sequential processes. *Theoretical Computer Science*, 58:249–261, June 1988.

[Reisig, 1985] W. Reisig. *Petri Nets: An Introduction*. Prentice-Hall, 1985.

[Reisig, 1987] W. Reisig. Place-transition systems. In *Advances in Petri Nets, 1986 Part I: Central Models and their Properties*, volume 254 of *Lecture Notes in Computer Science*. Springer-Verlag, 1987.

[Revuz, 1975] D. Revuz. *Markov Chains*. North-Holland/American Elsevier, 1975.

[Rishe, 1988] N. Rishe. *Database Design Fundamentals*. Prentice-Hall, 1988.

[Ross, 1977] D.T. Ross. Structured analysis: A language for communicating ideas. *IEEE Transactions on Software Engineering*, 3(1), 1977.

[Ross, 1983] S.M. Ross. *Stochastic Processes*. MacMillan, 1983.

[Ross, 1990] S.M. Ross. *A Course in Simulation*. Collier MacMillan, 1990.

[Rumbaugh et al., 1991] J. Rumbaugh, M. Blaha, W. Premerlani, F. Eddy, and W. Lorensen. *Object-Oriented Modeling and Design*. Prentice-Hall, 1991.

[Schek and Scholl, 1986] H.J. Schek and M.H. Scholl. The relational model with relation-valued attributes. *Information Systems*, 11:137–147, 1986.

[Schiffers and Wedde, 1978] M. Schiffers and H. Wedde. Analyzing program solutions of coordination problems by CP-nets. In *Mathematical Foundations of Computer Science*, volume 64 of *Lecture Notes in Computer Science*, pages 462–473. Springer-Verlag, 1978.

[Sernadas et al., 1991] C. Sernadas, P. Resende, P. Gouveia, and A. Sernadas. In-the-large object-oriented design of information systems. In [van Assche et al., 1991], 1991.

[Shannon, 1975] R.E. Shannon. *Systems Simulation : the Art and Science*. Prentice-Hall, 1975.

[Shipman, 1981] D.W. Shipman. The functional data model and the data language daplex. *ACM Transactions on Database Systems*, 6:140–173, 1981.

[Sibertin-Blanc, 1991] C. Sibertin-Blanc. Cooperative objects for the conceptual modelling of organizational information systems. In [van Assche et al., 1991], 1991.

[Sifakis, 1977] J. Sifakis. Use of Petri nets for performance evaluation. In H. Beilner and E. Gelenbe, editors, *Proceedings of the Third International Symposium IFIP WG. 7.3., Measuring, Modelling and Evaluating Computer Systems*, pages 75–93. North-Holland, 1977.

[Sifakis, 1980] J. Sifakis. Performance evaluation of systems using nets. In W. Brauer, editor, *Net theory and applications : Proceedings of the Advanced Course on General Net Theory, Processes and Systems*, volume 84 of *Lecture Notes in Computer Science*, pages 307–319. Springer-Verlag, 1980.

[Snepscheut, 1985] J.L.A. van de Snepscheut. *Trace Theory and VLSI Design*, volume 200 of *Lecture Notes in Computer Science*. Springer-Verlag, 1985.

[Sol and van Hee, 1991] H.G. Sol and K.M. van Hee, editors. *Dynamic Modelling of Information Systems*. North-Holland, 1991.

[Sommerville, 1989] I. Sommerville. *Software Engineering*. Addison-Wesley, 3rd edition, 1989.

[Spaccapietra, 1987] S. Spaccapietra. *Entity-Relationship Approach: Ten Years of Experience*. North-Holland, 1987.

[Spivey, 1987] J.M. Spivey. *Understanding Z. A Specification Language and its Formal Semantics*. Cambridge University Press, 1987.

[Spivey, 1989] J.M. Spivey. *The Z Notation: A Reference Manual*. Prentice-Hall, 1989.

[Teorey et al., 1986] T.J. Teorey, D. Yang, and J.P. Frij. A logical design methodology for relational databases using the extended entity-relationship model. *Computing Surveys*, 18(2):197–222, 1986.

[Thompson, 1991] S. Thompson. *Type Theory and Functional Programming*. Addison-Wesley, 1991.

[Tsichritzis and Lochovsky, 1982] D.C. Tsichritzis and F.H. Lochovsky. *Data Models*. Prentice-Hall, 1982.

[Ullman, 1988] J.D. Ullman. *Principles of Database and Knowledge-based Systems*. Computer Science Press, 1988.

[van Assche et al., 1991] F.J.M. van Assche, B. Moulin, and C. Rolland, editors. *The Object Oriented Approach in Information Systems*, Proceedings of IFIP TC8 Working Conference. North-Holland, 1991.

[van Benthem, 1983] J.F.A.K. van Benthem. *The Logic of Time*. D. Reidel, 1983.

[van der Aalst, 1992] W.M.P. van der Aalst. *Timed Coloured Petri Nets and their Application to Logistics*. PhD thesis, Eindhoven University of Technology, 1992.

[van Hee and Verkoulen, 1991] K.M. van Hee and P.A.C. Verkoulen. Integration of a data model and high-level Petri nets. In *Proceedings of the 12th International Conference on Applications and Theory of Petri Nets*, pages 410–431, Gjern, Denmark, June 1991.

[van Hee and Verkoulen, 1992] K.M. van Hee and P.A.C. Verkoulen. Data, process and behaviour modelling in an integrated specification framework. In H.G. Sol and R.L. Crosslin, editors, *Proceedings of the Second International Conference on Dynamic Modelling of Information Systems*, Washington, D.C., USA, March 1992. North-Holland.

[van Hee et al., 1989a] K.M. van Hee, G.J. Houben, and J.L.G. Dietz. Modeling of discrete dynamic systems — framework and examples. *Information Systems*, 14(4):277–289, 1989.

[van Hee et al., 1989b] K.M. van Hee, L.J. Somers, and M. Voorhoeve. Executable specifications for distributed information systems. In [Falkenberg and Lindgreen, 1989], pages 139–156, 1989.

[van Hee et al., 1991] K.M. van Hee, L.J. Somers, and M. Voorhoeve. A formal framework for dynamic modelling of information systems. In [Sol and van Hee, 1991], pages 227–236, 1991.

[Ward and Mellor, 1985] P.T. Ward and S.J. Mellor. *Structured Development for Real-Time Systems.* Yourdon, 1985.

[Wilkstrom, 1987] A. Wilkstrom. *Functional Programming using ML.* Prentice-Hall, 1987.

[Woodcock and Loomes, 1988] J. Woodcock and M Loomes. *Software Engineering Mathematics.* Pitman, 1988.

[Wordsworth, 1992] J.B. Wordsworth. *Software Development with Z: A Pratcical Approach to Formal Methods in Software Engineering.* Addison-Wesley, 1992.

[Wymore, 1967] A.W. Wymore. *A Mathematical Theory of Systems Engineering: The Elements.* John Wiley and Sons, 1967.

[Yourdon, 1989] E. Yourdon. *Modern Structured Analysis.* Prentice-Hall, 1989.

[Zeigler, 1976] B. Zeigler. *Theory of Modeling and Simulation.* Wiley Interscience, 1976.

[Zeigler, 1982] B.P. Zeigler. *Multi facetted Modelling and Discrete Event Simulation.* Academic Press, 1982.

# Index